Ross Clifford

John Warwick Montgomery's Legal Apologetic

Christliche Philosophie heute
Christian Philosophy Today
Quomodo Philosophia Christianorum Hodie Estimatur

Band 5

Band 1
John Warwick Montgomery
Tractatus Logico-Theologicus

Band 2
John Warwick Montgomery
Hat die Weltgeschichte einen Sinn?
Geschichtsphilosophien auf dem Prüfstand

Band 3
John Warwick Montgomery
Jésus: La raison rejoint l'histoire

Band 4
Horst Waldemar Beck
Marken dieses Äons

Band 5
Ross Clifford
John Warwick Montgomery's Legal Apologetic

John Warwick Montgomery

John Warwick Montgomery's Legal Apologetic

An Apologetic for all Seasons

Christian Philosophy Today 5

Verlag für Kultur und Wissenschaft
Culture and Science Publ.
Bonn 2004

JOHN WARWICK MONTGOMERY'S LEGAL APOLOGETIC
An Apologetic for all Seasons

Copyright © 2016 Ross Clifford. All rights reserved. Except for brief quotations in critical publications or reviews, no part of this book may be reproduced in any manner without prior written permission from the publisher. Write: Permissions, Wipf and Stock Publishers, 199 W. 8th Ave., Suite 3, Eugene, OR 97401.

This edition published by Wipf and Stock Publishers in cooperation with Verlag für Kultur und Wissenschaft.

Wipf & Stock
An Imprint of Wipf and Stock Publishers
199 W. 8th Ave., Suite 3
Eugene, OR 97401

www.wipfandstock.com

PAPERBACK ISBN: 978-1-4982-6897-4
HARDCOVER ISBN: 978-1-4982-8991-7

Manufactured in the U.S.A.

Acknowledgments

This writer would like to express appreciation to the following people who have aided me in this endeavour. This book is based on my doctoral thesis.

Dr John Warwick Montgomery for providing me with materials, including his latest unpublished texts and for always being available to answer queries as I pursued this study. Also, for his encouragement to academically evaluate the teaching of one's mentors. His writings to me have been the 'hound of heaven'.

My doctoral supervisor throughout this study Dr Bill Andersen, who personifies what it is to be a Christian academic. Two other doctoral supervisors worked with me for part of the time: Dr Graham Cole and Geoff Moore LL.M., Barrister-at-Law. Their valuable contribution is also much appreciated.

The faculty, staff, and College Council members at Morling Theological College who were always encouraging. In particular Mrs Nancy Connell for her endless hours of typing and computer work; and Philip Johnson for his incessant probing.

My wife Beverley whose encouragement, support and giving of her time in this project was invaluable, and my children Briony and Joel for their understanding.

Contents Page

Acknowledgments 5
Contents Page 7
Introduction 11
Background and Focus of the Study 11
Aims and Structure 14
Limitations 16
Chapter 1 19
Historical Background 19
The Early Church 19
Grotius, Sherlock, Greenleaf 21
Links to the Historical Apologetic 24
Common Sense 26
Influence on General Christian
and Non-Christian Apologetic Works 27
A Fourfold Taxanomy 32
General Observation 40
The Model and its Development 41
Intended Audience 45
Potential Difficulties 46
New Development 47
Epistemological Matters 48
Chapter 2 57
The Evidence 57
Documents 58
'Ancient Documents' Rule 59

Legal Hermeneutic 72
Hearsay 80
Hostile Witnesses 80
Multiple Hearsay 82
First-Hand Admissible Hearsay –
'The Devil's Advocate' Position 86
A Point for Further Research: Letter of James 102
Luke's Gospel 104
Non-Technical Legal Apologetic 106

Chapter 3 109
Testimony 109
The Competency and Truthfulness of a Witness 110
Limitations Surrounding Eyewitness Testimony 139
Things 144
Circumstantial Evidence 147
The Circumstantial Case 148
Reframing the Legal Apologetic 158
The Technical Apologetic 159
The Non-Technical Apologetic 162
'Commonly Agreed Facts' Apologetic 163

Chapter 4 166
'New Spirituality' 166
Background to 'New Spirituality' 167
Apologetic Models in Relation to 'New Spirituality' 179
Montgomery's 'Incarnational' Model 181
Montgomery and the Apologist's Craft 185

The Legal Apologetic Model of
Montgomery in Relation to New Spirituality 189

The Resurrection and Circumstantial Evidence 189

Reframing the Circumstantial Apologetic 211

The Resurrection and Direct Evidence –
Montgomery and the Place of Story 217

Reframing the Direct Evidence 223

Faddishness 224

Conclusion: An Apologetic Case Study Approach 226

Chapter 5 .... **229**

Strenghts of the Legal Paradigm 229

Scriptural Support 229

Historical Precedent 238

Other Factors Supporting the Application
of the Legal Method to Ultimate Questions 238

Perceived Limitations of the Legal Paradigm Analogy 248

Law and Astonishing Events 249

Eternal Facts in Issue 254

A Legal Formalist Approach 259

Conclusion **267**

Appendix 1 Table of Lawyers' Apologetic Writings **269**

Resurrection and Reliable Gospels 269

Bible (not just the gospels) Reliability 269

Creation and Evolution 270

Trial of Jesus 270

Miracles, Historico-Philosophical Attacks 271

Citing Fulfilled Prophecy 271
Apologetic Ethics
(the focus is on ethics in an apologetic format) 272
Worldview and Culture 272
Legal Forms (for example wills and contracts)
to Apologetically Explain Theological Motifs 272
Theodicy 272
Personal Testimony 273
Bibliography **274**
Primary Sources 274
Cases 279
General Bibliography 280

Introduction

Background and Focus of the Study

A review of this generation's apologetics indicates the prominent role played by the legal apologists[1]. Montgomery is today's leader of those committed to this apologetic paradigm. In this genre the resurrection of Jesus, based on reliable New Testament records, is the primary focus.[2] Lawyers' verbal testimony, articles or books on the objectivity of the Christian truth claims are seen as affirming the historicity of the resurrection. Typical citations in popular apologetic works are those of Sir Edward Clarke and Sir Lionel Luckhoo:

> As a lawyer I have made a prolonged study of the evidences for the events of the first Easter day. To me the evidence is conclusive, and over and over again in the High Court I have secured the verdict on evidences not nearly so compelling.[3]

> I have spent more than forty-two years as a defence trial lawyer appearing in many parts of the world and am still in active practice. I have been fortunate to secure a number of successes in jury trials and I say unequivocally the evidence for the resurrection of Jesus Christ is so overwhelming that it compels acceptance by proof which leaves absolutely no room for doubt.[4]

This legal line of 'proof' has become so broadly based and influential it is appropriate to classify legal apologetics as an apologetic school: a school related to the historical argument for the resurrection of Jesus, yet with its own characteristics. In the nineteenth century the lawyer Francis Wharton asserted, 'Christian apologists have at all times been disposed, if not to adopt juridical tests, at least to appeal to juridical standards.'[5] Remarkably the significance of this school has largely gone unnoticed, perhaps because of its link to the historical apologetic.[6] Admittedly Craig, Dulles and Geisler have brief entries on one or two legal apologists, but not in the context of identifying any common legal paradigm or

---

[1] See chapter one and Appendix one.
[2] Cf. Phillip E. Johnson, *Darwin on Trial* (Downers Grove: InterVarsity, 1991). There will be further discussions on other models in chapter one and the Appendix.
[3] Michael Cassidy, *Chasing the Wind* (London: Hodder and Stoughton, 1985), 117-118.
[4] John Ankerberg and John Weldon, *Ready with an Answer* (Eugene: Harvest House, 1997), 106.
[5] Francis Wharton, 'Recent Changes in Jurisprudence and Apologetics', *The Princeton Review* 2, 1 (July-December 1878): 149. Wharton published a number of seminal texts on international civil and criminal law.

juridical school.⁷ Likewise Boa and Bowman in their recently published apologetic handbook have abbreviated entries on a small number of apologists who utilise the juridical model, under the heading 'The Rise of the Legal Evidence Model'.⁸

This study commences by analysing John Warwick Montgomery's legal apologetic. There are a number of reasons for the concentration on Montgomery.

1. Over the last forty years he has been one of the 'classic protagonists' for the apologetic methodology of evidentialism and the majority of legal apologists are evidentialists.⁹

---

⁶ For example the legal apologetic is overlooked in the following standard introductory texts on apologetics: Gordon Lewis, *Testing Christianity's Truth Claims* (Chicago: Moody, 1976); Bernard Ramm, *Varieties of Christian Apologetics* (Grand Rapids: Baker, 1961); L. Russ Bush, *Classical Readings in Christian Apologetics AD 100 --1800* (Grand Rapids: Zondervan, 1982); Norman Geisler, *Christian Apologetics* (Grand Rapids: Baker, 1976); Alister McGrath, *Bridge-Building: Effective Christian Apologetics* (Leicester: Inter-Varsity, 1992); Peter Kreeft and Ronald K. Tacelli, *Handbook of Christian Apologetics* (Downers Grove: Inter-Varsity, 1994). Even Frederic R. Howe who has a short section on legal evidence does not mention any legal apologists in *Challenge and Response* (Grand Rapids: Zondervan, 1982), 111-114.

⁷ William Lane Craig refers to Hugo Grotius in *Apologetics: An Introduction* (Chicago: Moody, 1984); Avery Dulles refers to Hugo Grotius, Thomas Sherlock and William Warburton in *A History of Apologetics* (Philadelphia: Westminster Press, 1972); Norman L. Geisler has entries on Simon Greenleaf and Thomas Sherlock in the *Baker Encyclopedia of Christian Apologetics* (Grand Rapids: Baker, 1999). Geisler here has a reference to Montgomery but not as to his legal apologetic even though Montgomery's legal apologetic was well established by the time of publication. Admittedly in *Miracles and the Modern Mind*, rev. ed. (Grand Rapids: Baker, 1992), 132-139, Geisler briefly refers to Greenleaf and Montgomery in a legal evaluation of witnesses. And in a text Geisler co-edited with a lawyer he uses the courtroom jury paradigm as a guide for truth finding. See Norman L. Geisler and Paul K. Hoffman, eds., *Why I am a Christian* (Grand Rapids: Baker, 2001), 7-12. Montgomery concurs that the legal apologetic is often neglected in contemporary apologetic assessments. See John Warwick Montgomery, *Defending the Gospel Through the Centuries: A History of Christian Apologetics*, Contemporary Apologists 11, audiotape (Newport: Institute for Law and Theology, 1980); John Warwick Montgomery, 'Neglected Apologetic Styles: The Juridical and the Literary' in *Evangelical Apologetics*, Michael Bauman, David Hall and Robert Newman, eds. (Camp Hill: Christian Publications, 1996), 119-126.

⁸ Kenneth D. Boa and Robert M. Bowman, *Faith has its Reasons: An Integrative Approach to Defending Christianity* (Colorado Springs: NavPress, 2001), 161-169.

⁹ Gary R. Habermas, 'Greg Bahnsen, John Warwick Montgomery, and Evidential Apologetics', *Global Journal of Classical Theology* 3, 1 (March 2002): 1, <http://www.trinitysem.edu/journal/toc_v3n1.html>. Montgomery has indicated that the legal style of proof is now his preferred method. See John Warwick Montgomery, 'A Lively Exchange on Evidentialism and Presuppositionalism', *Philosophia* 1, 4 (8 April 1999) on line at <http://www.trinitysem.edu/philosophia.html>.

Background and Focus of the Study

2. As a legal apologist his projects such as the Simon Greenleaf School of Law (now Trinity Law School) have influenced a new generation of apologists who interact with the legal method.[10]

3. As indicated in the 'Taxonomy' in chapter one, the legal apologetic for the resurrection of Jesus comprises a broad evangelical apologetic school but a critical assessment of all its layers lies beyond the scope of one thesis. Hence, the need for a critical consideration of one of its chief protagonists, as this approach will also bring insights and criticisms of the school as a whole.

4. Montgomery's legal apologetic is to date a paradigm for this discipline. Firstly, as one would expect of a lawyer, it succinctly and persuasively sets out the means of proof; documents, hearsay, testimony, things, circumstantial evidence[11] in support of the evidentiary fact in issue:

> *Jesus of Nazareth was executed by Roman authorities upon a cross at Golgotha. The said Jesus was some days later seen alive by various witnesses. It is claimed Jesus rose from the dead.*

James Fairbanks says of Montgomery's legal apologetic, 'the tightly constructed and highly logical arguments are indeed impressive.'[12] Secondly, it builds its case appropriately, beginning with the documents. Religious sceptic and lawyer Richard Packham, in the most extensive critique of Montgomery's legal apologetic to date concurs, 'I agree wholeheartedly that the first question to be answered is, "Are the historical records of Jesus (the canonical New Testament writings) solid enough to be relied on (to establish the claims of Christianity)?"[13] Thirdly, following on from the second point it establishes its case on primary

---

[10] For example Francis Beckwith, Kerry McRoberts, Craig Parton, John Weldon and Dan Story. All are referred to in the Bibliography and throughout this thesis. His legal-historical apologetic has also influenced leading established popular apologists. See Josh McDowell, *The Resurrection Factor* (San Bernardino: Here's Life, 1981); Don Stewart, *You be the Judge* (San Bernardino: Here's Life, 1983). Don Stewart has stated that John Warwick Montgomery is the apologist who has had the most influence on his own apologetic approach. Interview by the author (Eastwood, NSW, 8 August 1997).
[11] For the legal understanding of the means of proof see J.D. Heydon, *Cross on Evidence*, 5th Aust. ed. (Sydney: Butterworths, 1996), 46-59.
[12] James D. Fairbanks, review of *Christians in the Public Square*, by C.E.B. Cranfield, David Kilgour, John Warwick Montgomery, in *Fides et Historia* XXIX, 1 (Winter/Spring 1997): 177.
[13] Richard Packham, 'Critique of John Warwick Montgomery's Arguments for the Legal Evidence for Christianity', <http://www.infidels.org/library/modern/richardpackham/montgomery.html>, 5. See also McGrath, *Bridge-Building*, 160-165. McGrath states that two major reasons that cause people to stumble over the resurrection are 'the improbability of the event, the unreliability of the New Testament witness to the event' (160).

source data (the gospels) with limited but constructive use of secondary sources.[14] Fourthly, although a 'popular' apologetic, it provides extensive endnotes for the more 'academic' reader to investigate Montgomery's legal-historical apologetic and authorities relevant to the points being made.[15] Fifthly, the apologetic addresses the two basic questions a lawyer/tribunal has about inferential evidence: Is the relevant evidence admissible? Is the evidence credible? The rules and principles of law that Montgomery relies on for the first question, and the criteria he pleads for the second concern, will be considered at length in chapters two and three. Sixthly, it calls for a response. It pleads the main and subordinate facts in issue to the satisfaction of a reasonable person. Seventhly, it is a model with application beyond faith. Consistent with his monistic philosophy of knowledge Montgomery justifies the scriptures, Christian ethics, and a Christian understanding of human rights on the basis of the resurrection via the legal apologetic.[16]

Aims and Structure

The study has five main aims and the structure of the thesis corresponds to these aims. Firstly, I endeavour to outline the historical nature of the legal apologetic school and, via a taxonomy, evaluate Montgomery's model in comparison to other legal apologists. This occurs in chapter one. Secondly, I set out possible epistemological concerns as they relate to Montgomery's legal apologetic and indicate that the evidence admits a hearing, not a verdict, and the quantum of proof should be a civil standard where a special amount of evidence may be required. This also takes place in chapter one. Thirdly, the study is partly about showing Montgomery's adequacy in his apologetic approach to the evidences, but also about a progressive assessment of his approach. This results in an attempt not only to reframe Montgomery's legal apologetic, but also the legal apologetic paradigm as a whole. Such contribution can be seen to be relevant to the concerns of the 'modernity' style of thinking or what Montgomery categorises as the thinking of the 'tough-minded' enquirer.[17] This process occurs in chapters two and three.

---

[14] John Warwick Montgomery, *Human Rights and Human Dignity* (Grand Rapids: Zondervan, 1986), 137.
[15] Montgomery is often criticised for his 'popular' style. However, this is his basic apologetic model, and the criticism fails to recognise the exhaustive endnotes for the reader who wants to investigate further. See for example, John Warwick Montgomery, *Where is History Going?* (Minneapolis: Bethany, 1972).
[16] For example, Montgomery, *Human Rights*, 158-160.

Aims and Structure 15

The reframing of Montgomery's legal apologetic stresses, in part, that for a 'technical' apologetic the setting should be a *prima facie* case where the primary documentary evidence is admissible first-hand hearsay, not remote hearsay. In this regard John's gospel and Paul's resurrection account (1 Corinthians 15:8) are material documentary evidence in support of Christ's resurrection appearances. I explore the weight to be given to the book of James and Luke's gospel. Also I attempt to show how the admissible first-hand eyewitness testimony for the death and resurrection of Jesus passes Montgomery's criteria for credibility. With respect to the circumstantial evidence it needs to answer the criticism of the empty tomb hypothesis, for it deemed to be adequate. Further, I argue there is no 'real' evidence ('things') for the resurrection. I seek to present a reframing for the more general 'non-technical' apologetic relying on the principles outlined in the technical apologetic. As the role of evidences is not limited to evidentialism, but is found in most apologetic methodologies,[18] this reframing in some measure is seeking to speak to apologetic study as a whole.

Fourthly, to a probable response that Montgomery's apologetic persuasiveness for those exploring 'Postmodern Spirituality' or 'New Spirituality' is problematic, I seek to show, interacting with his literary and subjective evidential apologetic, its adequacy in that context as well. This is a direction Montgomery has not directly taken. This reframing indicates that the cumulative case for the resurrection commences with the human predicament of existential anxiety, and one of its main strands is the circumstantial evidence of common subjective experiences. I endeavour to establish by this reframing that Montgomery's legal apologetic has a broad application. This is considered in chapter four. Finally I aim to establish why Montgomery's juridical paradigm is an appropriate analogy.

---

[17] In the spirit of William James and Herbert Feigl the expression 'tough-minded' means for Montgomery respect for facts, open-mindedness, antagonistic approaches and an experimental trial and error attitude. See John Warwick Montgomery, ed., *Christianity for the Tough Minded* (Minneapolis: Bethany, 1973), 9-16. This is not a study on 'modernity' and 'postmodernity'. However the study acknowledges that with respect to religious truth claims there are those today who are attracted to a more reasoned, rational, cognitive thought-system which emphasises the scientific method. This is often labelled a 'modernity' style of thinking. In contrast others operate more out of a framework of 'New Spirituality' or 'postmodern' style of thinking with its commitment to story, experience and psychic unity. In chapter four this approach is considered. Further it is suggested that many are influenced by both thought patterns. For apologetic purposes there are those today who are more influenced by a rational defence and there are others who begin with how this connects to their subjective experiences.

[18] Gary R. Habermas 'Evidential Apologetics' in *Five Views on Apologetics*, Steven B. Cowan, ed. (Grand Rapids: Zondervan, 2000), 93-94. For a criticism of Habermas' evidentialism, yet an acceptance of his understanding of a role for evidences in other apologetic methodologies, see pages 122-145. See also Habermas, 'Bahnsen, Montgomery', 4-6.

In the three considered categories of scripture, history (tradition) and other factors there are bases for justifying the legal apologetic. This is the substance of chapter five.

Limitations

A focus on Montgomery's legal apologetic for the resurrection of Jesus means there are a number of delimitations. This would be true of any assessment of Montgomery's work as he writes and operates in so many disciplines. Mohler states that Montgomery, 'has developed one of the most varied resumes in the evangelical world'.[19] As will be outlined some of his fields of endeavour have already been subject to academic study. The legal apologetic is a study in itself.

1. This is not a study of the *bona fides* of Montgomery's methodology of evidentialism and its related epistemology.[20] In this regard see Boa and Bowman's evaluation in *Faith has its Reasons*.[21] Montgomery comments that in this text his 'evidentialist method is very fairly presented and (unlike many who have treated it ...) Boa and Bowman have actually read and assimilated most of the author's central publications on the subject'.[22] There are a number of other evaluations of his evidentialism.[23] Therefore this thesis is pursuing internal questions as to the adequacy of Montgomery's evidential legal apologetic.

2. This study is neither a study of Montgomery's historical method,[24] nor his renowned historical apologetic[25] for the resurrection of Jesus which have

---

[19] See Richard Albert Mohler, 'Evangelical Theology and Karl Barth: Representative Models of Response' (Ph.D. Thesis, The Southern Baptist Theological Seminary, 1989), 39.

[20] For example see John Warwick Montgomery, *Faith Founded on Fact* (Nashville and New York: Thomas Nelson, 1978), esp. 107-127. Cf. John W. Frame, *Cornelius Van Til: An Analysis of His Thought* (Phillipsburg, New Jersey: Presbyterian and Reformed, 1995), 299-309.

[21] Boa and Bowman, *Faith*, 159-206.

[22] John Warwick Montgomery, 'Editor's Introduction', *Global Journal of Classical Theology* 3, 1 (March 2002): 1, <http://www.trinitysem.edu/journal/toc_v3n1.html>.

[23] See for example Kenneth Dale Boa, 'A Comparative Study of Four Christian Apologetic Systems' (Ph.D. Thesis, New York University, 1985), chaps. vi and xii; W. Gary Phillips, 'Apologetics and Inerrancy: An Analysis of Selected Axiopistic Models' (Th.D. Thesis, Grace Theological Seminary, 1985), chap. 3; Greg Bahnsen, 'A Critique of the Evidentialist Apologetical Method of John Warwick Montgomery', *Covenant Media Foundation*, <http://www.cmfnow.com/cgi-bin/nextpg?cmd=NextPg!1172&dir=s7!articles&tpl=PA016.htm>. See the response to Bahnsen: Habermas, 'Bahnsen, Montgomery'. See also the theses mentioned in endnote 26.

[24] See John Warwick Montgomery, *The Shape of the Past: A Christian Response to Secular Philosophies of History,* rev.ed. (Minneapolis: Bethany, 1975); Montgomery, *Where is History Going?*

[25] See John Warwick Montgomery, *History and Christianity* (Downers Grove: InterVarsity, 1971).

already been the subject of numerous evaluations.[26] Montgomery's historical apologetic preceded his legal apologetic, which developed with his increasing interest and qualifications in the law.

3. As Montgomery is an evangelical and his apologetic influence is on the large world of evangelical apologetics this study analyses his legal apologetic within that framework. It is about Montgomery's adequacy in his evangelical legal apologetic approach.

4. This study is neither a defence of the laws of evidence nor a history of evidence. These are clearly thesis topics in themselves. It is therefore not considering as such the status of legal evidence: documents, hearsay, testimony, things, circumstantial evidence. The first emphasis is on the methodological question of how the legal criteria used by Montgomery and the legal apologists to test the admissibility and credibility of the evidence generally, applies to the particular case of Christ's death and resurrection.[27]

5. This study is not a biography[28] of Montgomery nor a bibliography of his work.[29] Montgomery is viewed by some as a 'controversialist' and within evangelical and Lutheran circles there have been many discussions over his

---

[26] See the following theses: Martin Batts, 'A Summary and Critique of the Historical Apologetic of John Warwick Montgomery' (Th.M. Thesis, Dallas Theological Seminary, 1977); Stephen D. Rook, 'Historical Objectivism: The Apologetic Methodology of John Warwick Montgomery' (M.A. Thesis, Harding Graduate School of Religion, 1985); Keith Andrew Mascord, 'Faith, History and the Morality of Knowledge: The Contrasting Views of J.W. Montgomery and V.A. Harvey' (M.Th. Thesis, Australian College of Theology, 1993); Kerry McRoberts, 'Faith Founded on Fact: The Apologetic Theology of John Warwick Montgomery (M.C.S. Thesis, Regent College, 2000). See also the debate on Montgomery's historical method in *Fides et Historia*. Ronald J. VanderMolen, 'The Christian Historian: Apologist or Seeker', *Fides et Historia* 3, 1 (Fall 1970): 41-56; William A. Speck, 'Herbert Butterfield on the Christian and Historical Study', *Fides et Historia* 4, 1 (Fall 1971): 50-70; John Warwick Montgomery and James R. Moore, 'The Speck in Butterfield's Eye: A Reply to William A. Speck', *Fides et Historia* 4, 1 (Fall 1971): 71-77; Steven A. Hein, 'The Christian Historian: Apologist or Seeker?- A Reply to Ronald J. VanderMolen', *Fides et Historia* 4, 2 (Spring 1972): 85-93; W. Stanford Reid, 'The Problem of the Christian Interpretation of History', *Fides et Historia* 5, 1-2 (Spring 1973): 96-106; Timothy Paul Erdel, 'Stigma and Dogma: A Reply to Earl William Kennedy on Behalf of John Warwick Montgomery', *Fides et Historia* 6, 1 (Fall 1974): 26-32. See also Paul D. Feinberg, 'History: Private or Public? A Defense of John Warwick Montgomery's Philosophy of History', *Christian Scholar's Review* 1, 4 (Summer 1971): 325-331; Stephen J. Wykstra, 'The Problem of Miracle in the Apologetic from History', *Journal of the American Scientific Affiliation* 30, 4 (December 1978): 154-163.

[27] A detailed focus on criteria used rather than the status of a model, be it legal, philosophical or historical is not uncommon in light of limitations of research. For a thorough and recent discussion on the status of testimony in Jesus' time see Samuel Byrskog, *Story as History as Story* (Tübingen: Mohr Siebeck, 2001), 203-223.

theology and alliances. Liefeld's study well sets out Montgomery's story within such a context.[30].

Therefore, this study seeks to evaluate the adequacy of Montgomery's legal apologetic, to critique it, and by attempting to reframe it, show that it is *an apologetic for all seasons*.

---

[28] However, it is of some importance to note that Montgomery has a number of postgraduate degrees in the fields of theology (with an apologetic perspective) and law. (A.B., Cornell University; B.L.S.; M.A., University of California; B.D., S.T.M., Wittenberg University; M.Phil. in Law, University of Essex; LL.M., LL.D., Cardiff University; Ph.D., University of Chicago; Th.D., University of Strasbourg.) Further, he is a Barrister-at-Law in England and Wales and a member of the Bar of the Supreme Court of the United States. He is Emeritus Professor of Law and Humanities at the University of Luton. Montgomery specialises in human rights' law. See Montgomery, *Human Rights*; John Warwick Montgomery, *The Repression of Evangelism in Greece: European Litigation vis-à-vis a Closed Religious System* (Lanham, Maryland and Oxford: University Press of America, 2001).

[29] For an extensive bibliography see *Bibliography of Dr John Warwick Montgomery's Writings*, 3rd ed. (Edmonton: Canadian Institute for Law, Theology and Public Policy, 2000).

[30] David R. Liefeld, 'Lutheran Motifs in the Writings of John Warwick Montgomery' (M.Th. Thesis, Westminster Theological Seminary, 1986), esp. 1-91. For personal reflections on his life see James R. Moore, 'The Contributors' in *Christianity for the Tough Minded*, Montgomery, ed., 290-291.

Chapter 1

The History of the Legal Apologetic, a Taxonomy, Montgomery's Model, and Epistemological Concerns

Historical Background

Montgomery views Hugo Grotius, the 'father' of international law and the instigator of Protestant apologetics, as the founder of the legal apologetic that is based on the resurrection of Jesus. He then very briefly traces its life through Thomas Sherlock, Simon Greenleaf up to Sir Norman Anderson. He also notes the role played by the Apostle Paul as a rabbinic lawyer.[1] Not surprisingly, Montgomery concludes with a comment from his own theological mentor, Martin Luther, to add weight: 'If the world will not hear the divines, they must hear the lawyers, who will teach them manners.'[2]

In this section the condensed thoughts of Montgomery will be expanded on together with the offering of possible new insights and leads. Such an extensive overview is of some importance as it is not to be found elsewhere. However, the task of fully unravelling the origins of the legal polemic and the historical connection between the various apologists lies beyond the scope of this thesis. A future thesis could well focus on an historical analysis of the development of the legal argument for the resurrection.[3]

The Early Church

It argued at some length in chapter five that the legal paradigm has its roots in the early church, particularly in the gospel of John and Luke-Acts. I also document its connection to the Apostle Paul. The rabbinic reasoning method of Paul should not be understated. He was a student of the Torah. New Testament historian Paul Barnett asserts 'Paul was a brilliant man with a lawyers' mind'.[4] And this legal expertise found expression beyond Judaism. Alister McGrath argues that Paul's apologetic to the Romans in Acts 24-26 is not philosophical or theological, but conforms to the pattern of legal Roman proceedings well known in that period.[5]

---

[1] See John Warwick Montgomery, *The Law Above the Law* (Minneapolis: Bethany, 1975), 43-4; Montgomery, *Human Rights*, 133-154.

[2] Montgomery, *The Law Above*, 90.

[3] In fact individual theses on the legal apologetic of Simon Greenleaf and Sir Norman Anderson would be justified.

[4] Paul Barnett, 'Risen Christ is Historical Reality', *Sydney Morning Herald* (5 April 1994), 12.

Duncan Derrett surmises from his expertise in Oriental Law that the clue to understanding Paul does lie in his legal thinking and his ability to construct an apologetic letter anticipating the correspondent's objections.[6] He observes 'The rhetoric of the times expected the orator to anticipate objections and forestall them.'[7]. Whilst it is true that much of what Paul wrote was to Christian believers, his speeches in Acts contain apologetic data, as do parts of his letters.[8]

Apologists note this reliance on legal rhetoric is also found in early church apologists, particularly Tertullian.[9] This is not surprising as those preparing for a life in the civil service in the Latin speaking West often faced instruction in rhetoric and advocacy.[10] Tertullian probably also practised as a jurisconsult.[11] Now whilst Tertullian does not enter into a legal defence of the resurrection, in the *Apology* his legal training is most evident in his arguments defending the good citizenship of the Christians and the high calibre of Christianity as a religion in contrast to other world views.[12] Burrows, who explores Tertullian scholarship of the last 100

---

[5] Alister E. McGrath, 'Apologetics to the Romans', *Bibliotheca Sacra*, 155 (October-December 1998): 387-393.

[6] J. Duncan M. Derrett, *Law in the New Testament* (London: Durton, Longman and Todd, 1970), 461-463.

[7] ibid, 463.

[8] Paul Barnett states that when a Pauline letter contains historical information about Jesus, such information is given to make some apologetic or doctrinal point, *Jesus and the Rise of Early Christianity* (Downers Grove: InterVarsity, 1999), 416. See also James D.G. Dunn, *Romans 1-8* (Dallas: Word, 1988), lvi.

[9] Montgomery in his historical tape series spends time on an analysis of Grotius, Sherlock and Greenleaf as well as acknowledging the legal pedigree and role of Tertullian. See Montgomery, *Defending the Gospel*. Ambrose (Bishop of Milan), Amphilochius (Bishop of Iconium), Cyprian (Bishop of Carthage), Eusebius (Bishop of Doryleum) and pagan apologist Lucian of Samosata are a sample of some other possibilities. For initial reading see J.D. Douglas, ed. *The New International Dictionary of the Christian Church* (Exeter: Paternoster, 1974). With respect to Lucian also see William L. Lane, 'Unexpected light on Hebrews 13:1-6 from a second century source', *Perspectives in Religious Studies* 9, 3 (Fall 1982): 267-274. In the Eastern Orthodox tradition is George Scholarius (c.1400-c.1468). See Jaroslav Pelikan, *The Christian Tradition: A History of the Development of Doctrine*, Vol. 2 (Chicago and London: The University Press, 1974), 242.

[10] See for example J.N.D. Kelly, *Jerome* (Peabody, Massachusetts: Hendrickson, 1998), 10-17. Only in the twelfth century did law cease to be a subdivision of rhetoric. See John Warwick Montgomery, *Christ our Advocate* (Bonn: Verlag für Kultur und Wissenschaft, Culture and Science, 2002), 272. This book was not published at the time of completing this thesis.

[11] A. Cleveland Cox, 'Introducing note' in *The Ante-Nicene Fathers*, Vol. III, Alexander Roberts and James Donaldson, eds. (Grand Rapids: William B. Eerdmans, 1968), 3. Hans Von Campenhausen indicated that at the very least 'Tertullian thinks like a lawyer'. See *Ecclesiastical Authority and Spiritual Power in the Church of the First Three Centuries*, trans. J. A. Baker (London: Adam and Charles Black, 1969), 174.

[12] 'Tertullian's Apology is a brilliant application of Roman juridical principles to the defence of Christianity'. Dulles, *A History*, 40.

years and its forensic law court rhetoric links finds, 'Drawing upon an established form of forensic rhetoric in the *Apology* Tertullian acts as an advocate, bringing a carefully crafted and stylistically polished case for Christianity not simply before "the Roman Magistrates", but before the literate Roman audience of his day.'[13]

Grotius, Sherlock, Greenleaf

Despite these strong early roots, the structure of today's juridical apologetic with its legal terminology and resurrection focus is traced to Hugo Grotius.[14] In book two of *The Truth of the Christian Religion,* Grotius' argument is based on historical proof for the divinity of Christ on the basis of his miracles, including the resurrection.[15] His method here is consistent with early church apologists such as Eusebius and is in line with latter legal apologists such as Montgomery.[16] Phrases like 'The resurrection of Jesus Christ proved from credible testimony', 'founded upon sufficient testimony' and 'affirmed themselves to be eyewitnesses of it' have added meaning in light of his legal status.[17]

Now whilst it is true that the current legal apologetic is indebted to Grotius, its more obvious foundations are the writings of Thomas Sherlock and Simon Greenleaf. In response to Deists such as Thomas Woolston, Sherlock (1678-1761) used an actual legal model in his apologia, *Trial of the Witnesses of the Resurrection of Jesus.*[18] As Master of the Inner Temple Church, Sherlock was a pastor to the legal profession. Although not a lawyer himself, he creatively employed a legal moot to determine whether the witnesses to Christ's resurrec-

---

[13] Mark S. Burrows, 'Christianity in the Roman Forum: Tertullian and the Apologetic Use of History", *Vigilae Christianae* 42, 3 (September 1988): 214.

[14] Montgomery, *The Law Above,* 84. For background to Grotius see Oliver O'Donovan and Joan Lockwood O'Donovan, eds., *From Irenaeus to Grotius: A Sourcebook in Christian Political Thought* (Grand Rapids and Cambridge: William B. Eerdmans, 1999), 787-792.

[15] Hugo Grotius, *The Truth of the Christian Religion*, trans. John Clarke (London: William Baynes, 1825).

[16] Eusebius, *Demonstratio Evangelica*, 3.4. For discussion see William Lane Craig, *The Historical Argument for the Resurrection of Jesus During the Deist Controversy* (Lewiston: Edwin Mellen, 1985), 46-50.

[17] Grotius, *The Truth*, Book II, 82-85.

[18] Thomas Sherlock, *The Tryal of the Witnesses of the Resurrection of Jesus* is photoreproduced in John Warwick Montgomery, ed., *Jurisprudence: A Book of Readings* (Strasbourg: International Scholarly Publishers, 1974), 339-450. For a brief evaluation of eighteenth century apologists (Sherlock, Butler and Paley), who rely on the role of law and evidence see Jan-Melissa Schramm, *Testimony and Advocacy in Victorian Law, Literature and Theology* (Cambridge: Cambridge University Press, 2000), 32-37.

tion gave false evidence and whether therefore the resurrection was a fraud. Sherlock took his cue from Woolston's blasphemy trial and had the case 'reopened' after a friendly discussion among 'Gentlemen of the Inns of Court'.[19] Colin Brown observes that the summing up of the judge in Sherlock's moot puts the charges against the apostles in two main categories. 'The first (which anticipated Reimarus) was that the whole story was a piece of fraud and deceit.' The second (which anticipated Hume and Lessing) was that the evidence was insufficient to support so extraordinary an event.[20] In Sherlock's apologetic the jury found the apostles not guilty of giving false evidence. His book went through numerous editions and continues to be reprinted.[21] Sherlock's tome was answered by another deist Peter Annet with his *The Resurrection of Jesus Consider'd*. And it is in this eighteenth century literature war between Christians and Deists where Gilbert West's urbane harmonisation of the resurrection narratives, *Observations on the History and Evidence of the Resurrection*, appears. West, a clerk to the Privy Council[22] was awarded the Oxford Doctorate of Civil Law for his effort.[23]

Simon Greenleaf (1783-1853), after a distinguished career as a lawyer and court reporter, was appointed to The Royall Professorship of Law in the Harvard Law School. On the death of Joseph Story, Greenleaf was appointed as the Dane Professor in the same school. Greenleaf is recognised as the foremost North American authority on common law evidence in the nineteenth century[24] and he remains an established authority on evidence today.[25]

---

[19] Sherlock, *The Tryal*, 341-343.
[20] Colin Brown, *Jesus in European Protestant Thought 1778-1860* (Grand Rapids: Baker, 1985), 41-43.
[21] For discussion of Sherlock's role see Colin Brown, *Philosophy and the Christian Faith* (London: Inter-Varsity, 1969), 76-79.
[22] He was appointed extra clerk on 15 May 1729 and then as clerk on 21 April 1752. For the historical list of all the clerks of the Privy Council see <http://www.ihrinfo.ac.uk/publications/office/office1.html>.
[23] See Colin Brown, *Miracles and the Critical Mind* (Grand Rapids: William B. Eerdmans; Devon: Paternoster, 1984), 51-58; Craig, *The Historical*, 260-261, 348.
[24] For biographical details see Ross Clifford, *The Case for the Empty Tomb*, 2nd rev. ed. (Sutherland, NSW: Albatross, 1993), 41-55. Also published as *Leading Lawyers' Case for the Resurrection* (Edmonton: Canadian Institute for Law, Theology and Public Policy, 1996) and *Leading Lawyers Look at the Resurrection* (Sutherland, NSW: Albatross, 1991).
[25] Pamela Binnings Ewen, *Faith on Trial* (Nashville; Broadman and Holman, 1999), 10. His primary text on evidence was Simon Greenleaf, *A Treatise on the Law of Evidence* (Boston: C.C. Little and J. Brown, 1842). Publishers Gaunt Incorporated reprinted in 1997.

Historical Background 23

Greenleaf's main apologetic work is *The Testimony of the Evangelists*.[26] It is primarily a harmony of the gospels. The introductory section of the book, *An Examination of the Testimony of the Evangelists*,[27] is the apologetic section of most interest. In this apologetic Greenleaf was clearly influenced by clergy with a legal 'mind'. He cites Mark Hopkins' Lowell Institute lectures on a number of occasions.[28] The lectures were published in 1846 as *Evidence of Christianity*. Hopkins, a Congregational minister and not a lawyer, was interested in law and his book became a standard college textbook for many years. Hopkins uses such phraseology as 'we should hold ourselves in the position of an impartial jury, bound to decide solely according to the evidence.'[29] Greenleaf also often cites Thomas Hartwell Horne, an apologist, librarian and bible commentator. Horne was ordained in the Church of England in 1819 and had worked as a clerk to a barrister.[30]

In his apologetic Greenleaf carefully scrutinizes the gospels by principles of evidence, such as the 'Ancient Documents' rule, and finds a court of law would admit them and find their contents reliable. His work is the origin of what is identified in the next section of this chapter as the 'technical legal apologetic'. This technical legal apologetic will strongly influence the American legal apologetic, whilst the English tradition follows a more general legal reasoning format. Perhaps this is due to its connection to the marginally less 'technical', yet effective, approach of Thomas Sherlock.

Greenleaf's legal argument has been most influential and is replicated in apologetic works to the present time. Prominent apologists or lawyers who rely heavily on Greenleaf include: Charles Morrison,[31] Joseph Sagebeer,[32] Francis Lamb,[33] Walter Chandler,[34] Stephen Williams,[35] Howard Russell,[36] Irwin Linton,[37] Clarence Bartlett,[38], Montgomery,[39] and Pamela Ewen.[40]

---

[26] Simon Greenleaf, *The Testimony of the Evangelists* (Grand Rapids: Baker, 1984).
[27] ibid, 1-54.
[28] ibid, 3-6, 41.
[29] Mark Hopkins, *Evidences of Christianity* (Boston: Marvin, 1876), 39.
[30] See Greenleaf, *The Testimony,* 3-24; Thomas Hartwell Horne, *An Introduction to the Critical Study and Knowledge of the Holy Scriptures*, 4 vols. (Philadelphia: E. Littell, 1825).
[31] Charles R. Morrison, *The Proofs of Christ's Resurrection from a Lawyer's Standpoint* (Andover: Warren F. Draper, 1882).
[32] Joseph Evans Sagebeer, *The Bible in Court* (Philadelphia: Lippincott, 1900).
[33] Francis J. Lamb, *Miracle and Science: Biblical Miracles Examined by the Methods, Rules and Tests of the Science of Jurisprudence as Administered Today in Courts of Justice* (Oberlin, Ohio: Bibliotheca Sacra, 1909).
[34] Walter M. Chandler, *The Trial of Jesus from a Lawyer's Standpoint*, 2 vols. (New York: Federal Press, 1925).

Links to the Historical Apologetic

It is evident that the rise of the legal apologetic via Sherlock and Greenleaf is connected to the 'flowering' of the historical apologetic in the eighteenth century. Dulles observes that the eighteenth century apologetic almost exclusively focused on biblical and historical evidences.[41] William Lane Craig, whilst affirming this eighteenth century florescence, believes the 'flowering' of the historical evidential apologetic reaches back to Hugo Grotius.[42] His view here lends weight to Montgomery's position on the role of Grotius in historical-legal apologetics.

Craig indicates there are a number of reasons for the growth of the historical argument in the eighteenth century and these can be directly applied to the legal parallel. These include the rise of historical consciousness and historiography, the spread of Deism, and the strength of rationalism.[43] The Deist challenge called for a defence of the resurrection and the enlightenment spirit of the time was open to a rigorous apologetic model based on an epistemological common ground. Yet it was not a philosophical defence as few Deist disputants were philosophical rationalists and the debate focused on natural and revealed religion.[44]

It is interesting to note that whilst the historical apologetic declined in the nineteenth century due to the advance of biblical criticism, 'the tide of subjectivism', religious revival and romanticism,[45] the legal apologetic in Simon Greenleaf and others had its growth period in this same time right up until the mid twentieth century. With the development of jurisprudence the historical argument may have found another home.[46]

---

[35] Stephen D. Williams, *The Bible in Court or Truth vs Error* (Dearborn, Michigan: Dearborn, 1925).
[36] Howard Hyde Russell, *A Lawyer's Examination of the Bible* (Westerville, Ohio: Bible Bond, 1935).
[37] Irwin H. Linton, *A Lawyer Examines the Bible: An Introduction to Christian Evidences*, 5th edn. (Boston: W.A. Wilde, 1943).
[38] Clarence Bartlett, *As a Lawyer Sees Jesus: A Logical Analysis of the Scriptural and Historical Record* (New York: Greenwich, 1960).
[39] Montgomery, *Human Rights*, 137-150.
[40] Ewen, *Faith*.
[41] Dulles, *A History*, 155-257.
[42] Craig, *The Historical*, 71.
[43] ibid., 234-235, 317-321, 350-352.
[44] ibid, 234-235.
[45] ibid., 352-427.

In today's biblically critical world both schools are well represented.[47] And apologists such as Montgomery and Strobel use historical and legal insights in their apologetic and interact in some depth with both disciplines.[48]

One should not be surprised by this link between the historical and juridical apologetic, as in fact legal scholarship helped shape the development of the modern historical method.[49] Bebbington notes that Jean Bodin is just one French humanist who approached the study of history via legal studies:

> This group of writers seems to have had no well-known successors in France, although their legal approach to history became entrenched in southern Italy and affected seventeenth-century constitutional thought in Britain. Furthermore Bodin in particular undoubtedly influenced the greatest precursor of historicism, an early eighteenth-century Florentine professor of rhetoric, Giambattista Vico.[50]

Vico himself was an Italian jurist. Montgomery in his philosophical historiography argues for Vico's importance to Christianity together with the role he played in the anticipation of the historical method and the elevation of history to its proper place among the sciences.[51] Vico in his autobiography shows a further link to jurisprudence by noting his indebtedness to jurists Francis Bacon and Hugo Grotius. In particular he appreciated Grotius embracing in a system of universal law the whole of philosophy and philology.[52]

---

[46] Cf. Schramm who suggests the approximate end-point to the evidentiary apologetic, including one with a legal testimony emphasis, as being 1870. See *Testimony*, 31. The historical reliability argument for the New Testament is still found in classics like Alexander Balmain Bruce, *Apologetics or, Christianity Defensively Stated* (Edinburgh: T & T Clark, 1911); F.F. Bruce, *The New Testament Documents: Are They Reliable?*, 5th ed. (London: Inter-Varsity, 1960).

[47] See for example, Paul Barnett, *Is the New Testament History?* (Sydney: Hodder and Stoughton, 1986); Ewen, *Faith*.

[48] Montgomery, *History and Christianity*; Montgomery, *Human Rights*, 131-160; Lee Strobel, *The Case for Christ* (Grand Rapids: Zondervan, 1998). This is most evident in Montgomery's latest book. Montgomery combines here historical and legal insights in the form of propositions. See John Warwick Montgomery, *Tractatus Logico–Theologicus* (Bonn: Verlag für Kultur und Wissenschaft, Culture and Science, 2002), 3 – 3.691.

[49] Further, on the influence of rhetorical persuasion on Graeco-Roman literary and historical sources see Byrskog, *Story*, 203-223.

[50] David Bebbington, *Patterns in History* (Leicester: InterVarsity, 1979), 95.

[51] Montgomery, *The Shape*, 187-216. Cf. Robert Flint, *Vico* (Edinburgh and London: Blackwood, 1884), 44, 80-82.

[52] Frederick Copleston, *A History of Philosophy*, Vol. 6 (New York: Doubleday, 1985), 154-157.

This interconnectedness between jurists and the advancement of historical consciousness is paralleled in the development of the legal and historical polemic. Yet in apologetic study, the role of the legal paradigm has been regretfully absorbed by the historical apologetic.

Common Sense

In this historical overview there is one other well-documented tie that deserves mentioning. The nineteenth century American evangelical apologetic, including the legal apologetic, was unquestioningly influenced by Common Sense philosophy or Scottish Realism.[53] It had great impact upon Mark Hopkins and no doubt Simon Greenleaf as well who certainly relied on Hopkins.[54] Common Sense confidence in the scientific method and its commitment to realism was its empirical base. In this regard the influence of jurist and former Lord Chancellor Francis Bacon was strategic with his belief in objective fact finding and the inductive method applicable to a variety of disciplines.[55] As far as faith was concerned, those influenced by Common Sense philosophy touted a sure rational base for the truths of the bible and the ability to demonstrate the truths of Christianity to the honest enquirer.[56] Marsden brings this summary:

> Critical to the nineteenth century apologists' arguments for the authenticity of Scripture, for instance, was an appeal to the very down-to-earth and everyday reliability of human testimony. A law of our nature simply obliges us to believe the testimony of witnesses of known veracity. Courts of law in all cultures and all our knowledge of the past depend on such sources.

---

[53] For its impact on the Princeton school of apologetics see Raymond Cannata, 'History of apologetics at Princeton Seminary' in *Unapologetic Apologetics*, William A. Dembski and Jay Wesley Richards, eds. (Downers Grove: InterVarsity, 2001), 57-76.

[54] George M Marsden, *Fundamentalism and American Culture* (New York and Oxford: Oxford University Press, 1980), 13-17. See also Mark Ellingsen, 'Common Sense Realism: The Cutting Edge of Evangelical Identity', *Dialog*, 24 (1985): 197-205; Theodore Dwight Bozeman, *Protestants in an Age of Science: The Baconian Ideal and Antebellum American Religious Thought* (Chapel Hill: University of North Carolina Press, 1977).

[55] Marsden, *Fundamentalism*, 15, 55-62. For Bacon's reliance on Renaissance Law in his inductive method see Charles B. Thaxton, 'A Dialogue with "Prof" on Christianity and Science' in *God and Culture: Essays in Honor of Carl F.H. Henry*, D.A. Carson and John D. Woodbridge, eds. (Grand Rapids: William B. Eerdmans, 1993), 286-288 and endnote 17.

[56] Marsden, *Fundamentalism*, 15-16; Mark A Noll, 'Common Sense Traditions and American Evangelical Thought', *American Quarterly*, 37 (1985): 216.

All but the most hardened skeptics must agree that veracious testimony often is a legitimate ground for certainty. So ran the common argument for the authority of Scripture.[57]

Influence on General Christian and Non-Christian Apologetic Works

Since the time of Grotius it is apparent that legal reasoning has also made an impression on Christian apologists and evangelists whom one would not normally classify as being legal apologists. (In the next section it will be shown that legal apologists include both the legally and non-legally trained.) There are apologists, like Mark Hopkins, who have dipped into legal technology or reasoning without being identified as part of the legal apologetic school. There are some other prominent examples worthy of mention. There are the legal trials and legal ideas created by John Bunyan in *Pilgrim's Progress* and *The Holy War*.[58] Parkin-Speer says Bunyan actually shifts from these legal analogies to religious and scriptural levels. Bunyan portrays 'the hope of apocalyptic justice which will go beyond earthly, human justice.'[59]

Montgomery asserts Bishop Joseph Butler was, prior to C.S. Lewis, probably the greatest Anglican apologist.[60] In Butler's apologetic response to Deism, that reflects heavily on the phenomena of nature, there are phraseology and allusions that express his reading in the law. Butler speaks in legal terminology when he avers to: 'evidence from testimony', 'proof of Christianity', 'real weight', 'direct and circumstantial evidence'.[61] Butler was awarded the B.C.L. (Bachelor of Civil Law) in 1721 and the D.C.L. in 1733 from Oxford University. It is not possible to know exactly what in common law would have been studied for these degrees, as the then university records do not give any information about course content.[62]

---

[57] George M. Marsden, 'Everyone One's Own Interpreter? The Bible, Science and Authority in Mid-Nineteenth Century America' in *The Bible in America: Essays in Cultural History*, Nathan O. Hatch and Mark A Noll, eds. (New York and Oxford: Oxford University Press, 1982), 91.
[58] Diane Parkin-Speer, 'John Bunyan's Legal Ideas and the Legal Trials in His Analogies', *The Baptist Quarterly* XXXV, 7 (July 1994): 324-331.
[59] ibid., 330.
[60] John Warwick Montgomery, *Defending the Biblical Gospel, Study Guide*, Joseph P. Gudel, prepared (Edmonton: Canadian Institute for Law, Theology and Public Policy, 1999), 48.
[61] Joseph Butler, *The Analogy of Religion* (London: Bell and Daldy, 1871), esp. part II, chap. 7.
[62] This information is recorded in an email received from Alice Blackford, Assistant Keeper of the Archives (Oxford University, 19 March 2001). Also see Leslie Stephen, 'Joseph Butler' in *The Dictionary of Natural Biography*, Vol. III, Leslie Stephen and Sidney Lee, eds. (London: Oxford University Press, 1917), 519-525.

William Paley's *A View of the Evidences of Christianity* is the 'high water mark' of the historical apologetic.[63] It could be argued that the influence of the law on his treatise has been underplayed. Howson records how Paley, who became a justice of the peace, spent his spare time as a young man attending trials and that 'all through life he displayed marked cleverness in weighing evidence, and a great love of that kind of pointed investigation which is required in the cross-examination of witnesses.'[64] Lawyer Professor Blunt said of Paley 'it would not be in the power of the most suspicious lawyer at The Old Bailey to subject two witnesses to a stricter cross-examination than that by which Paley has tried the testimony of St Luke and St Paul'.[65] Further, he performed the role of chancellor of ecclesiastical courts and the canons required this person to be learned in the civil as well as the ecclesiastical law.[66]

There is intrinsic evidence of how Paley's interest in law affected his work. For example, when dealing with the alleged discrepancies between the gospel accounts he stated,

> The usual character of human testimony is substantial truth under circumstantial variety. This is what the daily experience of courts of justice teaches. When accounts of a transaction come from the mouths of different witnesses, it is seldom that it is not possible to pick out apparent or real inconsistencies between them. These inconsistencies are studiously displayed by an adverse pleader, but oftentimes with little impression upon the minds of the judges.[67]

Another sign in Paley's apologetic is the conclusion to his said book that reads as a legal summation. With respect to the miracle narratives he pleads they are written,

> By eyewitnesses of the scene, by contemporaries and companions of those who were so; not in one book, but four each containing enough for the verification of the religion, all agreeing in the fundamental parts of the history.

---

[63] Craig, *The Historical*, 352.
[64] J.S. Howson 'Preface' in William Paley, *Horae Pauline* (London: Society for Promoting Christian Knowledge, 1891), xi-xiii.
[65] ibid, xii.
[66] M.L. Clarke, *Paley: Evidences for the Man* (Toronto: University of Toronto Press, 1974), 33.
[67] William Paley *A View of the Evidences of Christianity*, rev. ed. (London: The Religious Tract Society, 1848), 319.

> We have these books, established by more and more stronger proofs than belong to almost any other ancient book whatever ...[68]

The revivalist Charles Finney, unlike Bunyan and Paley, had legal qualifications as he sat the bar examination.[69] His commitment to Christian ministry and the bible came as he read the scriptures in the context of his legal training.[70] Finney based his evangelistic preaching on the model of a lawyer before a jury.[71] And although Finney is not remembered as an apologist, he did address groups of sceptical lawyers and others of a like mind. On these occasions he set out 'to convince the lawyers' of the truth of the Christian worldview and biblical soteriology.[72]

R.A. Torrey did his undergraduate study at Yale with the intention of proceeding to law school, but was 'called' to Yale Divinity School.[73] He was the heir of D.L. Moody in evangelism and his apologetic for the intrinsic evidence for the reliability of the gospels is well pleaded.[74] Finally, Boa and Bowman argue that Richard Whately, James Orr and Clark Pinnock are apologists who were likewise influenced by the legal evidence model.[75]

In this post-Reformation period it is not only the traditional Christian apologists who have seen the benefit of the juridical method. Herman Reimarus' rationalistic apology that was published anonymously and posthumously in 'fragments' by Lessing, gave birth to the nineteenth century search for the historical Jesus. His influence permeated the twentieth century, with Albert Schweitzer affirming this 'most splendid achievement' and 'that we should recognise an historical performance of no mean order in this piece of Deistic polemics'.[76] In the fragment, 'On

---

[68] Paley, *A View*, 366.
[69] Charles G. Finney, *An Autobiography* (London: The Salvationist, n.d.), 4-6.
[70] ibid, 6.
[71] ibid, 68-71. For further discussion see Charles E. Hambrick-Stowe, *Charles G. Finney and the Spirit of American Evangelicalism* (Grand Rapids: William B Eerdmans, 1996), 6-10, 34-35. 'What struck many people about Finney's preaching was that he sounded like a lawyer arguing his case in court.'(35).
[72] Finney, *An Autobiography*, 298-305, 364-368.
[73] Roger Martin, 'R.A. Torrey – Defender of the Faith', *Simon Greenleaf Law Review*, VII (1987-1988): 165-197.
[74] R.A Torrey, *What the Bible Teaches* (New York: Revell, 1898), 166-167. For the role of the evidences for the resurrection see R.A. Torrey, 'The Centrality and Importance of the Bodily Resurrection of Christ from the Dead' in *The Fundamentals for Today*, Vol. 1, R.A. Torrey, ed. (Grand Rapids: Kregel, 1958), 265-279.
[75] Boa and Bowman, *Faith*, 161-169.
[76] Albert Schweitzer, *The Quest of the Historical Jesus*, trans. W. Montgomery (London: A. & C. Black, 1911), 22-23.

the resurrection narratives' Reimarus' aim is to prove the narratives are self contradictory. In his judicially styled argument he cites ten alleged contradictions. Reimarus states, 'Witnesses who differ so greatly in the most important points of testimony would not be recognised in any secular court as valid and legal ... to the extent that a judge could rely on their story and base his decision on it.' He poses the question: how could anyone justify their religion and salvation 'upon the testimony of four such varying witnesses'?[77] The legal metaphor is common in this monumental treatise.[78]

Sceptic Thomas Huxley, who was not a lawyer, also relied at times on the legal analogy. It is reported that at the Metaphysical Society in January 1876 he vacated the Chairman's chair for Gladstone and presented a forensic paper on Jesus' resurrection where in the style of a criminal court barrister he sought to destroy the case for the supernatural. His prosecution has been called 'the most notorious test case in the Metaphysical's history'.[79] It was this occasion that evoked the retort of John Henry Newman, 'I thank my lucky stars, that when asked to accept the honour of belonging to it (Metaphysical Society), I declined.'[80] As well in his essays he countered John Henry Newman's assertion that the gospel miracles are religious and moral events and therefore 'infidels' can't dismiss them on the basis you could not get a verdict for them in a court of Justice. Huxley's cry was that in light of the value placed on miracles, they are a significant issue and historical evidence and proof of a legal standard can be properly demanded. He pleaded for facts, sufficient evidence – legal proofs.[81]

In the setting of Victorian literature Schramm discusses Robert Browning's poem *A Death in the Desert* which explores the status of the apostle John's eyewitness

---

[77] H.S. Reimarus, 'Concerning the Intention of Jesus and His Teachings' in *Reimarus Fragments*, trans. Ralph S. Fraser, Charles H. Talbert, ed. (London: SCN, 1971), 176. Reimarus was influenced by Christian Wolff and English Deism. Wolff held that revelation may be above reason but not contrary to it, and reason establishes the criteria by which revelation may be judged. For discussion see Craig, *The Historical*, 363-391.

[78] ibid., 174: 'And I am definitely assured that if today in court four witnesses were heard in a case and their testimony was as different in all respects ... no case could be constructed on such conflicting testimony.' See also 197-200, 210-211. On Thomas Paine's allusions to legal analogy see Joseph P. Gudel, 'An Examination and Critique of Thomas Paine's *Age of Reason*', *The Simon Greenleaf Law Review*, I (1981-1982): 75-100.

[79] For a report of this 'sensational' meeting see Adrian Desmond, *Huxley: Evolution's High Priest* (London: Michael Joseph, 1997), 83-85; William Irvine, *Apes, Angels and Victorians* (London: Weidenfeld and Nicolson, 1956), 195-201. See for a response Walter Campbell Witcher, *Legal Proof Being an Answer to Thomas H. Huxley and Other Sceptics Demand for Legal Proof of the Resurrection of Christ from the Dead* (Fort Worth: Christian Forum, 1937).

[80] Ian Ker, *John Henry Newman* (Oxford: Oxford University Press, 1988), 732.

testimony.[82] And she reveals how William Gladstone's famous review of Mary Ward's *Robert Elsmere*, 'invokes the same legalistic model of evidence-based analysis as Ward'. Gladstone is not so much unhappy that Ward's novel put Christianity on trial 'as that it has not been adequately defended'.[83]

Clarence Seward Darrow was the trial lawyer who defended John T. Scopes in the famous 1925 'monkey trial' and his legal skills and reasoning are most evident in his written refutation of Christianity.[84] Then there is Anthony Flew's argument for the presumption for atheism based on equating the common law presumption of innocence with the onus of proof lying on the proposition, not the opposition. He attempts to establish a procedure for debate between believer and unbeliever. He argues from this legal analogy that the onus lies on those who support the proposition of God to bring forward sufficient reasons to warrant same.[85] Other sceptical legal works include Emery Scott West's, *Impeachment of the Bible*, George Luther Clark's, *A Lawyer Looks at the Bible*,[86] and Judge E.B. Docker's case for Jesus not dying on the cross.[87]

This juridical paradigm is not confined to the Christian world. There is ample evidence that other religions have been influenced by legal analogies, in particular the apologetic rhetoric of Islam and Baha'i.[88]

---

[81] For example, Thomas Huxley, 'Agnosticism and Christianity' in *Science in Christian Tradition: Essays*, Thomas Huxley (New York: D. Appleton, 1899), 334-342. For a discussion see Robert Shafer, *Christianity and Naturalism* (New Haven: Yale Press, 1926), 130-137. Huxley at best misunderstood Newman who certainly held the leading scriptural miracles, unlike some other miracles, were supported by an overwhelming amount of proof. See Richard A. Hutton, *Cardinal Newman* (London: Methuen & Co., 1905), 59-70. Montgomery even contends Newman's, 'Essays on Scripture Miracles' operates in the 'Legal Language Game' - *Defending the Biblical Gospel, Study Guide*, 60. Cf. Schramm, *Testimony*, 31.

[82] Schramm, *Testimony*, 165-173.

[83] ibid., 175.

[84] Clarence Darrow, *Why I Am an Agnostic and Other Essays* (Buffalo: Prometheus, 1984).

[85] Anthony G.N. Flew, *God, Freedom and Immortality* (Buffalo: Prometheus, 1984). This is a reissue of his 1976, *The Presumption of Atheism*. See also Terry Miethe and Anthony Flew, *Does God Exist? A Believer and Atheist Debate* (New York: Harper San Francisco, 1991), 11-18. Flew states on the presumption of atheism, 'in this coinage the word "presumption" is not – as on others lips it might be – a synonym for "presumptuousness". Instead it is intended to be construed as it is when we speak of innocence in common law' (11). David Prescott refutes Flew's alleged presumption in 'Anthony Flew's presumption of atheism revisited: a Christian lawyer's perspective', *Simon Greenleaf Law Review*, VII (1987-1988): 139-162.

[86] Emery Scott West, *Impeachment of the Bible* (Chicago: N. P, 1923); George Luther Clark's, *A Lawyer Looks at the Bible* (New York: Vantage, 1956).

[87] E.B. Docker, *If Jesus Did Not Die on the Cross? A Study in Evidence* (London: Robert Scott, 1920).

Summary

In this study and historical overview, it is not assumed all Christian lawyers have been open to a 'classical' legal apologetic. There are those who, because of their more presuppositional methodology or commitment to theological liberalism, would adopt other models.[89] An interesting example of the former is a nineteenth century Canadian monograph that is a dialogue between a judge and his guest. The judge advocates 'heart logic', not 'logic of the head', and any intellectual demands are primarily met by scriptural typologies, not evidences for the resurrection.[90] However it is evident John Warwick Montgomery's legal apologetic, which has inspired other current apologists, has a long and significant pedigree.

A Fourfold Taxanomy

When evaluating Montgomery's legal apologetic, it is useful to do so in comparison to the work of other apologists in this school.[91] This has not been done before. I am suggesting that the legal apologetic that focuses on the resurrection and the New Testament records can be divided into four major categories. The first category I have dubbed 'lawyer apologists using an evidential approach that often includes general legal principles.' The second, 'lawyer apologists using a

---

[88] See for example Shlomo Pines, 'Philosophy' in *Cambridge History of Islam*, Vol. 2B, P.M. Holt, Ann K.S. Lantern and Bernard Lewis, eds. (Cambridge University Press, 1977), 780-823. For a Jewish model see Harold M. Weiner (Barrister), *The Origin of the Pentateuch* (Oberlin, Ohio: Bibliotheca Sacra; London: Elliot Stock, 1910).

[89] Lawyers in the 'liberal' category would include: Peter Cameron, *Heretic* (Sydney: Doubleday, 1994); George Higinbotham and Hartley Williams (former Melbourne judges) – for references see Jill Roe, 'Challenge and Response: Religious Life in Melbourne 1876-86', *Journal of Religious History* 5, 2(1968): 149-166; James Albert Pike (Bishop), *What is This Treasure?* (New York: Harper & Row, 1966). For discussion on Pike see John Warwick Montgomery, *The Suicide of Christian Theology* (Minneapolis: Bethany, 1970), 32-61. In the presuppositional category Richard Packham, whose legal sceptical critique of Montgomery is referred to in this thesis, says one Australian Christian lawyer's response to his critique was to avoid the negative arguments raised and to simply attack Montgomery personally and conclude, 'it all comes down to a matter of faith'. Email received from Richard Packham (21 March 2000).

[90] Anonymous, *A Quaint Old Nova Scotian Judge's View of the Roman Governor's Question, 'What is Truth?'* (London: William Ridgway, 1878), 6-7, 13-18. The author, who may or may not be a lawyer, has the judge relying on the typology of Abraham's sacrifice of Isaac.

[91] The following legal apologetic books have been identified but not included as they require further investigation: Edward Joseph Ingram, *On the Witness Stand, He Who was Now is* (Los Angeles: Hoffman Press, 1931), also released as *Criminal and Illegal Trial of the Nazarene Peasant* (Fort Worth: World Co., 1924); Edward Deming Lucas, *The Logic and Reason in Christianity: A Brief by a Lawyer* (New York: Fleming Revell, 1945); George H. Pendarvis, *The Living Witness: A Lawyer's Brief for Christianity* (St Louis: B. Herder, 1912); Daniel Webster, *A Defense of the Christian Religion* (New York: M.H. Newman, 1844).

A Fourfold Taxanomy 33

technical legal approach'. The third, 'non-lawyer apologists citing a non-technical legal apologetic in support of their argument and/or arguing a non-technical apologetic themselves'. The fourth, 'non-lawyer apologists using a technical legal apologetic'.

Category one is an apologetic, based on general legal principles, that assists us in assessing whether a witness is lying, whether the gospels are reliable and/or what the circumstantial evidence is for the resurrection. Category two, in addressing the same issues, builds on the general legal reasoning and it is argued say that under the 'Ancient Documents' rule the gospels would be actually admitted into a court of law today. Then specific laws/presumptions of evidence are marshalled in support of the case for the resurrection. It is important to note that the differences between categories one and two will become more evident in chapters two and three. The historical development in their legal apologetic school is not from category one to two or three to four as technical apologists like Greenleaf date from the 18th century.[92] Rather the development has been in the acumen of the apologists in each particular category and in the evolution of the legal principles relied on.

In category one, one would place Hugo Grotius.[93] Other lawyers who are in this category include: Sir Norman Anderson,[94] Sir Robert Anderson (former chief of the Criminal Investigation Department, Scotland Yard),[95] Edmund H. Bennett (former judge, lecturer Harvard Law School and Dean, Boston School of Law),[96] Roger P. Booth,[97] Herbert C. Casteel (former judge),[98] Gerard Chrispin,[99] Charles Colson (Special Counsel to President Richard Nixon),[100] Thomas

---

[92] Simon Greenleaf, *The Testimony*, 1-54.
[93] Grotius, *The Truth*.
[94] J.N.D. Anderson, *The Evidence for the Resurrection* (London: InterVarsity, 1966); Norman Anderson, *Jesus Christ: The Witness of History* (Leicester: Inter-Varsity, 1985); Norman Anderson, *The Fact of Christ: Some of the Evidence* (Leicester: Inter-Varsity, 1979).
[95] In these lists brief reference is made in brackets to the role of these apologists apart from their being a lawyer. These roles are connected to their legal apologetic. Normally no reference is made if fuller biographical details appear in the body of the thesis. Robert Anderson, *A Doubter's Doubts About Science and Religion*, 3rd edn. (Glasgow: Pickering & Inglis, 1924), 95-103.
[96] Edmund H. Bennett, *The Four Gospels from a Lawyer's Standpoint* (Boston: Houghton, Mifflin, 1899).
[97] Roger P. Booth, *The Bedrock Gospel: Sifting the Sources, with Commentary* (n.p., England: Paget, 2001). Booth whilst acknowledging that on the balance of probability Jesus' body was not in the tomb his presuppositions on miracles lead him to conclude that his resurrection was a spiritual body and not a physical body (135-152).
[98] Herbert C. Casteel, *Beyond a Reasonable Doubt* (Joplin, Missouri: College Press, 1990).
[99] Gerard Chrispin, *The Resurrection: The Unopened Gift* (Epsom, Surrey: Day One Publications, 1999).

Erskine (1788-1870, Scotland's outstanding lay theologian),[101] Nicky Gumbel (leader of the Alpha evangelism movement),[102] Don Gutteridge[103] Lord Hailsham (former Lord Chancellor of England),[104] Frank Hanft (former Professor of Law, University of North Carolina),[105] Jeffrey C. Martin,[106] Charles Carrol Morgan,[107] Oliver Mowat (former Premier of Ontario),[108] Albert L. Roper,[109] Britton H. Tabor,[110] Francis Wharton,[111] Phineas Bacon Wilcox.[112] Mistakenly Frank Morison (Albert Henry Ross), has been viewed as a lawyer, and therefore one to be included in this category, because of the juridical nature of his monumental work *Who Moved the Stone?*[113]

Robert Anderson is one of the best known apologists and his central concern, unlike the others mentioned, is not the resurrection of Christ. His apologetic classics focus on the method of higher critics, the relationship between science and religion and fulfilled prophecy. He is more a negative or defensive apologist seeking to defend the faith. This is no doubt due to the fact that he is a presuppositionalist and has a certain disdain of arguing with positive Christian evidences. He limits the miracle apologetic to accrediting Jesus as the Jewish Messiah and it has no place in the gentile mission. There the gospel is simply preached. Yet paradoxically at times he allows for a resurrection apologetic '… the resurrection of Christ is a public fact accredited by evidence which will stand the test of discussion and verification.'[114]

---

[100] Charles Colson, *Loving God* (Basingtoke: Marshalls, 1983), 61-70.
[101] Thomas Erskine, *Remarks on the Internal Evidence for the Truth of the Revealed Religion*, 7th ed. (Edinburgh: Waugh and Innes, 1823).
[102] Nicky Gumbel, *Why Jesus?* (Eastborne: Kingsway, 1991).
[103] Don Gutteridge, *The Defence Rests its Case* (Nashville: Broadman, 1975).
[104] Lord Hailsham, *The Door Wherein I Went* (London: Collins, 1975), 28-47.
[105] Frank Hanft, *You Can Believe* (Indianapolis: Bobbs-Merrill, 1952).
[106] Jeffrey C. Martin, *A Lawyer Briefs the Big Questions* (Anderson, Indiana: Bristol House, 2000).
[107] Charles Carrol Morgan, *A Lawyer's Brief on the Atonement* (Boston: The Fort Hill Press, 1910).
[108] Oliver Mowat, *Christianity and its Evidences* (Toronto: Williamson, 1890).
[109] Albert L. Roper, *Did Jesus Rise From the Dead?* (Grand Rapids: Zondervan, 1965).
[110] Britton H. Tabor, *Skepticism Assailed* (Philadelphia: Monarch, 1895). The text includes the classic essay by jurist Lord Lyttelton, 'Treatise on the Conversion of St. Paul' (432-514).
[111] Francis Wharton, *A Treatise on Theism and on Modern Skeptical Theories* (Philadelphia: Lippincott; London: Trubner, 1859), 116.
[112] Phineas Bacon Wilcox, *A Few Thoughts by a Member of the Bar* (Columbus, Ohio: T.B. Cutler, 1836).
[113] Frank Morison, *Who Moved the Stone?* (Downers Grove: InterVarsity, 1982).
[114] Robert Anderson, *A Doubter's*, 101. For a discussion of Robert Anderson's apologetic see Ross Clifford, 'The Case of Eight Legal Apologists for the Defense of Scripture and the Christ Event' (M.A. Thesis, Simon Greenleaf School of Law, May 1987), chap. 3.

A Fourfold Taxanomy

The most influential apologist in this group is Norman Anderson. He is an authority on Islamic Law and was the Professor of Oriental Laws and the Director of the Institute of Advanced Legal Studies at The University of London.[115] Anderson also critiques the methodology of higher biblical critics. His apologetic for the historical nature of the resurrection of Jesus does take the form of one presenting a case. He answers the attempts that seek to explain the empty tomb; for example, the disciples stole the body. He finds that no hypothesis, apart from 'Christ is risen', fits the facts. The character of the witnesses and the nature of the narratives rule out the gospel account as invention or legend. He builds as well upon the circumstantial evidence including the institution of the Christian Sunday. Like Origen,[116] he rebuts the approach that the appearances of Christ could be due to hallucinations. He finds 'the empty tomb, then, forms a veritable rock on which all rationalistic theories of the resurrection dash themselves in vain.'[117]

Norman Anderson does not venture into the realm of category two. His more cautious use of legal principles draws this rejoinder from an otherwise supportive Montgomery, '(his books) employ no technical legal knowledge whatever and therefore offer little help in integrating theology and law.'[118]

Summary
Category one, with its general use of legal principles such as the basic criteria referred to in chapter three for testing whether a witness is telling the truth, has made an important contribution to apologetics. Its use of simple 'down to earth' legal arguments has meant it has provided apologists with tools to reach a wide audience. As a consequence it has historically attracted a broad range of apologists from a number of western countries. It is a model that the non-lawyer apologist can adopt with little difficulty. As will be shown in chapters two and three, it has had a tendency to overstate its case and create confusion through generalisations such as, 'the gospel testimony does not contain hearsay'. It will be argued here that the non-technical legal apologetic has to tighten and reframe its case.

In category two are the following lawyers: Clarence Bartlett (former circuit judge),[119] Clarrie Briese (former Chief Magistrate of NSW),[120] Walter Chandler,[121] Ross Clifford,[122] Pamela Binnings Ewen,[123] Dale Foreman,[124]

---

[115] Sir Norman's apologetic is considered in more detail in Clifford, *The Case for the Empty Tomb*, 82 -108.
[116] Origen, *Contra Celsum*, 2.60-2.61.
[117] J.N.D. Anderson, *The Evidence*, 20.
[118] John Warwick Montgomery, *Law and Gospel: A Study in Jurisprudence* (Oak Park, Illinois: Christian Legal Society, 1978), 46.
[119] Bartlett, *As a Lawyer*.

Simon Greenleaf,[125] Val Grieve,[126] Ken Handley (Justice, Court of Appeal, Supreme Court of NSW),[127] Roger Himes,[128] Francis Lamb,[129] Irwin H. Linton,[130] Sir Lionel Luckhoo,[131] John Warwick Montgomery,[132] Charles Robert Morrison,[133] Howard Hyde Russell,[134] Joseph Sagebeer,[135] John Ford Whitworth,[136] and Stephen Williams.[137] These apologists, like those in category one, focus on the resurrection of Jesus established by trustworthy documents, reliable eyewitness testimony and circumstantial evidence. However the courtroom is more clearly the setting. Specific rules of evidence are relied on for testing documents and testimony including the 'parol evidence rule' and Thomas Starkie's rules for determining whether witnesses are speaking the truth.[138] I will exhibit the technical features of this apologetic in the subsequent pages that focus on Montgomery's legal model. I will also appraise the relationship between the technical apologetic and the non-technical apologetic.

Some, like Val Grieve and Clarence Bartlett,[139] are closer to category one and speak of the evidence for the resurrection being of a form that would be accepted in a court of law today if the gospel eyewitnesses could be called. Others such as Foreman, Lamb, Linton and Montgomery go further and claim that the gospels

---

[120] Clarrie Briese, 'Witnesses to the Resurrection – Credible or Not?' (Sydney: Lawyers' Christian Fellowship, 1999), <http://www.lcf.pnc.com.au/Resurrection.htm>. Briese's apologetic is also found in part in Clifford, *The Case for the Empty Tomb*, 132-135.
[121] Chandler, *The Trial*.
[122] Clifford, *The Case for the Empty Tomb*.
[123] Ewen, *Faith*.
[124] Dale Foreman, *Crucify Him: A Lawyer Looks at the Trial of Jesus* (Grand Rapids: Zondervan, 1990).
[125] Greenleaf, *The Testimony*.
[126] Val Grieve, *Your Verdict* (Bromley: STL, 1988).
[127] Ken Handley, 'A Lawyer Looks at the Resurrection', *Kategoria*, 15 (1999): 11-21.
[128] Roger Himes, *Counsellor State Your Case!* (Denver: Accent, 1978).
[129] Lamb, *Miracle and Science*.
[130] Linton, *A Lawyer Examines*.
[131] Lionel A. Luckhoo and John R. Thompson, *The Silent Witness* (Nashville: Thomas Nelson, 1995).
[132] Montgomery, *Human Rights*, 131-160.
[133] Morrison, *The Proofs*.
[134] Russell, *A Lawyer's*.
[135] Sagebeer, *The Bible in Court*.
[136] John Ford Whitworth, *Legal and Historical Proof of the Resurrection of the Dead with an Examination of the Evidence in the New Testament* (Harrisburg, Pennsylvania: The United Evangelical Church, 1912).
[137] Stephen D. Williams, *The Bible in Court*.
[138] Montgomery, *The Law Above*, 84-90; Chandler, *The Trial*, 1: 6-70.
[139] Grieve, *Your Verdict*, 79; Bartlett, *As a Lawyer*, 124-169.

A Fourfold Taxanomy

with their record of Jesus' death and resurrection are actually admissible documents. They rely heavily on Simon Greenleaf and his pleading of the 'Ancient Document' rule.[140] Francis Lamb states:

> We have found a consensus of unnumbered decisions by those courts and by judges and jurists of the highest authority and standing in the civilized world, and they show that the Gospel of John, like the other books of the Scriptures, is clearly within the Ancient Document rule and law of evidence, and clearly satisfies the test and standard proposed, and show that that Gospel, tested by the principles and rules of the science of jurisprudence as administered in courts of justice in controversies between man and man, is competent and admissible as evidence.[141]

Yet whether it be a Val Grieve, Francis Lamb or Thomas Sherlock the reliance of those in categories two and four on legal principles is more ardent than those in categories one and three.[142]

Summary

Category two is a more sophisticated apologetic as it evaluates at a technical level issues such as the admissibility of the gospel documents and the hearsay nature of the gospel testimony. On the whole English legal apologists have not ventured into this area. Whilst the technical apologetic presents more formal arguments, apologists like Montgomery have shown it can still operate on a popular level. The technical legal apologetic continues to appeal to those seeking more detailed evidence for the resurrection. However, as will be argued later, its more technical approach raises deeper questions as to the actual legal strength of the evidence for the resurrection. As in category one, there has been a tendency to overstate the case. As a consequence I will further argue that the technical legal apologetic has to reframe its case.

With respect to category three there are many popular general or historical apologists that briefly use the legal apologetic. Two prominent examples are Paul Barnett and Michael Cassidy. Barnett in *The Truth about Jesus* states, 'the analysis of the resurrection belongs to disciplines which evaluate evidence, in particular those of the historian and the lawyer'.[143] He then cites English legal person-

---

[140] Greenleaf, *The Testimony*, 7-10.
[141] Lamb, *Miracle and Science*, 52.
[142] More detailed biographical information on Edmund Bennett, Sir Norman Anderson, Sir Robert Anderson, Lord Hailsham, Frank Morison, Simon Greenleaf and Sir Lionel Luckhoo may be found in Clifford, *The Case for the Empty Tomb*.

ality Sir Edward Clarke on the reliability of the gospel evidence for the resurrection. He concludes by taking the common investigative skills of the historian and lawyer to an implied informal jury setting.[144] Keith Mason, Solicitor General for New South Wales, comments that Barnett's process throughout the book in evaluating the evidence is very similar to how a lawyer would test the evidence.[145]

Michael Cassidy in his popular tract, *The Uniqueness and Divinity of Jesus Christ,* likewise gathers Sir Edward Clarke as well as Lord Darby as expert witnesses for the resurrection.[146] Other non-lawyers who use legal analogy include: John Blanchard,[147] Kenneth Boa and Larry Moody,[148] Michael Green,[149] John Penter,[150] W.M. Robertson,[151] Wilbur Smith.[152] Green, Boa and Moody, as does Montgomery, continue to make the mistake of referring to Frank Morison as an attorney in order to add weight to their legal argument.[153]

There are four general apologists who make a unique contribution to the legal apologetic in this third category. One is Don Stewart who has published a dedicated non-technical legal apologetic treatise.[154] Another is Harry Rimmer who offered financial rewards to anyone who could establish a scientific mistake in the bible. Two litigants took Rimmer to court claiming they had established their case and that Rimmer refused to pay. Rimmer, albeit on technical grounds, won both cases and published his version of the facts.[155] The third is C. Stephen Evans who bases his philosophic and cumulative case style apologetic on a legal approach to evidence.[156] The fourth is popular journalistic apologist Lee Strobel.

---

[143] Paul Barnett, *The Truth About Jesus* (Sydney South: Aquila, 1994), 150.
[144] ibid, 151.
[145] ibid, iv – v.
[146] Michael Cassidy, 'The Uniqueness and Divinity of Jesus Christ', *Theologically Speaking* (November 1996).
[147] John Blanchard, *Will the Real Jesus Please Stand Up?* (Darlington, Durham: Evangelical Press, 1989).
[148] Kenneth Boa and Larry Moody, *I'm Glad You Asked* (Wheaton: Victor, 1982).
[149] Michael Green, *Man Alive!* (Downers Grove: InterVarsity, 1967). Green adopts chapter headings such as 'The Witness-Box' and 'The Facts of the Case', 17, 29.
[150] Penter who uses a legal moot to address questions about the historical nature of the bible, miracles and the historical Jesus is more committed to critical biblical scholarship than most of the legal apologists. See John Penter, *Circumstantial Evidence* (San Francisco: Faraday Press, 1981).
[151] W.M. Robertson, *The Bible at the Bar* (London: Pickering & Inglis, n.d.).
[152] Wilbur Smith, *Therefore Stand* (Boston: Wilde, 1945), 423-425.
[153] Green, *Man Alive!*, 54-55; Boa and Moody, *I'm Glad*, 53. Montgomery also makes this error, see John Warwick Montgomery, 'A Lawyer's Case for Christianity', *Christian Legal Journal* 2, 3 (Spring 1993): 15.
[154] Stewart, *You Be*.
[155] Harry Rimmer, *That Lawsuit Against the Bible* (Grand Rapids: William B. Eerdmans, 1940).

A Fourfold Taxonomy 39

Strobel relies heavily on his legal reporting journalistic experience and on legal apologists from Greenleaf to Luckhoo. His argument at times borders on the technical apologetic.[157]

In category four are non-lawyers: Michael R. Licona,[158] Walter Martin,[159] Kel Richards,[160] Richard Riss,[161] Thomas Sherlock,[162] Dan Story,[163] William Webster,[164] Weldon and Ankerberg,[165] Robert Dick Wilson[166] and foremost popular apologist Josh McDowell.

McDowell for example in *The Resurrection Factor* includes an abstract from Walter Chandler's *The Trial of Jesus*. It includes discussion and technical findings like the following:

---

[156] C. Stephen Evans, *Why Believe? Reason and Mystery as Pointers to God* (Leicester: Inter-Varsity, 1996).

[157] Lee Strobel, *The Case* (in particular chapter two); Lee Strobel, *God's Outrageous Claims* (Grand Rapids: Zondervan, 1997), 166-183. Strobel holds a Master of Studies in Law degree from Yale Law School. Harvard law graduate and journalist William Proctor is another significant apologist in this journalistic apologetic school. Proctor develops principles from journalism rather than the law for evaluating the gospel testimony. See *The Resurrection Report* (Nashville: Broadman & Holman, 1998).

[158] Michael R. Licona, *Cross Examined* (Falls Church, Virginia: Truth Quest, 1998).

[159] Walter Martin and Jill Martin Rische, *Through the Windows of Heaven* (Nashville: Broadman & Holman, 1998), 230: 'More than five hundred witnesses testified to seeing Jesus *after* his resurrection ... If you presented this in any courtroom you could prove any case you wanted – its *evidence*.' Martin came from a family of lawyers and saw himself as 'theological lawyer', http://groups.google.com/groups?q=Walter+Martin&hl=en&safe=off&rnum=5&ic=18

[160] Kel Richards, *Jesus on Trial* (Kingsford, NSW: Matthias Media, 2001).

[161] Richard Riss, *The Evidence for the Resurrection of Jesus Christ* (Minneapolis: Bethany, 1977).

[162] Sherlock, *The Tryal*, 339-450.

[163] Dan Story, *Defending Your Faith* (Grand Rapids: Kregel, 1997).

[164] William Webster, *The Fitness of the Witnesses of the Resurrection of Christ Considered* (London: James Lacy, 1731) and *The Credibility of the Resurrection of Christ upon The Testimony of the Apostles* (London: J. Wilford, 1735). Both texts are reproduced in the *Simon Greenleaf Law Review*, VI (1986-1987).

[165] Ankerberg and Weldon, *Ready*, 102-109.

[166] Wilson was Professor of Semitic Philology at Princeton in the era of Hodge, Warfield and Machen. He employed legal reasoning and language to defend the reliability of the Old Testament. For example he stated, 'I shall seek to follow without prejudice the laws of evidence as laid down in Sir James Fitzjames Stephen's Digest of the Law of Evidence in so far as these laws relate to documents.' See Robert Dick Wilson, *A Scientific Investigation of the Old Testament* (Philadelphia: Sunday School Times, 1926), 65. It is interesting to note that apologist Warfield himself received a Doctor of Laws in 1892 from the College of New Jersey and a Doctor of Laws from Davidson College in 1892. See Samuel G. Craig, 'Benjamin B.Warfield' in *B.B. Warfield, Biblical and Theological Studies*, Samuel G. Craig, ed. (Philadelphia: Presbyterian and Reformed, 1968), xv.

These various considerations are the logical basis of that rule of law laid down by Mr Greenleaf under which the gospel histories would be admitted in a modern court of law, in a modern juridical proceedings.[167]

General Observation

As mentioned, Montgomery's legal apologetic focuses on Jesus' resurrection and argues for trustworthy gospels. This is the primary legal apologetic. There are other apologetic areas where lawyers have ventured and it is useful to note this as Montgomery certainly interacts with a broad range of issues. Appendix one sets out a table of the eclectic legal apologetic. Whilst a detailed analysis lies beyond the focus of this thesis, it is identified as another area for possible further research, when no doubt further legal apologists in these other fields will be identified. Not included in the table are non-apologetic authors, with legal backgrounds, like John Calvin, who have focused on biblical studies or systematic theology.

The trial of Jesus, which is a major area of interest for lawyers, is included in the appendix although in itself it has limited apologetic value. It is centred more on whether Jesus had due process. However, many of these 'trial' apologists consider issues as to the reliability of the New Testament text and the fact of the resurrection as their argument progresses.[168]

It will be evident that a number of legal apologists write in more than one area.

Summary
In the limited assessment in apologetic textbooks of the legal apologetic to date, a taxonomy of the different apologetic models has not occurred. Both the non-technical and technical legal apologetic models have influenced lawyer and non-lawyer apologists alike. Whilst Montgomery belongs to the technical school, it will be documented in chapters two and three that he at times moves into a non-technical argument. Future assessment of the legal apologetic needs to evaluate arguments at the technical and non-technical level.

---

[167] McDowell, *The Resurrection*, 177.

[168] For example see George W. Thompson, *The Trial of Jesus: A Judicial Revue of the Law and Facts of the World's Most Tragic Courtroom Trial* (Indianapolis: Bobbs-Merrill, 1927), 27-30. Others like Walter Chandler develop the argument of reliable New Testament documents and the resurrection to such a degree that they have been included in the legal apologetic categories in the above section.

The Model and its Development

Montgomery's brief is most fully set out in *Human Rights and Human Dignity* with a slightly altered version in *Christians in the Public Square*.[169] It is presented in the form of propositions in *Tractatus Logico–Theologicus*.[170] His work is one of the most original technical legal apologetics since Greenleaf's *The Testimony of the Evangelists*. James Fairbanks, says of Montgomery's legal apologetic in *Christians in the Public Square,* that it demonstrates 'why Montgomery enjoys the reputation of being one of the twentieth century's most renowned Christian apologists'. However he adds this rider that its, 'likely persuasiveness to those who have grown up in a post-modern world is unfortunately problematic.'[171] In chapter four of this thesis it will be shown that Montgomery's apologetic resonates with aspects of postmodern spirituality. He will be shown to be an apologist for all seasons. What follows is a summary of Montgomery's legal apologetic and its development. In chapters two and three, where there is an evaluation of his legal criteria, the substance of his argument is again addressed, and critiqued in detail.

Montgomery initially investigates whether the New Testament records of Jesus are historically reliable. His primary focus is the four gospels. Then he asks is the testimony in these records, which is offered as proof of the resurrection, solid enough on which to make a finding of fact?

If the documents and testimony are reliable, then there is 'decisive proof' of Jesus' claim to deity. If Jesus' deity is the finding, then the bible has a 'divine stamp' because of his pronouncements about same.[172]

---

[169] Montgomery, *Human Rights*, 131-160; John Warwick Montgomery, 'The Jury Returns: A Juridical Defense of Christianity' and 'A Lawyer's Case for Christianity' in *Christians in the Public Square*, C.E.B. Cranfield, David Kilgour, John Warwick Montgomery (Edmonton: Canadian Institute for Law, Theology, and Public Policy, 1996), 223-250, 269-282. 'The Jury Returns' is also found in John Warwick Montgomery, ed. *Evidence for Faith* (Dallas: Probe, 1991), 319-341. 'A Lawyer's Case for Christianity' is also found in *Christian Legal Journal* 2, 3 (Spring 1993): 10-16. Future references to the written version of 'A Lawyer's Case' will be based on the *Christian Legal Journal*. 'A Lawyer's Case' is a more condensed version. 'A Lawyer's Case' is based on a transcript of a lecture given by Montgomery at the University of Calgary, 15 November 1991. The audiotape of the lecture has additional and different material. At times the implication of this fact will be mentioned in this thesis.

[170] Montgomery, *Tractatus*, 3 – 3.8732.

[171] Fairbanks, review of *Christians*, 117-119.

[172] Montgomery, *Human Rights*, 136-137; Montgomery, *Tractatus*, 3.15. For the 'uniform testimony of the primary-source documents' that sets out Jesus' claim for divine status (for example John 14, John 20:28) see proposition 3.5.

Thus Montgomery's legal apologetic clearly rests on how good the New Testament records are, and how reliable is the testimony therein. With respect to the former, Montgomery succinctly presents the genesis of his historical apologetic:

> How good are these New Testament records? They handsomely fulfill the historian's requirements of *transmissional reliability* (their texts have been transmitted accurately from the time of writing to our own day), *internal reliability* (they claim to be primary-source documents and ring true as such), and *external reliability* (their authorships and dates are backed up by such solid extrinsic testimony as that of the early second-century writer Papias, a student of John the Evangelist, who was told by him that the first three Gospels were indeed written by their traditional authors.[173]

The liberal higher critics' position on the gospels is then countered by Montgomery. For example, he cites a specialist authority on Roman law, A. N. Sherwin-White.[174] Sherwin-White argued in the 1960-61 Sarum Lectures that the gospel narratives are no less promising than the sources relied on for Jesus' contemporary, Tiberius Caesar. And yet the more advanced form critics maintain the historical Christ is unknowable, a position he finds untenable. Habermas whilst not dismissing the advocacy of Sherwin-White does present a rider. Sherwin-White did not say myth could never make its way into the text, but that two generations is an insufficient time for myth to destroy the core historical material.[175]

Montgomery then moves into his specific legal apologetic with respect to the documents. His argument is pithy. This is consistent with a legal paradigm where the strongest case is presented. Reference is made to Simon Greenleaf as 'the greatest nineteenth-century authority on the law of evidence in the common-law world' and he relies on Greenleaf's understanding of the 'ancient documents' rule:

> ... ancients documents will be received as competent evidence if they are 'fair on their face' (ie offer no internal evidence of tampering) and have been maintained in 'reasonable custody' (ie their preservation has been consistent with their content).[176]

---

[173] ibid., 137.
[174] ibid., 138-139.
[175] Gary R. Habermas, 'Philosophy of History, Historical Relativism and History as Evidence' in *Evangelical Apologetics*, Bauman, Hall and Newman eds., 96.
[176] Montgomery, *Human Rights*, 137.

The Model and its Development

Montgomery correctly states Greenleaf's stance as being that as the gospels comply with this rule, they would be established in any court of law.[177]

The speculation that the gospels were faked some hundred years later, as suggested by Trevor-Roper, is answered by citing the former Lord Chancellor, Lord Hailsham.[178] Hailsham refers to one of his own cases on the nature of fakes where material was gathered which found that forgeries of a later age cannot fail to include stylistic or other material from the forger's own age which invariably leads to his work being detected for what it is. The implication is that if the gospels were late fakes, they would reveal intrinsic evidence, which they do not, of being second or third century writings.[179]

The historical soundness of the documents does not establish the veracity of the contents so Montgomery then considers the testimony therein. In his early writings Montgomery focused on document reliability, however he did seek to show that the testimony is not hearsay, and that it was 'cross-examined' in the very teeth of Jewish and Roman opposition.[180] He also republished Greenleaf's treatise on this issue.[181] Greenleaf appears to rely on Thomas Starkie when he states the rule as to the reliability of any particular testimony as follows:

> The credit due to the testimony of witnesses depends upon, firstly, their honesty; secondly, their ability; thirdly, their number and the consistency of their testimony; fourthly, the conformity of their testimony with experience; and fifthly, the coincidence of their testimony with collateral circumstances.[182]

Greenleaf's scrutiny of the gospel writers leads to his finding that they meet these five tests and that their testimony would therefore be given due weight by court of law.

---

[177] ibid. See Greenleaf, *The Testimony*, 7-11.
[178] ibid., 138.
[179] Lord Hailsham, *The Door*, 29-47.
[180] See Montgomery, *The Law Above*, 42-57,84-90; Montgomery, *Law and Gospel*, 34-37; John Warwick Montgomery, 'Legal Reasoning and Christian Apologetics', *Christianity Today* XIX, 10 (14 February 1975): 71-72. The last reference was revised and reprinted in *The Law Above*, 84-90. It is also used by Montgomery as a handout at apologetic seminars.
[181] Montgomery, *The Law Above*, 118-140.
[182] Greenleaf, *The Testimony*, 28. As I mention in 'The Case of Eight Legal Apologists' this is almost a direct quote from English authority, Thomas Starkie. See Thomas Starkie, *A Practical Treatise of the Law of Evidence and Digest of Proofs, in Civil and Criminal Proceedings*, Vol. 1, 2nd rev. edn. (London: J. and W.T. Clarke, 1833), 480.

In his later works, *Human Rights and Human Dignity* and *Tractatus Logico-Theologicus* Montgomery specifically develops the second prong of his legal apologetic by applying McCloskey and Schoenberg's fourfold test for exposing the gospel testimony to the charge of perjury.[183] The first test is internal defects in the witness which refer to personal characteristics or past history showing that the witness is inherently unreliable. Montgomery asserts there is no evidence that the apostolic witnesses had criminal records, were pathological liars or were people who could not be trusted. The second test is external defects in the witness which refer to motives to falsify. Montgomery notes that there was no financial or societal benefit in lying. The third test is internal defects in the testimony such as self-contradiction. Montgomery indicates the evidence is that the gospel writers present different but complementary accounts. The fourth test is external defects such as inconsistencies between the gospels and archaeology. Montgomery states that modern archaeology has confirmed the reliability of New Testament geography, chronology and general history. In summation Montgomery's finding is: on not one of the four elements of the perjury construct, 'can the New Testament witnesses be impugned.'[184]

Montgomery continues this legal line by citing Givens' standard text, *Advocacy*, and his insights that a witness engaged in deception must perform the most difficult act of juggling three things simultaneously in the witness box: He must ensure he does not contradict what his cross-examiner knows; he must take care that nothing he says can be checked against contradictory data; and he must tell a consistent lie. Montgomery's argument is that although the gospel writers were never put on the witness stand, the Jewish religious leaders had intimate contact with Jesus' ministry and the '*means, motive,* and *opportunity* to expose the apostolic witness as inaccurate and deceptive if it had been such, and the fact that they did not can only be effectively explained on the ground they *could not*'.[185]

It should be noted that Montgomery's legal apologetic is not confined to the primary sources – the gospels. He has consistently briefly referred to Josephus and other secondary sources; and to the circumstantial evidence, for example if Jesus did not rise, who stole the body?[186] In conjunction with the circumstantial evi-

---

[183] Patrick L. McCloskey and Ronald L. Schoenberg, *Criminal Law Advocacy*, Vol. 5 (New York: Matthew Bender,1984), para 12.01-12.03.
[184] Montgomery, *Human Rights*, 144; Montgomery, *Tractatus*, 3.44 – 3446.
[185] ibid, 144-148. See Richard A Givens, *Advocacy: The Art of Pleading a Cause* (Colorado Springs: Shepard's/McGraw Hill, 1980), 69-90.
[186] Montgomery, *Human Rights*, 151-152; Montgomery, 'A Lawyer's Case', 15.

dence he uniquely introduces proof by *res ipsa loquitur* into the legal apologetic, which is pleaded as follows:

> Res ipsa loquitur in typical negligence cases
>
> 1. Accident does not normally occur in the absence of negligence.
>
> 2. Instrumentality causing injury was under the defendant's exclusive control.
>
> 3. Plaintiff did not himself contribute to the injury.
>
> Therefore, defendant negligent: „the event speaks for itself."
>
> Res ipsa loquitur as applied to Christ's resurrection
>
> 1. Dead bodies do not leave tombs in the absence of some agency effecting the removal.
>
> 2. The tomb was under God's exclusive control, for it had been sealed, and Jesus, the sole occupant of it, was dead.
>
> 3. The Romans and the Jewish religious leaders did not contribute to the removal of the body (they had been responsible for sealing and guarding the tomb to prevent anyone from stealing the body), and the disciples would not have stolen it, then prevaricated, and finally died for what they knew to be untrue.
>
> *Therefore,* only God was in a position to empty the tomb, which he did, as Jesus himself had predicted, by raising Him from the dead: „the event speaks for itself."[187]

Intended Audience

Montgomery's legal apologetic is aimed at a popular audience as well as academics and fellow lawyers. The popular focus is evident in the debates in which Montgomery participates and in his public seminars.[188] It is also apparent from Montgomery's writings that whilst he adopts a technical legal apologetic he has the 'lay' reader in his mind as his argument is not immersed in deep, unexplained

---

[187] Montgomery, *Law and Gospel*, 35.
[188] For example, John Warwick Montgomery and Mark Plummer, 'Humanism or Christianity?', debate (Randwick, Sydney, 17 February 1986). For a report of the debate, see the *Sydney Morning Herald* (19 February 1986), 23.

legal jargon.[189] A particular strength of Montgomery is his ability to translate his popular legal apologetic writing to a wider academic and legal audience by the use of extensive, detailed footnotes and by the covering in his work of important legal and factual issues. This is certainly true of *Human Rights and Human Dignity* that operates not only at a very readable level, but also crosses over to a reader who has a more academic interest in the fields of law, human rights and jurisprudence.

There is further evidence of Montgomery's intending his legal apologetic for an academic audience. He uses a brief legal argument, including references to other legal apologists such as Norman Anderson, for the justification of the Christian worldview and the resurrection in his legal master's thesis on Marxism and human rights.[190] Montgomery's apologetic is also published in Christian legal papers which illustrates his desire to engage with his legal peers.[191]

Potential Difficulties

Montgomery's legal apologetic does include rejoinders to what have been perceived to be potential difficulties. The rejoinders that lie within the boundaries of this study will be considered. They are as follows. In the next section on 'Epistemological Matters' there is an evaluation of two issues. Firstly, Montgomery acknowledges that legal reasoning is probabilistic and then defends probability as the only justifiable basis for decision-making which is based on evidence.[192] This is discussed in the context of the nature of the legal understanding of proof. Secondly, he addresses the argument that more evidence is required to prove a resurrection. He suggests in *Human Rights and Human Dignity* that a supernatural event has no bearing on the weight of evidence required to establish it. If Jesus was dead at point A and alive at point B, then resurrection has occurred. Simply facts like that Jesus was seen eating fish at point B means he is now amongst the living.[193] In chapter two there is an assessment of Montgomery's argument that legal principles and legislation have reduced the problem that the apostolic testimony is hearsay, 'to the vanishing point'.[194]

---

[189] See Montgomery, *The Law Above*, 84-90.
[190] John Warwick Montgomery, 'The Marxist Approach to Human Rights: Analysis and Critique', *Simon Greenleaf Law Review*, III (1983-1984): 179-180. This is Montgomery's M. Phil. in Law Thesis at the University of Essex.
[191] For example Montgomery's, 'A Lawyer's Case'.
[192] Montgomery, *Human Rights*, 152-154; Montgomery, *Law and Gospel*, 34-35.
[193] ibid., 154-155.
[194] ibid., 149-150.

In response to Hume and others, Montgomery argues that the miraculous nature of the resurrection does not make it beyond investigation or intellectual belief.[195] Montgomery also answers Reformed philosophers, including Ronald Nash and classical apologists such as R.C. Sproul, who insist that an independent theistic structure must first be established to make any theological sense of the resurrection.[196] Montgomery is criticised here because of his claim that the Jesus resurrection apologetic is a proof for the existence of God. He responds: If Jesus is raised, then his claims about his own deity have warrant and therefore there is an historical theistic argument.[197] Montgomery argues that the eyewitnesses to the resurrection being friends or acquaintances of Jesus does not discredit them but rather adds weight to their testimony. He cites the legal text, *Eyewitness Testimony: Strategies and Authorities,* in support of the weight to be given to an unimpeached eyewitness identification of a prior acquaintance.[198] These particular matters are addressed in chapter three. Finally, Montgomery responds to the premise that facts are not 'brute' or self-interpreting by asserting 'that the very nature of legal argument (judgments rendered on the basis of factual verdicts) rests on the ability of facts to speak for themselves.'[199] Within the constraints of this thesis this issue will be limited to a discussion in chapter five on the legal formalist model.

New Development

The Christian philosopher Francis Beckwith expands the technical, legal apologetic of Montgomery by focusing in his thesis on similar legal principles as to the credibility and admissibility of evidence to judge current direct eyewitness testimony and circumstantial evidence of the miraculous. His reason for employing the legal method is twofold: firstly, legal science has developed meticulous legal criteria in distinguishing truth from error, and secondly there are the similarities between legal claims and miracle claims. In support of the second he holds that legal and miracle claims almost always involve the credibility of witnesses, that

---

[195] ibid., 151-152.
[196] ibid., 156-157.
[197] Montgomery, *Faith Founded*, 58-63. For critique see R.C. Sproul, John Gerstner and Arthur Lindsley, *Classical Apologetics* (Grand Rapids: Zondervan, 1984), 146-152; Geisler, *Christian Apologetics*, 95-98.
[198] Montgomery, *Human Rights*, 155. See Edward B. Arnolds, William K. Carroll, Melvin B. Lewis and Michael P. Seng, *Eyewitness Testimony: Strategies and Tactics* (New York: McGraw Hill, 1984), 400-401.
[199] ibid., 157.

legal and miracle claims involve non-testimonial evidence, that legal reasoning helps the evaluation of this, and that miracle claims like legal petitions often evoke counter claims.[200]

In support of the legal model Beckwith follows Montgomery in citing philosophers Toulmin and Adler, but adds Bruce Waller. He refers to the legal precedent of Greenleaf, Norman Anderson and Montgomery. He states: 'Montgomery is probably the most qualified twentieth century thinker to write on the integration of legal reasoning and miracle claims.'[201] Beckwith's case considers the evidence that would be required to support a finding that a miracle had taken place. He cites legal authorities including McCloskey, Schoenberg and Wigmore in evaluating such. His conclusion is that under the technical legal model certain miracles could today be verified. Beckwith notes that whilst a sceptic may still on probabilities read the evidence differently, he has 'no evidential grounds by which to claim that the theist has no epistemic right to describe the event as such.'[202]

Epistemological Matters

With respect to the legal apologetic for the resurrection there are some specific epistemological issues that are best dealt with now.

A major strength, as will be canvassed in chapter five, is the appropriateness of the legal paradigm for analysing the truth claims of Christianity. The sceptic Richard Packham, in his critique of Montgomery begins by 'wholeheartedly' agreeing that 'The Christian claims can be tested as to their truth by the very reasoning employed in the law to determine questions of fact.' He concurs that legal rules are open to many as 'reflections of natural reason'.[203]

Another matter is the question of proof. In my Introduction, 'proof' in a legal context has already been referred to. It was Luckhoo who spoke of the evidence

---

[200] Francis J. Beckwith, *David Humes' Argument Against Miracles: A Critical Analysis* (New York: University Press of America, 1989), 122-138. Beckwith studied under Montgomery at Simon Greenleaf. Also see the article of lawyer Paul K. Hoffman, 'A Jurisprudential Analysis of Hume's "In Principal" Argument Against Miracles', *Christian Apologetics Journal* 2, 1 (Spring 1999), <http://www.ses.edu/journal/issue2_1/2_hoffman-mn.htm>.
[201] ibid., 125.
[202] ibid., 133.
[203] Packham, 'Critique', 5. James Patrick Holding in his refutation of Packham wrongly asserts that Packham agrees with him that Montgomery was misguided in applying legal evidence to the gospels. Holding ironically then applies his own literary and historical insights. See 'Robert (Richard) Packham refuted', <http://www.tektonics.org/JPH_LLL.html>.

Epistemological Matters

for the resurrection being so 'overwhelming that it compels acceptance by proof which leaves absolutely no room for doubt'.[204] Montgomery writes of the 'ordinary standards of proof'.[205]

The mention of 'proof' here in a philosophical framework would be an unfortunate word as it is seldom used except in a syllogistic form, a deductive approach. Law takes no cognisance of this and the word 'proof' is most commonly used in an inductive paradigm. The international and Australian authority on legal evidence, *Cross on Evidence*, begins 'The evidence of a fact is that something which tends to prove it…'[206] Philosopher, C. Stephen Evans, supports the position that the legal level of proof is the most appropriate for apologetics and in evaluating religious truth claims. He advocates the court, juridical model. He holds that the philosophical standard seems impossibly high and 'seems unfair, since this is not the standard of proof we require for nonreligious areas'.[207]

In a court of law one also encounters the term 'moral certainty' when the degree of proof required for a finding is discussed. Certainty, like proof, in this context, in contrast to its common usage in philosophy, does not mean demonstrably true. Rather certainty, in a criminal trial setting, means beyond a reasonable doubt, as it is understood that no amount of factual evidence can yield certainty in an absolute sense.[208] As will be discussed, in a civil proceeding the quantum of proof required to prove a fact is the balance of probabilities. And as the scientist Dr David Snoke stresses, it is not only the law which speaks of certainty where 'perfect' certainty is not possible: 'For (working) scientists, a whole spectrum of degrees of certainty exists, with perfect certainty and complete ignorance as two ends of the scale.'[209]

---

[204] Lionel Luckhoo, *The Question Answered: Did Jesus Rise from the Dead* (n.p., n.d.), 28.
[205] Montgomery, *Tractatus*, 3.676.
[206] Heydon, *Cross*, 1.
[207] Evans, *Why Believe?*, 20. Cf. Thomas J. Richards, *The Language of Reason* (Sydney: Pergamon, 1980), 38-39. Richards cites a Fallacy of Unattainable Standards of Argument. He argues in mathematics a full rigorous proof in an argument is justifiable. In other areas of life, such as the causes of lung cancer, the best you could do is offer some message of support and it's not reasonable to expect conclusive proof in the logical deductive sense. Doubt based on the lack of conclusiveness is in such cases unreasonable – a fallacy. It is argued that the Christian truth claims by their nature, like the causes of lung cancer, are not capable of demonstrable proof.
[208] In support of this epistemological principle of legal method Montgomery quotes from Judge Shaw, 'The circumstances taken as a whole, and giving them their reasonable and just weight, and no more, should to a moral certainty exclude every other hypothesis.' *The Law Above*, 45.
[209] David Snoke, 'The Problem of the Absolute in Evidential Epistemology', *Perspectives on Science and Christian Faith* 47, 1 (March 1995): 8.

Allowing for the rich and varied use of words like 'proof' and 'certainty' within the various realms of apologetics - historical, scientific, journalistic, literary, philosophical, legal, is consistent with the role of language espoused by Ludwig Wittgenstein who noted its different rules according to the 'game'.[210] And law clearly defines and sets its own conditions for communication. Margaret Davies, Law School Flinders University, finds: 'If law is a game, it is essentially a language-game, because in any of the spheres in which it operates, it orders the field of play as well as the players.'[211] Montgomery also refers to Wittgenstein when discussing the role of language in the legal apologetic as different from the philosophical apologetic.[212]

There are those in the apologetic world who will continue to oppose Montgomery's 'probable' God. The issues raised really relate to whether evidentialism is justified which, as indicated in the Introduction, is beyond the scope of this thesis. It was noted that such methodological concerns have been well and truly canvassed by Montgomery and others. However, the fact is that if, as chapter five suggests, a legal apologetic paradigm is appropriate, such an apologetic will only address probabilities. 'Legal reasoning is probabilistic'.[213]

A more pressing issue for this thesis is the quantum of proof required to make a finding on the facts about the resurrection of Jesus. It is surprising that the majority of legal apologists do not seriously address the issue of quantum. They challenge the listener or reader to concede that the probabilities are strong enough to amount to legal proof, but they are divided over the issue of the quantum. In fact, in many cases no direction is given on whether one is making a finding beyond a reasonable doubt or by a preponderance of the evidence.[214] Some apologists use language that connects to a criminal standard whilst others use a civil standard.[215] In reality, the difference in quantum required is such that a case 'won' in a civil proceeding may be lost in a criminal court. In what court is Jesus tried?

The inconsistency does not extend to Montgomery. Montgomery, for example, in a legal master's thesis stipulates the higher standard of 'moral certainty, beyond reasonable doubt' as he does in his *magnum opus*.[216] In part he relies on

---

[210] Ludwig Wittgenstein, *Philosophical Investigations* (Oxford: Basil Blackwell, 1958), s.7.
[211] Margaret Davies, *Asking the Law Question* (North Ryde: The Law Book Company, 1994), 22.
[212] John Warwick Montgomery, *The Law Above*, 89. For a discussion on Wittgenstein's work on verification and language see Montgomery, *The Suicide*, 268-370.
[213] Montgomery, *Human Rights*, 152.
[214] Exceptions include Ewen, *Faith*, 15; Richards, *Jesus*, 84.
[215] For example see the Introduction where Clarke speaks more of probability and Luckhoo adopts a criminal standard.

Epistemological Matters

Swinburne who, applying mathematical tools of probability to his argument (Bayes' theorem of probability calculus), calculates the probability of Jesus' resurrection at 'a whopping 97%'.[217] Admittedly, in another place Montgomery uses language of 'more probable or less probable' and exhorts proof by *res ipsa loquitur* – a civil standard.[218] He also indicates that faith is the bridge between the gap of a 'high level of probability' and certainty.[219] However he is clearly prepared to operate at a standard used in a criminal court.

Although Prescott also pleads for proof beyond reasonable doubt,[220] C. Stephen Evans holds that we ought to make belief judgements that are in accordance with the preponderance of evidence.[221] He suggests this is the normal standard for making decisions in life. Further, he argues that 'beyond reasonable doubt' applies where there is a presumption of innocence. This is so in criminal trials. Blackstone's famous dictum operates here: 'it is better that ten guilty persons escape, than one innocent suffer'.[222] In rational enquiry into religious faith there is no assumed 'guilt' or 'innocence', hence there is no presumption in favour of theism or atheism.[223] The sceptic and the believer have an equal burden. In fact when one considers the eternal ramifications of disputing the resurrection of Jesus, it could be argued, using a concept from the law of torts, 'calculus of risk', that the unbeliever has the burden of proof.[224]

I believe the civil test is a more appropriate legal analogy[225]. Perhaps the legal apologists have opted for the higher burden because of the serious, eternal issues at stake. The fact is however, that this is an apologetic focusing on historical and circumstantial evidence, seeking to persuade opinion. To claim proof 'beyond

---

[216] Montgomery 'Marxist Approach', 124-125; Montgomery, *Tractatus*, 3.665 – 3.6651.

[217] Montgomery, *Tractatus*, 3.873. For a report see 'Editorial Apologetics: Probable Cause', *Christianity Today* 46, 8 (8 July 2002): 8.

[218] Montgomery, 'Neglected Apologetic', 121-123; Montgomery, *Defending the Biblical Gospel, Study Guide*, 41.

[219] Montgomery, audiotape, 'A Lawyer's Case'; John Warwick Montgomery, 'God & Other Law-Makers', *Beyond Culture Wars* (May/June 1993), <http://www.alliancenet.org/pub/mr/mr93/1993.03.MayJun/mr9303.jwm.lawmakers.html>.

[220] Prescott, 'Anthony Flew's', 162.

[221] Evans, *Why Believe?*, 20-24.

[222] William Blackstone, *Commentaries on the Laws of England*, Vol. IV (Oxford: Clarendon Press, 1769), 352.

[223] Evans, *Why Believe?*, 20-21.

[224] Prescott, 'Anthony Flew's', 158-161.

[225] Ewen, *Faith*, 15. This does not stop the apologist using the analogy of the listener or reader being a member of a jury. In America juries are still part of the civil trial system and in other English speaking countries they are still found in some civil suits, for example defamation cases. See John G. Fleming, *The Law of Torts*, 7th ed. (North Ryde, Sydney: The Law Book Company, 1987), 280-285.

reasonable doubt' is to promise too much. And Montgomery has shown, through commissioned surveys, that in both England and the United States very few people would decide 'beyond reasonable doubt' on the basis of less than 75% certainty. In fact a considerable number of the sample surveyed said they would require 100% certainty.[226]

What does one mean by balance of probabilities? According to David Hamer, rationality dictates that a mathematical standard of greater than 50 per cent should be adopted.[227] For the marshalling of evidence this will be the position taken in this thesis. Some judges insist, whilst agreeing the tribunal can operate under this understanding of proof, that it still must feel the persuasion of the occurrence or existence of any fact in issue before it can be found.[228] In other words proving a fact is realistically often more than the meeting of some mathematical formula. All the apologist can do is present the evidence and, in theological terms, the intuition will be one of inner conviction.

One matter concerning Montgomery's legal epistemology that raises discussion is his view that there is no special amount of evidence required to establish a miracle such as a resurrection. He cites approvingly the former master of the Temple Church, Thomas Sherlock, and says Sherlock, 'is certainly correct that a resurrection does not in principle create any insuperable evidential difficulty.'[229] In Sherlockian language he continues,

> Thus the eating of fish is sufficient to classify the eater among the living, and a crucifixion is enough to place the crucified among the dead. In Jesus' case, the sequential order is reversed, but that has no epistemological bearing on the weight of evidence required to establish death or life. And if Jesus was dead at point A, and alive again at point B, then resurrection has occurred: *res ipsa loquitur*.[230]

---

[226] 37.5% English and 18.7% United States respondents required the 100% certainty. See John Warwick Montgomery, 'The Criminal Standard of Proof', *New Law Journal* 148, 6837 (24 April 1998): 582 – 585.
[227] David Hamer, 'The Civil Standard of Proof Uncertainty: Probability, Belief and Justice', *Sydney Law Review* 16, 4 (December 1994): 506-536. In torts if two hypotheses are evenly poised, the plaintiff has not discharged the onus incumbent on her. See Fleming, *The Law*, 299.
[228] ibid., 508-512.
[229] Montgomery, *Human Rights*, 154.
[230] ibid., 155. See John Warwick Montgomery, 'The Search for Ultimates: A Sherlockian Inquiry', *Christian Legal Journal* 2, 3 (Spring 1993): 8. Reprinted in John Warwick Montgomery, *The Transcendent Holmes* (Victoria, British Columbia: Calabash, 2000), 119-135.

Epistemological Matters

This 'minimal facts' position of Montgomery has not arisen with his legal apologetic. It is grounded in his historical evidentialism. At a much earlier time he stated that to prove a supernatural event, 'The case demanded is no less than, but also no greater than, that required for events in general.'[231] Admittedly, elsewhere Montgomery posits a qualification to his position when he states one needs enough evidence to convict as in other 'comparable cases'.[232]

Montgomery, in this issue, has his sights firmly fixed on David Hume. He is addressing the Humean argument that common experience of non-supernatural events reduces the probability of the supernatural to such a point that incredibly greater evidence (which is for Hume clearly not available) would be needed to establish an alleged supernatural event.[233] In countering Hume however, one has to exercise some caution. To be open to the possibility that a miraculous event in time and space would admit evidence does not mean one should in such a case rely on the same amount of evidence as needed to prove a natural event. Beckwith illustrates his concerns with Montgomery's position:

> The problem with this response is that it is simply not realistic. For example, if my next door neighbor tells me that his father passed away last night, that would be sufficient reason in most cases to believe that the event had occurred. On the other hand, if this same neighbor a week later tells me with no additional evidence that his 'dead' father came by for dinner that evening, I would be acting reasonably if I did not believe him. I would probably doubt either my neighbor's sanity or the accuracy of his first report (i.e. that his father died). Now if other factors, such as doctors' reports, numerous other witnesses, a missing body, etc., began and continued to converge upon the event, at some point I would have to give up my skepticism in order to remain rational.[234]

In law, the nature of the issues to be decided has a bearing on the rules that govern that finding and the factual evidence required.[235] Even in civil trials the unlikelihood of a plaintiff's version will mean it takes more evidence for the plaintiff to

---

[231] John Warwick Montgomery, *Principalities and Powers* (Minneapolis: Bethany, 1981), 193-194, endnote 41.
[232] Montgomery, audiotape, 'A Lawyer's Case'. Montgomery does not make this qualification in the transcript of the lecture. See also Montgomery, *Tractatus*, 3.1171 – 3.1172 and 3.6765.
[233] ibid. Cf Beckwith, *David Hume's*, 121-138.
[234] Beckwith, *David Hume's*, 135-136, endnote 22.

reach the level of balance of probabilities. The Australian High Court Justice Dixon noted:

> The seriousness of an allegation made, the inherent unlikelihood of an occurrence of a given description, or the gravity of the consequences flowing from a particular finding are considerations which most affect the answer to the question whether the issue has been proved to the reasonable satisfaction of the tribunal.[236]

Further one could argue that Jesus' own actions in giving more and more 'convincing proof' to his disciples, even after initial resurrection appearances, confirmed that he also saw the need for weighty evidence, in view of the immensity of the actual event.[237]

The legal apologetic school needs to reconsider its general stance on the weight of evidence for the resurrection when it engages in epistemic discourse. The 'sceptic', be he or she a sceptical judge or jury member, is entitled to have more confidence in testimony within his or her own range of experience, and to expect more evidence for a supernatural event which he or she may well believe natural law data makes improbable. In light of the alleged semantic strength of the Christian truth claim and the value that is placed upon it, this is doubly so. Richard Packham shows some movement from a Humean position when he suggests 'I would have no difficulty accepting as fact any number of very improbable events, if the weight of the evidence were consonant with the inherent improbability of the event claimed.' A lack of such evidence for Packham is a defeated for belief.[238]

However, as will be mentioned in our critique of Cavin in chapter five in the section 'Eternal Facts in Issue', Montgomery is right in holding that this higher level of proof does not mean the legal apologetic must ground itself on a never-ending

---

[235] Legal apologist Jeffrey E. Bauer further acknowledges, 'Generally speaking in a court of law, the more numerous and varied the individual facts upon which a conclusion is based, the more likely it is to be correct'. Jeffrey E. Bauer, 'The Logician's Model of Judgment and the Resurrection of Christ', *Simon Greenleaf Law Review*, VII (1987-1988): 129.

[236] *Briginshaw v Briginshaw* 1938 CLR 60 at 361-362. For further discussion see chapter five, 'Law and Astonishing Events'. For proceedings in quasi-judicial tribunals see Heydon, *Cross*, 9-12.

[237] The New Testament acknowledges this, for example in Acts 1:3. See F.F. Bruce, *The Book of the Acts, The New International Commentary on the New Testament* (Grand Rapids: William B. Eerdmans, 1980) 33: 'Jesus appeared at intervals to His apostles in a manner which could leave no doubt in their minds that He was alive again, risen from the dead.'

[238] Packham, 'Critique', 14. See also Schramm, *Testimony*, 62.

Epistemological Matters

pursuit of data. And the truth is that whilst Montgomery pleads his more minimalist epistemic point of view in his theoretical discourse, he offers much more by the way of evidence than Jesus eating fish.

Admits a hearing, not a verdict

There is one other matter which is a major premise of this thesis. It relates to legal apologists, on the whole, framing their case in such a way that they suggest that either directly or indirectly, all the relevant evidence has been heard or pleaded. The listener or reader is therefore now in the position of a judge or jury: to consider his or her verdict.[239] Val Grieve is representative of the legal apologetic school when he concludes, 'Lawyers may present the evidence, but every legal case ends with the judge turning to the members of the jury and saying, "Ladies and gentlemen of the jury, the verdict is yours" .... It's your turn now. What is your verdict about Jesus? Did he rise from the dead? And if he did, what are the implications for you, and your own life and death?'[240]

After the research had been completed for this thesis, I concluded that the implication that the listener or reader was in a position of a judge or jury to consider a verdict was to claim too much. This is certainly so for the technical apologetic. It is understandable why the paradigm has functioned this way as traditionally apologetics has sought to lead the listener or reader to a response.[241] However, throughout chapters two and three it will be argued that the listeners or readers are not in the position of a judge or jury to consider their verdict. The reasons for this include that there are evidentiary issues concerning these: the admissibility of the New Testament records; the admissibility, credibility, and weight of the New Testament testimony for the resurrection. As will be argued, the legal apologist would be very confident that these issues would be addressed in any trial, but whether this is so is a matter of debate. How the testimony of Peter, John and others, which includes alleged discrepancies over the resurrection appearances, would be weighed after a rigorous cross-examination, is beyond our real knowledge.

For these reasons the legal apologists should reframe the legal apologetic to one in which the evidence admits a hearing, not a verdict. I will argue that the legal apologist does have a case for the death and resurrection of Jesus and, therefore, can be responsible in asking for a hearing. Moreover the sceptic who refuses to

---

[239] For example Stewart, *You Be*, 105-106; Russell, *A Lawyer's*, 227-250. Russell concludes, 'Men and women of the jury, I ask you now to write your ballot in this case' (250).
[240] Grieve, *Your Verdict*, 112-113; Montgomery, *Human Rights*, 148-149.
[241] Acts 17:29-34.

give the apologist a hearing is irresponsible in so doing. Apart from the possible rejoinders over the submitted evidence being a reason for the legal apologist to limit his case to a hearing, there is epistemic humility. There is much more epistemic humility in an apology that advocates a hearing than in 'the evidence demands a verdict' approach. By 'hearing', one means 'a *prima facie* case' approach whether it be a lawyer preparing a brief for trial, or a preliminary hearing (in appropriate jurisdictions that allow for this). By 'preliminary hearing' one does not mean a 'grand jury' if that implies a one way street for the prosecution, but 'a hearing' where the evidence is submitted, and where there is some sifting of the evidence 'pro and con'.[242]

The purpose of a preliminary hearing is not to reach a verdict but to decide whether there is sufficient evidence for a trial: a case to answer. A preliminary hearing in some jurisdictions is conducted on the basis of the documentary evidence.[243] Whether it be preparing a case for trial or a preliminary hearing, the evidence will have to be marshalled, and the possible rejoinders outlined and considered, but the trial is still to come. This approach is responsible in that it does not elongate the legal apologetic to an inappropriate level. The listener or reader will be still called to consider the evidence, but cannot avoid doing so on the basis of the apologist overstating his or her case.

In legal fiction there are numerous examples of writers who have not taken their story to trial but who have centred their novel on a preparation for trial or a preliminary hearing.[244] The legal apologist will not be limited in presenting his or her case by a novel or story, as is suggested in chapter four, if only the evidence admits a hearing, rather than a verdict. There is definitely a case to answer.

---

[242] See Barry Reed, *The Indictment* (New York: St Martin's, 1994), 301-302.
[243] For discussion see for example Brett, Waller and Williams, *Criminal Law: Text and Cases*, 6th ed. (Sydney: Butterworths, 1989), 20-23.
[244] For example, Perri O'Shaughnessy [Pamela and Mary O'Shaughnessy], *Obstruction of Justice* (New York: Island, 1998); D.W. Buffa, *The Prosecution* (Crows Nest, NSW: Allen and Unwin, 2001); Patricia D. Benke, *Cruel Justice* (New York: Avon, 1999); Christine McGuire, *Until Proven Guilty* (London: Mandarin, 1994).

Chapter 2

Evaluation of Montgomery's Legal Apologetic:
The Criteria Part I

The legal apologetic is a C – inductive model. The probability of an actual thing or event is 1. Given the balance of probabilities as the appropriate standard, a probability range between 0.5 and 1 is required for a finding on the facts. It is true an argument (P – inductive) may in itself raise the probability of a conclusion above 0.5. It is more likely in a fact-based historical legal paradigm that several arguments (C – inductive) operating in tandem will be required to show that a conclusion is probable. In law it is not necessary for each item of fact to stand on its own as proof of the issue. It is said to be enough if each item of evidence shows the fact in issue is more probable. In a cumulative case therefore each item creates a cord that is one strand of a rope.

The biblical model for the resurrection is a C – inductive argument and it has been the same for the legal apologetic: for example reliable witnesses, empty tomb, and personal testimony. This C – inductive argument is inferential as the resurrection event itself cannot be presented (presumptive evidence). Inferential evidence for such consists of two forms: direct or testimonial evidence, indirect or circumstantial evidence.[1] This inferential evidence in the legal apologetic is 'activated' evidence as it used to support the resurrection hypothesis. The C – inductive paradigm of Montgomery, and the legal apologists as a class, has evident strengths and potential weaknesses. (This is true of any apologetic method.) These strengths and potential weaknesses will be the focus of not only this chapter, but also chapters three and four.

The Evidence

The main question is whether the pleaded inferential evidence for the resurrection is admissible, credible, relevant (material and probative value)[2] and leads to a verdict. The legal criteria used to prove documents, hearsay, testimony, things and circumstantial evidence will be considered. As the legal apologetic has its home in the Anglo-American world the authorities relied on are those of common law countries and the legal system that is adopted is the Anglo-American adversarial trial process, rather than the European inquisitorial system. In this chapter

---

[1] See John H. Wigmore, *Treatise on Evidence,* Vol. 1 (Boston and Toronto: Little, Brown, 1904), 13.
[2] The question is whether the evidence is material to the case and does it help establish the truth of the facts. See Ewen, *Faith,* 13.

documents and hearsay will be the focus. In chapter three the other three strands of evidence are evaluated. This chapter relates more specifically to issues surrounding the technical legal apologetic and the criteria in chapter three have a more general application to both the technical and non-technical model. Chapters two and three are particularly applicable to the concerns of the 'modernity' style of thinking. In chapter four the evidence is again considered in the context of an apologetic to 'New Spirituality'.

Documents

As previously mentioned in the Introduction and chapter one the New Testament accounts are the primary evidence for the facts in issue: the death and resurrection of Jesus. The legal apologist's primary focus is the four gospels. Sceptic Packham concedes the New Testament records are most relevant to the case and if they are not solid enough to be relied upon, other key questions become moot.[3] So one is left to investigate whether they are admissible and credible. It is the authenticity of the gospels (admissibility) that will be discussed. The evangelists' testimony (credibility) will be evaluated in the next chapter.

There is another issue though. Christian truth claims are often dismissed on the basis that they lack direct oral evidence in support, and that they rely on documentary statements that are considered inferior. Law can be of assistance here. In judicial science, whilst there is considerable debate over the weight to be given to documentary evidence in comparison to oral evidence, it is viewed highly. McEwan acknowledges the regulations that operate in some jurisdictions which require the maker of a document to be available to give evidence, unless he is dead, or unfit to attend indicates a preference for oral evidence in those tribunals.[4] However, she rightly argues that this alleged superiority of oral evidence is not universally accepted. She states, 'Like historians, continental jurisdictions prefer documentary sources'.[5] They are perceived as less subjective. Brown also notes that although documents cannot be cross-examined, one considerable advantage they possess over oral evidence is that their contents do not alter once in evidence. He concludes, 'This certainty of content is often a real benefit in the shifting sands of forensic evidence.'[6]

---

[3] Packham, 'Critique', 5.
[4] Jenny McEwan, *Evidence and the Adversarial Process* (Oxford: Blackwell Business, 1992), 212-218.
[5] ibid., 193.
[6] R.A. Brown, *Documentary Evidence in Australia*, 2nd ed. (North Ryde, NSW: LBC, 1996), 2.

Honoré has shown that neither kind of evidence is inherently more reliable than the other, although oral testimony has a tactical advantage rather than one of merit as a called witness is a 'self-authenticating and self-defending document'. Honoré concludes though, 'neither law nor history can afford any favourite other than truth'.[7] In this spirit Magner asserts that there is no absolute answer as to whether oral or documentary evidence is the best evidence, and that circumstances will dictate what the best evidence is in an individual case.[8]

Without question, documentary evidence is legally good evidence provided the records are worthy of trust.[9]

'Ancient Documents' Rule

The major legal criteria Montgomery uses to prove the New Testament books, and in particular the gospels are authentic is the 'Ancient Documents' rule. In chapter one (in the historical overview) it was shown Montgomery is in a long line of technical legal apologists who are indebted to Simon Greenleaf in this regard. The said rule is a major plank in this apologetic. Montgomery states, 'ancient documents will be received as competent evidence if they are "fair on their face" (i.e. offer no internal evidence of tampering) and have been maintained in "reasonable custody" (i.e. their preservation has been consistent with their content)'. He cites approvingly Greenleaf's assertion that under this rule the competence of the New Testament documents would be established in any court.[10] Montgomery concludes, 'the burden of proof thus rests upon the unbeliever to disprove the testimonial value of these apostolic books, not upon the Christian to build up support for documents already having *prima facie* legal authority'.[11] A well reasoned defence of Montgomery's argument, presented by lawyer Boyd Pehrson, is found in the internet journal of which Montgomery is the general editor.[12]

---

[7] Tony Honoré, 'The Primacy of Oral Evidence?' in *Crime Proof and Punishment: Essays in Memory of Sir Rupert Cross*, C.F.H. Tapper, ed. (London: Butterworths, 1981), 192. In this article Honoré outlines historically the debate between common law countries and continental law countries over the primacy of oral evidence.

[8] Eilis S. Magner, 'The Best Evidence – Oral Testimony or Documentary Proof?', *The University of New South Wales Law Journal* 18, 1 (1995): 93-94.

[9] McEwan, *Evidence*, 192.

[10] Montgomery, *Human Rights*, 137; Montgomery, *Tractatus*, 3.291 – 3.29111.

[11] Montgomery, 'Neglected Apologetic', 122.

[12] Boyd Pehrson, 'How Not to Critique Legal Apologetics: A Lesson from a Skeptic's Internet Page Objections', *Global Journal of Classical Theology* 3, 1 (March 2002): 1-9, <http://www.trinitysem.edu/journal/toc_v3n1.html>.

This pleading of the 'Ancient Documents' rule has also had a great impact upon general apologetics. One example is Norman Geisler who avers that because of this rule the New Testament 'should be considered authentic'.[13] Another is Ankerberg and Weldon's citing of William Burns Lawless, a former Justice and Dean of Notre Dame Law School, who stated Greenleaf's conclusions on the admissibility of the gospels is as 'valid in 1995 as it was in 1842'.[14]

The significance of the 'Ancient Documents' rule lies in the fact that the gospels are hearsay evidence. With regard to documents the rule of evidence with respect to hearsay is as follows: '... assertions in documents produced to a court when no witness is testifying, are inadmissible as evidence of the truth of that which was asserted'.[15]

The primary reason for the exclusion of hearsay evidence is that the adverse party is denied the opportunity to cross-examine the declarant and to test the declarant's perception, memory, sincerity and ability. Strategically, the 'Ancient Documents' rule is an exception to hearsay rule. The rule is as cited above, with the normal proviso that the said document be at least twenty years old. It is a common law principle that in many jurisdictions has been codified.[16] Its primary justification is that in such cases it is not feasible or practical to call the maker of the document. It is presumed that, although the document may not be corroborated or authenticated by any *res gesta* act, it is unlikely that any fabrication or forgery would have escaped exposure over such a period of time. Such instruments it is said 'prove themselves'.[17]

Ancient documents are not automatically admitted. They must meet the requirements of a necessity for the evidence and a guarantee of the evidence's trustworthiness.[18] The guarantee of trustworthiness in this context is that the documents are 'fair on their face' and have been maintained in 'reasonable custody', also known as 'natural' or 'proper custody'. It is accepted that there may be other 'natural' places of custody and no one custody is the necessary one.[19] As indicated in

---

[13] Geisler, *Miracles and the Modern Mind*, 133.
[14] Ankerberg and Weldon, *Ready*, 106.
[15] Rupert Cross and Nancy Wilkins, *An Outline of the Law of Evidence*, 3rd ed. (London: Butterworths, 1971), 96.
[16] See Edward W. Cleary, ed., *McCormick on Evidence*, 3rd ed. (St Paul: West Publishing, 1984), s. 223, 692-694; Heydon, *Cross*, s. 5, 1019-1020. Cross notes it's an ill-defined exemption. United States Federal Rules of Evidence 803 (16) – Hearsay exemptions, 'Statements in a document in existence twenty years or more the authenticity of which is established'.
[17] Spencer, A. Gard, *Jones on Evidence*, 4 vols., 6th ed. (Rochester: The Lawyers Co-operative; San Francisco: Bancroft–Whitney, 1972), 3: 286-288.
[18] *Sherrill v Estate of Plumley* 514 SWR 2d 286 at 286-291.

chapter one, legal apologists like Montgomery seek to establish that the gospels are 'fair on their face' by countering 'liberal' criticisms of the gospels' pedigree and by proving they are not fakes. Greenleaf holds, with respect to 'reasonable custody', that one would expect the New Testament records to be found in the church in the care of Christians. They are so found.[20] In support there is case law that the proper custody for baptismal registers or vicar's books includes the church.[21]

There is however a major procedural matter in this reliance on the 'Ancient Documents' rule, that requires further attention. The admissibility of the gospel evidence is a matter of law to be decided by a judge. 'Average' listeners or readers are not in a position to judge on questions of law, at least not without a good deal of equipping. Apologetically they are members of a jury, or triers of fact. Rarely is this distinction made and readers or listeners are left with the assumption that they could reasonably hold the gospels are admissible on the limited data given to them. And certainly they don't have all the indicia before them that a judge would have.

Admittedly in response it could be argued that the control of the judge is limited. Packham in his critique of Montgomery's use of the 'Ancient Documents' rule places considerable weight on the authority of Wigmore on evidence.[22] Such reliance is warranted and Wigmore's assessment of the rule is one of the most extensive.[23] Wigmore's inference is that once a tendered document is taken to be sufficiently evidenced as to its genuineness of execution it is submitted to the jury.[24] It could be pleaded that 'sufficiently evidenced' is 'unsuspicious appearance' (fair on their face) and from 'natural custody'.[25] Further, it appears that only a *prima facie* showing is required.[26]

In light of this limited burden of proof upon the plaintiff, there is considerable justification for the pleading of some legal apologists, including Montgomery, that once such documents are admitted under this criterion the burden lies with

---

[19] See M.N. Howard, Peter Crane and Daniel A. Hochberg, *Phipson on Evidence*, 14th ed. (London: Sweet & Maxwell, 1990), 952-954.
[20] Greenleaf, *The Testimony*, 7-9.
[21] See Howard, Crane and Hochberg, *Phipson*, 953.
[22] Packham, 'Critique', 6-8. Pehrson's article is a response to Packham. See 'How Not'.
[23] John Henry Wigmore, *Evidence in Trials at Common Law*, Vol. 7, rev. James H. Chadbourn (Boston and Toronto: Little, Brown, 1978), 721-745.
[24] Wigmore, *Evidence*, 7: 721-745. See also sections 2128, 2135.
[25] ibid., 721-728.
[26] ibid., 721-723, s. 2135. Wigmore cites *United States v Tellier* 255 F. 2d 441 (2d Cir. 1958) and notes 'that only a prima facie showing is required'.

the adverse party to either impeach, or otherwise render doubtful, the documents and their recitals.[27]

So what is the procedural concern? It lies in the fact that even if a judge found on the evidence offered above that a *prima facie* case had been made as to 'fair on their face' and 'reasonable custody', the matter would not rest there. There are still contentious issues that the legal apologists don't fully address. Even if the adverse party was stopped from raising these objections at the *voire dire*[28] on admissibility they would certainly alert the jury to this fact. As well, a judge in her summation to the jury would certainly address the weight to be given to the evidence and instruct on the objections raised that do relate to questions of law.[29] And in a hearing without a jury, a judge may simply prefer to provisionally admit such documents, subject to final rulings as to admissibility and consideration of weight.

It is not simply a case of satisfying two basic criteria and moving on as the burden has shifted. Dale Foreman is one who takes this course even though he admits it 'begs the question' of whether the ancient writings (gospels) are reliable.[30] The legal apologist in future should acknowledge the rigorous debate that would accompany a request to tender the gospels relying on the 'Ancient Documents' rule, be it to a judge or to judge and jury.[31] Two examples highlight the depth of such debate. The first is the ground breaking *Mabo* case. Documentary evidence was tendered in the form of three hundred and thirteen exhibits. The historical works included first contact with the Torres Straits, archival notes and volumes of an anthropological expedition. Keon-Cohen notes, 'These (documents) generated much argument concerning admissibility, weight and relevance.'[32]

---

[27] Greenleaf, *The Testimony*, 8: 'The burden of showing them to be false and unworthy of credit, is devolved on the party who makes that objection.' See also Montgomery, *Human Rights*, 140; Russell, *A Lawyer's*, 44-45. It is not unusual in law for the proponent's duty to be discharged by establishing a *prima facie* case. See *William Henry Bailey v Charles Lindsay Bailey* (1924) 34 C.L.R. 558 for this evidentiary principle with respect to a probate suit involving testamentary capacity.

[28] *Voire dire* is used here in the English trial context of a trial within a trial.

[29] Heydon, *Cross*, 298-299.

[30] Foreman, *Crucify Him*, 67-68.

[31] In fact Montgomery and Greenleaf imply that once the gospels have satisfied the two basic criteria they have a presumption of innocence – it is assumed they are genuine until proved otherwise. Greenleaf, *The Testimony*, 7-8; Montgomery, *Human Rights*, 137-140.

[32] B.A. Keon-Cohen, 'Some Problems of Proof: The Admissibility of Traditional Evidence' in *Mabo: A Judicial Revolution: The Aboriginal Land Rights Decision and its Impact on Australian Law*, M.A. Stephenson and Suri Ratnapala, eds. (St Lucia: University of Queensland Press, 1993), 188.

The second is the case *West v Houston Oil Co*. In this suit the court ruled that even if there is sufficient evidence for an ancient document to go to a jury, if the defendant comes forward with other evidence to the contrary then there is no artificial probative force as to the genuineness of the document simply because it has been admitted. The jury still hears the arguments and it is for the jury to weigh and determine what is the ancient document's value and probative force.[33]

It is the technical and untried issues such as the 'Ancient Documents' rule that warrant the legal apologetic in future limiting its case as one of preparing for trial, or perhaps a preliminary hearing rather than a fully constituted hearing. However, as we will shortly see the 'Ancient Documents' rule does have a place, but firstly there are some common objections that are likely to be raised.

Objections relating to the 'Ancient Documents' rule[34]
One possible objection of the adverse party is that the original gospels have been lost. In rejoinder, it would be argued that the 'Ancient Documents' rule makes provision for the admissibility of copies of documents.[35] *McCormick on Evidence* states, 'The preferable and majority view is that satisfaction of the ancient document requirements will serve to authenticate an ancient copy of an original writing.'[36] However, the onus lies on the party tendering the secondary document to show it is the most reliable evidence available.[37]

A second and more substantial objection relates to the authentication of the copies. The originals were not signed and therefore the copies bear no signature. Legislators often deem that it is mandatory for admissibility that statements by witnesses are handwritten or signed.[38] However, legal apologist Francis Lamb pleads that judicial science for centuries has held one must take into consideration what may be reasonably expected in all the circumstances, and courts have

---

[33] *West v Houston Oil Co*. 56 Tex. Civ. App. 341, 120 S.W. 228. Cited in Charles T. McCormick, Frank W. Elliott and John F. Sutton Jr., *Cases and Materials on Evidence* (St. Paul: West Publishing, 1981), 680-682.

[34] These objections could even be raised at a preliminary hearing if the case was dependent on the admission of documentary evidence. Some of these objections are referred to in Clifford, 'The Case of Eight Legal Apologists', 14-19. The argument here is more critical, developed and further objections are raised.

[35] Packham, 'Critique', 7.

[36] Cleary, *McCormick*, 694; Lamb, *Miracle and Science*, 40-43. For a discussion of 'reform' legislation that has resulted in the fact that in many jurisdictions it is no longer a condition of admissibility that the document be original or even authenticated see Magner, 'The Best Evidence', 81.

[37] For a discussion on the relationship between copies of documents and oral evidence see Cleary, *McCormick*, 720-722.

[38] Heydon, *Cross*, 1044.

accepted documents that have not been executed.[39] This is certainly true, of say, historical reports that by the nature of their genre differ from the rigid execution principles that apply to land deeds. Similarly with wills in some jurisdictions execution criteria are not essential to their operation. An example is section 18A of the *Wills Probate and Administration Acts* (NSW) as amended, which allows for probate of a will in circumstances where the informal testamentary instrument does not comply with the legislative requirements of signature, witnesses, and dating and may not even counter these limitations by being hand written.[40] It could also be argued under the 'Ancient Documents' rule that there is a presumption of due execution provided the historical document is 'fair on the face' and from 'reasonable custody'.[41] In fact Greenleaf asserts that the entire text of Corpus Juris Civilus is received as an authority in Continental Europe on 'much weaker evidence of its genuineness'.[42]

Of more interest with respect to authentication of copies is the issue of provenance. Arguing against the gospels' provenance Packham refers to Wigmore's citing of *Carter v Wood* where a copy of a deed was not admitted as the copier knew nothing of its genuineness. However he fails to mention that Wigmore then cites *Dickson v Smith* where an ancient map was admitted as it was found to come from the register's custody.[43] So the principle is that in the absence of corroborative evidence of the original's duplication, one must establish a probable chain of evidence to the originals. This process is similar to the conveyancer in an old system real property structure who for the conveyance to be effective must trace the ownership of the property and a clear description of the land to a 'good root of title'. Now, Packham is mistaken in his view that as the gospels have gone through 'many hands' provenance cannot be established.[44] Sir Frederick Kenyon, one time librarian and director of the British Museum is just one who states:

> The interval, then, between the dates of original composition and the earliest extant evidence becomes so small as to be in fact negligible, and the last foundation for any doubt that the scriptures have come down to us substantially as they were written has now

---

[39] Lamb, *Miracle and Science*, 33-38. See also Pehrson, 'How Not', 1-3.
[40] This practice was confirmed by Ruth Pollard, Legal Officer, Public Trustee of NSW. Interview by the author (Darling Harbour, NSW, 3 November 2000).
[41] R.A. Brown, *Documentary*, 57; Wigmore, *Evidence*, 7: 596.
[42] Greenleaf, *The Testimony*, 8-10.
[43] Wigmore, *Evidence*, 7: 595. See *Carter v Wood* 103 Va 68, 48 S.E. at 553; *Dickson v Smith* 134 Wis. 6, 114 N.W. at 133.
[44] Packham, 'Critique', 7.

been removed. Both the authenticity and the general integrity of the books of the New Testament may be regarded as finally established.[45]

Montgomery pleads:

> Competent historical scholarship must regard the New Testament documents as coming from the first century and as reflecting primary-source testimony about the person and claims of Jesus.[46]

A number of the legal apologists place some weight on this issue and develop the argument.[47] Ewen briefly works from the earliest papyri to Codex Sinaiticus and to later manuscripts.[48] Morrison also notes quotations from the 'New Testament' by the Apostolic and Church Fathers such as Justin Martyr, Clement and Tertullian and how they favourably compare with the canonical gospels.[49] New Testament scholar Metzger states that so extensive are these citations that if all other sources of our New Testament were destroyed they would be sufficient alone for reconstruction of practically the whole New Testament.[50] Montgomery, in his legal apologetic in *Human Rights and Human Dignity*, relies on one of his three-fold techniques of historical analysis: 'transmissional reliability' (their texts have been transmitted accurately from the time of writing to our own day).[51] In his magnum opus Mongomery sets out fully the case for transmissional reliability in proposition form.[52]

He finds 'Between the dates of original composition and earliest complete texts of the Gospels which we possess (*Codex Sinaiticus* and *Codex Vaticanus*), there are extant fragments, quotations, and lectionary readings going back to the first

---

[45] Frederick Kenyon, *The Bible and Archaeology* (New York & London: Harper, 1940), 288-289.
[46] Montgomery, *History and Christianity*, 34.
[47] See also Ross Clifford and Philip Johnson, *Sacred Quest*, rev. ed. (Sydney: Albatross, 1993), 147-169. Here we endeavour to show that new spirituality texts on Jesus' missing years (13-30 age), based on Nicholas Notovitich's *Unknown Life of Jesus Christ,* fail to establish a probable claim of provenance and lacked the credibility of the gospels.
[48] Ewen, *Faith*, 17-20.
[49] Morrison, *The Proofs*, 63-73. See for similar approach Russell, *A Lawyer's*, 41-63.
[50] Bruce M. Metzger, *The Text of the New Testament* (New York and Oxford: Oxford University Press, 1968), 86.
[51] Montgomery, *Human Rights*, 137.
[52] Cf. Montgomery, *Tractatus*, 3.24 – 3.258.

century and possibly earlier'[53] Montgomery's approach is replicated in other legal apologetic works and Greenleaf simply concludes, that the gospels 'are entitled to an extraordinary degree of confidence'.[54]

Justice Ken Handley, although not relying on the 'Ancient Documents' rule, has a brief but effective rejoinder on provenance.[55] He asks if the gospels are authentic records and suggests the reader is entitled to know if they have been corrupted by constant recopying or if one can find a 'good root of title'. He refers to documents from the early partial papyrus manuscripts (from 130 – 150 AD) to later complete manuscripts (Sinaiticus, 5000 extant Greek manuscripts). He favourably compares the dates and the large number of copies of the surviving early manuscripts for the New Testament with those of classical works of Greece and Rome (Caesar's Gallic Wars, Herodotus, Arrian on Alexander the Great). The large number of early New Testament manuscript copies is important as it allows one to determine the accuracy of the copying of the manuscripts since having a number of variant copies aids scholars in reconstructing the original document and determining what passages are authentic. As a consequence New Testament authority Stephen Neill finds, 'We have a far better and more reliable text of the New Testament than of any other ancient work whatever, and the measure of uncertainty is really rather small.'[56]

Handley also notes external data such as archaeological evidence (existence of Nazareth) and non-Christian sources (Suetonius, Tacitus, Josephus, Talmud) that confirm the gospel accounts and their trustworthy transmission. Lord Hailsham and some other legal apologists go into some detail on the external material and discuss possible concerns such as the variant Josephus accounts, and the alternative reports in the gnostic gospels and the apocryphal New Testament. With respect to Josephus they find that whether one accepts his 'statements' verbatim, there is no doubt he did chronicle the fact that Jesus lived and died and that he gives us a neutral account.[57] The gnostic and apocryphal sources simply do not have the transmission reliability of the gospels.[58]

---

[53] ibid., 3.253. See also *History, Law and Christianity* – full details.
[54] Greenleaf, *The Testimony*, 9.
[55] Handley, 'A Lawyer', 11-17.
[56] Stephen Neill, *The Interpretation of the New Testament* (Oxford: Oxford University Press, 1964), 78.
[57] Hailsham, *The Door*, 28-33; Clifford, *The Case for the Empty Tomb*, 70-81. For a discussion of the external evidence see Robert E. Van Voorst, *Jesus Outside the New Testament* (Grand Rapids: William B. Eerdmans, 2000); Barnett, *Jesus and the Rise*, esp. 143-151; E.M. Blaiklock, *Jesus Christ: Man or Myth?* (Nashville: Thomas Nelson, 1974), 19-31. For external evidence and reliable transmission of the gospel see Barnett, *Is the New Testament History?*

In conclusion Handley finds Christians are entitled to have confidence in the transmission of the gospels.[59] As indicated the reader who researched Montgomery's work would find he argues likewise as he submits the gospels to the tests of transmission, and internal and external reliability.[60] Montgomery also does this effectively in public debates with sceptics.[61] Legal apologists must follow Montgomery's lead and focus on such arguments for provenance in their reliance on the 'Ancient Documents' rule if they wish to plead the admissibility of the gospels under it.

A third objection is that the 'Ancient Documents' rule is limited to real property instruments and other commercial leases. This is a plausible objection as most of the references to the rule relate to land recitals and property rights disputes.[62] In rejoinder there are good authorities that establish that the scope of the rule applies to all documents, public or private.[63] Also one would expect the focus to be on property disputes, as that is the field that would attract finance for litigation. Wigmore notes the rule's application to land, and then states it applies to 'all sorts of documents whatever'.[64]

A fourth objection is one Packham understandably makes a lot of and it relates to the content of the document. The 'Ancient Documents' rule is about admissibility or authentication of the document. Yet admissibility falls short of demonstration. Packham claims Montgomery does not make this distinction, 'but leaves the impression with the lay reader that if the document is "authenticated" and "admissible", it is to be believed. That, in my opinion, is a dishonest distortion'.[65]

---

[58] J.B. Phillips, *Ring of Truth* (Basingstoke, Hants: Lakeland, 1984), 123-124; James M. Robinson, ed., *The Nag Hammadi Library* (Leiden and New York: E.J. Brill, 1998). Robinson states that with respect to documents like the Gospel of Thomas, 'The number of unintentional errors is hard to estimate, since such a thing as a clean control copy does not exist; nor does one have, as in the case of the bible, a quantity of manuscripts of the same text that tend to correct each other when compared.' (2).
[59] Handley, 'A Lawyer', 14-17.
[60] Montgomery, *Where is History Going?*, 44-74. See also Montgomery's *History, Law and Christianity* which brings together his historical and legal apologetic. It features his *History and Christianity* and the legal apologetic in *Human Rights*. This text is the appropriate starting point. For a comprehensive defense of Montgomery's use of these three criteria see Craig Hazen, '"Ever Hearing but Never Understanding": A Response to Mark Hutchin's Critique of John Warwick Montgomery's Historical Apologetics', *Global Journal of Theology*, 3, 1 (March 2002): 1-10.
[61] For example, Montgomery and Plummer, 'Humanism'.
[62] Heydon, *Cross*, 1019-1020.
[63] See Howard, Crane and Hochberg, *Phipson*, 952.
[64] Wigmore, *Evidence*, 7: s. 2145.
[65] Packham, 'Critique', 8.

Packham's criticism is unjustifiable. Montgomery and others openly acknowledge admissibility does not equate to a demonstration of truthfulness. Montgomery's case has a first step of proving historical documents, and a second of asking 'how good is their testimony to Jesus?'[66] This two stages approach is common in the legal apologetic.[67] Russell succinctly states, 'Whether a volume is authentic and whether credible are two very separate questions – neither necessarily implying the other'.[68]

There is however an issue the legal apologists do not raise with respect to the content of the document which is fundamental. The 'Ancient Documents' rule at common law has traditionally related more to the authentication of the document than with the admissibility of its contents. It does not automatically lead to admission of the substance of the document irrespective of its credibility.[69] (It can be argued this is even true today for the United States, even though the *Federal Rule of Evidence 803 [16]* states statements in Ancient Documents are admissible as exemptions to hearsay).[70] Greenleaf takes no cognisance of this position and asserts that when an instrument is admitted under the said rule the court is bound to receive into evidence its substance as well unless the opposing party is able to impeach it.[71] Other legal apologists have taken Greenleaf's stance.[72]

In contrast Martin states 'the judicial authorities are in sharp conflict concerning the extent to which statements in an ancient document, and particularly those in a nondispositive writing, are receivable as an exemption to the hearsay rule'.[73]

In some jurisdictions there is little doubt the said rule operates as an exception to the hearsay rule and the contents of the documents are received into evidence to be tested as to their truthfulness. In this regard there is common agreement that statements in land deeds are in this category where there is corroborating evi-

---

[66] Montgomery, *Human Rights*, 139-150; Montgomery, *Tractatus*, 3.2912.
[67] For example, Ewen, *Faith*, 17-142; Bartlett, *As a Lawyer*, 39-43, 130-168; Williams, *The Bible in Court*, 1-43.
[68] Russell, *A Lawyer's*, 42.
[69] Cleary, *McCormick*, 903-904. Wigmore, *Evidence*, 7: s. 2145a. Wigmore cites from *Town of Ninety Six v Southern Ry* 67 F. 2d 579 (4th Cir. 1959) at 583: 'The fact that an instrument is an ancient document does not affect its admissibility in evidence further than to dispense with proof of its genuineness.'
[70] Not all jurisdictions in the United States take the position that the hearsay exemption applies to the substance of an Ancient Document. See F.W. Binder, *Hearsay Handbook*, 2nd ed. (Colorado Springs: Shepard's/McGraw-Hill, 1983), 232.
[71] Greenleaf, *The Testimony,* 10-11.
[72] Chandler, *The Trial*, 1: 5-9; Lamb, *Miracle and Science*, 51-59.
[73] Michael M. Martin, *Basic Problems of Evidence*, 6th ed. (Philadelphia: American Law Institute – American Bar Association, 1988), 422. See also for case law Gard, *Jones*, 3: 286-290.

dence of possession of the property.[74] The question is to what extent, 'recitals in such documents as letters, maps, etc. ... become admissible?'[75] It is in this kind of category that the new Testament records fall and the sceptic could raise here a cogent objection to the admissibility of their contents. It could also be argued that there is no rule that applies absolutely and each case would have to be argued separately.[76]

The issues a judge could consider are to what extent the ancient document recitals are firsthand hearsay and whether the age of the original writing predates the controversy at issue. The latter is one of the rationales underlying the exception to the hearsay rule.[77] As the declarant is not able to be cross-examined as to a motive to falsify the document and/or if they have been influenced by partisanship, the predating of the controversy is of some importance. This is especially so in cases where the authors of documents are 'parties to the proceedings', as it could be argued is the case with the New Testament writers.

The question as to first-hand hearsay will be addressed in the hearsay section of this chapter. Few legal apologists specifically address the predating issue. Pamela Ewen is one who does, and answers it by arguing the gospel writers had no motive or plan to falsify their history.[78] These arguments will be discussed in the next chapter. And whilst such arguments will be shown to add considerable weight to the credibility of the gospel testimony, and whilst they may be of consideration for admissibility of the content of documents such as the gospels, they do not directly address the issue. The gospels do not predate the controversy. One illustration suffices. Matthew apologetically counters the allegation that the disciples themselves had stolen Jesus' body.[79] Craig argues that in this pericope 'we have a good illustration of how early Christians argued for the fact of Jesus' resurrection, upholding it against the Jewish polemic'.[80] The point is that an adverse party could reasonably plead to judge and/or jury that the admissibility of the substance of the documents under the said rule is problematic.

In the see-sawing arguments over the admissibility of the contents from a hearsay and predating perspective, the Wigmorian theory of 'circumstantial probability

---

[74] Wigmore, *Evidence in Trials at Common Law*, Vol. 5, rev. James H. Chadbourn (Boston and Toronto: Little, Brown, 1974), 527.
[75] ibid., 525-526.
[76] Wigmore, *Evidence*, 7: 744-745.
[77] Cleary, *McCormick*, 903-905.
[78] Ewen, *Faith*, 21-22.
[79] Matthew 28:11-15.
[80] Craig, *The Historical*, 5-6.

of trustworthiness' should be voiced in support.[81] The court may take into account when determining the reliability of the hearsay the existence of evidence which provides independent corroboration, the circumstances in which the statement was made, and the creditworthiness of the declarant. In this regard the appeal of Montgomery and some other legal apologists to Roman authors Suetonius, Tacitus and Pliny the Younger, and the Jewish authors Josephus, Rabbi Eliezer and the Talmud for the existence of corroborative data, is appropriate.[82]

It is also in this context of circumstantial probability that Ewen's point could be raised, viz. that there was no plan of falsification of evidence formed and, even if there were desires to falsify, the danger of easy detection would probably counteract its force.[83] Montgomery states that a plan of falsification 'would at once be exposed by those who would be only too glad to do so'[84]. The legal apologists tend to leave such matters to the credibility of the testimony, however they have a role in the actual admissibility of it.[85]

The question as to whether the authentication of the gospels under the 'Ancient Documents' rule leads to receiving their substance into evidence is contentious. Yet, it could be strongly pleaded there is justification for doing so.

A twofold role
Is there a place for the 'Ancient Documents' rule in the legal apologetic, or should one abandon this technical legal apologetic? The 'Ancient Documents' rule has a twofold role. Firstly, it can be used to show at a *prima facie* level the gospels are probably admissible. This is a 'modernity' foundation that the listener or reader will find helpful. It rightly evidences that the burden is on the adverse party as well as on the apologist when it comes to gospel reliability. It highlights the issues that even at a preliminary hearing level should be discussed in openly considering the reliability of historical documents. Montgomery's focus on this rule is most appropriate.

There is a second apologetic role which has not previously been raised. The 'Ancient Documents' rule shows that a court of law is not adverse to admitting ancient records. If authenticity can be established, ways are looked for to over-

---

[81] Wigmore, *Evidence*, 5: s. 1422. For discussion see Andrew Palmer, 'The Reliability-Based Approach to Hearsay', *Sydney Law Review* 17, 4 (December 1995): 525-540.
[82] Handley, 'A Lawyer', 11; Montgomery, *Human Rights*, 137; Montgomery, *Tractatus* 3.21 – 3.212
[83] Wigmore, *Evidence*, 5: s. 1422.
[84] Montgomery, *Tractatus*, 3.4525
[85] For example, Russell, *A Lawyer's*, 65-79.

'Ancient Documents' Rule

come hearsay and other objections. It simply is the best evidence available, and the danger of treating 'unreliable' hearsay as evidence on this best evidence criteria is accounted for by the criteria of provenance, 'fair on the face' and 'reasonable custody'.[86]

Two actual cases that are relevant to these considerations are *Dallas County v Commercial Union Assurance Co.* and *Administration of Papua and New Guinea v Daera Guba*. In the former case the defendants produced a newspaper article of more than fifty years to support their position. It was the reporter's eyewitness account of a fire and the only substantial evidence on the disputed facts. The reporter was not present to give evidence. The Court of Appeal affirmed that the District Court was correct in admitting and relying on the newspaper report. It was stated by the appellate court:

> To our minds, the article published in The Selma Morning-Times on the day of the fire is more reliable, more trustworthy, more competent evidence than the testimony of a witness called to the stand fifty-eight years later.
>
> ... We do not characterize this newspaper as a 'business record', nor as an 'ancient document', nor as any other readily identifiable and happily tagged species of hearsay exception. It is admissible because it is trustworthy, relevant and material, and its admission is within the trial judge's exercise of discretion in holding the hearing within reasonable bounds.[87]

The second case is referred to by Justice Handley.[88] It concerns the purported purchase in 1886 of five acres of Port Moresby land by officers of the Crown from 'the natives'. The official records consisted largely of annual reports made in 1886 and 1888, despatches and communications and survey plans. Chief Justice Barwick wrote:

> Having read and reread the official documents to which reference has been made in the case, I see no reason to doubt both their general accuracy and the veracity of those who compiled them. Indeed, the more I have read them, the better opinion I have

---

[86] See Andrew L-T Choo, *Hearsay and Confrontation in Criminal Trials* (Oxford: Clarendon Press, 1996), 189-191. Choo outlines what constitutes 'best evidence' and the dangers of same.

[87] *Dallas County v Commercial Union Assurance Co.* 286 F.2d 388 (5th Cir. 1961) at 398.

[88] Handley, 'A Lawyer', 11-17.

formed of the capacity of those who prepared them and the more convinced I am that they speak of events which actually took place as they are related in the reports and despatches.[89]

Justice Handley concludes, 'For nearly 2,000 years Christians have been saying the same thing about the historical books of the New Testament'.[90] Handley's argument is that the gospels can be shown to be just as trustworthy.

In both cases the court did not see the need to rely on the 'Ancient Documents' rule. The historical records were simply admitted as 'relevant and material'. The 'Ancient Documents' rule, it can be argued, establishes that courts would be open to admission of the New Testament records upon proof of their authentication, provenance, and circumstantial probability of trustworthiness irrespective of any hearsay exemption category. In fact it could be argued the court could be asked to take judicial notice of the historicity of Christ (i.e. take cognisance of matters which are so clearly established that no formal evidence is necessary). Apart from judicial notice the argument could take the form that history affirms beyond reasonable doubt the life of Jesus as it is a matter of public notoriety. Judicial and historical knowledge are often interrelated and the court may take judicial notice after acquainting itself with the historical evidence.[91]

However, in view of the disputed notoriety with respect to the resurrection of Jesus it is far more likely that the adverse party and the court would seek a debate over admissibility of the New Testament records and their recitals, than that they would rely on the general accepted 'facts of history'.

In the circumstances it is best to speak of the case for the admissibility of the New Testament records and their contents admitting a hearing, rather than a verdict.

Legal Hermeneutic

Montgomery critiques at some length 'post-Bultmannians' or 'the New Hermeneutic'. He defends the subject-object distinction against the drift to the epistemological pattern of the 'existentially grounded interpreter'.[92] Lengthy consideration of biblical hermeneutics lies beyond the scope of this thesis. However, his

---

[89] *Administration of Papua and New Guinea v Daera Guba* (1972-1974) 130 CLR 353 at 378-379.
[90] Handley, 'A Lawyer', 17.
[91] See Heydon, *Cross*, s. 3040. The court in this context is not receiving the documents into evidence, but acting on its own refreshed historical knowledge.
[92] See for example, John Warwick Montgomery, *Crisis in Lutheran Theology* (Minneapolis: Bethany, 1967), 45-109.

argument does briefly surface in the context of the legal apologetic. Here he explores some legal canons for the proper construction of legal documents and statutes and applies them to the New Testament documents. His aim is to demonstrate that in law, whilst the interpreter brings her own apriori assumptions and bias, it is the text that judges one's prejudices. The meaning of the text is not established by extrinsic considerations, although they may be helpful to clarify ambiguity. The text must be allowed to 'interpret itself', meaning that the text must be understood in its original sense. Such a hermeneutic is proffered first as a restraint on the higher biblical critic who may advocate extra-biblical material to create some other interpretation; and secondly as an appropriate apologetic method in assisting the listener or reader to discern Jesus' words and story.[93]

One legal canon Montgomery relies heavily on in support of his argument is the 'parol evidence' rule which he states as follows: external oral testimony or tradition will not be received in evidence to add, subtract from, vary or contradict an executed written instrument such as a will.[94] Packham criticises Montgomery's use of the said rule on two grounds. Firstly, Wigmore limits its operation to the 'formation and constitution of jural acts'.[95] Historical documents and biographies are not jural acts as there is no intended legal effect. The ambit of the rule is enforceable written wills, contracts, promissory notes as well as judicial records.[96]

Secondly, Packham notes that even if the rule as to exclusion of extrinsic evidence is applied to the gospels, it contains many exceptions. The rule can't be used to allow a document to hide from issues of being void because of fraud, mistake or illegality. And none of these issues can be determined by mere inspection of a document.[97] Extrinsic evidence is also admissible to prove the true nature of

---

[93] See John Warwick Montgomery, 'Legal Hermeneutics and the Interpretation of Scripture' in *Evangelical Hermeneutics*, Michael Bauman and David Hall, eds. (Camp Hill, Pennsylvania: Christian Publications, 1995), 15-29. See also, Montgomery, *The Law Above*, 84-90; Montgomery, *Law and Gospel*, 23-26. An interesting case in this regard is *Deeks v Wells et al* [1930] 4 D.L.R. 513 at 541. In this suit Deeks claimed H.G. Wells' book the *Outline of History* plagiarised her work. The appellate judges agreed that a lot of the extrinsic evidence of the literary critics that was presented was worthless and almost an insult.
[94] Montgomery, *The Law Above*, 87; Montgomery, *Tractatus*, 4.93201 – 4.933.
[95] Packham, 'Critique', 17.
[96] Heydon, *Cross*, 1163-1166.
[97] Packham, 'Critique', 16-17. In support of Packham's position see P.J. Hocker, Ann Duffy and Peter G. Heffey, *Cases and Materials on Contract*, 5th ed. (North Ryde, NSW: The Law Book Company, 1985), 254. For discussion on a narrow and broad view of admissibility of extrinsic evidence in such issues see D.W. Grieg and J.L.R. Davis, *The Law of Contract* (North Ryde, NSW: The Law Book Company, 1987), 440-444.

the agreement, for example: Is this a conveyance or merely a mortgage?[98] Such an exemption could have a bearing in determining whether the gospels are biography or of another genre. In fact an adverse party to the legal hermeneutic could argue that because of the rigidity of this canon there is evidence of some strong judicial dissatisfaction with the rule against *ex post facto* interpretation. This dissatisfaction is not confined to radical jurists.[99] If Packham had conducted further research he would have discovered that Montgomery addresses a number of these issues.[100]

In answer to Packham's first objection it could be said that he himself misses the point. A text Packham does not cite is *Law and Gospel* where Montgomery acknowledges that the said rule, or its equivalent, applies specifically to contractual instruments and the construction of wills, and his argument is therefore based on a legal analogy.[101] It is an appropriate analogy. The gospels as part of the New Testament are caught up in the traditional understanding of testament: a covenant (contract) between God and his people. This is a covenant that in a non-technical sense has incredible 'legal' effect as it binds people to God and his laws and promises. And as Montgomery notes, the gospels also include the motif of eternal inheritance (will).[102] Further, in chapter five, the legal apologetic nature of parts of the New Testament is discussed. The gospels lend themselves to such broad legal principles and analogy.

Montgomery's species of analogical reasoning could also be developed to counter Packham's second objection. The exceptions to the 'parol evidence' rule, that can lead to the admissibility of external evidence of a document being void, are substantially answered in the previous section on the transmission and provenance of the gospels. And it needs to be remembered that in common law, to establish the element of falsity, it is not enough that a document simply contains a falsehood. The document must purport to be that which it is not: tell a lie about itself.[103] Also allowing extrinsic evidence to determine the nature of gospels will simply confirm an historical *bioi* component.[104]

---

[98] A.A. Guest, gen. ed., *Chitty on Contracts*, 25th ed. (London: Sweet & Maxwell, 1983), 813. For a full discussion on exemptions to rule see 806-833.

[99] J.W Carter, *Breach of Contract* (North Ryde, NSW: The Law Book Company, 1984), 23-25. The Law Commission: The Parol Evidence Rule (working paper No. 70, 1976) states. 'It is a technical rule of uncertain ambit ... We accordingly make the provisional recommendation that it should be abolished.' See J.W. Carter, D.J Harland and K.E. Lindgren, *Cases and Materials on Contract Law in Australia* (Sydney: Butterworths, 1988), 300-302.

[100] For example see Montgomery, *Law and Gospel*, 24 – 26.

[101] ibid., 24.

[102] ibid., 24 – 25.

Further, whilst there may be some judicial concerns over rigidly applying such a rule, there is a definite form of construction when assessing the meaning of the parties to a document or statute. Australian High Court Chief Justice Murray Gleeson states it is a rare judge who strays from the ordinary canons of construction.[105] For example, the principles of construction with respect to wills are as follows. Firstly, look at the face. Secondly, look for a plain, common interpretation, whilst acknowledging there may be a legal interpretation of some words, such as 'devise', that has already been determined by the appropriate court. (In looking for the common interpretation of certain words and phrases it is legitimate for the court to place itself in its thinking in the same 'factual matrix' of the parties.[106] In this case this would be the religious background of that era.)[107]

A third principle is that if there is a conflict in the will between clauses, the second clause will usually dominate. However, extrinsic evidence may be allowed to reverse this, such as the solicitor's will instruction sheet, the solicitor's memory, evidence from the notes of the deceased, or evidence from those who talked to the deceased. The primary point is that preference is given to finding the meaning of the will from within the text and where possible resolving ambiguity intrinsically.[108] An hermeneutical principle that asks the listener or reader to initially read the gospels as given.

Norman Anderson is another who supports this legal analogy for hermeneutics. Citing Odgers' *Construction of Deeds and Statutes,* he pleads common sense

---

[103] David Lanham, Mark Weinberg, Kenneth E. Brown and George W. Ryan, *Criminal Fraud* (North Ryde, NSW: The Law Book Company, 1987), 176-179.

[104] For the gospels as lives of Jesus see R.A. Burridge, *What are the Gospels?* (Cambridge: Cambridge University Press, 1995), 208-209. For a discussion on whether the gospels defied the pattern of *bioi* of that general era with respect to Christ's death see Paul Barnett, *Jesus and the Logic of History* (Grand Rapids: William B. Eerdmans, 1997), 159-161. For the gospels belonging in the subgenre of the *bios* even allowing for the extent of the lawsuit motif in Luke and John see Andrew T. Lincoln, *Truth on Trial: The Lawsuit Motif in the Fourth Gospel* (Peabody, Massachusetts: Hendricksen, 2000), 169-171. For the suggestions that biographies by non-professionals were most likely to have been written by someone with a personal acquaintance with the subject and involved eyewitness informants see Burridge and Peter M. Head, 'The Role of Eyewitnesses in the Formation of the Gospel Tradition', *Tyndale Bulletin* 52, 2 (2001): 275-294.

[105] Gleeson is specifically addressing here statutory interpretation. See Murray Gleeson, *The Rule of Law and the Constitution, 2000 Boyer Lectures* (Sydney: ABC Books, 2000), 130-132.

[106] Daniel Khoury and Yvonne S. Yamouni, *Understanding Contract Law*, 2nd ed. (Sydney: Butterworths, 1989), 92-93; *Reardon Smith Line Ltd. v Yngvar Hansen-Tangen* [1976] 1 W.L.R. 989 at 997.

[107] John W. Drane, 'The Religious Background' in *New Testament Interpretation*, I. Howard Marshall, ed. (Exeter, Paternoster, 1977), 117-125.

[108] This construction was confirmed by Pollard, Interview.

rules that are applicable to the scriptures and that have guided courts for centuries. He states the rules as follows:

> The meaning of a document or of a particular part of it is to be sought for in the document itself ...
>
> Words are to be taken in their literal meaning (the grammatical and ordinary sense of the words are to be adhered to, unless that would lead to some absurdity or inconsistency with the rest of the instrument) ...
>
> The deed is to be construed as a whole ...[109]

Sir Norman likewise acknowledged that extrinsic evidence is admissible where there is ambiguity, not to construe the deed, but to translate for the courts the terms used by the parties.[110] On this important question of ambiguity Ford and Lee aver extrinsic evidence is admissible, 'not to contradict or vary a document, but to resolve an ambiguity. It is not admissible to create an ambiguity. If the language of the document has a definite and unambiguous meaning, extrinsic evidence is not admissible to show that the maker of it meant something different from what was said.' However, if after examining the document as a whole the language of the disponer in part appears to be susceptible of more than one meaning, then the circumstances behind this are relevant and admissible extrinsic evidence.[111]

Norman Anderson in summary pleads that some theologians, conservative and liberal, and some critics,

> ... seem to me to pay singularly little attention to any such canons of interpretation ... Many of them, indeed, seem to accept or reject biblical evidence on what appears to be a purely subjective basis. They will not only quote, but also treat as authoritative and decisive, a passage which suits their thesis, yet they will completely ignore other passages which run counter to their argument. Again, they often appear to take singularly little trouble to interpret the document as a whole, and reject the elementary presump-

---

[109] Norman Anderson, *A Lawyer Among the Theologians* (London: Hodder and Stoughton, 1973), 16-20. See Gerald Dworkin, *Odger's Construction of Deeds and Statutes*, 5th ed. (London: Sweet & Maxwell, 1967), 28-56.
[110] ibid., 16-18.
[111] H.A.J. Ford and W.A. Lee, *Principles of the Law of Trusts* (North Ryde, NSW: The Law Book Company, 1990), par. 207.

tion that an author is intrinsically unlikely to have contradicted himself. Instead, they seem positively to swoop, on occasion, on contradictions which do not – or do not necessarily – in fact exist.[112]

Another hermeneutical legal canon that Montgomery briefly mentions is harmonization. With respect to the gospels he states, 'Harmonization of apparent scriptural difficulties should be pursued within reasonable limits, and when harmonization would pass beyond such bounds, the interpreter must leave the problem open ...'.[113] He further pleads that with respect to the individual gospel authors the harmonization principle implies that the benefit of doubt is given to the author. It is common sense to assume that authors do not blatantly contradict themselves and the burden is on the adverse party to prove otherwise.[114] Norman Anderson, relying on his legal expertise states:

> Is it not a matter of plain commonsense to make a reasonable attempt to resolve apparent inconsistencies in any of web of evidence before jumping to the premature conclusion that the witnesses – or, indeed, one and the same witness – have presented us with 'glaring' and 'irreconcilable' contradiction?[115]

In support of Montgomery's position it is true that courts understand that witnesses tell their story differently and a sensible approach to the 'reunionistic method' is followed in most hearings.[116] Robert Anderson is another legal apologist who pleads from his legal-detective experience and practice that harmonization is an appropriate canon to initially apply to the gospels' apparent inconsistencies and ambiguities.[117] This issue is critically discussed in more detail in the next chapter in the section 'Testimony: internal defects in the testimony itself'.

A principle that Montgomery and the other legal apologists do not refer to, but is pertinent to legal canons of interpretation, is that of 'User under Ancient Documents'. It is stated thus:

---

[112] Norman Anderson, *A Lawyer Among*, 19-20.
[113] Montgomery, *Law and Gospel*, 25; Montgomery, *Tractatus*, 3.4443 – 3.4444.
[114] See John Warwick Montgomery, 'The Wounded Watson' in Montgomery, *The Transcendent Holmes*, 65-66.
[115] Norman Anderson, *A Lawyer Among*, 111.
[116] Gleason C. Archer, *Encyclopedia of Bible Difficulties* (Grand Rapids: Zondervan, 1982), 315.
[117] Robert Anderson, *The Bible and Modern Criticism*, 5th ed. (London: Hodder and Stoughton, 1905), 221-222.

> In the case of very ancient documents, there may be great difficulty in deciding on the meaning of the words employed, and in that case evidence of usage is admissible to show what was the meaning attached to the document soon after its execution by those interested in its interpretation. There is a probability that at least some of these persons would have insisted on a proper interpretation of the instrument, and if a certain interpretation has been adopted and acquiesced in for a long period of years this affords a probability of its correctness. This is what is called 'contemporaneous interpretation' or 'contemporanea expositio'.[118]

The principle allows for extrinsic evidence for translating words and pericopes, but primarily takes notice of the understanding of those persons closest to the execution of the document. This is consistent with the form for construction of a will when there is ambiguity as mentioned above: in which case one first goes to the notes or memory of the instructing solicitor. This principle has apologetic rebuttal value for the listener or reader who is confronted with the supernatural nature of 'the Christ event' in contrast to the rationalistic critics who wish to reinterpret and demythologize the same miracle. Those closest to the miracle event don't translate or even theologise the idea from history.[119]

Legal canons for the proper construction of legal instruments offer reliable and tested tools for the listener or reader to objectively interpret the gospels. Such contribution can be seen to be particularly relevant to the concerns of a 'modernity' style thought-system. Packham criticises the argument as it stands, but when it is presented as an analogy it can be enhanced to offer useful and proven hermeneutical criteria for documents. It provides tools that could form part of the debate on the science of theological hermeneutics, and that at least interact with diverse matters such as: the interpreter's theory of language, relationship to the text, and worldview.[120]

Montgomery in part offers his legal hermeneutic as a correction to the hermeneutic of Critical Legal Studies.[121] Yet, one would imagine that a postmodern lis-

---

[118] Dworkin, *Odger's*, 83. I mention this principle briefly in Clifford, 'The Case of Eight Legal Apologists', 97.
[119] For discussion on the expressions of faith of the first Christians being in a dialectic relationship with one's language expressions of faith today see James D.G. Dunn, 'Demythologizing – The Problem of Myth in the New Testament' in *New Testament Interpretation*, Marshall, ed., 285-307.
[120] Gerhard Maier, *Biblical Hermeneutics* (Wheaton: Crossway, 1994), 15-64, 207-370; James W. Volz, *What Does This Mean? Principles of Biblical Interpretation in the Post-Modern World*, 2nd ed. (Saint Louis: Concordia, 1995), 13-52.

Legal Hermeneutic

tener or reader with emphasis on a reader-response orientated criticism would not be totally convinced by this method. The importance of the reader[122] as well as the text in the hermeneutical process would be stressed.[123] These issues are addressed in more detail in chapter five in the section 'A Legal Formalist Approach'.

However, in hearing some of the criticisms of a postmodern reading of the gospels, one does not need to concede that the text has no inherent or determinate meaning. In chapter five it is Twining who reminds us that whilst social, political and reader-response construction is widely accepted, theorists who deny the existence of objective truth are 'rare birds'.[124] Only ideological manipulations of the text removes the listener or reader from the inherent meaning. Further, Tremper Longman presents evidence that the cutting edge of current literary practice is 'varied' and 'eclectic'. A variety of approaches is utilised at the same time. And with New Historicism advocating the historical setting of texts, be it with an openness to theological and ideological questions, it could well be argued that there is a place for consideration of the legal hermeneutic in literary studies.[125] Longman concludes, 'Though the avant-garde has moved far beyond formalism, some scholars still find it productive.'[126]

Montgomery acknowledges that much work is yet to be done on the relationship between legal canons and biblical hermeneutics.[127] Yet his argument, in this context, adds considerable weight to the call of legal apologists that the listener or reader ought to be encouraged to follow 'ordinary canons of construction'. It is a creative and appropriate argument that enhances the legal apologetic.

---

[121] Montgomery, 'Legal Hermeneutics', 21-29; Montgomery, *Tractatus*, 2.55 – 2.59.

[122] For discussion see Edgar V. McKnight, *Postmodern Use of the Bible* (Nashville: Abingdon, 1988).

[123] Edgar V. McKnight, 'A Defence of a Postmodern Use of the Bible' in *A Confessing Theology for Postmodern Times*, Michael S. Horton, ed. (Wheaton: Crossway, 2000), 68-73; Michael J. Gorman, *Elements of Biblical Exegesis* (Peabody, Massachusetts: Hendricksen, 2001), 11-33; Garrett Green, *Theology, Hermeneutics, and Imagination* (Cambridge: Cambridge University Press, 2000), 173-186.

[124] William Twining, *Rethinking Evidence: Exploratory Essays* (Oxford: Basil Blackwell, 1990), esp. chap. 4.

[125] Tremper Longman III, 'Literary Approaches to Old Testament Study' in *The Face of Old Testament Studies*, David W. Baker and Bill T. Arnold, eds. (Grand Rapids: Baker, 1999), 97-115.

[126] ibid, 111.

[127] Montgomery suggests this is another field for postgraduate apologetic research. Interview by the author (Strasbourg, France, 26 July 1996).

Hearsay

To date the technical argument has focused on the admissibility of the gospels on the basis of the 'Ancient Documents' rule or alternatively the openness of courts to admitting trustworthy instruments.

Hostile Witnesses

Montgomery offers another reason why the gospel testimony should be received. He cites F.F. Bruce who states,

> (And) it was not only friendly eyewitnesses that the early preachers had to reckon with; there were others less well disposed who were also conversant with the main facts of the ministry and death of Jesus. The disciples could not afford to risk inaccuracies (not to speak of wilful manipulation of the facts), which would at once be exposed by those who would be only too glad to do so. On the contrary, one of the strong points in the original apostolic preaching is the confident appeal to the knowledge of the hearers; they not only said, 'We are witnesses of these things,' but also, 'As you yourselves also know' (Acts 2:22). Had there been any tendency to depart from the facts in any material respect, the possible presence of hostile witnesses in the audience would have served as a further corrective.[128]

Montgomery's argument continues along the lines that the presence of these hostile witnesses has the functional equivalence of cross-examination. His legal argument is not without precedent and is propagated by Linton and others.[129] So for Montgomery the occasionally voiced objection that the apostolic testimony would be rejected by modern courts as hearsay is answered. He argues that the gospel witnesses were subjected, as it were, to searching cross-examination and this reduces the problem of hearsay evidence 'to the vanishing point'.[130]

On a less technical basis Strobel posits this 'adverse witness-test' in his interview with New Testament scholar Craig Blomberg. Blomberg affirms, 'we have a pic-

---

[128] Montgomery, *Human Rights*, 148; Montgomery, *The Law Above*, 88-89. See Bruce, *The New Testament*, 46..
[129] Linton, *A Lawyer Examines,* 51-54.
[130] Montgomery, *Human Rights*, 148-150; Montgomery, 'The Search for Ultimates', 6-8; Montgomery; *Tractatus*, 3.452 – 3.461.

ture of what was initially a very vulnerable and fragile movement that was being subjected to persecution. If critics could have attacked it on the basis that it was full of falsehoods or distortions, they would have ... that's exactly what we don't see'.[131] And Russell develops the argument by bringing to the bar later hostile 'witnesses' such as Voltaire and Paine and interacting with their perceived objections.[132]

Packham is scathing in his reply, 'we have now left the realm of legal evidence and are in the never-never land of apologetics'.[133] He challenges Montgomery to cite a single case where 'inherently incredible' evidence was admitted on a 'functional equivalent' of cross-examination. He protests that it is the purest speculation that anything like juridical cross-examination took place in the presence of hostile witnesses. Further, he pleads that even if the 'functional equivalent' of cross-examination took place it doesn't add weight to the Christian case as the Jews rejected it. If they had the opportunity to examine the case, they were not persuaded.[134] Packham's argument finds support in Martin's legal apologetic. He admits the evidence as submitted leaves a number of issues an opposing counsel could explore.[135]

I believe Montgomery should vacate his 'hostile witnesses' argument as it relates to admissibility. It's not required. The case for the admissibility of the gospel testimony best rests on the arguments raised in the previous section on documents.

The analogy of cross-examination of the apostolic witnesses runs into difficulties at a technical level as the possible presence of 'hostile witnesses' cannot really be equated to a full and detailed cross-examination, where a variety of 'traps' would be employed to ascertain if the witness was lying.[136]

Yet the argument of Montgomery and Strobel has real merit. It should be raised on the issue of weight as Montgomery does in his public lectures.[137] When the court considers the admissibility of the gospels its position will resemble that of real evidence. Here the court must be satisfied about the security of the transmis-

---

[131] Strobel, *The Case*, 51.
[132] Russell, *A Lawyer's*, 25-45.
[133] Packham, 'Critique', 12.
[134] ibid., 12-13.
[135] Martin, *A Lawyer Briefs*, 108-113. Martin refers to the alleged resurrection appearance discrepancies and Matthew's account that when Jesus died on the cross many holy people were raised to life in Jerusalem.
[136] For a listing of the 'traps' that can expose a lying witness (such as detailed cross-examination on unforeseen detail) see Givens, *Advocacy*, 69-92.
[137] Hear audiotape Montgomery, 'A Lawyer's Case'.

sion of the document finding that it has not been altered since it was composed, just as it must be clear that a murder weapon is in the same state as when it was found at a crime scene. With respect to the credibility of the written testimony it will speak more as oral evidence.[138] The court will be concerned with the author's truthfulness, integrity and accurate observation. The court no doubt would take a practical approach bringing all relevant and admissible evidence to bear.[139] In this empirical investigation counter-evidence is considered as are the surrounding circumstances. Now the expert insights of Bruce and Blomberg would be relevant and the counter evidence of Packham produced. Montgomery could be confident of the integrity and relevance of the evidence in such a discourse.

Multiple Hearsay

A significant issue few technical legal apologists address is whether the entire gospel record is admissible or only those parts which are first-hand hearsay? Inadmissible parts of a tendered document should be excised.[140] Whilst this issue particularly impacts the technical legal apologetic, it is also of relevance for a non-technical apologetic as the admissibility status of the entire gospel testimony is usually a given in both models, even if an actual court setting for the resurrection is not relied on.

First-hand hearsay is an assertion in a document that if the declarant appeared he would be competent to testify to the truthfulness of that assertion. Therefore, it is an assertion of which the New Testament writer had first hand knowledge.[141] There are parts of the gospels that are not first-hand hearsay. For example the virgin birth narratives and the book of Luke.

Montgomery is open to a brief that includes certain second-hand hearsay. He notes that in continental civil law the hearsay rule does not exist. He goes on to say the hearsay rule is almost being swallowed up in Anglo-American countries by exceptions such as the 'Ancient Documents' rule. Further in civil trials some

---

[138] Honoré, 'The Primacy of Oral Evidence', 186-192.

[139] Greenleaf implies this approach, see *The Testimony*, 54. On the weight to be accorded to documentary statements Brown illustrates from the *N.S.W. Evidence Act 1898 (repealed)*. Section 14c(1) states that regard shall be had to all the circumstances from which any inference can be reasonably drawn as to the accuracy or otherwise of the statement, as to whether the statement was contemporaneous with the existence of the facts stated, and as to whether the maker of the statement had any incentive to conceal or misrepresent facts. See R.A. Brown, *Documentary*, 201-202.

[140] R.A. Brown, *Documentary*, 177.

[141] See Binder, *Hearsay Handbook*, 231-232.

jurisdictions are freeing themselves from hearsay restraints and allowing for second-hand hearsay.[142] He balances this with the preference 'that a witness ought to testify "of his own knowledge or observation", not on the basis of what has come to him indirectly from others.' As well he concedes this second-hand hearsay liberalisation applies to civil trials, without a jury, where a judge presumably has the ability to sift the evidence.[143] So he acknowledges the pluses and minuses for second-hand hearsay accounts.

Let us now turn to Montgomery's three points that appear to be raising the possibility of second-hand hearsay admissibility. With respect to Continental civil law it is true that in principle hearsay is admissible in French and German civil courts, though if oral hearsay is suspect the court may decline to hear it.[144] In other words, the relation of the evidence to the witnesses' knowledge may still be relevant. As to the 'Ancient Documents' rule, whilst it may lead to the admissibility of the substance of the document it certainly does not mean second-hand hearsay is always covered by the exemption. Binder in his assessment of American case law concludes, 'an exemption contained in an ancient document will not be excepted to the hearsay rule if it appears that the declarant would be incompetent to testify to the assertion if he were present in court.'[145]

There is considerable justification for Montgomery's third point of civil jurisdictions seeking to free themselves of hearsay restraints. No doubt the hearsay rule will continue to be liberalised in certain jurisdictions. Judge Adrian Roden Q.C. noted that as a general rule hearsay is less reliable, yet much can be of value.

He quoted Lord Diplock's judicial candour, 'The array of statutory exceptions now to be found in various jurisdictions is further evidence of the unsatisfactory nature of the rule.'[146]

In contrast to civil law practice the criminal law position on second-hand hearsay is less welcoming. For example the Australian *Evidence Act 1995 (Cth)(NSW)* states that in criminal hearings there be no remote hearsay and Palmer pleads, 'The common law should demand no less'.[147] In this context the Australian Law Reform Commission held that second-hand hearsay can be unreliable.[148] Palmer

---

[142] Montgomery, *Human Rights*, 149. See also Pehrson, 'How Not', 4-5.
[143] ibid., 150.
[144] Honoré, 'The Primacy of Oral Evidence?', 188-189.
[145] Binder, *Hearsay Handbook*, 231.
[146] Adrian Roden, 'The Place of Individual Rights in Corruption Investigations', Paper delivered to The Fourth International Anti-Corruption Conference (Sydney, 16 November 1989), 19. See also Howard, Crane and Hochberg, *Phipson*, 584-592.

continues that if the declarant is only reporting what someone else claims to have perceived, then the possible causes of mistake are increased.[149]

Although I have in this study advocated that we ought to make belief judgements that are in accordance with the preponderance of evidence (civil standard), I hold that Montgomery, and the legal apologists, should also consider submitting an apologetic not based on second-hand hearsay even though civil jurisdictions are being liberated from many hearsay restraints. Shortly, it will be shown that Montgomery is supportive of this direction. There are a number of reasons for this. Firstly, is the alleged semantic strength of the Christian truth claim and the value placed upon it. It warrants the best evidence. Secondly, even if the New Testament second-hand hearsay reports were admitted there is still the question of weight. We just don't know, after the rigours of a trial, what probative value a judge or jury would place on this testimony. Thirdly, as mentioned the liberalisation applies frequently to civil trials without a jury where the verdict rests with a judge who has the skills to sift the evidence. The listener or reader is unlikely to have these skills.[150] This concern is supported by the *Evidence Act 1995* which provides for a judge 'warning' a jury regarding second-hand hearsay.[151] Fourthly, is the fact that not all civil jurisdictions are necessarily open to second-hand hearsay where the evidence is documentary, rather than oral.[152] Fifthly, is the nature of the second-hand evidence for the resurrection of Jesus. In many jurisdictions this removing of the hearsay rule is not without boundaries. In the Australian legislation the second-hand oral or documentary exemption is with regards to a representation 'that is given by a person who saw, heard or otherwise perceived the representation being made'.[153] For example, a wife being able to give evidence on what her now deceased husband had seen and what he told her whilst it was still fresh in his memory. If such a provision were applied to the gospels one would have to show that the author was the one who received the representation. A reading of the gospels indicates that this is not explicitly stated in the multiple hearsay accounts.[154] As will be indicated there are first-hand hearsay

---

[147] For discussion see Palmer, 'The Reliability-Based', 532-534. However, remote hearsay is allowed, to a limited extend, in some jurisdictions in preliminary criminal hearings. See Perri O'Shaughnessy [Pamela and Mary O'Shaughnessy], *Presumption of Death* (London: Piatkus, 2003), 312.

[148] Stephen Odgers, *Uniform Evidence Law*, 3rd ed. (North Ryde, NSW: LBC, 1998), 185.

[149] Palmer, 'The Reliability-Based', 532-534.

[150] It is because of this that Howe in his apologetic handbook, whilst relying on legal evidence to assess Christian truth claims, 'does not follow' to a verdict. Howe, *Challenge*, 110-117.

[151] s. 165.

[152] Heydon, *Cross*, 1090-1093.

[153] s. 63-64.

accounts in the New Testament for the death and resurrection of Jesus. The other hearsay reports may not even be secondary and are too remote for consideration in a claim of this nature.

In all the circumstances a legally informed listener or reader is more likely to be persuaded by an argument relying on first-hand hearsay. Support for this position comes from the lawyer John Mortimer who, through Montgomery's favourite legal fictional character Rumpole, reveals the perils of tribunals relying on multiple hearsay when someone's well being is at stake. This corpulent defender of sinful humanity cries out that hearsay evidence in such situations is 'worthless' and this is no mere 'legal quibble'.[155] As one could imagine, Packham claims the legal apologetic's flirting with hearsay evidence is a defeater for belief.[156]

Pamela Ewen is one of the few legal apologists who interacts with this hearsay issue. She affirms that the normal requirement, 'that a witness giving testimony should have first-hand knowledge remains an important standard for determining the credibility, or the actual value, that the jury will give to that (gospel) testimony.' She cites US *Federal Rule of Evidence* 602 in support.[157] Ewen then proceeds rightly to explain that the courts have interpreted first-hand knowledge with some flexibility to permit either a showing of first-hand knowledge or showing that circumstances were sufficient to support such a finding. These circumstances include the author having the opportunity to observe the events, and living at that time and in that place, as well as other evidence that appears to corroborate personal observation. This 'flexibility' is particularly relevant to documentary testimony. Ewen concludes, 'In a situation in which the evidence that the witness had an adequate opportunity to observe the facts is uncertain, the evidence will be admitted and the jury will decide the issue.'[158] Odgers records the codification of such 'flexibility'. The Australian *Evidence Act 1995* section 62 states that it only has to be 'reasonably supposed' to be first-hand knowledge.

---

[154] Mark 16:1-8, Matthew 28:1-15, Luke 1:1-4. John will be considered in the next section on first-hand hearsay. Also, whilst Luke purports to undertake an investigation of the facts on the basis of handed down eyewitness reports, it is not clear where Luke stands in this chain of reporting. With respect to these particular Matthew and Mark accounts Byrskog is correct in his assessment that they do not claim to be the direct report of the practice of autopsy, i.e. the author is not the eyewitness and further we do not know to whom the eyewitness report was made. See Byrskog, *Story*, 246-253.

[155] John Mortimer, 'Rumpole and the Children of the Devil' in *The Best of Rumpole* (New York: Penguin, 1994), 219-222. On even nineteenth century authors, such as Charles Dickens, resisting an over-reliance on hearsay material see Schramm, *Testimony*, 7-8.

[156] Packham, 'Critique', 12-14.

[157] Ewen, *Faith*, 36. See Cleary, *McCormick*, 1080-1081.

[158] Ewen, *Faith*, 36-37.

He comments that consequently a party does not have to show that the observation was so based, only that it 'might reasonably be supposed' to be so. If an adverse party claims that it was not so based, the burden will shift to that party to persuade the court that the evidence is not first-hand hearsay.[159] As mentioned, it will be argued that the legal apologetic should follow the paradigm of a *prima facie* case. This 'flexibility' of interpretation is of particular significance in such an analogy.

Ewen then does what most other legal apologists have not done. She submits the gospels to a first-hand hearsay test to determine what is admissible. This should be the paradigm for future technical legal apologists. Having said that, a major flaw in Ewen's case is that she does not consider whether sections of each gospel should be excised. She merely looks at each gospel as a whole and her lack of micro analysis of the gospel pericopes in her technical legal apologetic is an oversight. She acknowledges the need to do so when she finds that, 'when a witness testifies partly to things that he or she has actually seen or heard, and partly from what was told by another, a practical compromise under the rules governing evidence is to admit the information based on first-hand knowledge and exclude the remaining testimony.' Then without micro analysis she finds, 'Matthew, John and Peter (speaking through Mark) all purport to have actually observed the resurrection of Jesus'.[160] Her conclusions do not give due weight since certain passages read as if the gospel authors were not present and had no personal observation (for example Matthew 28:2-10).

First-Hand Admissible Hearsay – 'The Devil's Advocate' Position

In *The Case for the Empty Tomb* I briefly set out the first-hand hearsay evidence for the resurrection.[161] And Montgomery has shown support for my position of relying on first-hand hearsay. Pehrson's article in defence of Montgomery's legal apologetic was 'commissioned' by Montgomery. Pehrson states 'Ross Clifford has written a fine essay on the admissibility of the New Testament texts as evidence of a hypothetical trial. He plays devil's advocate and strictly enforces the hearsay rule.' Pehrson then continues his argument along the same premise. The first-hand hearsay evidence tendered was only part of the case.[162]

---

[159] Odgers, *Uniform Evidence*, 158-159.
[160] Ewen, *Faith*, 69.
[161] Clifford, *The Case for the Empty Tomb*, 85-98, 141-142.
[162] See, Pehrson, 'How Not', 4 - 5.

The structure of the argument follows Montgomery's apologetic. All the evidence tendered is circumstantial in the sense that there was no eyewitness present in the tomb. The relevant legal evidence is twofold. Firstly, one must prove Jesus was dead – beyond resuscitation – at point A. Secondly, it must be shown that he was alive at point B.

Was the death sentence carried out? I indicate the gospel of John records the execution and the author confirms he was a witness to it and he knows it happened (John 19:28-35). The evidence also supports Peter being there. He heard some of the inquisitions of Jesus and there is evidence he did not flee after Jesus' arrest. It is argued that Mark was most probably a 'scribe' for Peter[163] and a clear first-hand account is found in Mark 15:22-37. Matthew also testifies to the death of Christ (Matthew 27:38-50). Although the disciple Matthew fled after Jesus' arrest the eyewitness nature of his chronicle points to the probability of his return to the scene, a fact Luke supports (Luke 23:49). However, even if the author of Matthew's gospel is not one of the twelve disciples he, like 'Mark', writes as one who was there, or from the context it may be 'reasonably supposed' that is the case.[164]

With respect to Jesus being alive at point B the documentary evidence supports John's gospel being an eyewitness account (John 20:1-8, 19-28).[165] I now hold that the situation with Matthew and Mark is more problematic. Matthew's only first-hand account is the 'Great Commission' which is given to the eleven disciples, but that is only a first-hand eyewitness account if Matthean authorship is justified (28:16-20). I discuss this matter further in the next section on 'Dating and Authorship'. The pericope is matter-of-fact reporting, but the integrity, and apparent personal touch and observation of the reporter is evident in the poignant statement, 'but some doubted'. In *The Case for the Empty Tomb* the debate over the ending of Mark is raised, including the fact that there is no first-hand observation in the shorter ending. It is suggested that even if one concludes Mark at chapter 16 verse 8 other writings affirm Peter's presence at the resurrection appearances.[166] This argument is dubious in a technical sense. Peter is not responsible for the other documents that record his observations apart from 2

---

[163] Clifford, *The Case for the Empty Tomb*, 20 - 27.
[164] See Briese, 'Witnesses', 1-2.
[165] For a discussion on whether chapter 21 of John is original or a later edition see Leon Morris, *The Gospel According to John* (Grand Rapids: William B. Eerdmans, 1971), 858-860. Morris holds that even if it is a later edition, it is more probable that it is by the same author of the rest of John, rather than someone else altogether. Chapter 21 also contains strong eyewitness testimony.
[166] Clifford, *The Case for the Empty Tomb*, 93.

Peter (see 1:16-18). And 2 Peter moves one into the contentious area of authorship, canon and the context of the term 'eyewitnesses of his majesty' which term relates more to Jesus' transfiguration and baptism than his resurrection.[167] Further, there is little apologetic option but to conclude Mark's gospel at verse 8 of chapter sixteen. To include the so called 'shorter ending of Mark' or verses 12 to 20 involves one in major textual problems. Codices Vaticanus and Sinaiticus support the conclusion of Mark ending at verse 8. Admittedly a number of other manuscripts support 'the short ending' and verses 12 to 20, but Lane argues textually the language and style of these verses do not support Marcan authorship.[168] It is more likely that the other endings are mutilations of the original last page. It is true that the evidence for the resurrection of Jesus in Mark is not confined to chapter sixteen. The structure of Mark, that is followed by Matthew and Luke, has Jesus before his disciples strategically foretelling his resurrection (8:31-38, 9:30-32, 10:32-34). This evidence indicates the state of mind of Jesus, but is not proof of the fact itself. In conclusion, the legal apologist should not tender verses 9-20 and strategically verses 1-8 have no first-hand observation.

However, in a legal apologetic, as Montgomery argues, the eyewitness evidence of Paul in 1 Corinthians 15 verses 3 to 8 is significant.[169] It is the earliest written evidence for the resurrection and can be dated between 52-57 AD.[170] Handley says that Paul here 'appeals to the evidence of eyewitnesses, including himself. This is a remarkable piece of historical evidence written at an early date, when eyewitnesses were still alive'.[171] The fact that Paul's encounter was a personal and actual event, and not a mere vision is evidenced by Paul's claim that Jesus

---

[167] Ray Summers, *2 Peter, The Broadman Bible Commentary*, Vol. 12 (Nashville: Broadman, 1972), 178-179.

[168] For a discussion on the conclusion of Mark see William L. Lane, *Commentary on the Gospel of Mark*, (Grand Rapids: William B. Eerdmans, 1974), 601-605.

[169] Montgomery, 'A Lawyer's Case', 11-13. Cf. Montgomery, *Human Rights*, 133-134. See Gary R. Habermas, 'The Resurrection Appearances of Jesus' in *In Defense of Miracles*, R. Douglas Geivett and Gary R. Habermas, eds. (Downers Grove: InterVarsity, 1997), 262-275. John Gill indicates Lord Lyttelton's treatise, *Observations on the Conversion and Apostleship of St. Paul. In a Letter to Gilbert West esq.*, was a novel departure in that it focused the resurrection argument on Paul rather than the gospel writers. John Gill, '"Of Miracles", Lord Lyttelton, and Alexander the Miracle Worker', http://arts.adelaide.edu.au/philosophy/jgill/miracles.htm.

[170] For a discussion on whether Paul was endeavouring to prove the resurrection historically see the section 'Scriptural Support', in chapter 5 of this thesis. For discussion on dating see Raymond F. Collins, *First Corinthians, Sacra Pagina Series*, Vol. 7 (Collegeville, Minnesota: The Liturgical Press, 1999), 20-24.

[171] Handley, 'A Lawyer', 12. Habermas documents that even leading sceptics such as G.A. Wells acknowledge the eyewitness status of Paul. See Gary R. Habermas, 'Why I Believe in Miracles' in *Why I am a Christian*, Geisler and Hoffman, eds., 111-124 at 117-118.

clearly spoke to him face to face during the episode.[172] Lockwood asserts that Paul's linking of this encounter with Jesus with his being abnormally born is best understood as Paul suggesting he had a premature spiritual birth, 'he had not had the benefit of a full gestation period; he had been thrown into his discipleship in a sudden and unexpected fashion. Yet even he ... had been given the privilege of becoming an eyewitness of the resurrected Christ'.[173]

William Lane Craig in his debate with Gerd Lüdemann on the fact of Jesus' resurrection makes an unwarranted concession. He pleads in this apologetic context that Jesus' postmortem appearance to Paul does not count. Paul's was a vision of Christ and not an appearance of Christ.[174] His argument has two main premises, one being that the appearances of Christ, in contrast to the veridical visions of Jesus, involved an extramental reality that all those present could experience. Only Paul 'saw' the Lord.[175] The argument is shallow in light of the private nature of most of the resurrection appearances, that is they were restricted to future committed followers, and not all who saw the Lord initially recognised him (for example, John 20: 10-18). Further, all the postmortem appearances of Christ were unpredictable. One senses that Craig's primary objection is in response to Lüdemann's position. Lüdemann holds that Paul knew nothing of the empty tomb tradition and that Jesus was not raised. In 1 Corinthians 15 verses 5 to 8 Paul uses the same verb ὤφθη (*ōphthē*) ('he was seen') for himself as he does for the apostles.[176] In other words he claims to have experienced the same appearances as the others before him. Lüdemann argues that as Paul's experience was clearly visionary, so was theirs. Craig in response is arguing that Paul's encounter is different, in order to protect the physical nature of the postmortem gospel appearances. Stephen Davis is of similar mind and like Craig suggests Luke seems to limit resurrection appearance to the period between his crucifixion and some forty days later. Any encounter with Jesus after that is to be classified as a

---

[172] Acts 22:7-20, 26:14-18, Galatians 1:16. Paul Barnett, *1 Corinthians* (Ross-shire, Great Britain: Christian Focus, 2000), 279-280.
[173] Gregory J. Lockwood, *1 Corinthians, Concordia Commentary* (Saint Louis: Concordia, 2000), 556-557. Cf. Ben Witherington, *Conflict and Community in Corinth* (Grand Rapids: William B. Eerdmans; Carlisle: Paternoster, 1995), 300. And see Anthony C. Thiselton, *The First Epistle to the Corinthians, the New International Greek Testament Commentary* (Grand Rapids, Cambridge: William B. Eerdmans; Carlisle: Paternoster, 2000), 1208-1211. Thiselton argues the emphasis of Paul in verses 8 and 9 lies primarily not on his place amongst the witnesses, but on the undeserved grace of God.
[174] Paul Copan and Ronald K. Tacelli, *Jesus' Resurrection Fact or Fiction? A Debate Between William Lane Craig and Gerd Lüdemann* (Downers Grove: InterVarsity, 2000), 57-92, 180-181, 197.
[175] ibid., 196-198.
[176] ibid., 40-51, 60-62.

vision or a different sort of experience. Davis cites Acts 1 verse 3 in support, however a reading of that text does not support directly or indirectly his premise. Now the fact that Paul's encounter may have been an appearance, does not mean that other post Pentecost encounters must also be appearances, an issue that concerns both Craig and Davis (Acts 7:53-56, Revelation 1:12-18).[177] In law each case is judged on its own merits and a hypothesis is drawn from the facts rather than from a presupposition.

The weakness in Craig's argument is apparent. In the debate he observes that the historian's task is very much like that of a trial lawyer, 'to examine the witnesses in order to reconstruct the most probable cause of events'.[178] He constantly however advocates the primacy of the appearance traditions in the gospels as corroborated by the Pauline list of 1 Corinthians 15 verses 3 to 7.[179] He fails to understand the secondary hearsay nature of much of this testimony. This fact is not lost on Roy W. Hoover's critical response to Craig's overall argument. Hoover states, 'In comparison with Paul's firsthand testimony, what the Gospels' authors report about the resurrection would rank no higher than hearsay.'[180] As we will see Hoover clearly overstates his case but his position is more solid than Craig's. Robert H. Gundry is just one of the respondents to the debate who critiques Craig on Paul's encounter. He argues that Paul's use of ὤφθη indicates he is linking his experience to the other witnesses. However, Lüdemann is incorrect in his assumption that they are therefore all visionary. Gundry argues that in the New Testament this Greek verb translated 'appeared' or 'was seen by' implies neither nonphysical substance nor heavenly location.[181] He concludes, 'The substance, the location and the origin depend on other factors; Paul's citation contains no hint of exaltation to God's right hand. Therefore Lüdemann lacks a good basis for his opinion that the earliest tradition concerning the risen Christ has him appearing from heaven in a nonphysical form.'[182] And on Craig's reservations Gundry responds, 'Whether seen on earth or in heaven, Jesus remains as physical after resurrection as he was before resurrection. Against both Lüdemann and Craig then, the heavenliness of a vision does not imply nonphysicality.'[183]

---

[177] Stephen T. Davis, '"Seeing" the Risen Jesus', in *The Resurrection*, Stephen T. Davis, Daniel Kendall and Gerald Collins, eds. (Oxford: Oxford University Press, 1997), 126-147. Davis does not totally rule out that Paul's vision may count as a resurrection appearance, although he believes it is contrary to what Luke is saying. In any event he holds it cannot be used as a grid to be imposed on the other pre-ascension appearances (139).
[178] Copan and Tacelli, *Jesus' Resurrection*, 31.
[179] ibid., 18-182.
[180] ibid., 129.
[181] ibid., 115-120.
[182] ibid., 117.

Clearly Paul saw his encounter of the risen Christ as being in the line of the apostles.[184] Like them, Jesus appeared to him (compare Acts 13:31 with 1 Corinthians 15:8).[185] He includes himself in the witness list as an eyewitness of the fact. He does not ask to stand aside. Norman Anderson is impressed by the quality of Paul's evidence. His finding is more in line with the evidence than Craig's. He stresses that Paul's encounter, 'was just as real and "objective" as that of the other apostles, not that theirs were as "visionary" as his.'[186] Montgomery concludes, that the efforts of Lüdemann to discount the historical considerations that surround the resurrection 'fail and fail miserably'.[187]

The argument to date suggests that the technical legal apologetic can submit that, as to the death of Jesus, Matthew, Mark (Peter) and John had adequate opportunity to observe the facts, and with respect to the resurrection John, Paul and perhaps Matthew give accounts for a jury to consider. The argument is supplemented by the fact that each of the authors wrote as one who had first-hand knowledge or it can be 'reasonably supposed' that that is the case. The legal apologists as a class are certain of that. Magistrate Clarrie Briese had many years on the bench and his comments are representative, 'the people who wrote them put themselves forward as witnesses, indeed as eyewitnesses to many of the events and incidents they record'.[188] Montgomery stresses clearly they had 'intimate contact' with Jesus throughout his three year ministry.[189] Admittedly, at times the testimony includes personal thoughts and interpretation, but in the context of this genre it is admissible as it linked rationally to what was observed, and the court is not being asked to place any weight on these thoughts.[190]

---

[183] ibid., 116.

[184] Byrskog, *Story*, 226-227.

[185] Gundry also argues that Paul was not alone in his encounter with Jesus being one that happened after Jesus ascended into heaven. John's gospel implies Jesus ascended on the Sunday of Easter and then he returned to the disciples. Evidence in part for this is the fact that Jesus told Mary Magdalene not to touch him as he had not ascended to his Father. A week later Thomas was invited to handle him. As well Jesus bestows the Spirit in John, which is evidence of his glorification. See Copan and Tacelli, *Jesus' Resurrection*, 117. On the New Testament presenting a unified view of the nature of Jesus' resurrection see Robert H. Gundry, 'The Essential Physicality of Jesus' Resurrection According to the New Testament' in *Jesus of Nazareth: Lord and Christ*, Joel B. Green and Max Turner, eds. (Grand Rapids: William B. Eerdmans, Carlisle: Paternoster, 1994), 204-219.

[186] Norman Anderson, *Jesus Christ: The Witness*, 135. See also Norman Anderson, *The Fact*, 3-8; Gordon D. Fee, *The First Epistle to the Corinthians, the New International Commentary on the New Testament* (Grand Rapids: William B. Eerdmans, 1987), 732.

[187] Montgomery, *Tractatus*, 3:63.

[188] Briese, 'Witnesses', 1-2.

[189] Montgomery, *Tractatus*, 3.62332.

[190] Ewen, *Faith*, 65.

Dating and authorship
However, this is not the end of the argument or the matters to be considered. Succinctly, Montgomery refers to the questions of dating and authorship of the gospels. These are thesis topics in themselves and likewise can only be pithily addressed as they specifically relate to a legal argument. As usual, Montgomery cites a number of texts that tackle the said questions in more detail, including his own University of British Columbia lectures 'Jesus Christ and History' that are reproduced in *History and Christianity*.[191] Firstly, dating and a related issue, the memory of the witnesses will be considered, then authorship and the matter of sources.

The question of whether the gospel writers had personal knowledge of the Christ event to some extent depends on the *date* of the documents. Certainly it must be proved that they were written within the lifetime of the apostles. Ewen addresses this issue in detail in her legal apologetic. Her case is initially based on the intrinsic evidence. Her later extensive reliance on the 'Magdalen fragments' and the dating of Carsten Thiede betrays the nature of Ewen's treatise at times as 'out on a limb'. Montgomery would say that relying on such contentious material is far from ideal.[192] She argues from the intrinsic evidence that the gospels were written by AD70. She is more confident than apologist and historian Paul Barnett who, whilst acknowledging the evidence for such a date, notes differing opinions on same and concludes, 'All that can be said in these matters, however, is that a case can be made but not proved. The problem is that the evidence is circumstantial and sometimes ambiguous.'[193] The question must be asked what Barnett means by 'proved'? If he means requesting a court to find on the balance of probabilities, rather than finding on overwhelming consensus, then many legal apologists such as Montgomery and Ewen would strongly argue that a case can be made. That the evidence is intrinsic and circumstantial in itself is not a defeater. Barnett, however, does assert that the gospels were definitely in circulation by about

---

[191] Montgomery, *Human Rights*, 137, 293. Texts referred to include Bruce, *The New Testament*; Gary R. Habermas, *Ancient Evidence for the Life of Jesus* (Nashville: Thomas Nelson, 1984).
[192] Ewen, *Faith*, 41-52. Montgomery is committed to 'never giving people (unnecessary) problems', rather always presenting the best evidence. See Montgomery, *Defending the Biblical Gospel, Study Guide*, 9-10. Richard N. Ostling also critiques this aspect of Ewen's work. See Clergy/Leader's mail-list, No 1-059, clergy@pastornet.net.au.
[193] Barnett, *Is the New Testament History?*, 38. In support of a date later than AD70 see for example David E. Garland, *Reading Matthew: A Literary and Theological Commentary on the First Gospel* (New York: Crossroad, 1993), 3-4; John Riches, 'Matthew' in *The Synoptic Gospels*, John Riches, William R. Telford and Christopher M. Tuckett (Sheffield: Sheffield Academic Press, 2001), 83-88.

AD90 as there are other documentary references to same. He is not in any way precluding a much earlier date, and he documents the evidence that the gospels were circulating during the lifetime of the authors.[194]

In her argument from intrinsic evidence Ewen, like Morrison and other legal apologists, argues that the gospels are silent on the destruction of Jerusalem in AD70, the Nero persecutions in AD67 and the deaths of Peter and Paul (compare John 21:19).[195] She notes that John A.T. Robinson has given the further example that the gospel of Matthew seven times warns against the influence of the Sadducees whose power really declined after AD70, and it reflects a need to continue to co-exist with a current Jewish culture that struggled after AD70.[196] Whilst Montgomery affirms the general thrust of Ewen's argument, his succinct historical and legal apologetic for an early dating of the gospels also relies on the affirmation of William Albright.[197] In his recent historical-legal apologetic Montgomery includes the following precise intrinsic argument:

> [Where > signifies 'must have occurred later than':] Paul dies in A.D. 64-65 > Book of Acts (which does not refer to Paul's death but would have done so had he already died) > Gospel of Luke (which constitutes 'part one' of Acts and is referred to in the preface of Acts as written earlier) > Gospel of Mark (which was employed as one of the sources of Luke's Gospel), and probably Matthew as well (tied in content, as it is, to Mark and Luke) > Jesus' ministry (*ca.* A.D. 30).[198]

In rejoinder it could be argued that Jesus' eschatological discourse in Matthew and Luke indicates a date after AD70. Robinson has argued that on the face of it the synoptics do not so read. The eschatological discourse is at least *prima facie* foretelling and doesn't mention actual prophetic fulfilment.[199] And as Wenham

---

[194] ibid., for example, 78.
[195] Ewen, *Faith*, 38-40; Morrison, *The Proofs*, 79.
[196] John A.T. Robinson, *Redating the New Testament* (London: SCM, 1976), 103-104.
[197] William F. Albright the late W.W. Spence Professor of Sematic languages at John Hopkins University stated, 'In my opinion, every book of the New Testament was written by a baptised Jew between the forties and the eighties of the first century AD (and very probably sometime between AD50 and 75'. Interview, 'Toward a More Conservative View', *Christianity Today* 7, 8 (18 January 1963): 3. For the citing of Albright in Montgomery's historical and legal apologetic see *History and Christianity*, 35 and the public audiotape lecture, 'A Lawyer's Case'.
[198] Montgomery, *Tractatus*, 3.2771. For a discussion on the unity and relationship of Luke-Acts see Joseph Verheyden, 'The Unity of Luke-Acts: Where are we up to?' in *The Unity of Luke-Acts*, J. Verheyden, ed. (Leuven, Belgium: Leuven University Press, 1999), 3-56.
[199] John A.T. Robinson, *Redating*, 86-103.

and Dodd point out, the Lucan pericopes that some say show a knowledge of Jerusalem's destruction (Luke 19:42-44, 21:20-24) are probably more analogous with Old Testament prophetic literature and Nebuchadnezzar's assault on Jerusalem.[200] In such pleadings the work of Barbara Thiering is relevant. Her radical reappraisal of the 'Jesus of history' is conservative as far as dating is concerned. Her position is that the gospels are far too detailed, dependent on direct instruction and eyewitnesses in nature to be late. In fact she dates them before AD60.[201] Handley likewise holds that evidence supports a date by AD70 and certainly within the lifetime of the eyewitnesses.[202] It is a case the legal apologetic needs to make if it wishes to assert eyewitness testimony. Montgomery does so unequivocally.

There is another element to the dating issue that the listener or reader may raise. It is the matter of *memory*. As Palmer states in his assessment of reliability-based hearsay, 'it seems obvious that the shorter the lapse of time between a person's perception of an event and their narration of it, the less likely it is that any mistake will have arisen due to a failing memory'.[203] Odgers concurs by citing the Australian Law Reform Commission, 'The least unreliable account of events is likely to be that given at or shortly after the event'.[204] Even the dating of the gospels by Ewen or Montgomery has a lapse of a minimum thirty years before recording the event. The principle espoused however is rebuttable. Handley argues the case. He refers to survivors of the First World War who 81 years later remember vividly certain events. In case law he refers to the HMAS Voyager case. Survivors of the collision with HMAS Melbourne gave evidence thirty-two years after the disaster. As a judge in this significant case Handley notes, 'survivors gave evidence at the trial that had the clearest recollection of what had happened … the thirty-two years in this case was longer than the interval of twenty years or so to the date of 1 Corinthians'.[205] Jesus also had a monumental impact on the witnesses.

Norman Anderson critically analyses the disciples' 'memory' as it relates to the teachings of Jesus. Whilst dissatisfied with the evangelical arguments that the disciples committed Jesus' teaching and interpretations of the episodes of his life to exact memory,[206] he concludes the cultural milieu of the day suggests 'much

---

[200] John Wenham, *Redating Matthew, Mark and Luke* (London: Hodder & Stoughton, 1991), 224; C.H. Dodd, *More New Testament Studies* (Manchester: Manchester University Press, 1968), 72-79.
[201] Barbara Thiering, *Jesus the Man* (Sydney: Doubleday, 1992), 75.
[202] Handley, 'A Lawyer', 13-14.
[203] Palmer, 'The Reliability-Based', 533.
[204] Odgers, *Uniform Evidence*, 156.
[205] Handley, 'A Lawyer', 12-13.
[206] Norman Anderson, *The Teaching of Jesus* (Downers Grove: Inter-Varsity, 1983), 19.

of Jesus' teaching must have been comparatively easy to remember in considerable detail – vivid parables, striking aphorisms and hyperboles, controversies with critics and comments on miracles, for example ... a large number of eyewitnesses of the ministry of Jesus, and some of the apostles themselves, were in a position to contribute to, verify and check the oral traditions available to the evangelists and also, as many would claim, at least the earliest of the written records'.[207] Anderson is not claiming all of the teachings of Jesus were first-hand observation, but rather the parts which are capture the *ipsissima vox* if not the *ipsissima verba* of the sayings of Jesus. The witnesses could testify at times to the exact words and other times in their own words their sense of what actually happened or was said. Anderson's findings are not as conservative as those of Alan Millard, Professor of Hebrew and Ancient Semitic Languages, School of Archaeology, Classics and Oriental Studies, University of Liverpool, who suggests that some of Jesus' followers may well have had papyrus role, pen and ink with them to take down the words of this travelling teacher. He concludes as to the gospels, 'some, possibly much, of their source material was preserved in writing from that time (Jesus' lifetime), especially accounts of the distinctive teachings and actions of Jesus'.[208]

In debate over the evidence for the resurrection there may well arise an onus on the apologist to establish sufficient memory about the life and teaching of Jesus. However, as the focus is the resurrection, the major concern will be the witnesses' memory of these events. In light of the extraordinary nature of Christ's death and resurrection the onus therefore is not a heavy one. As Montgomery states 'the events of the last week of Jesus' earthly life – his trial crucifixion, and burial – were events of high interest...'[209] Further, Montgomery and Greenleaf argue, the presumption is that the witnesses are of sound mind and of ordinary intelligence who one would expect to remember such events clearly.[210] The case

---

[207] Norman Anderson, *The Teaching*, 19-20. See also D.A. Carson, *Scripture and Truth* (Grand Rapids: Zondervan, 1983), 124, 378. Carson notes research argues for some written records back to Jesus' ministry.
[208] Alan Millard, *Reading and Writing in the Time of Jesus* (Sheffield: Sheffield Academic Press, 2000), 223-224.
[209] Montgomery, *Tractatus*, 3.625
[210] Montgomery, *The Law Above*, 121-122. The issue of memory is not a new one. Row in support of the resurrection, used the analogy as to who, of those at the Battle of Trafalgar fifty or sixty years ago, 'would not be competent to hand down the events with sufficient accuracy to the next generation'. C.A. Row, *A Manual of Christian Evidences* (London: Hodder and Stoughton, 1892), 140. For an adult witness there are authorities for the presumption that they have the mental ability to observe, remember and report. See Magner, 'The Best Evidence', 72.

for their reliable memory is not unrelated to the following discussion on the capability and credibility of the witnesses.

The other related question is *authorship*. Montgomery argues for traditional authorship of the four gospels and footnotes historical apologists in support.[211] Such apologetic arguments normally set out the extrinsic evidence of Papias, Irenaeus and the Muratorian Canon[212] and interact with sources such as Q, Mark, 'M' and 'L'. They are well rehearsed by Montgomery, F.F. Bruce, E.M. Blaiklock and Paul Barnett.[213] They find the intrinsic evidence supports John as author as he is called the disciple whom Jesus loved and appears to be one of the inner circle (for example, John 21:19-25). The extrinsic evidence of the Muratorian Fragment and Irenaeus support the apostles' authorship. Barnett is representative when he finds, 'What cannot be denied is that all the evidence on the identity of the author, from both inside and outside the fourth gospel, points not to an unknown disciple but to John Zebedee, the beloved disciple'.[214] That the internal and external evidence point to the author being John the apostle is supported by New Testament evangelical scholars such as D.A. Carson and Leon Morris.[215] Their arguments evidence a reliance on Westcott's cumulative case that the author was: (1) a Jew, (2) a Palestinian, (3) an eyewitness, (4) an apostle, i.e. one of the twelve, (5) the apostle John.[216] Morris states the fact is that 'the massive argument of Westcott has not been decisively refuted'. For Morris, Westcott's position is even preferred to a middle ground of the gospel being authenticated but not written by John.[217] Admittedly, such conclusions are at variance with critical scholars, such as Culpepper, who view the origins of John's gospel from a sociological perspective and conclude the gospel comes not from one author, but a Johannine school.[218] George Beasley-Murray, an evangelical, is in substantial agreement and finds that the beloved disciple is not John the apostle, and that the

---

[211] Montgomery, *Human Rights*, 137.
[212] Montgomery, *History and Christianity*, 26-40.
[213] Bruce, *The New Testament*, 29-61; Blaiklock, *Jesus Christ*, 34-47; Barnett, *Is the New Testament History?*, 49-110. Montgomery is less inclined to concede sources such as 'M' and 'L'. For his brief critique of Documentary and Form Criticism see 'Why has God Incarnate Suddenly Become Mythical?' in *Christians in the Public Square*, Cranfield, Kilgour and Montgomery, 307-316; Montgomery, *Tractatus*, 3.3 – 3.394. Montgomery argues, 'no manuscripts of "pre-edited" material have ever been found; nor have any accounts been discovered which describe the redaction of books by churchmen or by early communities' (3.341)
[214] Barnett, *Is the New Testament History?*, 78.
[215] D.A. Carson, *The Gospel According to John* (Leicester: Inter-Varsity; Grand Rapids: William B. Eerdmans, 1991), 68-81; Leon Morris, *Studies in the Fourth Gospel* (Exeter: Paternoster, 1969), 139-292.
[216] Carson, *The Gospel*, 70-71.
[217] Morris, *Studies*, 264-265.

gospel was written by a master interpreter of the school of the beloved disciple.[219] A rejoinder of Carson is that Culpepper offers no criteria as to how one distinguishes this school from a group of Christians, 'who cherish the Evangelist's writings and commend them to others'.[220] In this debate the name of the author of John's gospel is not the essential element for the legal apologetic.[221] The key criterion here is whether the author is testifying from his own observation, or might be 'reasonably supposed' to be so doing.

Foreman's critical analysis of the gospels does not fit the caricature of a conservative evangelical apologist but his conclusions differ from Culpepper's school. With respect to the gospel of John he observes, 'So many details in this gospel are unique, credible and unmistakenly personal that it would be difficult to deny its being firmly rooted in a first-hand account.'[222] This is a typical finding of the legal apologists who in their legal practice daily interpret evidence and documents.[223] And as no doubt Montgomery would also argue this finding is consistent with the basic legal hermeneutical principle of initially not going behind the document, but looking at the face of the document, for a plain, common interpretation. Of interest, Foreman exempts Luke from the first-hand account category stating it is 'our one admittedly "hearsay gospel"'.[224]

The connection of Mark's gospel with Peter or what F.F. Bruce calls 'Petrine authority'[225] is based on Papias and the intrinsic work of scholars such as Guelich and Lane who observe, for example, that Peter's message in Acts 10 verses 34 to 43 has a framework of a primitive kerygma similar in content and chronology to the written gospel, especially Mark.[226] Even Barbara Thiering affirms that the evidence indicates 'Mark's gospel was written under the auspices of Peter'.[227] Ewen includes a legal argument establishing that documentary statements made

---

[218] R. Alan Culpepper, *John* (Edinburgh: T. & T. Clark, 2000), 56-58, 297-325; R. Alan Culpepper, *The Johannine School: An Examination of the Johannine School Hypothesis Based on an Investigation of the Nature of Ancient Schools* (Missoula: Scholars Press, 1975), 287-289. See also Lincoln, *Truth on Trial*, 263-266; Stephen S. Smalley, *John: Evangelist and Interpreter* (Exeter: Paternoster, 1978), 813.
[219] George R. Beasley-Murray, *John, Word Biblical Commentary*, 2nd ed. (Nashville: Thomas Nelson, 1999), lxx-lxxv.
[220] Carson, *The Gospel*, 80-81.
[221] This position has a strong history of support amongst apologists. See for example George Park Fisher, *Manual of Christian Evidences* (New York: Charles Scribner's Sons, 1888), 4.
[222] Foreman, *Crucify Him*, 66.
[223] For example Chandler, *The Trial*, 1: 26-27; Clarrie Briese, 'The Verdict', *Australian Presbyterian* (April 2000): 5-8.
[224] Foreman, *Crucify Him*, 64.
[225] Bruce, *The New Testament*, 36.

in Mark's gospel, that are determined to be Mark acting as an interpreter or helper for Peter, would be treated in law as statements by Peter and first-hand knowledge.[228] This does not mean the author of Mark's gospel was a mere scribe or amanuensis. There is conjecture that we can be assured that the author's own eyewitness observations are recorded for us, as he is the young man who fled naked on the night Jesus was arrested (Mark 14:51-52). This trivial, but personal, account is found in no other gospel.[229] Whether the author is this naked youth, tradition strongly supports the author as being John Mark[230] who accompanied Barnabas and Paul on a preaching mission (Acts 13:4-5) and his mother's house was a meeting place for the first Christian community (Acts 12:12). Byrskog states, 'whoever composed the Markan narrative – and evidence suggests John Mark – that person had indeed a special interest in Simon Peter'.[231] All this leads Barnett to justifiably conclude that the vivid detail and descriptions in the gospel indicate that it is the recollection of someone who had been present at many of the events and who could confirm what took place (for example 5:38-41).[232] The intrinsic and extensive evidence points to the 'author/s' being a person/s who might be 'reasonably supposed' to be testifying from their own observation as to the death of Christ.

The real issue is Matthew's gospel. This is because the 'M' fragment cited earlier (Matthew 28:16-20) that relates Matthew's first-hand observation of the resurrection is an encounter limited to the eleven disciples. If Matthew is not the author this is not first-hand knowledge. It can perhaps be argued that οἱ δὲ

---

[226] Robert Guelich, 'The Gospel Genre' in *The Gospel and the Gospels*, Peter Stuhlmacher, ed. (Grand Rapids: William B. Eerdmans, 1991), 173-208; Lane, *Commentary on the Gospel of Mark*, 7-12. C.H. Dodd initiated this view. See Dodd, *More New Testament*, 1-11; C.H. Dodd, *The Apostolic Preaching and its Developments* (London: Hodder & Stoughton, 1944), 46-52.

[227] Thiering, *Jesus*, 75. Cf. William R. Telford, 'Mark' in *The Synoptic Gospels*, Riches, Telford and Tuckett, eds., 133-137.

[228] Ewen, *Faith*, 57-69. See also *Evidence Act 1995 (Cth) (NSW)*, s. 63-64 which allows for the admission of a representation of what someone heard or saw and which is made directly to the author of the document. As previously mentioned this provision does not apply to Mark 16:1-8 as Peter is obviously not the one making the representation to 'Mark' as to what he personally observed.

[229] For discussion see Lane, *Commentary on the Gospel of Mark*, 526-528; Robert H. Gundry, *Mark: A Commentary on his Apology for the Cross* (Grand Rapids: William B. Eerdmans, 1993), 881-882.

[230] Martin Hengel, *Studies in the Gospel of Mark*, trans. John Bowden (Philadelphia: Fortress Press, 1985), 28-30.

[231] Byrskog, *Story*, 284.

[232] Barnett, *Is the New Testament History?*, 91-96. For a critical discussion see R.T. France, *The Gospel of Mark, The New International Greek Testament Commentary* (Grand Rapids and Cambridge: William B. Eerdmans; Carlisle: Paternoster, 2002), 35-41.

ἐδίστασαν raises whether others were present. This is unlikely due to the text more probably indicating that Christ appeared only to the eleven disciples.[233] The presence of doubt does not textually require others outside the eleven to be present, whether the doubt related to the fact of a resurrection or whether Jesus should be worshipped as Lord (Matthew 28:17). Doubt amongst the disciples was an experience that surrounded the resurrection appearances (Luke 24:1-34) and explains Jesus' many more convincing proofs in Acts chapter one.[234]

Montgomery, Ewen, Bruce and Blaiklock are confident about Matthew's authorship or editorship and rebut objections to same.[235] Legal apologist Bennett uniquely highlights the 'M' pericope of chapter seventeen, verses 24 to 27 that includes comment on the temple taxes and the king's taxes. He asks whether this is just such an observation as one would expect from a tax gatherer? It is solid intrinsic evidence.[236] (Montgomery brought Bennett's argument back into the apologetic domain by publishing his article in *the Simon Greenleaf Law Review*.)

Yet any attempt to admit Matthew as first-hand hearsay would raise numerous objections from an adverse party relying on contemporary scholarship. There would be Vincent Taylor's cry based on the synoptic problem that it would be, 'improbable in the extreme that an apostle would have used as a source the work of one (Greek Mark) who was not an eyewitness of the ministry of Jesus'.[237] The argument is, in a more general legal form: 'If this is Matthew the apostle, why did he have to rely on other sources, eyewitness or not?'[238] And Matthew's gospel does not claim to be the direct report of the practice of autopsy. Then there is the issue of the reliability of the extrinsic evidence of Papias who stated that Matthew 'compiled oracles in the Hebrew language' when the gospel has come to us in Greek. It is questions such as these that lead Barnett, a leading evangelical scholar, to conclude that although the author of Matthew is a responsible scribe

---

[233] See Floyd V. Filson, *The Gospel According to Matthew* (London: Adam and Charles Black, 1971), 304-305. Cf. Booth who in his legal text does not see the assertions in this passage as authentic, *The Bedrock Gospel*, 141-142.
[234] Filson suggests that the doubt was simply related to lack of recognition of the resurrected Jesus, ibid., 305. This position fails to appreciate the doubt that surrounded the nature of the resurrection event itself. In this regard see Robert H. Gundry, *Matthew*, 2nd ed. (Grand Rapids: William B. Eerdmans, 1994), 593-594; Frank D. Rees, *Wrestling with Doubt* (Collegeville, Minnesota: Liturgical Press, 2001), 204-207.
[235] Montgomery, *History and Christianity*, 32-34; Ewen, *Faith*, 54-55; Bruce, *The New Testament*, 38-40; Blaiklock, *Jesus Christ*, 41-45.
[236] Bennett, *The Four Gospels*, 10. For further intrinsic evidence (diction, stylistic features, Old Testament phraseology) that Matthew himself composed this story see, Gundry, *Matthew*, 355-357.
[237] V. Taylor, *The Gospels*, 4th ed. (London: Epworth, 1938), 92.
[238] Riches illustrates this point from a current legal case, 'Matthew', 54-58.

and does not exaggerate the sources at his disposal, we are uncertain as to who the final author or editor was.[239] Such a conclusion is, of course, still conservative in view of the position of many New Testament scholars that 'Matthew' formulated his gospel in the context of the needs and the development of his community, in a post - AD70 Judaism.[240]

As mentioned legal and historical apologists rebut such objections. The rejoinders for the similarities between Matthew and other sources are not that the author copied, but rather that such similarities arise out of the fact of the individual author's closeness to Christ and the ability of the authors to hear the same oral teachings.[241] Also, there is no obvious objection as to why a witness could not use in his compilation of facts a previously written transcript which he himself accepted as accurate.

With respect to Papias, Bruce sees the most probable explanation being that the oracles (Logia) refer to a collection of Christ's sayings that underline the 'Q' material constructed on the lines of prophetical Old Testament books.[242] There is no reason that Matthew could not have translated these and used them in compiling the gospel.[243]

Is it necessary to enter the debate over the authorship of Matthew? The issue mainly relates to the resurrection, as Matthean authorship is not essential for the proof of Christ's death since there are the Marcan and Johannine accounts in support and it is not essential that the Matthean eyewitness testimony be that of Matthew the apostle. As to the resurrection there are already the eyewitness testimony of the event in John's gospel, and Paul's affirmation, and these two sources meet legal and biblical standards of corroboration.[244] (However, it is perhaps a surprising finding that the admissible documentary evidence for the resurrection is not focused on the synoptic gospels.) Further, as indicated, the legal apologetic case for Christ's resurrection on a technical or non-technical basis does not rest on this first-hand evidence alone. It is a cumulative case.

---

[239] Barnett, *Is the New Testament History?*, 102-109. For a discussion on authorship see also Richard S. Ascough, 'Matthew and Community Formation' in *The Gospel of Matthew in Current Study*, David E. Aune, ed. (Grand Rapids: William B. Eerdmans, 2001), 96-126.

[240] Riches, 'Matthew', 82-100.

[241] Ewen, *Faith*, 72-75. This position is supported by Barbara Thiering, *Jesus*, 75-76.

[242] Bruce, *The New Testament*, 38-39.

[243] Greenleaf, *The Testimony*, 12.

[244] The evidence of two eyewitnesses is difficult to overcome, see Ewen, *Faith*, 68. With respect to the biblical requirements see chapter 5 'Scriptural Support'. As well corroboration is about the quality of the witnesses, not the number of witnesses. See Heydon, *Cross*, 366-369.

First-Hand Admissible Hearsay – 'The Devil's Advocate' Position   101

If the legal apologists wish to use Matthew as first-hand source on the resurrection, more work will need to be done in presenting a succinct and probable argument on Matthean authorship.[245] A possible direction in this regard is to focus on the material that is unique to Matthew. This, as indicated, includes Jesus' teaching on tax and his commission to the disciples. On the basis of the intrinsic and extrinsic evidence a strong case can be made for Matthean involvement.[246] What needs to be remembered is that it does not have to be shown that 'M' is based on such first-hand knowledge but only that it might be reasonably believed so to be. This applies to all evidence relied on.

In discussions on authorship the role played by 'Q' and other possible *sources* arises. It is claimed at times that these alleged sources, that underlay the gospels and their consequential synoptic relationships, mitigate against the reliability and first-hand nature of the gospels that the technical legal apologists propagate. As to the first-hand observations of the resurrection the argument has no base. If the focus is on John's gospel, Paul and 'M', the sources don't apply to it. As to the death of Christ, where both the accounts of Mark and Matthew may be pleaded, there may be an issue. The legal apologists as a whole are aware of the debates but rarely enter into them.[247] No doubt this is so because from a legal perspective they would anticipate that a legal suit based in part on documentary evidence would have sources that influence them, such as a solicitor's instruction sheet, will form, or a conveyance based on some standard contract. The alleged sources may assist in understanding the structure of the document,[248] but don't preclude direct testimony about the author's first-hand knowledge or observation of the facts addressed in the document. The witness may well be examined as to her reliance on some source and its influence on her memory, but that does not estop the author being called. Further, Montgomery and Greenleaf claim that the discrepancies between Matthew and Mark in their accounts and their own arrangement of facts mitigate against the probability that the gospels are mere copies of each other or that they simply rely on common sources.[249]

Ewen makes a unique contribution to the synoptic problem as it relates to the possible interdependence of the authors.[250] She isolates three possible types of sim-

---

[245] As has been indicated the only possible first-hand eyewitness resurrection account in Matthew is the 'Great Commission' (28:16-20), and for it to be so Matthew the disciple must be the author.
[246] Blaiklock, *Jesus Christ*, 43-44.
[247] See for example Handley, 'A Lawyer', 13-14.
[248] ibid.
[249] Montgomery, *Human Rights*, 142-143. See also Greenleaf, *The Testimony*, 16-17; Montgomery, *The Law Above*, 106-107.

ilar passages: those with common themes and no identical wording; those that contain parts of sentences with identical structure or words, with the remainder of the sentence different; and those that focus upon identical, or almost identical, wording of entire sentences or passages. She concludes that in a court of law only the third category is an issue. The first two categories would have great credibility because of their independence. As to the third category *if* the jury deemed the accounts to be interdependent then only one witness could be credited with that particular testimony. She highlights that that decision will be made by the jury taking into consideration the credibility of the testimony as a whole. Then Ewen makes a finding against the facts with respect to the third category as it relates to the gospels: 'the majority of these types of sentences or passages are quotations of Jesus'.[251]

She does not include the crucifixion accounts of Matthew and Mark in this third category when the textual evidence could be said to support such a finding of interdependence.[252] Ewen's legal argument when applied to the passion narratives means that a jury may decide only Mark or Matthew is relevant evidence on the fact of Jesus' death.

Certainly, the legal apologist could argue against such a scenario on the basis of the credibility of both witnesses and that the original evidence of both as to certain of the events surrounding the life and character of Christ supports their both being heard.[253] However, it may well be that with the first-hand evidence of John, only the documentary evidence of Mark or Matthew would be admitted.

A Point for Further Research: Letter of James

Whilst Montgomery and the legal apologists have based their case on the New Testament gospels, Peter and Paul, further research should consider the letter of James. There are two reasons for this. The first is the hypothesis that the 'James' who stands behind the letter is the brother of Jesus.[254] As a consequence Byrskog states, 'We have a unique opportunity to study an early Christian eyewitness at work in the letter of James'.[255] He observes that virtually no one doubts that the

---

[250] Ewen, *Faith*, 74-83. Holding argues Montgomery's legal apologetic should have addressed this issue. See Holding, 'Robert (Richard) Packham', 4.
[251] ibid., 80.
[252] On the relationship between chapters 26-28 of Matthew and chapters 14-16 of Mark see Allan Barr, *A Diagram of Synoptic Relationships* (Edinburgh: T & T Clark, 1938).
[253] For example, Matthew 5-7.
[254] Byrskog, *Story*, 168-176.

A Point for Further Research: Letter of James

prescript of 'James, servant of God and of the Lord Jesus Christ' (1:1) refers to the Lord's brother.[256] There are three or four other persons in the New Testament who carried this name but they are largely unknown apart from James the son of Zebedee who died a martyr's death in AD44. Byrskog's conclusions are supported by other New Testament scholars such as Moo and Adamson who likewise answer the critics who argue that despite the prescript, the language of the letter and its tawdry reception into the canon point to another author and that it was written late because of its post-Pauline separation of faith and deeds.[257] Having said this Byrskog is open to the position of Davids and others that there was an editorial process that was based on James' teaching.[258] In any event there is at least at a *prima facie* level a good argument for the initial author being an eyewitness. Whilst there is no direct eyewitness narrative in James there is the utterance 'our glorious Lord Jesus Christ' (2:1). Here James acknowledges not only Jesus as the Messiah but Lord. In the context, Lord has implications of divine status and δόξης (*doxēs*) suggests at least an exaltation to a heavenly sphere.[259] This utterance is consistent with the claim that James was one who doubted but saw the resurrected Christ (1 Corinthians 15:7).

The second reason for legal apologists to consider the letter of James is its 'profound familiarity with Jesus' teaching',[260] (for example compare 5:12 with Matthew 5:34-37). Byrskog argues that most scholars today agree that James did not rely on the synoptic gospel narratives.[261] This notable similarity between accounts points to the reliable manner in which eyewitness testimony was handed down.

In future assessments of the legal apologetic the letter of James as a possible *prima facie* corroboration of other New Testament eyewitness accounts should be considered.

---

[255] ibid., 167.
[256] ibid., 168.
[257] Douglas J. Moo, *James, Tyndale New Testament Commentaries* (Leicester: Inter-Varsity; Grand Rapids: William B. Eerdmans, 1985), 19-30; James B. Adamson, *James: The Man and his Message* (Grand Rapids: William B. Eerdmans, 1989), 3-52.
[258] Peter Davids: *Commentary on James, New International Greek Testament Commentary* (Exeter: Paternoster, 1982), 10-13.
[259] Richard Bauckham, 'James and Jesus' in *The Brother of Jesus: James the Just and his Mission*, Bruce Chilton and Jacob Neusner, eds. (Louisville: Westminster/John Knox Press, 2001), 131-135; Moo, *James*, 88-89.
[260] Byrskog, *Story*, 171.
[261] ibid., 172.

Luke's Gospel

What about Luke's gospel? The legal apologists have been aware of hearsay difficulties surrounding Luke's gospel since the time of Greenleaf and they haven't avoided the issue.[262] Greenleaf and Montgomery plead that the gospel could be technically admitted as 'satisfactory evidence of the matters it contains'.[263] They argue from a general common law exemption to multiple hearsay that allows for the admissibility of a relevant and trustworthy 'inquest of office, or of any other official investigation'.[264]

Other contemporary apologists take a similar line seeking to show Luke would be admissible as an enquiry undertaken by a person of competent intelligence at the request of someone in authority or for a public benefit.[265] If Luke were so admissible its contents would be corroboration of the first-hand hearsay.

There is real merit in this argument of legal apologists. Numerous jurisdictions have codified regulations that provide for multiple hearsay for business and public records.[266] Luke writes as one carrying out an investigation (Luke 1:1-4) and in chapter five of this thesis his commitment to eyewitness testimony is documented. Debate continues as to Ramsey's confirmation of Luke's acumen as a 'first rank' historian 'who should be placed along with the very greatest historians'.[267] Leon Morris, whilst acknowledging the debate, still holds, 'There is widespread recognition that Luke is a reliable historian.'[268] And for our purposes it can be properly asserted that Luke set out with diligence, and as a responsible scribe, to collect the account of the first witnesses.

However, there is a difficulty in this argument and it goes beyond the theological motifs evident in Luke's writings that one would not expect in an unbiased public report.[269] It is that whilst this multiple hearsay category exists, it could be argued that to be covered by this category it must be shown that the author of the report

---

[262] Greenleaf, *The Testimony*, 19-21.
[263] ibid., 21; Montgomery, *The Law Above*, 111. Montgomery here indicates his support of Greenleaf's position by his use of his apologetic and his citing of Greenleaf's argument.
[264] ibid., 20-21; Montgomery, *The Law Above*, 109-111.
[265] Ewen, *Faith*, 67; Foreman, *Crucify Him*, 30.
[266] See Beazley, 'Hearsay', 50-66 for commentary on Australia's *Evidence Act 1995*, sections 69-71, 182. See Howard, Crane and Hochberg, *Phipson*, 589-593 for commentary on England's *Civil Evidence Act* 1968.
[267] W.M. Ramsay, *The Bearing of Recent Discovery on the Trustworthiness of the New Testament* (Grand Rapids: Baker, 1953), 81, 221. Montgomery cites Ramsay in response to Tübingen school's critical attitude towards Luke, *History and Christianity*, 31-32.
[268] Leon Morris, *Luke* (London: Inter-Varsity, 1974), 33.
[269] ibid., 28-47.

not only exercised some neutrality, but set out to investigate the claims of all the parties including any adverse parties. One case speaks of a State Highway Patrolman's accident report being admissible for a number of factors including the following: 'The evidence showed that Sgt. Hendrickson gathered all the evidence that he could from all sources. There is no indication that he neglected any one source or impermissibly preferred one over another.'[270] As well, the definition of what is a 'record' is not without difficulty. Phipson states it has been doubted whether a file of correspondence is a record. And it is assumed there is a duty to keep the record.[271] The legal apologist would have to counter such uncertainties and argument in light of Luke's credible, but not diverse or duty bound, investigation.

In view of the above, the preferred option for legal apologists in the future is not to argue the admissibility of Luke but to submit that Luke is an 'historical' document the court could refer to in refreshing its memory about the facts concerning Jesus. The standing of Luke is certified by prominent jurists from Greenleaf to Montgomery, to Herron, to Handley.[272] It is a substantial document that with other extraneous evidence records the circumstances of Christ's death. A court could also refer to Luke with respect to the resurrection, not as we have argued previously on the fact of the resurrection, but as to what is claimed to be the state of mind of the disciples and the eyewitnesses. Luke-Acts in this capacity is confirmation of the first three minimal facts of the resurrection argument of Habermas and Moreland: Jesus' death by crucifixion, the earliest disciples' experiences that they thought were appearances of the risen Christ, and their subsequent transformation.[273] As Habermas asserts, there are few critical biblical, historical scholars who do not support the presence of such evidence.

For practical apologetic purposes there is another significant role for Luke.[274] It is that together with Acts, it justifies the legal apologetic. It could be said that

---

[270] *Baker v Elcona Homes Corp.* 588 F.2d 551 (6th Cir. 1978) at 558. For a discussion of the admissibility of public records and reports see McCormick, Elliott and Sutton, *Cases and Materials*, 934-939.

[271] Howard, Crane and Hochberg, *Phipson*, 591-592.

[272] For Greenleaf and Montgomery see references in this section. Handley, 'A Lawyer', 12-17; Sir Leslie Herron, *The Trial of Jesus of Nazareth from a Lawyer's Point of View*, Paper, The Australian Lawyer's Christian Fellowship, Sydney. (22 March 1970), 1.

[273] For the further evaluation of this minimal facts argument and its role in a legal apologetic see the section 'Reframing the Legal Apologetic' in the next chapter. Gary R. Habermas and J.P. Moreland, *Immortality: The Other Side of Death* (Nashville: Thomas Nelson, 1992), 69-70.

[274] It appears Barnett is close to viewing Matthew as in the same genre as Luke. If Matthew is excluded as first-hand hearsay consideration could be given to its linkage with the genre of Luke's gospel. See Barnett, *Is the New Testament History?*, 99-110.

Luke is the first secondary legal apologist in that he presents his case on the basis of the eyewitness testimony of others. The testimony, it could be argued, included first-hand reports (for example Paul and Peter) and secondary accounts. It is a legal, apologetic paradigm.[275]

Non-Technical Legal Apologetic

The above considerations on documents and hearsay as admissible evidence, that are directly related to the technical legal apologetic, have a bearing on the non-technical legal apologetic. The role of 'hostile witnesses' must not be overplayed in the context of the admissibility of the evidence. The said apologetic should avoid generalisations such as that 'the gospels do not contain hearsay'. Certainly it is appropriate to create a witness list comprising the disciples, Paul, 'the 500', Mary Magdalene, the other Mary, and the followers on the road to Emmaus, and imply that if a court hearing were taking place in Jesus' day, they are the witnesses who could be called to testify to their first-hand observations.[276] This is what the apostle Paul did for the hearers in his day.[277] Apologists such as Luckhoo creatively take the witness list further and create a moot.[278] It is then relevant to follow Montgomery's lead and highlight the presence of so called hostile witnesses. And further some legal apologists when discussing the hearsay exception of the 'Ancient Documents' rule instruct how in a non-technical way there are other recorded hearsay exemptions in the gospels. An illustration is the cry of Mary Magdala's 'I have seen the Lord.' It is an 'excited utterance' and as such is a possible '*res gesta*' exception to the hearsay rule.[279]

However, all claims that the substance of the gospels recording the above representations would be admitted in their entirety today, even in a non-technical

---

[275] John W. Mauck, *Paul on Trial: The Book of Acts as a Defense of Christianity* (Nashville: Thomas Nelson, 2001), 221-226. Mauck sees Luke-Acts as an 'evangelistic legal brief'.
[276] For example Casteel, *Beyond a Reasonable Doubt*, 167-170.
[277] 1 Corinthians 15:3-10. However, Paul in supplying such a witness list was not facing the hearsay problems of today as conceivably his witnesses could be called.
[278] Luckhoo and Thompson, *The Silent Witness*.
[279] Professor L. Donoghue, formerly of Simon Greenleaf School of Law is one who has lectured and even in examinations sought a response to this proposition. See mid term examination paper, Evidence II, Simon Greenleaf School of Law, California, 1983. However, it must be clearly explained this is a non-technical illustration of what could happen in legal proceedings in Jesus' day. This Johannine statement is second-hand hearsay. Also on a technical basis it could be argued that the proposition that courts place more weight on such statements, which are without cross-examination and without testing the assumption of truthfulness, in times of crisis or confrontation is debatable. See W.A.N. Wells, *Evidence and Advocacy* (Sydney: Butterworths, 1988), 104-105.

Non-Technical Legal Apologetic 107

sense must in future be avoided. Legal sceptics, or anyone with a knowledge of the law, may well assert that it is a misrepresentation. Hence it is counter-productive.[280]

The need for clarity and caution over what is admissible evidence is especially required for the more technical apologists who understandably at times cross over into a non-technical 'witness list' paradigm in their apologetic discourse. For example Val Grieve in his popular apologetic includes an extensive witness list and calls it direct evidence of first-hand testimony, not hearsay. He then examines the witnesses by evidentiary principles of credibility which will be considered in the next chapter.[281]

It is basically the Greenleaf paradigm[282] that argues that *all* of the testimony of the four evangelists would be admissible today[283] and then examines the witnesses' credibility. It is misleading.

Summary

The best paradigm as far as the New Testament documents and their recitals is concerned, is for the legal apologist to present a case for the resurrection of Jesus which succinctly outlines the arguments for the admissibility of the documents and the probable admissibility of their first-hand hearsay. There are two significant reasons for the focus on admissible first-hand hearsay. Firstly, it is the best evidence. There is an old adage, closely adhered to by trial lawyers: 'always lead with your best witness'.[284] Also in light of the alleged semantic strength of the truth claim and the value that is placed upon it, the listener or reader is entitled to the best evidence. Secondly, the typical listener or reader is not a judge or someone legally trained to the extent that he or she can sift the second-hand evidence. The relevant and admissible first-hand hearsay evidence at a *prima facie* level, is a foundation for the credibility and objectivity of the Christian message. It admits a hearing. From there it can be shown to the listener or reader how the other testimony is of a nature that would delight any first-century lawyer even if not admissible today. These technical and non-technical considerations are relevant in the general argument about the eyewitness and historical nature of the gospels and their resurrection accounts. Apologetic issues such as the virgin birth, whilst

---

[280] See Packham, 'Critique'.
[281] Grieve, *Your Verdict*, 61-77. See also for example, Bartlett, *As a Lawyer*, 59-71.
[282] Greenleaf, *The Testimony*.
[283] ibid., 9-10.
[284] So affirms Barry Reed, a chairman of the Massachusetts Trial Lawyers' Association, in his legal fiction book, *The Indictment*, 324.

of much interest to many legal apologists,[285] do not benefit from the technical legal apologetic paradigm, as all the witnesses are well removed from the authors.

In conclusion, Montgomery has considerably reformed and developed the technical legal apologetic. He has cemented its place in today's apologetic endeavours. Further consideration needs to be given to the matters raised above on documents and hearsay as the next generation of apologists build on his work. In a following chapter a model legal apologetic will be outlined that seeks to give due consideration to the matters raised to date.

---

[285] Bartlett, *As a Lawyer*, 66-68.

Chapter 3

Evaluation of Montgomery's Legal Apologetic:
The Criteria Part II

In this chapter the focus will be on the legal criteria used to prove testimony, things and circumstantial evidence. The issues considered have relevance for both the technical and non-technical apologetic. Whilst the non-technical legal apologists rarely discuss the admissibility of the gospels and hearsay, they usually interact with one if not all three of these means of proof.

Testimony

In Montgomery's apologetic there are two substantial matters with respect to the credibility of testimony that impact the legal apologetic as a whole. These are, the competency and truthfulness of a witness and the difficulties associated with eyewitness testimony. This is an appropriate point to reiterate that in this thesis we are not considering as such the status of testimony, nor the status of documents, hearsay, things and circumstantial evidence.[1] This is not a defence of the laws of evidence. Our focus is on the methodological question of how legal criteria, used to test the reliability of testimony generally, applies to the particular testimony of the New Testament witnesses.

However, with respect to the status of eyewitness testimony it is appropriate to draw attention to Byrskog's recently published thorough treatment on the value of sight and eyewitness reports in Graeco-Roman literary sources and in first century Judaism.[2] Montgomery also makes a case for the status of eyewitness testimony at the time of Christ's earthly ministry.[3] After an examination of primary sources, Byrskog concludes that many ancient historians adhered to the dictum of Heraclitus, 'eyes are surer witnesses than ears'.[4] He states:

> The ancient historians exercised autopsy directly and/or indirectly, by being present themselves and/or by seeking out and interrogating other eyewitnesses; they related to the past visually.

---

[1] For a philosophical discussion on the epistemological status of testimony and its being justification of belief in the same sort of way as perception, memory and inference see C.A.J. Coady, *Testimony: A Philosophical Study* (Oxford: Clarendon Press, 2000), 3-151.
[2] Byrskog, *Story*. See also A.W. Mosley, 'Historical Reporting in the Ancient World', *New Testament Studies* 12, 1 (October 1965): 10-26.
[3] Montgomery, *Tractatus*, 3.12512 – 3.12514.
[4] Byrskog, *Story*, 64.

> Autopsy was the essential means to reach back to the past. They acted very much like oral historians, aiming to hear the living voices of those who were present.[5]

Historians were aware of issues such as bias and inaccurate recollection among eyewitness information which lead to suspicions about the quality of the observation.[6] They primitively interacted with the kind of evidentiary questions that the rest of this chapter addresses.[7] They also understood that the informant is a social and psychological being and that we cannot simply bypass their own feelings and prejudices. Yet interestingly personal involvement in the event being observed was preferred as, 'a person involved remembers better than a disinterested observer'.[8] Whilst it would be incorrect to suggest that there is an exact comparison between Graeco-Roman rhetoric and today's legal criteria, the fact is that eyewitness testimony had status in the time of Christ and was subject to critical assessment.[9]

The Competency and Truthfulness of a Witness

A major contribution of the legal apologetic is the criterion developed to test the competency and truthfulness of the witnesses to Christ's resurrection. Simon Greenleaf's criteria are the common tests as they are used by Montgomery,

---

[5] ibid. History Professor, E.A. Judge, in his assessment of ancient historical standards, adds further weight here to the legal analogy:
'No contemporary historian would for a moment have accepted the apostles as historians. History was an art form designed to present the past usefully and impressively. The question of fact was not the ultimate criterion. In this, ancient history writing, as any history writing which concentrates upon form, was incipiently mythopoeic. For the same reason, the apostles would not have accepted the role of 'historian'. What they presented was news and evidence, and a burning conviction of its authenticity, that has no parallel in ancient literature except perhaps in the law courts and in the popular concern with portents.'
Cited in P.F. Jensen, 'History and the Resurrection of Jesus Christ – III', *Colloquium* 3,4 (May 1970): 349-350. Whilst Judge's position does not agree with Byrskog on the status of eyewitness testimony in historical sources, it does lend support to the legal apologetic in its treatment of the apostle's eyewitness testimony as legal evidence.

[6] Byrskog, *Story*, 176-198.

[7] ibid., 145-190.

[8] ibid., 165-166.

[9] Byrskog acknowledges that it is probable that New Testament eyewitnesses existed and that they functioned as informants during the emergence and development of the gospel tradition. These witnesses he sees as Peter, James, the women at the cross and tomb and the family of Jesus and he is critical of the gospels of John and Matthew being personal eyewitness accounts. *Story*, 65-91.

Foreman, Chandler, Linton, Bartlett, Ewen and many others.[10] These criteria are also adopted by non-lawyer apologists.[11] Greenleaf, relying on Thomas Starkie, cites the following rule of municipal law:

> The credit due to the testimony of witnesses depends upon, firstly, their honesty; secondly, their ability; thirdly, their number and the consistency of their testimony; fourthly, the conformity of their testimony with experience; and fifthly, the coincidence of their testimony with collateral circumstances.[12]

Greenleaf then evaluates the four evangelists by these five criteria to determine what weight should be given to their testimony. The five tests can also be applied to a non-technical apologetic and its broader witness list which usually includes all the disciples, the two disciples on the road to Emmaus, James, Paul and the female witnesses,[13] that is those whom Montgomery states had direct contact with the events surrounding Christ's life and who in consequence 'knew the score'.[14] The criteria do not relate to the admissibility of the testimony, discussed in the previous chapter, but to its credibility.

The tests of Greenleaf, if not definitive criteria for confirming evidence, are most appropriate. (As previously stated written testimony will speak as oral evidence when its credibility is being evaluated.) These criteria for assessing oral evidence are still valid and operative today. Clarrie Briese states that these tests 'would prove profitable reading for those of us who are called to be magistrates in this State'.[15] Other more current authorities use criteria which are not dissimilar. Roberts claims that the qualification to give evidence involves two faculties in a witness, 'the moral faculty and the cognitive faculty'. He asserts that the moral faculty is the inner source of the obligation to tell the truth (honesty); the cognitive faculty, broadly speaking being that which enables the witness to understand what was observed, to recall it and to order it and present it logically when giving

---

[10] Montgomery, *The Law Above*, 118-140; Foreman, *Crucify Him*, 68-71; Chandler, *The Trial*, 1: 12-70; Linton, *A Lawyer Examines*, 40-44; Bartlett, *As a Lawyer*, 127-168; Ewen, *Faith*, 85-142.
[11] For example, Josh McDowell relies on Chandler who follows Greenleaf. See McDowell, *The Resurrection*, 137-178.
[12] Greenleaf, *The Testimony*, 28.
[13] Grieve, *Your Verdict*, 61-77. Grieve subjects these witnesses to *Phipson on Evidence* criteria which are similar.
[14] Montgomery, 'Neglected Apologetic', 125-126.
[15] Briese, 'Witnesses', 1.

evidence (ability, conformity with experience, consistency). In addition the witness must possess the physical faculties necessary to communicate: the ability to hear and speak (ability).[16]

Montgomery in his later legal apologetic creatively uses the fourfold criteria of McCloskey and Schoenberg for exposing perjury. The tests are the *internal and external defects in the witness himself on the one hand and in the testimony itself on the other*.[17] Montgomery also translates this schema into diagrammatic form as a construct for exposing perjury.[18]

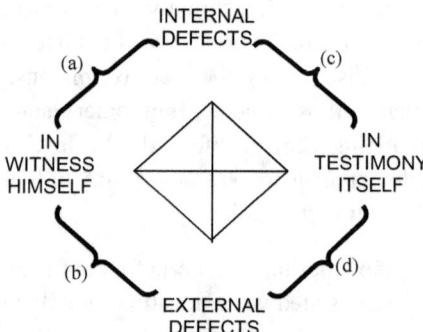

Whilst these tests specifically relate to asking whether the reliability of a witness can be impeached, they interact with Greenleaf's criteria, which Montgomery also affirms, and so the two models will be considered together. Montgomery focuses on assessing whether the testimony is perjury. This is because he commences with an axiom that testimony is truthful, unless it is otherwise exposed. In this section the critical assessment of the criteria centres on the legal questions that come to the fore.

Internal defects in the witness himself; <u>or</u> honesty (moral faculty) <u>and</u> ability (cognitive faculty)
With respect to the *honesty* of the resurrection witnesses Montgomery begins with a presumption of truthtelling. He asserts that there is a presumption in law

---

[16] Graham Roberts, *Evidence: Proof and Practice* (North Ryde, NSW: LBC, 1998), 261. Cf. Schwartz six 'notes' of the 'testimonial scale' in Louis E. Schwartz, *Proof, Persuasion and Cross-examination*, 2 vols. (Englewood Cliffs, New Jersey: Executive Reports Corporation, 1976), 1: 105-107.
[17] Montgomery, *Tractatus*, 3.44 – 3.446.
[18] Montgomery, *Human Rights*, 140-144. See McCloskey and Schoenberg, *Criminal Law*, 5: s. 12.

that, 'admissible testimony is considered truthful unless impeached or otherwise rendered doubtful'.[19] Swinburne argues similarly when he states, 'The principle of testimony, that we should believe what others tell us that they have done or perceived – in the absence of counter-evidence – is also *a priori*'.[20] In Montgomery's case the burden of proof, as far as the truthfulness of the gospel witnesses is concerned, is with the sceptic. Montgomery does not rest his case here for the gospel witnesses, since he places their testimony under a rigorous 'legal microscope' in order to evaluate its truthfulness and competency. No doubt he is reacting to the internecine methodology of some critics who appear always to assume the worst of biblical testimony.

This epistemic status of the truthfulness of testimony is common in the legal apologetic, and finds its roots in Simon Greenleaf. Greenleaf, relying on Starkie, furnishes the following municipal law: 'In the absence of circumstances which generate suspicion, every witness is to be presumed credible, until the contrary is shown; the burden of impeaching his credibility lying on the objector'.[21] He proceeds from this law to argue, 'that the testimony of the evangelists should be admitted to be true, until it can be disproved by those who would impugn it'.[22] Greenleaf goes so far as to suggest that this presumption is applied in courts of law, even to witnesses whose integrity is not wholly free from suspicion.[23] Others who advocate such a presumption include Val Grieve and Clarence Bartlett.[24]

On reflection I believe the term presumption here is too strong. It implies there exists an actual rebuttal presumption in law, while in reality there is no commonly accepted one.[25] At best, there is a defacto 'presumption' of truth in the absence of any other evidence tendered. And in any event, Packham notes Montgomery's concession that the said presumption does not apply if the

---

[19] Montgomery, *Human Rights*, 140.
[20] Richard Swinburne, 'Evidence for the Resurrection' in *The Resurrection*, Davis, Kendall, O'Collins, eds., 192. Cf. N. Wolterstorff, 'Can Belief in God be Rational if it has no Foundations?' in *Faith and Rationality*, A. Plantinga and N. Wolterstorff, eds. (Notre Dame: University of Notre Dame Press, 1983), 157-162. See also Coady, *Testimony*, 122-124 on the 'Propensity to Speak the Truth'.
[21] Greenleaf, *Testimony*, 25.
[22] ibid., 26.
[23] ibid., 28.
[24] Val Grieve, *Verdict on the Empty Tomb* (London: Falcon Booklet, 1970), 11-13; Bartlett, *As a Lawyer*, 127.
[25] Further evidence in support of my position is Howard, Crane and Hochberg, *Phipson*, 83-95. Phipson does not include this said presumption in its extensive list of presumptions. See also McEwan, *Evidence*, 204-205. McEwan argues there is no basis in fact for an assumption that what an individual says against himself may fairly be assumed to be true.

testimony is 'rendered doubtful'. Relying on *Jones on Evidence* and other authorities he pleads that doubtful, and therefore impeached evidence, includes testimony that is improbable or impossible, as well as testimony arising out of hysteria, hallucinations and delusions. The latter case of testimony arising out of hysteria and the like does not work against Montgomery's argument as the burden of showing that the evidence is so affected still lies on the adverse party.[26] However, the point is that concerns about the extraordinary supernatural nature of the gospel evidence probably would be raised by the judge, or in the pleadings of the adverse party, or in the testimony of other sceptical witnesses, and therefore any so-called presumption is unlikely to apply.[27] Hence it is doubtful whether a court would presume the truthfulness of testimony for an event such as a resurrection.

In law, what one can ask is that a judge and jury give a witness a fair hearing. To do this, they should not assume that a witness is untruthful.[28] Montgomery is on the mark when he puts it, 'a witness is assumed to be innocent'.[29] The same openness to a witness can be asked of an unbeliever in a legal apologetic, but there is no specific legal presumption that requires the unbeliever to hold initially that the gospel witnesses are truthful. In the former situation, the witness is initially heard with openness and respect. In the latter scenario, the burden on the doubter is much more onerous, and it does not reflect the way personal testimonies are perceived in real life, especially with regard to astonishing stories.[30]

Phillips, in his critique of Montgomery, argues there is another difficulty when one relies on such presumptions: there is nothing stopping the apologists of other faiths claiming the same for their witnesses and documents.[31] The focus in presenting the testimony of the resurrection witnesses should be on the criteria for the competency and truthfulness of the witnesses as referred to above, and not 'presumptions' that may be seen to weigh the argument in one's own favour. The former position is consistent with the heart of Montgomery's apologetic. And as Russell expresses it: if a witness solemnly testifies to a fact and is uncontradicted and unimpeached, then one can speak of a presumption of truth.[32]

---

[26] Heydon, *Cross*, 202-203.
[27] See Packham, 'Critique', 10. See also Gard, *Jones*, 4: 170-171.
[28] Bauer, 'The Logician's Model', 123-125. Lawyer Booth states in *The Bedrock Gospel*: 'In a court of law the presumption that all his testimony is *prima facie* untrue is not even applied to the recidivist!'(11).
[29] Montgomery, 'A Lawyer's Case', 13.
[30] Cf. Coady, *Testimony*, 123.
[31] Phillips, 'Apologetics and Inerrancy', 205.
[32] Russell, *A Lawyer's*, 75.

The Competency and Truthfulness of a Witness 115

With respect to the gospel witnesses' honesty or truthfulness, Montgomery is on solid ground when he argues, 'their simple literalness and directness is almost painful' and there is no evidence they were persons who could not be trusted.[33] Packham objects that being simple, literal and direct could also apply to Joseph Smith (Mormons).[34] Montgomery would respond that all the criteria need to be considered including, in Joseph Smith's case, the criteria relating to internal and external defects in the testimony itself. These tests would focus on the scientific and archaeological evidence that conflicts with Joseph Smith's account.[35] As a consequence Montgomery finds, 'The Book of Mormon lacks historical credibility, Joseph Smith's "witnesses" to its supposed divine origin hardly instill confidence..'[36]

Furthermore, Montgomery argues that one engaged in deception must say nothing that can be checked against contradictory data if he wants to remain undetected.[37] A lying witness is very coy about details. Significantly, the gospel testimony does not evidence such restraint. In fact, Russell finds as follows: 'A lawyer reading the narrative with care will be struck with the careful and abundant details of its statements. This is a quality of truth in testimony'.[38] And Chandler argues that the character of Jesus that is presented by the witnesses and that one is encouraged to emulate, is totally inconsistent with the values of questionable witnesses.[39]

However, as to the honesty of the witnesses the legal apologists should concede that we are speaking at a *prima facie* level as none of the witnesses has been subjected to the honesty traps of a seasoned cross-examiner.[40] Humphrey Palmer documents that cross-examination, viewed as the ultimate test for telling a good (honest) witness from a bad one, was developed in the Greek law courts and was employed by the first Greek historians.[41] This absence of cross-examination is especially relevant for the non-technical legal apologetic where many biblical witnesses are paraded and their testimony is presented as unimpeached.

---

[33] Montgomery, *Human Rights*, 140-141.
[34] Packham, 'Critique', 10.
[35] See John Bracht, *Let's Talk About It: A Letter to the Members of the Church of Jesus Christ of Latter-Day Saints* (Mortdale, NSW: n.p., 1993), 12-20. Bracht is a former Mormon with two postgraduate degrees in Mormon doctrine.
[36] Montgomery, *Tractatus*, 3.14313.
[37] Montgomery, *Human Rights*, 140-144.
[38] Russell, *A Lawyer's*, 73.
[39] Chandler, *The Trial*, 1: 14.
[40] Givens, *Advocacy*, 69-89.
[41] Humphrey Palmer, *The Logic of Gospel Criticism* (London: MacMillan, 1968), 32-33.

As mentioned in the previous chapter, Montgomery and others often claim that the functional equivalency of cross-examination can legitimately be found in the hostile Jewish leaders who had the means, motives and opportunity to expose the apostolic witnesses. But, whilst this argument has real merit in considering the weight to be given to the testimony, it is not the equivalent of a strong court room cross-examination. In a technical apologetic, it could be asserted that the limited admissible documentary testimony that is referred to in chapter two is not subject to the same reservations. It is common sense that the admissible documentary testimony of one who is deceased or someone who is otherwise unable to give evidence, is not subject to cross-examination. In this case the hostile Jewish leaders' argument also has a prominent place in considering the weight to be given to this testimony. Nevertheless it is hard to imagine in a technical or non-technical context an adverse party sitting timidly by as this criterion was offered to prove the credibility of the testimony. The adverse party would seek to interact with the admissible evidence, and to investigate both duplicity and the unreliability of the testimony, via similar internal and external criteria, and critical New Testament scholarship.

Further, there are three witnesses whose character and propensity for honest reporting would raise some concerns for an advocate in his preparation for the case. One is Matthew who was probably a small tax leaseholder. The social position and character of such a person could negatively be equated to that of 'sinner' and prostitute (Mark 2:16-17; Matthew 21:31-32); and Stegemann and Stegemann refer to Levi as the calling of a 'notorious' tax collector. Few respected the honesty of such a person.[42] The second is Mary Magdalene from whom 'seven demons had gone out' (Luke 8:2). Mary's stability and character is put under further trial by those who equate her with the sinner portrayed in Luke 7 verses 36 to 50.[43] The third is the apostle Peter. Under pressure he denied Christ (Mark 14:53-72, Matthew 26:57-75, Luke 22:54-62, John 18:15-27).

Whilst Perkins' observations that Peter's denial 'awakens a sympathetic chord in contemporary readers' and that in some sense he was 'playing out a divinely ordered script' may be justified, the fact is that Peter lied under 'cross-examination' in events surrounding Jesus' trial.[44]

---

[42] For a discussion on the social and economic status of a tax collector see Ekkehard W. Stegemann and Wolfgard Stegemann, *The Jesus Movement: A Social History of its First Century*, trans. O.C. Dean (Minneapolis: Fortress Press, 1999), 200-201.

[43] John Wenham, *Easter Enigma*, 2nd ed. (Grand Rapids: Baker, 1992), 22-33.

[44] Pheme Perkins, *Peter: Apostle for the Whole Church* (Edinburgh: T. & T. Clarke, 2000), 31-32.

It can be fairly argued that apart from the concerns mentioned above, on a *prima facie* level there is no substantial evidence that warrants an assumption that the witnesses are dishonest and not worthy of a fair hearing. Irrespective of one's view of the resurrection, Greenleaf's and Montgomery's assertion that the internal evidence points to the witnesses being good people seeking to testify about what they believed they had observed is a warranted one.[45] Such a factual finding is in contrast to the assumptions and interpretations of Reimarus, the Jesus Seminar, Dominic Crossan, and others, who belong to the radical school of the quest for the historical Jesus.[46] Crossan's explanation that Jesus' first followers knew almost nothing about the process of his death and that their gospel accounts are 'prophecy historicized', leaves a lawyer with a tale of witness deception, no matter how honourable the motives.[47]

From a legal perspective our discussions about the *ability* of the witnesses of the resurrection need only be brief. Swinburne asserts an *a priori* principle that memories in testimony are to be trusted in the absence of counter-evidence.[48] In law it means a witness is presumed to be of sound mind, reasonable memory and of an ordinary degree of intelligence in relation to recall and observation.[49] Montgomery and Greenleaf rightly plead this for the gospel witnesses.[50] The gospel witnesses were present during the life, death and resurrection of Jesus, so one could assume they could properly and soundly testify from their own knowledge and observation. The New Testament documents make the fact of their presence clear.[51]

The legal apologists often address the social standing of the witnesses to counter the often heard objections that they were illiterate peasants, or as Bartlett records it, 'a band of "ignorant fisherman"'.[52] At times the legal apologists 'strengthen'

---

[45] Greenleaf, *The Testimony*, 30-31.
[46] See the previous discussion on Reimarus in chapter one. Further, for discussion on the claims of the fraudulent and duplicitous nature of the gospel testimony in the Reimarus' fragments see Colin Brown, *Jesus in European*, 1-10.
[47] John Dominic Crossan, *Jesus: A Revolutionary Biography* (San Francisco: Harper San Francisco, 1994), 140-152. The integrity of the evangelists in a legal context is likewise unnecessarily compromised by the Jesus Seminar's conclusions that, 'the evangelists *frequently* attributed their own statements to Jesus' (emphasis mine). Robert W. Funk, Roy W. Hoover, and the Jesus Seminar, *The Five Gospels: The Search for the Authentic Words of Jesus* (New York: Macmillan, 1993), 23.
[48] Swinburne, 'Evidence for', 191-193.
[49] Briese, 'Witnesses', 4.
[50] Montgomery, *The Law Above*, 121-122 which reproduces Greenleaf's, *The Testimony*, 31-32; Montgomery, 'Neglected Apologetic', 121.
[51] See for example, Luke 23:49, 24:1-53, 1 Corinthians 15:3-8.
[52] Bartlett, *As a Lawyer*, 135-136.

their case by centring on the apparent 'professional' status and skills of Matthew (tax collector) and Luke (doctor).[53] Another course is to admit that many of the witnesses were not wealthy, and that they were unimportant people, arguably belonging to that culture's lower stratum.[54] However, in fairness, the position of the fishermen disciples is not totally clear. Unlike labourers and farm hands they probably owned their means of production and a case could be made for their being members of a lower middle class.[55] And in fact some of the witnesses, for example Joanna (Luke 8:3) and Joseph of Arimathea (Mark 15:43) were from the upper classes.[56] So there is a broader cross-section of social standing of the witnesses than critics often allow. As Greenleaf notes, we may well suppose that they 'were like the generality of their countrymen, until the contrary is shown by an objector'.[57] Yet in reality, whilst this argument may appeal to the lay person when considering the weight to be given to the testimony, in fact the social status of witnesses has little relevance to their ability to observe and recall.[58] The other often heard objection that the evangelists, who probably spoke in a Galilean Aramaic dialect, would not have had the bilingual skills to write in Koine Greek is simply unsubstantiated and demeaning. Koine Greek had by that time been disseminated throughout the eastern Mediterranean region.[59] Alan Millard states:

> The surviving examples of writing from Herodian Palestine and the available literary references show that writing in Greek, Aramaic and Hebrew was widespread and could be found at all levels of society. Writing was used to label jars, send messages, keep accounts and legal deeds and to preserve and propagate teaching and literature. Although the villages and hillsides of Galilee were the scene for much of Jesus' teaching, it is a mistake to insist this was an uncouth, isolated rural setting where people 'displayed only tenuous connections with literate culture'.[60]

---

[53] ibid., Ewen, *Faith*, 94-96; Clifford, *The Case for the Empty Tomb*, 46.
[54] Stegemann and Stegemann, *The Jesus Movement*, 199-201 and 382-387.
[55] Gerd Thiessen, *Sociality, Reality and the Early Christians* (Minneapolis: Fortress Press, 1992), 64-66.
[56] Christopher Burchard, 'Jesus of Nazareth', in *Christian Beginnings*, Jünger Becker, ed. (Louisville: Westminster/John Knox Press, 1993), 43-51.
[57] Greenleaf, *The Testimony*, 31.
[58] Foreman, *Crucify Him*, 69-70; Schwartz, *Proof, Persuasion*, 2: 1711-1712. Schwartz also discusses the benefits and drawbacks of education and intelligence on memory and reconciliation. They appear to balance themselves out. He states one's native retentiveness is unchangeable and no amount of culture would seem capable of modifying it.
[59] Barnett, *Jesus and the Rise*, 197.
[60] Millard, *Reading and Writing*, 210.

The Competency and Truthfulness of a Witness 119

External defects in the witness himself; or honesty as to motive (moral faculty/ state of mind)
Montgomery's response to this criterion is representative of the legal apologists. He states:

> Surely no sensible person would argue that the apostolic witnesses would have lied about Jesus for monetary gain or as a result of societal pressure. To the contrary: they lost the possibility both of worldly wealth and of social acceptability among their Jewish peers because of their commitment to Jesus. Might that very affection for and attachment to Jesus serve as a motive to falsify? Not when we remember that their Master expressly taught them that lying was of the Devil.[61]

Montgomery notes that this argument is iterated by classical apologists, including Hugo Grotius.[62] Subject to one reservation, Montgomery and the legal apologists are justified in adopting their common sense approach to this criterion. The reservation again relates to an ongoing premise of this thesis that the legal apologetic should restrict itself to a case that admits a hearing. The witnesses appear to have little to gain from fabricating the resurrection account. However, the credibility of the witnesses could be impugned by a cross-examination as to lies and motive. Normally evidence as to credibility of a witness is not admissible, but in many jurisdictions and in common law there is an exemption for evidence that may prove that a witness is biased or has a motive for being untruthful. Often that evidence has to be adduced otherwise than from the witness concerned, and such evidence can be rebutted, but the rule remains nevertheless.[63] Any committed defence counsel would like to show, or seek to prove, that witnesses of this nature are biased.[64] However, he would need to be cautious and fair in his questioning, as any attacks on a witness on such personal grounds must be well founded for if it fails, it will reflect adversely on the attacking party.[65] No doubt a defence counsel would consider calling witnesses who could testify as to the emotional, spiritual and physical commitment of Jesus' followers to their Lord. Also with

---

[61] Montgomery, *Human Rights*, 142. For example, Roper, *Did Jesus Rise?*, 37-39.
[62] ibid., Grotius, *The Truth*, Book II, 85-88. Since the eighteenth centry even the higher critics of the Bible have been reluctant to criticise the sincerity of 'The Testimony' where martyrdom of the first disciples has been established. See Schramm, *Testimony*, 146.
[63] For example see Odgers, *Uniform Evidence*, 280-301; Heydon, *Cross*, 521-522. For procedural limitations in cross-examination to show bias see Gard, *Jones*, 4: 138-140.
[64] For example see Hugh Selby, *Winning in Court* (Melbourne: Oxford University Press, 2000), 162-165.
[65] J.L. Glissan and S.W. Tilmouth, *Advocacy and Practice* (Sydney: Butterworths, 1998), 105.

respect to a possible basis for bias, a defence counsel could point to the spiritual prestige and other leadership advantages associated with being identified as a witness for the resurrection, should the substance of such matters be denied in the direct evidence of gospel witnesses. As already indicated this character evidence could be strongly rebutted, but that does not stop the issues being raised before a jury or judge. It is a position many unbelievers would surely anticipate.

Not unrelated to this issue is the fact that in some jurisdictions there is a disqualification of the evidence if the written statement was made by, 'a person interested at a time when proceedings were pending or anticipated involving a dispute as to any fact which the statement might tend to establish'.[66] The adverse party may seek to argue that the gospel writers wrote their material in anticipation of 'proceedings' (debate) involving this matter. It has been held in some jurisdictions that a person interested could simply be someone with an interest in distorting the truth.[67] This is a more technical issue and is unlikely to be raised in a non-technical apologetic. And it is worth noting that in more recent evidence legislation this concept of 'a person interested' is often absent.[68] Lord Denning reflects, 'It (also) seems incredible now but under the old common law every person having an interest, however remote, in the result of proceedings was barred from being a witness.'[69] However, the point of all this is that to stretch the legal analogy beyond a *prima facie* case is to fail to give due consideration to possible rebuttal evidence.

Summary

It can be fairly argued that the testimony of the resurrection witnesses, at a *prima facie* level and on the basis of a preponderance of the evidence, would pass Montgomery's criteria of internal and external defects in the witness, Greenleaf's criteria of honesty and ability, and Roberts' moral criteria. Much of the apologetic argument about the honesty and ability of the resurrection witnesses is uncomplicated and self evident.

Internal defects in the testimony itself; or their number and the consistency of their testimony, and the conformity of their testimony with experience (cognitive faculty)

---

[66] For a discussion of common law, English and Australian law see R.A. Brown, *Documentary*, 194-201.
[67] ibid., 194.
[68] For example, ibid., 201.
[69] Lord Denning, *Landmarks in the Law* (London: Butterworths, 1984), 208-209.

The *number* of eyewitnesses should not detain us. As argued in the previous chapter, on a technical level there is corroboration, and the non-technical witness list reveals numerous eyewitnesses. It is therefore a matter Montgomery and the legal apologists don't address in detail.[70] Montgomery quotes Plautus:

> One eyewitness is worth more than ten purveyors of hearsay; those who only hear about things say what they've heard, but those who see know the score![71]

Packham highlights what for him is an important internal defect — *material omissions*. He asserts that such omissions are just as fatal to the trustworthiness of testimony as are outright contradictions. He argues that the gospels are full of material omissions, for example John does not refer to the ascension.[72] His argument is dubious. The gospel writers, apart from Luke to some extent (Luke 1:1-3, Acts 1:1-2), do not claim they are seeking to record all of the events in Jesus' life, in fact John places one on notice that that is not his intention (John 20:30). Montgomery argues that no one gospel was ever intended to contain the complete account of Jesus' three year ministry.[73] Also, the so called omissions in the four gospel accounts may well be found to be insignificant if the witnesses were called to give their full evidence-in-chief. And really the issues Packham highlights, that is the absence of an ascension account in John and Mark's man inside the tomb not being specifically identified as the angel in Matthew and John, are not material omissions.[74] A more challenging omission an adverse party could raise is Paul's statement that the resurrected Jesus 'appeared to Cephas, then to the twelve' (1 Corinthians 15:5). Only Luke records this appearance to Peter before the other disciples (Luke 24:34). It appears from the brevity of the report that Luke had not investigated the account personally (Luke 1:3). Paul's statement in verse five probably belongs to tradition he had received (1 Corinthians 15:3)[75] which could have been designed to ensure Peter's primary role in the early church. In any event it could be argued that it is not a material omission as John in his resurrection account also notes the primary place of Peter in the resurrection appearances and that Peter was an eyewitness (John 20:1-10, 19-23). Foreman concludes that such 'omissions' in the gospel testimony do not discount the substance.[76] Further, even if one could challenge in cross-examination the

---

[70] Montgomery, *Human Rights*, 140-144; Ewen, *Faith*, 99-100.
[71] Montgomery, 'Neglected Apologetic', 125.
[72] Packham, 'Critique', 12.
[73] Montgomery, *Human Rights*, 142; Montgomery, *Tractatus*, 3.4443.
[74] Packham, 'Critique', 12.
[75] Fee, *The First Epistle*, 721-729.

resurrection witnesses over certain omissions in their prior statements (the gospels) one would still have to establish that each witness knew how to prepare good reports, and that he knew the information was important enough to be included.[77] There is little of substance in this alleged defeater.

A more significant issue is the *consistency* of the testimony. I am arguing here that it is helpful to approach this test on three levels. The first is the technical, legal apologetic for the resurrection appearances. In the previous chapter we argued that the admissible testimony are the first hand observations in John's gospel, Paul's account in 1 Corinthians chapter 15 verses 8 to 9 and possibly the 'M' pericope (Matthew 26:16-20). There is no contradictory evidence here and John's omission of an ascension narrative, which may be the setting of 'M' (Matthew 28:16-20) is discussed above.

The second level is an historical, popular apologetic for Christ's death and resurrection. There the alleged minor discrepancies and contradictions in the gospel accounts are answered by statements such as that of John Drane, 'These who criticise the gospel writers on grounds of inconsistency are just being unfair by imposing outmoded standards of logic that would never be applied to any other literature'.[78] Montgomery has a similar argument in his historical apologetic.[79] And one of the historians Montgomery likes to cite, Marc Bloch, gives the example of Napoleon's defeat at the Battle of Waterloo. Bloch holds that whilst one would expect the witnesses to the battle to agree on the fact of the defeat, one would doubt their testimony and dependence if they agreed exactly in their descriptions of the battle.[80] Drane also uses the legal metaphor of a personal court case where his recollections differed from other witnesses and he concludes: 'The judge did not say, "Because I have heard several stories of what happened, this accident could not have taken place." ... To do so would have been absurd, and we all recognise this. Yet this is exactly the sort of crazy conclusion that otherwise intelligent people seem to reach when talking about the New Testament.'[81]

---

[76] Foreman, *Crucify Him*, 70.

[77] Thomas A. Mauet, *Fundamentals in Trial Techniques*, 2nd ed. (Boston & Toronto: Little, Brown, 1988), 242-251. Mauet is commenting on the U.S. *Federal Rules of Evidence* as regards to prior inconsistent statements.

[78] John Drane, *The Bible Phenomenon* (Oxford: Lion, 1999), 133-134. See also Paley, *A View*, 319.

[79] Montgomery, *Where is History Going?*, 194-197. See also Montgomery, *Tractatus*, 3.64 – 3.642.

[80] Marc Bloch, *The Historian's Craft*, trans. Peter Putman (Manchester: Manchester University Press, 1954), 115.

[81] Drane, *The Bible*, 130. For a similar argument see Raymond E. Brown, 'A Between-the-Lines Look at Jesus', *U.S. Catholic* 53, 3 (March 1998): 14.

The third level will be our focus and that is the non-technical legal apologetic and its witness list as well as the technical legal apologetic for the death of Christ (Matthew, Mark and John). Here one deals from a legal perspective with allegations of numerous minor discrepancies and contradictions in the testimony. It is traditionally answered along the lines of the historical, popular apologetic, but with a distinctive legal justification. Two examples from leading authorities and practitioners who span the years, suffice. Greenleaf asserts, 'the discrepancies between the narratives of the several evangelists, when carefully examined, will not be found sufficient to invalidate their testimony.' Greenleaf pleads that many of the accounts can be harmonised and that far greater discrepancies can be found in various reports of legal judgements, without rejection on the part of lawyers.[82] Handley states,

> Courts expect that evidence given by honest and reliable witnesses will agree in substance but differ in detail, and they view with suspicion witnesses who give the same evidence word for word. This always suggests that they have put their heads together to make up their story. The gospels are four substantially independent accounts of the events which agree in substance, but differ in detail, and they pass this test.[83]

Whilst Greenleaf and Handley refer specifically to the four gospel writers, this evidentiary discourse is traditionally applied by the legal apologists to the testimony of all the witnesses in the gospels.[84] Montgomery who focuses his argument on the four gospels, concurs with this argumentation and states that if the gospels gave verbatim accounts, 'that fact alone would make them highly suspect, for it would point to collusion'. He continues that the gospel witnesses present different, but complementary accounts, 'just as veridical witnesses to the same accident will present different, but complementary accounts of the event'.[85]

He advises, 'there is nothing I like more than to have opposing counsel put on the stand four witnesses who tell exactly the same story of an accident. This is wonderful! I take my client out and negotiate for a higher fee ...'.[86]

There are *three issues raised on this third level*: Is this expectation of difference in detail a valid legal argument? Are the legal apologists arguing against the facts

---

[82] Greenleaf, *The Testimony*, 34-36.
[83] Handley, 'A Lawyer', 8.
[84] For example Grieve, *Your Verdict*, 61-77.
[85] Montgomery, *Human Rights*, 142.
[86] Montgomery, 'A Lawyer's Case', 14.

when one considers the verbatim gospel accounts for the death of Christ? Are the discrepancies and contradictions of a kind that would be covered by this alleged test? These are issues one would expect a listener or reader to raise in rebuttal.[87] One assumes they are also significant questions for those operating apologetically at the historical, popular level.[88]

Packham denies that this expectation of difference in detail is a valid legal argument. He states that it is not based on any rule of evidence, and is inconsistent with the very valid rule of evidence, 'that testimony which is inconsistent with other evidence, or contradictory, or self-contradictory, may be disregarded as unreliable'.[89] He asserts that the maxim is 'false in one thing, false in all'.[90] Packham does not cite the said valid rule of evidence on which he is relying. He does acknowledge that the harshness of the said rule has been softened in most jurisdictions, but a jury is free to view such inconsistent testimony as suspect and disregard it.[91]

In practice Montgomery's principle is a valid one. Trial lawyer and legal fiction writer Barry Reed illustrates:

> My witness was tripped up by the DA, a minor discrepancy. Said he was fifteen feet from the scene of the accident. The DA proved he was thirty feet away.
>
> I asked the jury, 'How many light fixtures are there over your heads – and please don't look up.' ...
>
> 'Madam forelady', I said, 'you might say six. You, sir' – I pointed to the guy next to her – 'might say three. Actually, there are none. Now you've been here for three days, coming and going. The entire room was in plain view, but the light fixtures weren't important to you. Just because you didn't guess correctly doesn't mean you weren't here!'

---

[87] See Packham, 'Critique', 8-13.
[88] Palmer, *The Logic of Gospel Criticism*, 33. Palmer states an historian in part asks, 'whether their story fits in with the other evidence'. See also Louis Gottschalk, *Understanding History* (New York: Alfred A. Knopf, 1960), 150.
[89] Packham, 'Critique', 11.
[90] ibid., 9. Whilst inerrancy is not a concern of this thesis it is interesting to note that Montgomery argues the same way when defending his commitment to this doctrine. John Warwick Montgomery, ed. *God's Inerrant Word* (Minneapolis: Bethany, 1974), 30-40.
[91] ibid.

> I get it; the jury got it. Just because Clancy was off by one hundred percent didn't mean he wasn't at the scene. Footage wasn't important; the accident was.'[92]

As mentioned, the principle is relied upon by legal apologists of considerable standing academically and as practitioners. Bauer even asserts, 'Generally speaking in a court of law, the more numerous and varied the individual facts are upon which a conclusion is based, the more likely it is to be correct.'[93] Montgomery's argument is valid, with a significant rider. And that is that though there may be differences in the telling of the events, contradictions and inconsistencies that bring into dispute the material fact in issue will have a profound effect on the weight given to the testimony, or even lead to its impeachment.[94] However, the issue must be significant and/or material.[95] *Cross on Evidence* states that the questions of a cross-examiner that may discredit a witness include questions, 'revealing errors, omissions, inconsistencies, exaggerations or improbabilities'.[96] And in such a cross-examination *Hampel on Advocacy* reminds that it is not usually necessary to do more than highlight the conflict between the witnesses to obtain the benefit of an apparent contradiction.[97]

The question is whether the differences in the testimony are significant and/or material and this will be considered shortly.

It could be argued against Montgomery that the gospel accounts do include verbatim accounts and therefore according to his own test this points to collusion.[98] In a non-technical apologetic the issue is a moot one as the long witness list for the death and resurrection of Jesus includes those whose experiences and observations would not lead to verbatim testimony. For example one has only to compare the possible testimony of Peter with Mary Magdalene, or with Joseph of Arimathea (Mark 15-16, John 18-20). For a technical apologetic with respect to the death of Christ there are issues, as indicated in the previous chapter, because of the similarities between the accounts of Matthew and Mark. Montgomery should restate his case and indicate that whilst lawyers prefer independent accounts verbatim stories are not *ipso facto* collusion.[99] Rather, they allow an

---

[92] Reed, *The Indictment*, 419-420.
[93] Bauer, 'The Logician's Model', 129.
[94] Ewen, *Faith*, 99-100.
[95] Glissan and Tilmouth, *Advocacy*, 106.
[96] Heydon, *Cross*, 480.
[97] Max Perry, *Hampel on Advocacy* (n.p. Victoria: Leo Cussen Institute, 1996), 60.
[98] Packham, 'Critique', 11.
[99] ibid.

adverse party in cross-examination of the witnesses to raise questions of collusion[100] and to seek to uncover inconsistency in the detail not fully covered in the prior testimony (gospel records). Witnesses in their collusion often fall into the standard trap of not covering all aspects of their story.[101] Obviously this cross-examination cannot happen with the witnesses whose accounts are found in ancient documents, and in such situations one has to rely on the general character of the witnesses as investigated in the earlier section – 'Internal defects in the witness himself'. In this regard the apologists can argue there are no grounds for collusion. However as was argued in the previous chapter, although the fact that Matthew and Mark are interdependent and perhaps rely on similar sources is not in itself a case of collusion, the verbatim nature of their testimony could mean that legally only one account could be used to substantiate John's account. This Montgomery and the legal apologists can concede.

The third issue is the most significant and it raises the issue as to whether the discrepancies and contradictions in the testimony of the non-technical legal apologetic are of the kind that one would expect in process of different witnesses telling their story, or whether they are significant and/or material discrepancies and contradictions that indicate the witnesses are confused or lying about what took place? As this is hardly a new issue in apologetics *per se*, the focus in this section will be on the legal implications.

John Shelley Spong outlines the common complaints.[102] John only has Mary Magdalene at the tomb, whilst the synoptics refer specifically to other women but appear to differ if Salome was one of them. (Matthew and Luke don't follow the Mark account here.) Spong acknowledges this contradictory data is not terribly significant, but it sets the scene. Then there is Mark's young man found at the tomb in contrast to Matthew's angel and Luke's two angels. As to the resurrection appearances, the gospels differ over what the women saw the first day of the week and with respect to the disciples there are different locations and times when Jesus appears and that Luke for example 'specifically denied the Galilean tradition'.[103] Spong holds, 'These texts reveal that within at most two generations of the original apostles, the Christian community could not agree on where the

---

[100] This is well illustrated by former trial lawyer D.W. Buffa. In one of his novels a witness goes through her story three times, including twice on cross-examination. 'When she repeated it a third time word for word, everyone knew she was telling a lie.' D.W. Buffa, *The Legacy* (Crows Nest, NSW: Allen and Unwin, 2002), 276.
[101] Givens, *Advocacy*, 73-75.
[102] John Shelley Spong, *Resurrection: Myth or Reality*? (New York: HarperSan Francisco, 1994), 101-105.
[103] ibid., 103.

foundational moment for that community's life had taken place. Where is reality? Objectivity? Truth?'[104]

Spong is correct that in isolation the contradictory data is often not significant, but on a cumulative basis there are at face value considerable differences in the accounts of what the witnesses allegedly saw. There are three principles that deal with this apparent conflict between witnesses that are consistent with Montgomery's general argument. These are: Is the alleged conflict of significance in the overall tenor of the case? Can the apparent inconsistencies in reality be explained by limited opportunities for observation, or genuine and honest mistake? Is it possible to reconcile these apparent conflicting accounts?[105] However, it must be remembered, 'a true inconsistency can effectively destroy a witness, and sometimes a whole case'.[106] In response to the three principles, a legal apologist can honestly state that the material fact in issue, the resurrection of Jesus, is affirmed by all the witnesses and that is the overall tenor of the case; that naturally the witnesses had at times limited and different opportunities for observation; and that scholars such as John Wenham and a number of legal apologists have shown how the resurrection accounts can be reasonably reconciled.[107] Montgomery also pleads the harmonisation principle as a legal hermeneutic in assessing the reliability of the gospel testimony.[108] In my legal apologetic supporting this approach I stated in part:

> The most detailed account of the empty tomb happenings is found in John. The other Gospels record part of what John states. While some have one angel and others two, there are simple explanations for this, one being there were different appearances; another, that one angel acted as spokesperson.
>
> One particular resurrection account of interest is Luke chapter 24. Unlike John, Luke does not record any appearance of the risen Christ in Galilee. Luke chapter 24 need not be a continuous narrative ... If that is so, there is sufficient time for the Galilean appearances. There was no obligation on Luke to schedule all of Jesus' resurrection appearances.[109]

---

[104] Ibid., 104.
[105] Perry, *Hampel on Advocacy*, 60.
[106] Glissan and Tilmouth, *Advocacy*, 106.
[107] Wenham, *Easter Enigma*; Robert Anderson, *The Bible and Modern Criticism*, 221-274; Greenleaf, *The Testimony*, 55-584. Montgomery also cites Wenham – *Tractatus*, 3.4444.
[108] See chapter 3, 'Legal Hermeneutic'; Montgomery, *Law and Gospel*, 25.
[109] Clifford, *The Case for the Empty Tomb*, 64.

Can the legal apologist confidently leave the matter there? I believe not. When the legal analogy is pushed beyound a *prima facie* case to an actual court hearing it fails to give due consideration to the process of cross-examination. Martin, focusing on the four gospel writers, illustrates one line of questioning:

> John, in your deposition only Mary Magdalene went to the tomb initially. Were there other women, as the other gospel writers testified? Can you explain why Jesus told Mary not to touch him as he had not yet returned to the Father, but then told Thomas to put his hands into Jesus' pierced body? And what were your sources for the story about the miraculous fishing trip, which appears only in your account of the risen Jesus? Did Peter or his family ask you to rehabilitate his reputation with this fabulous story?[110]

If the non-technical legal apologetic were focusing on the witness list rather than the gospel authors, another line of questioning could be:

> Q. Mary Magdalene it is your testimony that you were the first to the empty tomb. Is that accurate? (John 20:1-18).
>
> A. Yes
>
> Q. And it was your testimony that after that you immediately ran to Peter and another disciple and told them that 'They have taken the Lord out of the tomb, and we do not know where they have laid him.' (John 20:3). Is that accurate?
>
> A. Yes
>
> Q. Then after that you returned to the tomb and then Jesus appeared to you?
>
> A. Yes.
>
> Q. The witness known as the other Mary (Matthew 28:1-10) testified earlier that she was with you. Is that accurate?
>
> A. Yes.
>
> Q. Why didn't you testify to this when you first reported the incident. It is significant isn't it?

---

[110] Martin, *A Lawyer Briefs*, 110.

A. I simply then spoke of my own observations.

Q. Mary testified that you both saw Jesus before you went to Peter. That does not correspond with your recollection. Is that correct?

A. ...

In such questioning the points are made for argument later before a judge or jury, when focusing on such inconsistencies is a valuable impeachment technique.[111] The legal apologist would be very confident that the alleged inconsistencies could be harmonised[112] and answered in direct evidence or re-examination, or otherwise that the inconsistencies would not colour the tenor of the case and the weight given to the testimony. *After all the gospel witness list indicates that the testimony in support of the material fact in issue would be overwhelming.* As well it is only one aspect of a cumulative case. Yet it should be acknowledged that to hold that the alleged discrepancies in an actual juridical setting would not be significant, and have no bearing on the weight, is really beyond our experience. One's confidence in the testimony and character of the witnesses can still be firmly asserted in a non-technical apologetic, provided the legal analogy is not overstated.

'Conformity of the testimony with experience'. Montgomery does not interact with this criterion of Greenleaf in any detail in the third test of his fourfold criteria[113] but, as it will be shown, he is most aware of the significance of the issue. The test asserts that the veracity of the evidence in part depends on whether the facts testified about ordinarily occur in human experience.[114] This test is of significance in light of the supernatural nature of the resurrection event.

The legal apologists regularly encounter the argument that the astonishing resurrection event must be explained away as 'some form of hallucination or some pathological or psychic phenomena'.[115] This assertion can be answered in a negative apologetic framework by insisting that those who wish to legally impeach

---

[111] Leonard Packel and Dolores B. Spina, *Trial Advocacy: A Systematic Approach* (Philadelphia: American Law Institute-American Bar Association, 1984), 85.

[112] For example Matthew 28:1-8 enlarges on the events recorded in John 20:1-2. Matthew does not record the disciples going to the tomb (John 20:3-10) and takes up the story with Jesus appearing to the women (verses 9-10). There is in this case a gap between verse 8 and verses 9-10. See Orville E. David, *A Harmony of the Four Gospels*, 2nd. ed. (Grand Rapids: Baker, 1996), 211-215.

[113] However, as previously indicated Montgomery reproduces Greenleaf including this test. See Montgomery, *The Law Above*, 125-128.

[114] Greenleaf, *The Testimony*, 36.

the witnesses on such grounds carry the burden of proof.[116] As a mass hallucination is not a normal phenomenon it would be most difficult to prove. Habermas establishes that no sceptic has proved how the hundreds of witnesses to the resurrection could share in exactly the same subjective visual perception.[117] One is not confronting here an alleged mass suggestion (hypnosis) but an alleged mass visual experience that took place at different times and at different places.[118] In contrast to this lack of proof of hallucination, the legal apologist rightly points to the factual nature of the testimonial evidence. Montgomery maintains that the kind of evidence, which is considered in chapters two and three, reveals that the resurrection did happen in time and space and supports a biological miracle – not a psychological miracle.[119] He argues that clearly the intimate contacts that the eyewitnesses had with the resurrected Jesus, 'were not visions of the clouds whirling around and that sort of thing'.[120] Admittedly some legal apologists have taken a more positive apologetic approach to the hallucination theory by seeking to prove the resurrection is not an hallucination. Their arguments however have shown only a rudimentary understanding of the issues surrounding psychology and hallucinations.[121] The best apologetic legal model is to point to where the burden of proof lies with respect to hallucinations, and to then follow Montgomery and list the evidence in support of the resurrection.

Does the occasional lack of recognition of Jesus by the witnesses indicate that the gospel testimony does not conform to experience? Davis notes that there are several layers of explanations for this including: distance (John 21:4); confusion and lack of light (John 20:11-15); the suddenness of the appearances (Luke 24:36-37); the disciples own anguish, 'the fact that seeing Jesus alive again was the last thing they expected'; that their eyes were kept from recognising him (Luke 24:13-16), which one could argue is in itself not unlikely if the evidence supports the resurrection being a supernatural event![122] Admittedly such apparent satisfac-

---

[115] J.N.D. Anderson, *The Evidence*, 20. See also Craig, *The Historical*, which documents this is not a new argument and was responded to by apologists such as Paley (528-530).

[116] Magner, 'The Best Evidence', 72.

[117] Gary R. Habermas, 'Explaining Away Jesus' Resurrection: The Recent Revival of Hallucination Theories', *Christian Research Journal* 23, 4 (2001): 26-31, 47-49. Montgomery, *Tractatus*, 3.6341. Montgomery says of the sceptics' attempts, '"Plausible"? Hardly the critic attempts to practise psychology without a license.'

[118] Montgomery, *Tractatus*, 3.634 – 3.63413.

[119] Montgomery, *Human Rights*, 152.

[120] Montgomery, 'A Lawyer's Case', 15. See also Tabor, *Scepticism Assailed*, 274.

[121] J.N.D. Anderson, *The Evidence*, 20-23.

[122] Davis, '"Seeing" the Risen Jesus', 136-137.

tory explanations are another likely source an adverse party would pursue in cross-examination.

The more serious debate does not revolve around hallucinations, or lack of recognition, but simply whether the resurrection as an alleged supernatural event is automatically ruled out by this criterion. This is not the occasion to canvas all that Montgomery has written on miracles and the responses of other scholars to same. However, for background information, a brief uncritical outline of Montgomery's position on miracles, evidence and faith is in order before critically considering matters that relate specifically to the legal analogy. The best snapshot of Montgomery's thought is found in his paper 'Science, Theology and the Miraculous'.[123] There Montgomery states that a miracle is best regarded phenomenally as a *'unique, nonanalogous occurrence'*.[124] He defends the miracle apologetic against Hume's 'unalterable experience' argument, Flew's 'sophisticated' philosophical argument that miracles cannot be known historically, and McKinnon's resolve to treat all events as natural law. His own methodology in this context he applies to both the historical and legal apologetic:

> (1) the historian's knowledge of the general is never complete, so he can never be sure he ought to rule out an event or an interpretation simply because it is new to him, and (2) he must always guard against obliterating the uniqueness of individual historical events by forcing them into a Procrustean bed of regular, general patterns. Only the primary-source evidence for an event can ultimately determine whether it occurred or not, and only that same evidence will establish the proper interpretation of the event.[125]

---

[123] This paper was originally delivered at the Lee College Symposium on the Theological Implications of Science in 1977 and is reprinted in Montgomery, *Faith Founded*, 43-73. See also Montgomery, *Principalities,* 43-46; Montgomery, *Tractatus*, 3.671 – 3.691. For a response to Montgomery see Wykstra, 'The Problem', 154-163. Wykstra's article is a critique of Montgomery's miracle historical apologetic as found in *Where is History Going?; The Shape.* Montgomery's paper 'Science, Theology and the Miraculous' is also reprinted in the same volume of JASA (145-153). A further critique of Montgomery is Colin Brown's, *Miracles,* esp. 206-210. See also Mascord, *Faith, History,* esp. 65-80. For a legal assessment of the fact of miracles that relies in part on Montgomery's legal apologetic see Beckwith, *David Hume's,* 121-140.

[124] ibid., 50. Montgomery holds that a miracle can no longer be understood as a violation of natural law and following the lead of Holland redefines a miracle. See R.F. Holland, 'The Miraculous', *American Philosophical Quarterly* 2, 1 (January, 1965): 49.

[125] ibid., 57; Montgomery, *Human Rights,* 151-153.

Montgomery finds support for his argument in the fact that there are many significant historical happenings which are quite non-analogous to our present experience. One illustration of this that he proffers is Richard Whately's, *Historic Doubts Relative to Napoleon Buonaparte*, a tongue-in-cheek apologetic in response to Humean principles. Montgomery holds this to be a 'superlative tour de force' in apologetic literature[126] and Coady is likewise affirming when he states it is, 'a very amusing and perceptive application' of Hume's principles.[127] Whately writes:

> All the events are great, and splendid, and marvellous, great armies, - great victories, - great frosts, - great reverses, - 'hairbreadth scapes', - empires subverted in a few days; everything happened in defiance of political calculations and in opposition to the *experience* of past times; everything upon that grand scale, so common in Epic Poetry, so rare in real life; and this calculated to strike the imagination of the vulgar, and to remind the soberthinking few of the Arabian Nights. Every event, too, has that *roundness* and completeness which is so characteristic of fiction; nothing is done by halves; we have *complete* victories, - *total* overthrows, - *entire* subversions of empires, - *perfect* re-establishments of them – crowded upon us in rapid succession. To enumerate the improbabilities of each of the several parts of this history, would fill volumes; but they are so fresh in every one's memory, that there is no need of such a detail: let any judicious man, not ignorant of history and of human nature, revolve them in his mind, and consider how far they are conformable to Experience, our best and only sure guide. In vain will he seek in history for something similar to this wonderful Buonaparte, 'nought but himself can be his parallel'.[128]

Brown defines apologists who affirm Whately, such as Montgomery, Carnell and Geisler, as those who in this case rely more 'on the history of rhetoric and light entertainment' than serious scholarship.[129] He asserts they have confused two

---

[126] Montgomery, *The Suicide*, 43-44; Montgomery, *Tractatus*, 3.6721.

[127] Coady, *Testimony*, 187.

[128] Richard Whately, *Historic Doubts Relative to Napoleon Buonaparte*, 6th ed. (London: B. Fellowes, Ludgate Street, 1837). The monography is reprinted by legal apologist Craig Parton in his *Richard Whately: A Man for All Seasons* (Edmonton: Canadian Institute for Law, Theology, and Public Policy, 1997), 70-71. Parton did his M.A. Thesis on Whately under Montgomery.

[129] Colin Brown, *Miracles*, 146-147, 204.

categories of uniqueness: on the one hand there are reports of events without strict parallels that fall within the range of the normal experience, and on the other are events like miracles without any analogy with normal experiences.[130] Brown's objection may be relevant to the question of weight of evidence when one is engaged in epistemic discourse. It has already been argued that the legal apologetic should concede that more evidence is required to establish an event like a miracle than a report that may be within our range of normal experience, but without analogy. However, as Beckwith points out, for the evidentialist the argument is that events without analogy, whether they be astonishing events or not, unlike logically impossible events such as square-circles cannot be ruled out *a priori*.[131] Coady puts it, 'The point is that the lack of a suitable explanation of (astonishing) reports, other than their truth is a consideration against rejecting them, but it is only one consideration and is defeasible in various ways'.[132] Montgomery and the legal apologists as an evidential school properly see one such way as being reliable testimony as well as other categories of legal evidence.

A major premise behind Montgomery's position on miracles is that the shift from a deterministic Newtonian world view to an Einsteinian world view militates against Hume's argument that a miracle is contrary to an 'unalterable experience' and that Einsteinian relativity makes it inappropriate to speak of a miracle as a violation of a natural law as we are unable to assert that physical laws are absolute and unalterable.[133] Wykstra's response to Montgomery is that the 'correct epistemological moral to draw from the Einsteinian revolution is thus not: "Aha, now we see that miracles are possible after all!"; rather it is: "If we can no longer claim to *know* what natural processes in themselves are capable of producing, how can we know whether any startling anomaly is a miracle?"'[134] Montgomery no doubt again would reply in part on the fact that he is not advocating the Einsteinian world view to prove his case as such, but he is advocating that miracles cannot be ruled out *a priori* and 'the sheer nonanalogous uniqueness of Good Friday and Easter morning' stands before us an event of 'inherent, concrete character'.[135] It is because the evidence requires a biological rather than psychological miracle that he has taken that route.[136]

---

[130] ibid., 147.
[131] Beckwith, *David Humes'*, 95.
[132] Coady, *Testimony*, 198.
[133] Montgomery, *Faith Founded*, 49.
[134] Wykstra, 'The Problem', 156.
[135] Montgomery, *Faith Founded*, 72 and 51.

As to our focus, the legal apologetic, there are <u>four</u> not unrelated legal matters that arise with respect to the conformity of the testimony for the resurrection with experience. The first is the nature of the evidence itself. As will be discussed in chapter five in the section 'Law and Astonishing Events' Greenleaf and Montgomery rightly rely on the fact that the evidence was of an 'ordinary' kind that involved the senses. The witnesses saw, heard and touched the risen Christ. There is substantial evidence for the resurrection that doesn't require a prior commitment to a supernatural agency. It is empirical evidence that is based on observation that conforms with our own experience.[137] It is the meaning or inference the tribunal or jury draw from the facts that is the issue. Secondly, Ewen argues along similar lines to Montgomery's argument above, that is, the complexity of our universe and our biological systems, that at times defies understanding, does not stop scientists studying these. She notes that science has 'accepted that physical facts, or events, may exist without an understanding of their physical cause'. Therefore today, as science and history have advanced, the 'unknownable have become part of our everyday personal experience'.[138] Montgomery reflects, 'Unless we are willing to suspend "regular" explanations at the particular points where these explanations are inappropriate to the data, we in principle eliminate even the principle of discovering anything new.'[139]

Thirdly, as Greenleaf implies, this criterion is not irrebuttable: it is just one aspect of an extensive fivefold test, and a verdict that is against the evidence would be liable to be set aside. The plain testimonial evidence is that the resurrection occurred.[140]

The <u>fourth</u> matter is the most significant when considering this test and Montgomery's legal case on miracles. It is Montgomery's apparently insightful argument that collateral generalities cannot be introduced as evidence to obscure concrete evidence. Just as evidence of a person's character is not admissible for proving that he acted in conformity therewith on a particular occasion, similarly inadmissible is 'the ground that regular events in general make a particular miracle too "improbable" to consider'.[141] So just as a character trait is inadmissible

---

[136] ibid., 57; John Warwick Montgomery, *How Do We Know there is a God?* (Minneapolis: Bethany, 1973), 32-33; John Warwick Montgomery, 'The Reasonable Reality of the Resurrection', *Christianity Today* 24, 7 (4 April 1980): 16-19.
[137] Grieve, *Your Verdict*, 75; Greenleaf, *The Testimony*, 36; Montgomery, *The Law Above*, 125-131.
[138] Ewen, *Faith*, 105-106. See also a response to Hume on this point in Russell, *A Lawyer's*, 101-111.
[139] Montgomery, *Faith Founded*, 56.
[140] Greenleaf, *The Testimony*, 41-42.
[141] Montgomery, *Law and Gospel*, 34-35; Montgomery, 'Neglected Apologetic', 121.

to prove someone acted as a thief, so the arguments of Hume and others on the regular traits of the universe are inadmissible in deciding whether the resurrection occurred. Whilst this legal argument has merit there is a limitation that the legal apologists have not addressed: That is subordinate or collateral facts in certain circumstances may be in issue, for example, the evidence of a relationship that may make a witness biased.[142] And, as will be argued in chapter five, in the section on 'Law and Astonishing Events', there is some legal precedent for a tribunal not relying on evidence that is 'inherently incredible', i.e. something that does not appear to fit with what we know about the universe. By implication it could be argued that some tribunals may well be open to 'collateral generalities' as to the nature of the universe when considering an event such as the resurrection. Whilst Montgomery is entitled to argue against such a situation occurring, the reality is that some courts, even at the highest level, may well hold otherwise.

As a consequence, I believe Montgomery and the legal apologist cannot avoid the question of what in other circles is called background evidence. Background evidence may be equated to Montgomery's collateral generalities and is not the causal public evidence of detailed historical data. It is 'evidence from a wide area supporting a theory or theories about what normally happens'.[143] The classical argument of Hume of an 'unalterable experience' is background evidence. Once such background evidence is admissible, it will be a question legally of balancing it against the causal evidence. Swinburne's own position is that the solid causal evidence for the resurrection does not outweigh the background evidence if the latter is construed only on the basis of the laws of nature.[144] In a naturalistic world it is hard to find that a dead man could rise. However, Swinburne asserts Hume's 'worst' mistake was not to consider whether the laws of nature 'depend on something higher for their operation'.[145] Swinburne finds that the providential ordering of the world in various ways is best explained by the agency of God and the inductive evidence for his existence is more probable than not.[146] In light of the collateral evidence that supports both nature and God Swinburne concludes, 'I can only say that my own belief is that the historical evidence is quite strong, given the background evidence, to make it considerably more probable than not that Christ rose from the dead on the first Easter day.'[147]

---

[142] Heydon, *Cross*, 14-15.
[143] Swinburne, 'Evidence for', 194.
[144] ibid., 202.
[145] ibid., 198.
[146] ibid., 202. See also Richard Swinburne, *The Existence of God* (Oxford: Clarendon Press, 1979).
[147] ibid., 207.

Montgomery who is committed to the evidential approach of Swinburne, could join him to the extent of at least acknowledging that there is a need to allow for such background evidence. Montgomery has constantly opposed what he views as ultimately a presuppositionalist and/or Calvinist push of contemporary apologists to insist that, 'an independent theistic structure must be established to make any theological sense out of Jesus' resurrection'.[148] One of the reasons for Montgomery's reticence is that the historical resurrection apologetic operates for him as a proof for the existence of God. The verification of Christ's divine claims by his resurrection, proves there is a God.[149] And as I have briefly argued elsewhere, the critique of Sproul and others who argue the resurrection is not a valid proof raises an important question.[150] How is it they can offer the traditional theistic proofs (Cosmological and Teleological arguments) and Montgomery cannot offer an historical argument? All Montgomery is doing is arguing from effect (order of knowledge) to cause (order of reality) as they do themselves.[151] However, this is also another matter for consideration in its own right. Suffice it to say that, for the legal apologetic for the resurrection, Montgomery should concede that to pass the criterion of 'conformity of the evidence with experience', the background evidence is important. I am not suggesting here that he concede in other contexts his epistemological objections to a theistic structure. However without allowing for the possibility of discussion of the background evidence some sceptics will simply walk away from the legal apologetic, and with some justification, if the apologetic argument is relying on this particular criterion of the 'conformity of the testimony with experience'.[152] In this particular legal test the question of whether God exists is important, and it comes logically prior to considering other evidence. Practically this changes Montgomery's apologetic little as many unbelievers allow for the 'agency of God'.[153] And for those for whom the question of the existence of God is a necessary consideration he already has an appropriate apologetic in his repertoire that relies on arguments apart from the resurrection.[154] Inadvertently the secular legal fiction writer D.W.

---

[148] Montgomery, *Human Rights*, 156.
[149] Montgomery, *Faith Founded*, 58-63.
[150] Clifford, 'The Case of Eight Legal Apologists', 121-122.
[151] See Sproul, Gerstner and Lindsley, *Classical Apologetics*, 146; Norman L. Geisler, *Miracles and Modern Thought* (Grand Rapids: Zondervan, 1982), 66-75.
[152] Winfried Corduan, 'Recognizing a Miracle' in *In Defense of Miracles*, Geivett and Habermas, eds., 99-111.
[153] George Barna, *Evangelism that Works* (Ventura, California: Regel, 1995), 53-59.
[154] John Warwick Montgomery, 'Is Man his own God?', in *Christianity for the Tough Minded*, Montgomery, ed., 20-34. Beckwith who includes a legal defense of miracles adopts this approach based on a developed 'Kalam Cosmological Argument'. See *David Hume's*, 71-138.

Buffa provides one with a possible way forward. In a trial scene there is a debate over D.N.A. and the genetic code that leads the defence lawyer to suggest to an expert science witness, that God is the best explanation for this enormously complicated genetic design.[155] Clarrie Briese is one legal apologist who takes a similar route to Buffa,[156] and, as we will see in the next chapter, a simple teleological type 'proof' also appeals to the 'New Spirituality' seeker.[157] An argument for God's existence therefore can be naturally fitted into a legal apologetic, if required.

In his recently published text *Tractatus Logico-Theologicus* Montgomery has basically adopted the approach outlined in the above paragraph. Interacting with Swinburne he advocates 'interlocking natural theology' with the historical-legal case for the resurrection.[158] He states, 'That with all its limitation, the evidence supplied by what has been traditionally called "natural theology" is very powerful in supporting the existence of a transcendent God and in underscoring the meaningfulness of Jesus' historically attested claims to divinity.'[159] However, in his openness to the background evidence for the historical-legal apologetic he still vigorously opposes the classical apologist who insists that initially 'an independent Theistic Structure must be established to make sense of Jesus' claim to Deity and to give probative force to his resurrection'.[160] What Montgomery is clearly advocating is using 'natural theology' where it assists the discourse, as with respect to this legal criterion of 'conformity with experience'.

He is not conceding that such an 'interlocking' is a prerequisite to any apologetic, nor that one must begin one's apologetic by establishing a theistic structure. Whether one uses a theistic argument will depend on the circumstances and the questions of the listener or reader.[161]

---

[155] D.W. Buffa, *The Judgment* (Crows Nest, NSW: Allen & Unwin, 2001), 401-402. See also Charles Colson and Ellen Vaughn, *Gideon's Torch* (Dallas, London, Vancouver, Melbourne: Word, 1995), 517-519.
[156] Briese, 'Witnesses', 8-10.
[157] For example Wayne W. Dyer, *There's a Spiritual Solution to Every Problem* (Sydney: HarperCollins, 2001), 201-202.
[158] Montgomery, *Tractatus*, 3.8 – 3.8732.
[159] ibid., 3.87.
[160] ibid., 3.811.
[161] Montgomery's position is consistent with most evidentialists who are 'separate from classical apologists in that they think that a one-step argument from historical evidences (such as miracles) to God is feasible, and they often use this as their favorite argument. This does not, however, keep evidentialists from advocating the use of many other sorts of evidences and techniques, as their writings reveal'. Habermas, 'Evidential Apologetics', 98.

External defects in the testimony itself; or the coincidence of the testimony with collateral circumstances (cognitive faculty)

Chandler notes, as in this case, that this is the key test of credibility when a witness is dead and her evidence has been reduced to writing.[162] As no cross-examination of the witness is possible, testing the testimony against collateral external data is approaching functional equivalency. The reliability and trustworthy nature of the witness can be cross checked. Montgomery's argument here is symptomatic of the legal apologetic. It emphasises that unlike untruthful witnesses who seek to avoid detail that could lead to exposure, the gospel accounts and resurrection testimony are, 'replete with explicit references to secular personages, places and events'.[163] Collateral circumstances can be tested against the evidence. Montgomery illustrates by the fact that the doubts about Pontius Pilates' historicity were answered by the 1961 discovery at Caesarea of the 'Pilate inscription'.[164] Montgomery in his argument relies heavily on rightly-reputed evangelical scholars such as Blaiklock and Yamauchi.[165] Handley refers to the external evidence for existence of the village of Nazareth in the discovery in 1962 of a fourth century Jewish inscription near Caesarea, and that archaeological work in the old city of Jerusalem has confirmed much of the detail in the gospels and Acts.[166] To this type of list is often added data such as the references of Josephus and Tacitus to the person and death of Christ and in Josephus' case the belief about his resurrection.[167] Ewen has the most extensive analysis of this particular test.[168]

One is not seeking here to 'prove' the bible or to establish by this material that Jesus arose from the dead, but simply that the gospel writers and witnesses do not avoid detail, and much of what they record and say has been shown to be consistent with external data. Perhaps, in cross-examination Luke's census decree issued by Caesar Augustus (Luke 2:1-3) may come under examination, but it

---

[162] Chandler, *The Trial*, 1: 52.
[163] Montgomery, *Human Rights*, 143-144; Briese, 'Witnesses', 10-11.
[164] ibid., 144.
[165] Montgomery, *Human Rights*, endnote 269; E.M. Blaiklock, *The Archaeology of the New Testament* (Grand Rapids: Zondervan, 1970); Edwin M. Yamauchi, *The Stones and the Scriptures* (Grand Rapids: Baker, 1981).
[166] Handley, 'A Lawyer', 16. Handley in support cites Barnett, *The Truth*, see esp. 29-35; Bruce, *The New Testament*, 94.
[167] For example, Hailsham, *The Door*, 28-33; Roper, *Did Jesus Rise?*, 18-21. See Flavius Josephus, *Antiquities* XVIII 3.3; Cornelius Tacitus, *Annals* XV44.2-8. This historical detail is referred to in the previous chapter.
[168] Ewen, *Faith*, 107-142.

needs to be remembered Luke is not presenting as a witness as such, and this data is not relevant to Christ's resurrection.[169]

Summary

Montgomery's third and fourth tests affirm the life-like nature of the testimony of the resurrection witnesses. It can be properly argued that their 'discrepancies' have the 'ring of truth'. However, it should be noted that the character of the discrepancies could be tested in a cross-examination which again points to the apologetic advantages of limiting the legal analogy to a preliminary hearing. Conformity of the evidence with experience is a criterion legal apologists need not fear if their argument allows for the background evidence. Also the coincidence of the testimony of the resurrection witnesses with external accounts of personages, places and events in those days adds weight to their testimony.

Limitations Surrounding Eyewitness Testimony

A creative dimension Montgomery brings to the legal apologetic is his discussion as to the accuracy and reliability of eyewitness testimony.[170] He refers to genuine dangers that psychologists such as Elizabeth Loftus have identified in eyewitness testimony[171] Legal fiction writer Kate Wilhelm illustrates the problem:

> 'Mrs Leiter, you've made a positive identification, yet you can't say anything what he was carrying. Are you sure you got a good look at him?' 'Yes', she said. 'I really did. I saw him all over –

---

[169] However, it could be argued the accuracy or otherwise of the census details goes to the reliability of Luke as an historian and in his compiling of the witnesses' testimonies. Barnett argues despite the serious historical problems raised regarding the integrity of Luke 2:1-3, such as the absence of corroborative evidence of any decree from Augustus for a universal census, and the Josephus evidence of a Quirinius' census in Judea in AD 6/7, the possibility of Luke's historical accuracy should be kept open. Amongst other reasons for this is the fact that there are grounds for a case for an unknown census, including that such a census fits with Augustus' known practice, and that prōtē in Luke 2:2 in certain contexts has the nuance of 'former', and therefore Luke could be pointing to a less well known census than that conducted in A.D.6 (Acts 5:37). Barnett, *Jesus and the Rise*, 97-99. See also Montgomery, *Tractatus*, 3.44521 and Archer, *Encyclopedia*, 365-366. J.A. Thompson, former Chair of the Department of Middle Eastern Studies, University of Melbourne confirms Luke's general reliability. See *The Bible and Archaeology*, rev. ed. (Exeter: Paternoster, 1973), 405: 'Luke is shown to be a most careful recorder of information, whether it be matters of geography and political boundaries ... titles of local officers ... Asian or European towns'. Cf. Colin J. Hemer, 'Luke the Historian', *Bulletin of the John Rylands University Library*, 60 (1977): 35-37.
[170] Montgomery, *Human Rights*, 155-156.
[171] ibid., 155.

you know his whole body, the black pants and white shirt, but then I guess I really only looked at his face. That's how I am.'

During the recess, Frank said to Shelley, 'She's (Mrs Leiter) the worst possible witness. Honest, no axe to grind, no hidden agenda, just a good American housewife, who happens to be wrong, and will go to her grave convinced she's right.'[172]

Apart from Loftus there are a number of specialists and psychologists who, over the last hundred years or so, have entered the debate and who have carried out tests as to how well we observe people and their actions, as well as conducting extensive research on the difficulties surrounding eyewitness testimony. They have found the factors that influence its accuracy include: the difficulties people have in distinguishing among people of other races;[173] the stress and violence that often accompanies the observed event as well as the often brief duration of observation;[174] an unconscious transference where a person seen in one situation is mistakenly remembered by a witness as being in a different situation;[175] the high emotional loading of the incident that effects the error prone mechanism of perception and memory.[176] The number of witnesses involved does not necessarily alleviate the problems as research has shown that an observer can be persuaded to the majority opinion and that 'people can agree in error as easily as in truth'.[177]

Montgomery's presentation is that of an advocate before a jury. He affirms that eyewitness testimony, 'remains the cornerstone of legal evidence'.[178] Do the adverse findings on the strength of eyewitness testimony work against the case for Christianity or is there a category of eyewitness testimony that transcends this critical debate? The answer he gives is that there is. He notes there is one form of

---

[172] Kate Wilhelm, *For the Defense* (London: HarperCollins, 1997), 404-405.

[173] Elizabeth F. Loftus, 'Eyewitnesses: Essential but Unreliable', *Psychology Today* 18, 2 (February, 1984): 22.

[174] A. Daniel Yarmey and Hazel P. Tressillian Jones, 'Is the Psychology of Eyewitness Identification a Matter of Common Sense', in *Evaluating Witness Evidence*, Sally M.A. Lloyd-Bostock and Brian R. Clifford, eds. (Chichester, New York, Brisbane, Toronto and Singapore: John Wiley, 1983), 15-33.

[175] Elizabeth F. Loftus, *Eyewitness Testimony* (Cambridge, Massachusetts; London: Harvard University Press, 1979), 136.

[176] Brian R. Clifford and Ray Bull, *The Psychology of Person Identification* (London, Henley and Boston: Routledge & Kegan Paul, 1978), 214.

[177] Robert Buckhout, 'Eyewitness Testimony', *Scientific American* 231, 6 (December 1974): 28. Richard Ackland 'There's Life in the Marsden Monster Yet', *Sydney Morning Herald* (29 June 2001), 14: 'The Marsden judgement shows this (number of witnesses) could be faulty thinking. There is no safety in numbers, only in "facts"'.

[178] Montgomery, *Human Rights*, 155.

Limitations Surrounding Eyewitness Testimony 141

eyewitness testimony that is very difficult to impeach and that is the identification of a prior acquaintance. That is the testimony we have in the gospels, for example the disciple Thomas, and such testimony will withstand the 'power of persuasion' of an advocate that the witness identified the wrong person.[179] Those who identify the resurrected Christ were not mistaken as they knew him well previously and their eyewitness testimony is solid. This was either Jesus dead at point A and alive at point B or an hallucination. It could not be a case of mistaken identity resulting from a glimpse of some other passing figure.

The argument also indirectly answers the claim that as the resurrection was 'private' in nature and the appearances were to believers only, the testimony in support of the resurrection is less reliable.[180] In fact as Montgomery argues, the opposite is the case. The fact that the majority of the resurrection witnesses were prior acquaintances of Christ legally adds weight. They knew well the one they identified. It is appropriate to add to this argument of Montgomery's the fact that the appearances to Paul, the crowd of five hundred, James and Thomas indicate that not all the appearances were private and not all those who saw the risen Christ were initially believers (1 Corinthians 15:6-8, John 20:24-28). His resurrection appearances may not have been 'great and grandiose' but they were not simply of a nature private to those who were already convinced. There is a balanced testimony from both prior acquaintances and some outside of Jesus' circle.[181]

There are a number of issues, that emerge from Montgomery's argument, which are not addressed elsewhere. The first is the valid criticisms that can be made of the findings of psychologists such as Loftus. As many of the apologists who use the legal paradigm do not have Montgomery's legal mind, these criticisms need to be addressed to avoid their uncritically adopting his arguments. One criticism is the fact that the findings of psychologists in this area of eyewitness testimony are not uniform and there are contradictory results in testimony research.[182] Another criticism consists in methodological problems. Coady identifies, in this testimony research, *endemic* interpretative flaws and a strong ideological bias in much of the work.[183] His critique of the research of Loftus and her colleagues is

---

[179] ibid., 155-156.
[180] See Copan and Tacelli, *Jesus' Resurrection*, 134-135; Gerald O'Collins, *Jesus Risen* (New York/Mahwah: Paulist Press, 1987), 118-121.
[181] Davis, '"Seeing" the Risen Jesus', 131-132.
[182] David M. Saunders, Neil Vidmar, Erin C. Hewitt, 'Eyewitness Testimony and the Discrediting Effect' in *Evaluating Witness Evidence*, Lloyd-Bostock and Clifford, eds., 57-80.
[183] Coady, *Testimony*, 266-276.

extensive. He highlights one test that Buckhout advocates. A group of observers are given a brief glance of a display of twelve playing cards. They are asked, 'how many aces of spades did you see?' Most people report seeing three. Actually there are five in the display. Because people know aces of spades are black they tend to miss atypical red ones placed amongst the twelve. The conclusion is: 'prior conditioning and experience influence (eyewitness) perception'.[184] However, as Coady states, given the 'meaning-assigning conventions' of the poker pack there can be no red aces of spades. Hence, since there are only three (unambiguously definite) aces of spades, most of the subjects were right.'[185]

The above criticism of the 'witness of psychology' should not be taken as denying that there have been sensible findings, as listed above, that point to the conditions under which eyewitness testimony could be misleading. This is a fact which lawyers on the whole are aware of and accepting.[186] In the *Turnbull* case, whilst there appears overall confidence in eyewitness testimony, there are clear guidelines that include requiring the judge to withdraw the case from the jury if the case consists solely of poor quality evidence, such as a 'fleeting glimpse'.[187] However, this is a long way from claiming, as one hears some apologists say today, that 'eyewitness testimony of non prior acquaintances has been proved to be dangerous, so isn't it good (even providential) that the case for the resurrection is not based on this?' Such a generalisation is a likely defeater for any listener or reader with any legal background. Eyewitness testimony is not *a priori* unreliable; in fact the eyewitness identification of a non prior acquaintance may be reliable. Judges and juries will sift through the strengths and weaknesses of such evidence before reaching a decision about its weight.[188] So a concern is that some Christian apologists will be inadvertently misled by Montgomery's premise into overstating the case for the resurrection eyewitnesses in light of the possible limited nature of other cases of eyewitness testimony.

As Montgomery has brought into the debate concerns that psychology raises about the reliability of eyewitness testimony, at least in certain conditions, he faces three further issues. They raise questions that could work against his thesis

---

[184] Buckhout, *Eyewitness Testimony*, 25.

[185] Coady, *Testimony*, 271.

[186] McEwan, *Evidence*, 95-100. McEwan discusses the work of Loftus and the relationship between psychology and the law including the Devlin Report on the evidence of identification. For a critical assessment on psychol-legal reciprocity see William Twining, 'Identification and Misidentification in the Legal Process: Redefining the Problem' in *Evaluating Witness Evidence*, Lloyd-Bostock and Clifford, eds., 255-283; Clifford and Bull, *The Psychology*, 212-217.

[187] *R. v Turnbull and Others* 1976 3 All ER 549.

[188] Coady, *Testimony*, 275.

Limitations Surrounding Eyewitness Testimony

and as a result may indirectly support the hallucination theory. Has he opened Pandora's box? These issues need to be answered.

The first further issue is with respect to the gospel witnesses. Could it not be argued that the stress and emotional factors surrounding Christ's death makes their identification less plausible? As previously mentioned the number of witnesses does not necessarily assist here. Whilst this position could be argued, it is not likely to be given any weight. The fact that the resurrection appearances were not simply 'fleeting glimpses' but continued over a period of time; and the physical nature of them, as for example in Thomas' case (John 20:24-28), militates against such an adverse argument. Here the fact that the majority of the witnesses were prior acquaintances is most significant.

The second issue is of more weight. It relates to the appearance to Paul. It has been argued that Paul plays a significant part in the technical legal apologetic as, unlike the synoptic gospels, he offers admissible hearsay evidence for the resurrection. By turning to specialists and psychologists to support his case, has Montgomery inadvertently weakened the case for the reliability of the testimony of Paul? Do the length of time of Paul's observation, the less than ideal observation, conditions of light brighter than the sun (Acts 26:12-13), and Paul's own physical condition, (perhaps being tired from the journey he was on) as well as his being under the emotional and physical stress that one could presume accompanied his role as prosecutor and persecutor of Christians (Acts 26:9-11), act against his eyewitness identification of the risen Christ?[189] And Paul was not a prior acquaintance. One in rejoinder could argue that in Paul's case there was also a significant conversation with the risen Christ that identified the subject as well as the certainty of Paul's testimony. However, as seen in Kate Wilhelm's story, confidence in itself is no indicator of accuracy.[190] There is another important consideration and that is whether there is corroborating evidence.[191] The technical case for the resurrection does not turn solely on Paul's evidence or the other eyewitness testimony, and there is substantial circumstantial evidence that will be evaluated shortly which helps build a cumulative case for the resurrection. However, it again appears that to stretch the legal apologetic beyond the analogy of a *prima facie* setting is inappropriate in light of the conditions surrounding Paul's encounter. One can have great confidence in Paul's testimony, but there are questions that would inspire a robust cross-examination.

---

[189] Buckhout, 'Eyewitness Testimony', 24-26.
[190] McEwan, *Evidence*, 96.
[191] ibid., 96-97; Loftus, *Eyewitness Testimony*, 188.

The third issue relates to the testimony of prior acquaintances and the weight Montgomery places on this. In support of his argument he cites the text *Eyewitness Testimony*.[192] However, the authors of it do note that a lawyer for an adverse party is not without a line of argument in such a scenario. They state that a lawyer seeking to overturn the eyewitness testimony of a prior acquaintance could point out a human tendency, 'shared by all to some degree, to believe that we have seen what we expected to see, even though we in fact observed something or someone quite different'.[193] In Christ's case the nature of evidence, the numbers of witnesses involved, as well as the character of the 'prior acquaintance' relationships strongly militates against this argument, but it should be countered when arguing the case.

Montgomery's delimitation, on eyewitness identification of non-acquaintances, is a unique and potentially valuable contribution to the legal apologetic. In a non-technical apologetic it can be argued that one has good reliable eyewitness evidence for the resurrection as it is that of prior acquaintances. However, the legal apologist must not overstate the difficulties surrounding other eyewitness testimony. And for the legal apologetic the introduction of psychological and specialist insights on eyewitness testimony inadvertently raises issues about Paul's testimony that would provoke debate as to its reliability. These are issues that the technical legal apologist must address because of the primacy of Paul's evidence.

Things

Cross on Evidence defines things or 'real evidence'[194] as, 'anything other than testimony, admissible hearsay or document, the contents of which are offered as testimonial evidence examined by the tribunal as means of proof'.[195] According to Phipson, the preferred definition is, 'material objects, other than documents, produced for the inspection of the court'.[196] The real evidence in Cross's broader definition would incorporate the demeanour of the witnesses for the resurrection, or a 'view' of the actual tomb, and while such evidence would be applicable 2000 years ago, it is not evidence that today's apologist can produce.[197] There is one material object, exhibit, that some apologists rely on as real evidence. It is the Shroud of Turin. If it can be proved to be the burial clothes of Jesus, the myste-

---

[192] Montgomery, *Human Rights*, 155-156.
[193] Arnolds, Carroll, Lewis and Seng, *Eyewitness Testimony*, 387.
[194] Also called autoptic preference.
[195] Heydon, *Cross*, 59.
[196] Howard, Crane and Hochberg, *Phipson*, 4.
[197] Heydon, *Cross*, 49-50.

rious Shroud would be admissible for inspection, since any relevant kind of fact, 'cognizable by the senses of the tribunal may thus be offered'.[198] It would be the equivalent of the blood stained knife in a murder trial.

Val Grieve, relying on Stevenson and Habermas argues there are eight parallels between the death of Jesus and the 'death' of the figure on the Shroud.[199] Grieve wrote before the 1988 carbon-14 dating tests, although he was aware of the decision of the Catholic Church to allow these. He concluded, 'In the meantime, it can be argued that there is so far strong evidence to suggest that the Shroud is that of Jesus, through which he passed when he rose from the dead'.[200] Interestingly, Habermas still retains the Shroud in his apologetic even if he uses the more cautious language of, 'The Shroud may supply some additional scientific evidence for Jesus' resurrection'.[201] Ewen is another who makes a case for the Shroud, however she includes it in her discussion on the coincidence of the gospel testimony with collateral circumstances.[202]

Montgomery does not plead real evidence and there is no discussion about the Shroud. No doubt this is because Montgomery's commitment in his legal apologetic is to rely on the best evidence and not to 'muddy the waters' with contentious material that is of questionable value.[203] Montgomery is correct in not calling any 'things' in support of his case. The Shroud if used at all would at best be an 'appendix'. It is not an item of evidence, or proof, showing that the fact in issue is more probable. The listener or reader is unlikely to rate the Shroud that highly when making belief judgements. If he or she is not aware of the material that disputes the alleged origins of the Shroud, an adverse party would soon correct that. The list of witnesses would include Walter McCrone, an expert in microanalysis and painting authentication, whose chemical tests on the Shroud found that the blood image area consists of dilute paints of common usage during the Middle Ages.[204] Another would be Vaughn Bryant, Professor of Anthropol-

---

[198] Wigmore, *Evidence in Trials at Common Law*, Vol. 4, rev. James H. Chadbourn (Boston and Toronto: Little, Brown, 1974), 327.
[199] Grieve, *Your Verdict*, 86-96. See Kenneth D. Stevenson and Gary R. Habermas, *Verdict on the Shroud* (Ann Arbor: Servant, 1981).
[200] ibid., 95.
[201] Habermas, *The Historical Jesus: Ancient Evidence for the Life of Christ* (Joplin, Missouri: College Press, 1996), 282 and see 177-184, 254. See also Phillip H. Wiebe, 'Evidence for a Resurrection', *Journal of Christian Theological Research* 6, 2 (2001), http://home.apu.edu/~CTRF/jctr.html. Wiebe states the Shroud has value in showing that Jesus died as it is evidence of a person having 'weakly dematerialized'.
[202] Ewen, *Faith*, 131-137.
[203] Montgomery, *Defending the Biblical Gospel, Study Guide*, 9-10.

ogy and Director of the Pollen Laboratory at the Texas A. & M. University. Bryant critiques Max Frei's method of collection of the pollen samples off the Shroud which are the basis for his much relied on findings that the Shroud was in Palestine and Turkey. Ewen relies in part on the pollen images.[205] Bryant's own conclusion is that he does not believe that the current pollen studies can be used to authenticate the Shroud. His finding is in part based on the following observation about Frei's methodology:

> I have spent more than 30 years in pollen research and in the teaching and training of graduate students. For over a decade I have been conducting forensic pollen studies for federal, state and private agencies both in the United States and abroad. I have sometimes used sticky tape pulls to collect surface pollen and dust from a crime scene, and I have found that making precise pollen identifications from such sticky tapes is often problematic at best.[206]

Other expert witnesses from the laboratories at Oxford University, University of California at Berkeley, University of Arizona and the Zurich Institute for Middle Energy Physics could be called to show that their radiocarbon procedure dated the shroud to an average of AD.1325 ± 65 years.[207] There is also the substantial issue of the Shroud's provenance. Unlike the gospels, the Shroud cannot be traced back to the event in issue. Real evidence is of little value unless accompanied by evidence identifying it as the object in question: the graveclothes of Jesus Christ.[208] Also, if one cannot establish its provenance, there is little weight in asserting that the image upon the Shroud corroborates that Christ was crucified in a way consistent with his time. Even the Shroud's leading advocate, Ian Wilson, concedes the Shroud has only been 'historically known' for six hundred years.[209] No doubt in response to these expert witnesses others could testify positively to the pollen evidence and to the problems surrounding the radiocarbon

---

[204] Walter C. McCrone, *Judgement Day for the Shroud* (Chicago: McCrone Research Institute, 1996), 145-149.
[205] Ewen, *Faith*, 135.
[206] Vaughn M. Bryant, 'Does Pollen Prove the Shroud Authentic?', *Biblical Archaeology Review* 26, 6 (November/December 2000): 41-42. Bryant is responding to a more favourable response to the pollen evidence published by the Missouri Botanical Gardens. See Avinoam Danin, Alan D. Whanger, Uri Barueh and Mary Whanger, *Flora of the Shroud of Turin* (St. Louis: Missouri Botanical Garden Press, 1999).
[207] ibid., 39.
[208] Heydon, *Cross*, 50. See John 20:6-7.
[209] Ian Wilson, *The Blood and the Shroud* (London: Weidenfeld & Nicolson, 1998), 111-123.

dating, such as that the heat of the 1532 fire which scorched the Shroud and that may, as a consequence, have increased the carbon 14 content of the linen resulting in a misleading finding.[210] Yet, even with such rebuttal evidence, this material object is still surrounded with mystery. And the apologist who enters this field will then have to field questions from those who have read the more sensational tomes that claim everything from the Shroud being the work of Leonardo da Vinci to finding that it establishes Jesus was still alive when he was laid in the tomb and that therefore Paul's atonement doctrine is an unwarranted embellishment.[211]

In the legal apologetic one should follow Montgomery's lead and not plead the Shroud as real evidence. It no doubt is of interest to many and still may play a limited 'appendix' role in apologetics. In addition, the legal apologist may well find himself in a negative apologetic paradigm refuting the writings of those who use the Shroud to counter the case for orthodoxy.

Circumstantial Evidence

The case for the resurrection to date has rested on the facts in issue (Jesus dead at point A and alive at point B) being perceived, either by a group of eyewitnesses (non-technical apologetic) or else by the maker of a statement which is admissible under the ancient documents exception to the law against hearsay (technical apologetic). However, as in most actual cases, the admissible, relevant and credible evidence relied on by the legal apologists is not just proof from testimony and documents, but one that incorporates circumstantial evidence. Circumstantial evidence can be defined as any fact (evidentiary fact) from the existence of which the jury or judge may infer the existence of a fact in issue (principal fact). It usually consists of a number of items pointing to the same conclusion.[212] Grieve comments on the strength of circumstantial evidence:

> In fact, sometimes it is even better, as direct evidence can be more easily fabricated than a strong chain of circumstantial evidence (e.g. proof of purchase of a gun by an accused charged with murder, his finger prints on the gun which is the murder weapon), which is nearly always conclusive.[213]

---

[210] For discussion of the testing procedures see ibid., 179-194.
[211] See Lynn Picknett and Clive Price, *Turin Shroud in Whose Image?* (London: Corgi, 2000); Holger Kersten and Elmar R. Gruber, *The Jesus Conspiracy: The Turin Shroud and the Truth About the Resurrection* (Shaftesbury, Dorset; Rockport, Massachusetts; Brisbane: Element, 1994).
[212] Heydon, *Cross*, 16-17.

For some the word 'chain' is not the most appropriate metaphor. Justice Handley illustrates by stating that in Australia the standard direction to juries about circumstantial evidence has been that given by Chief Baron Pollock in *Regina v Exall*:

> It has been said that circumstantial evidence is to be considered as a chain, and each piece of evidence as a link in the chain, but that is not so, for then, if any one link break, the chain would fall. It is more like the case of a rope comprised of several cords. One strand of the cord might be insufficient to sustain the weight, but three stranded together may be quite of sufficient strength. Thus it may be in circumstantial evidence – there may be a combination of circumstances, no one of which would raise a reasonable conviction, or more than a mere suspicion; but the whole taken together may create a conclusion of guilt with as much certainty as human affairs can require or admit of.[214]

For circumstantial evidence to be sufficient, the 'rope' of evidence must be more probable than any other alternative and the inference sought must outweigh all other contrary inferences.[215]

The Circumstantial Case

In some sense, even the direct evidence for the resurrection is circumstantial. There is no direct eyewitness testimony of the event itself. The direct evidence is of Jesus being alive after the event, and a resurrection is an inference. However, when the legal apologists speak of circumstantial evidence they are focusing on the 'evidentiary facts' concept referred to above. I have listed elsewhere,[216] the circumstantial argument which normally includes a number, if not all, of the following strands:

> 1) The empty tomb and the only hypothesis that fits the facts is that Christ arose.[217]

---

[213] Grieve, *Verdict on the Empty Tomb*, 14.
[214] *R. v Exall* (1866) 4 F & F 922 at 929 (176 ER 850 at 853). See Handley, 'A Lawyer', 19-20.
[215] Gard, *Jones*, 4: 301-304.
[216] Clifford, 'The Case of Eight Legal Apologists', 139-140.
[217] Crispin, *The Resurrection*, 17-32.

The Circumstantial Case   149

2) The fact that Christians worship on Sunday and not the Sabbath. Only an event of deep significance could cause Jewish observers to make such a commitment.[218]

3) The fact that the tomb of Christ was not subject to early pilgrimages of worship.[219]

4) The existence of the Church (Christianity) whose origins can be traced to the resurrection of its founder.[220]

5) An unbroken chain of testimony from the disciples to today of changed lives that find their new meaning in the resurrection.[221]

Not all of the legal apologists place equal weight on the circumstantial evidence in their argument. The Greenleaf 'school' appears to focus more on the testimony and documentary evidence[222] in line with Greenleaf's own argument.[223] One can speculate on why this is so, but perhaps it is nothing more than the fact that as in Greenleaf's case, the defence of scripture and its gospel accounts against Deists or the likeminded is their primary mission. Montgomery, as one in this 'school', also does not develop the circumstantial case to the extent others do. An exception is his argument from the empty tomb where he relies on Frank Morison.[224] In Montgomery's case one may further speculate that he limits his excursion into circumstantial evidence[225] because his Lutheran roots ensure his preference is *Sola Scriptura*.[226]

Enhancing the case

With respect to Montgomery's circumstantial evidence apologetic, I believe there are a number of ways to enhance his case whilst still focusing on the pri-

---

[218] J.P. Moreland, 'The Circumstantial Evidence' in *The Case for Christ*, Strobel, 250-252.
[219] J.N.D. Anderson, *The Evidence*, 24.
[220] Grieve, *Your Verdict*? 83-85.
[221] Handley, 'A Lawyer', 17-18.
[222] For example, Ewen, *Faith* has little argument (160-165). Russell, *A Lawyer's* likewise has little discussion, but does mention the growth of Christianity and its effects upon the world (171-201).
[223] Greenleaf, *The Testimony*.
[224] Montgomery, 'A Lawyer's Case', 15-16; Montgomery, *Law and Gospel*, 35; Montgomery, *Human Rights*, 151-153; Montgomery, 'Neglected Apologetic', 122-123. See Morison, *Who Moved the Stone*? 146-166.
[225] Montgomery, *Tractatus*, 3.12511.
[226] John Warwick Montgomery, 'Lutheran Theology and the Defense of the Biblical Faith' in Montgomery, *Faith Founded*, 129-153. Also Montgomery points to the Jewish tribunals first century preference for direct evidence, not circumstantial evidence. See Montgomery *Tractatus*, 3.12514

macy of the direct eyewitness, documentary evidence. The first is that he could give more weight to the circumstantial argument. With the exception of point one above (the empty tomb), the argument is unlikely to receive criticism from biblical/historical scholarship as the stated evidentiary facts are difficult for even a sceptic to deny. They are straightforward matters. It does not require the critical assessment that the documentary and testimonial evidence calls for. In the next chapter it will also be argued that aspects of the circumstantial case are significant in the apologetic to 'New Spirituality'.[227] Historical apologists such as Paul Barnett effectively argue that the significant facts of transformation in the disciples and the existence of Christianity are best understood in the light of the momentous event of the resurrection which is the principal fact in issue. Admittedly, one could argue that causally these two facts could be interpreted as simply proving the early Christians' belief that Jesus was risen (psychological state).[228] However, the most probable explanation in light of the five cords of evidence is an actual resurrection event and this is confirmed by the direct evidence.[229] Norman Anderson is just one legal apologist to effectively argue this way from the circumstantial evidence.[230] Swinburne expands the fact of worship on the Sunday argument to include the sacrament of communion. His position is that this undisputed early historical event is a fact from which it can be inferred that the apostolic eyewitnesses celebrated and acknowledged that Jesus had risen from his death on that day. His argument has a further step which actually brings this evidentiary fact closer to the ultimate inference drawn from the principal fact in issue, and by so doing he increases the force of his circumstantial argument and limits the number of possible causes (explanations).[231] He asks, who is the likely source of this Sunday tradition?

He suggests the post-resurrection eucharist meals in the Lucan tradition (Acts 10:41) provide evidence that the risen Jesus gave meaning to the synoptic accounts of the institution of the last supper. Further, Paul lists his eucharistic instruction as being from Jesus (1 Corinthians 11:23) and as there is no synoptic evidence as to when the eucharist should be celebrated, a post-resurrection instruction is the most plausible.[232]

---

[227] See also Ross Clifford and Philip Johnson, *Riding the Rollercoaster: How the Risen Christ Empowers Life* (Sydney: Strand, 1998), 35-51.
[228] Wiebe, 'Evidence for a Resurrection', s. 22 - 23.
[229] Bishop Dr Paul Barnett, interviewed by the author (radio station 2CH, 8 April 2001). See also Habermas, 'Evidential Apologetics', 114-115.
[230] J.N.D. Anderson, *The Evidence*, 24-28. For further references see the endnote references above in support of the five strands of circumstantial evidence.
[231] Heydon, *Cross*, 16.

The Circumstantial Case

The second suggestion relates to the empty tomb. Montgomery's *res ipsa loquitur* argument is set out shortly. The gist of it is that it would have been counter-productive for the Roman or Jewish authorities to remove the body, and the disciples would not have stolen it, 'then prevaricated, and finally died for what they knew to be untrue'.[233] His finding has influenced other evangelists and apologists[234] and is a standard approach in apologetic discourse.[235] This argument is a 'cord' of significant weight. It draws a strong finding by the legal apologists: 'The empty tomb, then, forms a veritable rock on which all rationalistic theories of the resurrection dash themselves in vain'.[236]

Montgomery and the legal apologists however need to briefly address possible rejoinders the listener or reader may raise as to the fate of Jesus' body. They would certainly surface in a 'hearing' with an adverse party. The source of the rejoinders are 'Christian' and the majority are available in the popular market. Both Crossan and Spong argue that Jesus was never in a tomb. Crossan asserts the custom was to leave the victim's body for the wild beasts and birds of prey.[237] Spong states the custom for common criminals was to place their body in a mass grave. He concludes, 'His (Jesus) body was probably dumped unceremoniously into a common grave, the location of which has never been known – then or now.'[238] If we can prove that he was buried in a tomb there is still the argument mentioned in the previous chapter that the earliest account, being the Pauline pericope of 1 Corinthians 15 verses 3 to 8, knows nothing of the empty tomb tradition. For Lorenzen God can raise up new bodies, as he will in the resurrection of the dead, without the material of the old. So, the theology of 1 Corinthians 15 does not require an empty tomb for Jesus' resurrection and is in fact absent in Paul.[239] Lorenzen concedes the empty tomb narratives serve 'a legitimate and theological function' but they do not provide historically verifiable proof and it is a late tradition.[240] And then there is the swoon theory. Montgomery does address this naturalistic theory, that is as old as Venturini, by interacting with Schofield's *Passover Plot*.[241] His response is appropriate. It is that the hypothesis

---

[232] Swinburne, *Evidence for*, 207-212.
[233] Montgomery, *Law and Gospel*, 35.
[234] For example, Joel Edwards, *The Cradle, the Cross and the Empty Tomb* (London, Sydney and Auckland: Hodder & Stoughton, 2000), 142-144.
[235] McDowell, *The Resurrection*, 90-102.
[236] J.N.D. Anderson, *The Evidence*, 20.
[237] Crossan, *Jesus: A Revolutionary Biography*, 123-127.
[238] Spong, *Resurrection*, 225.
[239] Thorwald Lorenzen, *Resurrection and Discipleship* (Maryknoll, New York: Orbis, 1995), 174-181.
[240] ibid., 180-181.

is possible, but it is not the most probable. It is inconsistent with the other testimony, documentary and circumstantial evidence and is not therefore in accord with the evidence. It is often the naturalistic brief for those sceptics who struggle to acknowledge the supernatural.[242] The swoon theory asserts that despite the massive injuries Jesus suffered – hit about the face with a staff, cruelly flogged, crucified with nails and a spear to the side – he boldly appeared in a few days pretending that he was resurrected. This argument is not a serious defeater for the experienced apologist. Even the leading sceptic David Strauss had this to say of the swoon theory:

> It is impossible that a being who had stolen half dead out of the sepulchre, who crept about weak and ill wanting medical treatment, who required bandaging, strengthening and indulgence, and who still at last yielded to his sufferings could have given the disciples the impression that he was a conqueror over death and the grave, the Prince of life: an impression which lay at the bottom of their future ministry.[243]

Justifiably Handley, in the spirit of Montgomery, answers rejoinders like those above with the following:

> Reputable historians and courts work with the evidence; they don't alter it. The theories of so-called scholars 2,000 years after the events of the first Easter, which are not based on the historical evidence and are inconsistent with it, do not deserve to be taken seriously.[244]

A more considered defence in answer to Spong and Crossan could cite Joseph of Arimathaea. He is a central figure in Christ's burial (John 20:28-42). Raymond Brown states, 'That the burial was done by Joseph of Arimathea is very probable, since a Christian fictional creation ... of a Jewish Sanhedrist who does what is right is almost inexplicable, granted the hostility in early Christian writings toward the Jewish authorities responsible for the death of Jesus'.[245] Paul Gwynne also states, 'Arimathaea is a very obscure place without the biblical significance

---

[241] Montgomery, *Human Rights*, 152-153. For a developed theory see Michael Baignet, Richard Leigh and Henry Lincoln, *The Holy Blood and the Holy Grail* (London: Jonathan Cape, 1982), 308-319.
[242] See Thiering's elaborate swoon theory in *Jesus*, 121-125.
[243] David Friedrich Strauss, *The Life of Jesus for the People*, Vol I, 2nd ed. (London: William and Norgate, 1879), 412.
[244] Handley, 'A Lawyer', 19. Cf. Montgomery, *History and Christianity*, 40.

or symbolic value that one might expect in an apologetically inspired legend'.[246] This tradition therefore has the 'ring of truth'.[247] If the burial story was a fabrication why not simply leave it to Jesus' family and friends? It is the extra data given that could be rebutted and one does not expect such from false accounts. Further, it could be argued that the disciples and followers would be interested in seeing Jesus properly buried. There was a Jewish custom of preserving the graves of their holy men and it is unlikely Jesus would have been left for the dogs or consigned to a common pit.[248] In fact the Jewish law required that the corpse of an executed criminal, 'shall not remain all night upon the tree, you shall bury him that same day' (Deuteronomy 21:22-23). Brown observes that in the Qumran Temple Scroll and the writings of Philo this legal requirement of immediate burial applied equally to a crucifixion.[249] These facts lead Brown to conclude, 'That Jesus was buried is historically certain.'[250]

The case for the burial of Jesus should then plead the *'sine qua non approach'*.[251] This states that the early proclamation in Jerusalem that Jesus is resurrected would have obviously been risky, ludicrous and impossible if his grave were still occupied or his body were known to have been lying around somewhere.[252] Montgomery states 'not a word of refutation' comes from external contemporary sources.[253] Gwynne finds this argument is potent, even allowing for the considerable diversity, 'in the way people imagined resurrection, reflecting the complex mix of groups and theological schools that comprised Jewish religious society'.[254] The evidence supports the fact that this plea by the disciples for resurrection would have involved in most people's mind a corpse being transformed (Matthew 28:11-15. Cf. Daniel 12:1-3).

---

[245] Raymond E. Brown, *The Death of the Messiah: A Commentary on the Passion Narratives in the Four Gospels*, the Anchor Bible Reference Library, Vol. 2 (New York, London, Toronto, Sydney, Auckland: Doubleday, 1994), 1240.

[246] Paul Gwynne, 'The Fate of Jesus' Body: Another Decade of Debate', *Colloquium* 32, 1 (May 2000): 8. Gwynne's article is a useful overview of the whole debate to which I am indebted.

[247] William Lane Craig, 'John Dominic Crossan and the Resurrection' in *The Resurrection*, Davis, Kendall and O'Collins, eds., 256-257.

[248] William Lane Craig, 'The Empty Tomb of Jesus' in *In Defense of Miracles*, Geivett and Habermas, eds., 251.

[249] Raymond E. Brown, 'The Burial of Jesus (Mark 15:14-47)', *Catholic Biblical Quarterly*, 50 (April 1988): 233-245.

[250] Raymond E. Brown, *The Death*, 2: 1240.

[251] Gwynne, 'The Fate', 16-21.

[252] Byrskog, *Story*, 192-194.

[253] Montgomery, *Tractatus*, 3.4524.

[254] Gwynne, 'The Fate', 17. See also James D.G. Dunn, *The Evidence for Jesus* (Louisville: Westminster Press, 1985), 66-67.

As to the Pauline account, Craig's rebuttal to critical scholarship on the empty tomb is that the grammatically unnecessary threefold 'and that' in 1 Corinthians chapter 15 verses 3 to 5 is meant to underscore Jesus' burial as well as his death, and resurrection appearances. Here the burial and resurrection are connected. As well Paul in his letters uses the analogy, 'we were entombed with him' (Romans 6:4, Colossians 2:12). Jensen asserts here, 'It was not merely from death that Christ was raised up, but from the tomb'.[255] Whilst these references probably relate to baptism, again it does not seem possible to argue that Paul knew nothing of the empty tomb of Jesus. Further, when one compares Paul's speech in Antioch (Acts 13:29-30) with the gospel accounts, there is a 'perfect concordance' with those narratives on Jesus' crucified body being laid in a tomb and it being resurrected, followed by appearances. This makes it beyond doubt that Paul handed on the tradition of Joseph laying Jesus' body in a tomb and that that body was resurrected.[256]

There is another hypothesis for the empty tomb that is not normally raised by Montgomery and the legal apologists but could be addressed. And that is that grave-robbers were responsible. Craig is one apologist who argues there is no real evidence for this theory, but there are positive considerations against it. The case against includes: there is no motive as little of value was interred with the body; only a small band of followers, and Joseph, knew the exact location of the tomb; the proposed theft would have had to have been decided on and carried out within twenty-four hours or so as the tomb was empty on the Sunday morning; The presence of grave clothes in the tomb argues against this hypothesis (John 20:6-7). As mentioned above it is hard to believe if this hypothesis is true it would not have surfaced in response to the early proclamation by the disciples of the resurrection.[257] Again as Montgomery would say, in light of the cumulative evidence, the theory is possible but not probable.

I believe the legal apologetic case is stronger when the case for the laying of Jesus' body in a tomb is argued in more detail. It should be pointed out that the critics of the New Testament accounts of the fate of Jesus' body are not in agreement in their hypotheses of what occurred. This makes light of their suggestion that their own individual hypothesis is the common understanding of what happened to Jesus' body, or of what they claimed was the common burial practice for criminals. The critics cannot agree amongst themselves.

---

[255] Jensen, 'History and the Resurrection', 348.
[256] Craig, 'The Empty Tomb', 249. Cf. Gerald O'Collins, 'The Resurrection: The State of the Questions', in *The Resurrection*, Davis, Kendall and O'Collins, eds., esp. 13-17.
[257] Craig, 'The Empty Tomb', 259-261.

The Circumstantial Case 155

The third point relates to Montgomery's use of the proof of *res ipsa loquitur* – the event (facts) speak for themselves. *Res ipsa loquitur* is not a rule of law but a principle of evidence that assists plaintiffs in negligence actions where there is an inability to establish the exact cause of the accident.[258] This was confirmed in a recent Australian High Court case, *Schellenberg v Tunnel Holdings Pty. Ltd.* where it was stated that the *res ipsa loquitur* principle is, 'not a distinctive, substantive rule of law, but an application of an inferential reasoning process, and that the plaintiff bears the onus of proof of negligence even when the principle is applicable.'[259] The *Schellenberg* case sets out a useful history of the doctrine. It is helpful to restate Montgomery's proof which is set out in chapter two:

Res ipsa loquitur in typical negligence cases

1. Accident does not normally occur in the absence of negligence.

2. Instrumentality causing injury was under the defendant's exclusive control.

3. Plaintiff did not himself contribute to the injury.

Therefore, defendant negligent: „the event speaks for itself."

Res ipsa loquitur as applied to Christ's resurrection

1. Dead bodies do not leave tombs in the absence of some agency effecting the removal.

2. The tomb was under God's exclusive control, for it had been sealed, and Jesus, the sole occupant of it, was dead.

3. The Romans and the Jewish religious leaders did not contribute to the removal of the body (they had been responsible for sealing and guarding the tomb to prevent anyone from stealing the body), and the disciples would not have stolen it, then prevaricated and finally died for what they knew to be untrue.

Therefore, only God was in a position to empty the tomb, which He did, as Jesus Himself had predicted, by raising Him from the dead: „the event speaks for itself."[260]

---

[258] David Baker, *Introduction to Torts* (North Ryde, NSW: The Law Book Company, 1985), 8-13.
[259] *Schellenberg v Tunnel Holdings Pty. Ltd.* [2000] HCA 18 (13 April 2000) 2 at 7 per Gleeson C.J. and McHugh J.
[260] Montgomery, 'Neglected Apologetic', 122-123.

Montgomery applies the rule in different contexts. At times he appears to be using it in a technical legal apologetic sense indicating the doctrine proves his point.[261] In other contexts the same argument appears to work more as an analogy showing how the nature of the thinking encapsulated in the principle can be applied to apologetic and theological reasoning.[262] In his primary legal apologetic in *Human Rights and Human Dignity* he does not use the terminology of *res ipsa loquitur* at all, nor is his presentation as detailed, however he still cites the argument that the Romans and Jewish leaders and the disciples would not have taken the body and concludes, 'Ergo – by process of elimination – Jesus rose from the dead just as the firsthand accounts declare.'[263]

As will be discussed, Montgomery's unique reliance on *res ipsa loquitur* should be focused on its educative role. There are a number of reasons for this. Firstly, this rule is limited to the law of tort and is not found in other civil or criminal courts.[264] It is a leap to place the case for the resurrection into a negligence suit with analogies of plaintiffs suing defendants for damages. The 'negligence' of God is not the issue here.

Secondly, as Montgomery acknowledges, the analogy requires the tomb to be under God's exclusive control.[265] The evidence he pleads in support is the tomb being sealed and that Jesus the sole occupant was dead. With respect to the sealing of the tomb Montgomery no doubt is relying on Matthew 27 verses 62-66, a section peculiar to Matthew. Here Matthew narrates how Pilate told the chief priests and Pharisees to take a guard and secure the tomb. It is a clear apologetic argument added by Matthew to refute criticisms that someone could have taken the body.[266] However, there are difficulties with this passage from a technical, legal apologetic perspective. Matthew's unique section is hearsay at a technical level. And this is true also at a non-technical level unless one is arguing that Pilate or a pharisee is added to the witness list, possibly as a hostile witness. As well whilst e;cete (*echoed*) is best and most logically translated *you may have* guards indicating Pilate supplied non-Jewish troops, it could be translated in the indicative indicating that the Jews were to supply their own temple guards.[267] The uncertainty about the guards raises questions over the nature of the seal. Many

---

[261] Montgomery, 'Neglected Apologetic', 122-123; Montgomery, *Tractatus*, 3.666 – 3.6662.
[262] Montgomery, *Law and Gospel*, 35.
[263] Montgomery, *Human Rights*, 152.
[264] Peter Gillies, *Criminal Law*, 2nd. ed. (North Ryde, NSW: The Law Book Company, 1990), 18-22.
[265] *Anchor Products Ltd. v Hughes* (1966) 115 CLR 493 at 497 per Windeyer J.
[266] David Hill, *The Gospel of Matthew, the New Century Bible Commentary* (Grand Rapids: William B. Eerdmans; London: Marshall, Morgan & Scott, 1972), 357.

apologists place great weight on the custom of the day with respect to the role of elite Roman guards and the security of a Roman seal.[268] Further Matthew acknowledges there was a gap between the time Jesus was placed in the tomb and the placing of the guards indicating there was a time when the tomb was not under God's exclusive control (Matthew 27:57-62). For the argument from *res ipsa loquitur* to be technically applicable the apologist must establish the exclusive control of the tomb. It is doubtful this stringent requirement can be proved. This does not mean a general apologetic and a legal apologetic cannot make note of the guards and seal in their cumulative case for the resurrection of Jesus.[269] Such argument has some weight irrespective of establishing exclusive control.

Thirdly, for the doctrine to be applicable the occurrence that gives rise to the alleged negligence must lie within the experience of the lay person or the 'common knowledge of mankind'. So for example an unexplained sway or jerk by a car travelling in an ordinary way in ordinary conditions is an occurrence within common experience. An empty tomb is not.

It could be argued that expert evidence is allowed to assign a probable cause to an occurrence not within one's experience, in this case the empty tomb, but then one would have to ask how far one should really push this legal analogy.[270]

Fourthly, by relying on this doctrine the legal apologist could be unwittingly creating an obstacle in the mind of the listener or reader. Irrespective of the merits of the case the general trend in negligence cases has been for verdicts more sympathetic to plaintiffs.[271] It could be argued therefore by an adverse party, that with an event of the semantic strength of the resurrection a more rigorous proof than one resting on a negligence principle like *res ipsa loquitur* is needed to establish probability. Finally, in some jurisdictions the maxim is treated as 'expired' and it is held that one should just weigh the circumstantial evidence with any direct evidence to determine the facts, without any reference to the maxim.[272]

However, in a general, legal apologetic Montgomery's argument has real validity as an educational tool on evidence. It would be best used in the circumstantial

---

[267] For a discussion see R.T. France, *Matthew, Tyndale New Testament Commentaries* (Leicester: Inter-Varsity; Grand Rapids: William B. Eerdmans, 1985), 404-405; Frederick Dale Brunner, *Matthew*, Vol. 2 (Dallas, London, Vancouver, Melbourne: Word, 1990), 1071.
[268] For example, McDowell, *The Resurrection*, 54-59.
[269] See Paul L. Maier, *First Easter* (New York: Harper & Row, 1973), 111-122.
[270] For a discussion on the law on this point see *Schellenberg v Tunnel Holdings Pty. Ltd.* at 11.
[271] Fleming, *The Law*, 292.
[272] *Fontaine v British Columbia* (Official Administrator) 1998 1 SCR 424 at 435.

case to illustrate that law is not adverse to making a determination where there is no direct evidence of the cause, in this case the cause of the resurrection. The principle could be used as a response to those who query: 'Where is the proof of cause?' Also it may assist in explaining the general method of legal thinking, that is the relationship between presumptions and facts, and further what relevant circumstantial facts need to be proved in order that the ultimate fact in issue can be deduced. In this event, rather than *res ipsa loquitur* operating as a proof its role is educative as to an inferential reasoning process. This model is more in line with the argument in *Human Rights and Human Dignity*. The circumstantial argument in a non-technical or technical apologetic therefore should not specifically rely on the proof of *res ipsa loquitur* but the evidentiary facts in support of the resurrection.[273] All the evidentiary facts should be pleaded, not just the empty tomb, as one strand of the cord may be insufficient, but the five stranded together are of quite a different strength.

Summary

Most legal apologists, technical or non-technical, call on the proof of testimony and circumstantial evidence. The Montgomery and Greenleaf criteria are strong apologetic tools to test the competency and truthfulness of same. However, serious issues will arise if one seeks to claim that the criteria take one further than a case to answer, or the avoidance of a non-suit. The criterion of the conformity of the testimony with experience requires the apologist to address, where necessary, the existence of God in his legal apologetic. When the circumstantial evidence is also fully pleaded the legal argument for the resurrection is certainly one that warrants an answer.

Reframing the Legal Apologetic

Our considerations allow us to reframe the technical and non-technical apologetic of Montgomery and the legal apologetic school and, by so doing, outline paradigms that are apologetically consistent with the legal analogy and the evidence. It is not the intention here to restate all the issues raised to date, since the detailed argument in support of the premises is found in chapter two and this chapter. This reframing is a broad outline of possible future directions. It applies

---

[273] A secondary role for the principle of *res ipsa loquitur* is not inconsistent with the law of evidence. It can operate as a fall back position if an attempt to establish negligence on direct proof fails. See Baker, *Introduction to Torts*, 11.

to both the *negative or defensive* apologetic (defence of the resurrection in response to critical arguments)[274] and the *positive or offensive* apologetic (presentation of the resurrection case).

The Technical Apologetic

The setting. A *prima facie* level, be it a lawyer preparing a hypothetical case for trial, or a preliminary hearing (in appropriate jurisdictions that legislate for this). In the latter case the question is posed, is there a case to answer and should this matter therefore proceed to trial or a full tribunal hearing?

The question of proof. 'Proof' here refers to a civil standard, i.e. the making of a belief judgement in accordance with the preponderance of evidence: namely, 'What is more probable?' In view of the semantic strength of the claim of the resurrection, and it being an astonishing report, it is acknowledged that a listener or reader may well be more cautious than is normal in determining whether the burden of proof has been met.

The brief. Firstly, the material facts are stated. They are that in or about April A.D. 33, Jesus of Nazareth was executed by Roman authorities upon a cross at Golgotha near Jerusalem. The said Jesus Christ was seen alive some days later by various witnesses. There is circumstantial evidence in support of the material issue of the resurrection.

Secondly, the apologist will prepare a case to answer for the death of Christ. The court will be asked if it will be taking judicial or historical notice of this fact. Historical documentary evidence that one could use to make such a finding, or to refresh one's memory, includes the writings of Tacitus, Josephus and Luke's gospel. The brief should indicate what should be pleaded if the court wants proof admitted into evidence. There is direct documentary evidence in support. The documentary evidence consists in the appropriate eyewitness sections in the books of Mark and John. Matthew is also tendered but it may not be admissible because of its interdependence with Mark.

Thirdly, the brief will set out that the best direct documentary evidence for the resurrection of Jesus is the testimony of John and Paul (not the synoptics apart possibly from the 'M' pericope of Matthew 28:16-20).[275] The evidence is rele-

---

[274] An aspect of Christian witness that is often overlooked is the element of readiness for cross-examination. See A.R. Tippett, *Verdict Theology in Missionary Theory* (South Pasadena: William Carey Library, 1973), 58-59.

vant as it is observations about the facts in issue. In the brief it is argued that one can have confidence that this testimony will be found to be competent and truthful when it is evaluated by the appropriate Montgomery criteria. The criteria are the *internal and external defects in the witness himself on the one hand and in the testimony itself on the other*. In a worldview that allows for God, the testimony is in conformity with experience. Considerable weight should be given to this testimony. Further, the testimony of John is unlikely to be mistaken eyewitness testimony in view of his being a prior acquaintance.

Fourthly, the brief should prepare an argument for why this hearsay evidence of Mark, (Matthew), John, and Paul should be admitted. These offer firsthand reports within admissible documents under the 'Ancient Documents' rule. Provenance is an essential issue in establishing the authentication, and therefore the admissibility, of ancient documents. Therefore a probable chain of evidence is outlined showing that the copies we now have can be linked to the originals. It is stressed that normally only the firsthand accounts within the documents are admissible. However, one only has to prove that it can be reasonably supposed to be firsthand. To establish the evidence as firsthand, the dating and authorship of Mark, John and 1 Corinthians are shown to support eyewitness accounts. Secondary sources such as Suetonius, Tacitus, Pliny the Younger, Josephus, Rabbi Eliezer and the Talmud are noted as providing some corroboration. The apologetic case can then show that this firsthand hearsay is not totally dependent on the 'Ancient Documents' rule for its admissibility. It could be argued that the evidence is admissible as an historical record because it has been shown to be trustworthy, relevant and material. Here again the provenance of the documentary evidence and the credibility and truthfulness of the witnesses is mentioned.

Fifthly, the technical apologist, following Montgomery, will avoid in the brief an argument or pleading relating to 'things' such as the Shroud of Turin.

Sixthly, the apologist will prepare a case for proof by the circumstantial evidence. The weighing of the documentary (direct evidence) and circumstantial evidence is what determines the facts. The circumstantial evidence is the existence of the church, the empty tomb, Sunday worship, the fact that the tomb was not subject to pilgrimages, and an unbroken chain of testimony. The empty tomb case needs to prove that Jesus was actually dead in the tomb and to do so will have to set out answers to critical arguments propounded by scholars such as Spong, Crossan, Thiering and Lorenzen. The role of Joseph of Arimathaea and the *sine qua non*

---

[275] Also possibly James – see chapter two 'A Point for Further Research: The Letter of James'.

The Technical Apologetic 161

approach are two strands in such a case. Montgomery's unique pleading of *res ipsa loquitur* as a helpful legal analogy for inferential reasoning should be cited.

Seventhly, a summation is stated that there is admissible, relevant and credible evidence that supports the fact that Jesus was dead at point A (beyond resuscitation) and alive at point B.

Rejoinders and apologetic integrity

Apart from the legal epistemological questions already referred to, there are a number of other matters the technical apologist should list as rejoinders or issues in his brief that one should address and be prepared for even at a preliminary hearing. This should form part of the apologetic.

Firstly, the brief must mention that the admissibility of the accounts under the 'Ancient Documents' rule is a matter of law to be decided by a judge. Even if a judge admitted the evidence on a *prima facie* level on the basis that it was 'fair on the face' and from 'reasonable custody', there would be considerable ongoing debate on admissibility and the weight to be given to this evidence. Therefore, to equip the listener or reader (jury) to decide on weight, the objections to the 'Ancient Documents' rule outlined in chapter two should be considered as they would surface in the case.

Secondly, caution should be exercised in implying that once an ancient document is found to be 'fair on the face' the onus is on the adverse party to rebut the evidence. Also the brief should avoid stating that there is a presumption of truthfulness for witnesses. However, In both the case of admissibility and truthfulness, the apologist can claim there is an equal burden on the adverse party in establishing her case against Christ. With respect to the reliability of the memory of the witnesses, the onus is on the apologist in the brief to establish sufficient memory of the events in issue. This is not a difficult task.

Thirdly, the technical apologetic, at its best, should focus on the firsthand accounts within the gospels and Paul. Multiple hearsay is inadmissible in some jurisdictions, and, if admissible, is unlikely to be given the same weight in such a significant issue.

Fourthly, the Montgomery criteria used to evaluate the trustworthiness of the testimony does raise issues as to honesty, motive, and discrepancy in the testimony. As well there are questions over Paul's observation in light of the psychological evidence that Montgomery has cited. Even at a *prima facie* level the rejoinder of a possible adverse party on such criteria should be identified and addressed even if it is unlikely to be raised before trial. This is important for the integrity of the apologetic argument and again it is the kind of material a lawyer would want in his brief so he would be prepared for the trial.

The Non-Technical Apologetic

The setting and **the question of proof** as for the technical apologetic.
The brief. Firstly, the witness list comprises the disciples, Paul, James, 'the five hundred', Mary Magdalene, the other Mary, the followers on the road to Emmaus. (If a trial concerning the resurrection had been held in Jesus' day, based on today's standard of proof, their evidence would have been admissible as they were eyewitnesses.) It is also appropriate to argue the substantial weight that should be given to the testimony of the women to the resurrection appearances. They give an unbroken chain of testimony to Jesus' death, burial and resurrection, evidence that has a 'ring of truth' as women were not considered reliable witnesses at that time.[276] This is relevant evidence as all the testimony consists in observations about the facts in issue.

It is trustworthy as it passes the Montgomery tests. A case is prepared with these witnesses to come before the court. Further, there is the fact that most of the witnesses are prior acquaintances and they would not be mistaken in their identification of the risen Christ.

Secondly, these witness accounts are found in reliable documents that show good provenance, transmission and corroboration from external sources. (The apologist should develop the documentary argument as outlined in the previous chapter in the section on provenance).

Thirdly, the case for the circumstantial evidence is developed in the brief along the same line as in the technical apologetic.

Fourthly, a summary is given that there is relevant and trustworthy evidence to support the fact that Jesus was dead at part A (beyond resuscitation) and alive at point B.

Rejoinders and apologetic integrity
Firstly, it should be acknowledged that much of this testimony is hearsay evidence. It is not covered by documentary exceptions to hearsay, and even if one

---

[276] See Pinchas Lapide, *The Resurrection of Jesus* (Minneapolis: Augsburg, 1983), 97-99.

'Commonly Agreed Facts' Apologetic

relies on the analogy of these witnesses being able personally to come before a court in Jesus' day, the witnesses were not cross-examined.

Secondly, the apologetic must not advocate, in its brief generalisations, the legal admissibility of all of the gospels and in particular of Luke's gospel.

Thirdly, as in the technical apologetic, the criteria used to evaluate the testimony of the witnesses raises issues of honesty, motive, and discrepancy in the testimony. Again, even at a *prima facie* level, the apologist in his brief should indicate to the listener or reader how these issues are to be addressed.

Fourthly, the preferred position is that the hostile witnesses to Jesus' death and resurrection are not pleaded as a cross-examination when discussing admissibility of the evidence. However, this fact can be raised when arguing for the honesty and motive of the witnesses as it goes to the weight to be given to the testimony.

'Commonly Agreed Facts' Apologetic

Mention has been made of Habermas' and Moreland's 'minimal facts' position.[277] The legal apologist could in future pursue its case on this paradigm as well. Habermas and Moreland suggest that there is a 'minimal facts' argument that both disproves naturalistic hypotheses, as well as establishing that the resurrection of Jesus is the most probable explanation of the data. They claim this 'minimal facts' position receives the support of critical biblical-historical scholarship and satisfies the standard of proof required for the Christ event. The five crucial facts are:

> (1) Jesus' death by crucifixion; (2) the earliest disciples' experiences that they thought were appearances of the risen Jesus; (3) their subsequent transformations to the point of even being willing to die for their faith; (4) the resurrection as the very centre of early apostolic preaching; and (5) the conversion and resulting transformation of Paul.[278]

Three of the five facts are already substantially dealt with in chapter two and this chapter. The first two are not subjects of great controversy. The three facts are: Jesus' death by crucifixion; the disciples' subsequent transformation; the conver-

---

[277] See the section 'Luke's Gospel' in chapter 2.
[278] Habermas and Moreland, *Immortality*, 69-70. See also Habermas, 'Evidential Apologetics', 114-115. In the later reference Habermas adds Jesus' brother James to point (5).

sion and transformation of Paul (and James). As the Pauline evidence is not about the nature of his encounter with the risen Christ, but his conversion experience, it also will not evoke much controversy. A technical or non-technical apologetic brief could readily argue the proof of these three facts at a *prima facie* level. A fourth fact is that the resurrection is at the very centre of early apostolic preaching, and this is also argued in chapter five in the section on 'Scriptural Support'. The final fact consists of the early resurrection experiences that the disciples thought were appearances of the risen Christ. At a technical level one has John's gospel. However, as one is arguing here about the disciples' mental state and not the fact of the appearances themselves, Mark and Matthew are relevant, non-hearsay accounts, provided authorship of the disciples is established. The possible difficulties relating to Matthean authorship have been canvassed, but the legal apologists would confidently assert Peter's influence on Mark's gospel, and here we see in Mark's description of the resurrection events something of Peter's state of mind about these events (Mark 16:1-8). Further, relying on what has already been argued in chapter two, one could argue that a court take historical notice of the disciples' state of mind as gleaned from the books of Luke and Matthew. It is not a fact that would demand firsthand hearsay, as it is not seeking to prove an astonishing report, but a state of mind. It is submitted that the 'minimal facts' position could be proven at a technical legal level.

The legal apologist in the future could well begin her case by presenting a technical legal apologetic based on the 'commonly agreed facts' paradigm. Arguably it could be in the context of a full hearing and not just at a *prima facie* level, as the issues surrounding the admissibility of the documents and the cross-examination of the witnesses are less likely to be a concern, when the fact of the resurrection appearances is not the issue. Yet one would still have to be prepared to openly interact with the issues surrounding the admissibility of the ancient documents and their provenance.

It is conceivable however, that a number of listeners or readers would still not be satisfied that the apologist relying on the 'minimal facts' premise had met the burden of proof in light of the semantic strength of the claim.[279] This is my own apologetic experience with 'tough minded' sceptics. And no doubt some would argue: 'If a broad spectrum of biblical scholarship accepts the "minimal facts" position, why is it that a substantial number of scholars still question the resurrection?'[280] So, a fairly argued technical or non-technical apologetic on the fact

---

[279] For a discussion see Habermas and Moreland, *Immortality*, 71-72.
[280] This point is made by Boa and Bowman in *Faith*, 218.

of the resurrection itself, rather than the witnesses' state of mind, is a necessary complementary argument for those who find that Habermas' and Moreland's case does not in itself warrant belief in the resurrection.

Chapter 4

Montgomery's Legal Apologetic and 'New Spirituality'

'New Spirituality'

One can imagine an anticipated reaction to the previous chapters being as follows: does Montgomery's legal argument hold any apologetic sway for the spiritual seeker of the third millennium? It has already been noted that James Fairbanks planted a doubt in his positive affirmation of Montgomery's legal apologetic which included the reflection that its persuasiveness to those in a postmodern world is 'unfortunately problematic'.[1] Whilst Fairbanks' initial impressions are understandable they are for two reasons not justified.

Firstly, a premise of this chapter is that not all postmodern spirituality is totally divorced from the possibility of some factual grounding. The guru of 'New Spirituality', Deepak Chopra, begins his influential book, *How to Know God* by dipping into the legal analogy: 'although it does not seem possible to offer a single fact about the Almighty that would hold up in a court of law, somehow the vast majority of people believe in God …'. He goes on to ask what the facts would be like if we had them.[2] Clearly, although Chopra is not aware of a proof at hand for God's existence that would satisfy the juridical test, he does not dismiss, *a priori*, such an approach.[3] In fact Chopra goes on to discuss how indicators like quantum physics, the big bang theory, and near death experiences give us insights about our unity with God as well as revealing that the universe is not simply mechanistic.[4] James Redfield in his New Age classic, *The Celestine Prophecy*, takes a similar apologetic course,[5] as does Wayne Dyer in acknowledging that his movement from a 'soft' agnosticism was the result of teleological 'proofs', even though he still holds that knowledge achieved by 'realization' (trusting our own personal experience) is of a higher order than intellectual reasoning.[6] The way some within 'New Spirituality' revert to, or rely on, some factual discussion will be

---

[1] Fairbanks, review of *Christians*, 177. See Introduction.
[2] Deepak Chopra, *How to Know God* (London, Sydney, Auckland, Johannesburg: Rider, 2000), 1.
[3] 'New Spirituality' advocate Trenoweth exhibits a similar outlook when she states, 'Yet Christianity requires a leap of faith of such magnitude that I feel that I must parcel up all reason and leave it on the far side of some rocky gorge.' See Samantha Trenoweth, *The Future of God* (Alexandria, NSW: Millennium, 1995), x.
[4] Chopra, *How to Know God*, 267-305.
[5] James Redfield, *The Celestine Prophecy* (Sydney, Auckland, Toronto, New York and London: Bantam, 1993), 41-43.
[6] Dyer, *There's a Spiritual Solution*, 201-202 and 6-7.

highlighted in the case study herein. My experience is that many seekers are 'both/and' and not 'either/or' when it comes to 'modernity' and 'postmodern' spirituality.[7] In fact DiZerega speaks of the 'enormous blessings' of the Enlightenment and talks of his pagan spiritual perspective in the context of offering a, 'fitting corrective to the excesses of the Enlightenment and post-Enlightenment modernity'.[8]

The second reason that Fairbanks' impressions are not justified is that Montgomery's legal apologetic can be reframed for this so called 'postmodern world'. Such a reframing will rely on gleanings from Montgomery's writings. From his early years Montgomery has had a broad interest in, and openness to, occult phenomena including para-psychologies, fairies, alchemy, astrology and theosophical writings that have led to his building an extensive library on occult topics.[9] And at this stage it is also interesting to note that Montgomery in the early 1970's was already predicting the need for a subjective apologetic in light of the alienation many felt from the 'juggernaut of scientific technology' and the 'ideals of scientific objectivity'.[10] The legal apologetic is just one model that can interact with this new quest for meaning. Further, in all of this Cole claims: 'our society is inhabited by modernists and postmodernists'.[11] The legal apologetic still speaks today as many are still influenced by reason and argument.

Background to 'New Spirituality'

Prior to a consideration of an apologetic model directed towards 'New Spirituality' based on Montgomery's own methodology, it is important to outline what one means by this term. The current phenomenon of 'New Spirituality' is not a field on which Montgomery has written substantially. Certainly, as stated, over the years he has looked into the occult and disciplines now found in 'New

---

[7] In support see Dan Story, *Christianity on the Offense: Responding to the Beliefs and Assumptions of Spiritual Seekers* (Grand Rapids: Kregal, 1998), 24.
[8] Gus DiZerega, *Pagans and Christians: The Personal Spiritual Experience* (St. Paul: Llewellyn, 2001), 224.
[9] Montgomery, *Principalities*, 11-21.
[10] John Warwick Montgomery, 'The Apologetics of Eucatastrophe' in *Myth, Allegory and Gospel*, John Warwick Montgomery, ed. (Minneapolis: Bethany, 1974), 20. In fact Montgomery's essay in this book, 'The Chronicles of Narnia and the Adolescent Reader' (97-118) which explores the literary apologetic and the place of subjective universal symbols in folklore and fairytales with their possible relationship to apologetics, first appeared in 1959. See *Religious Education* 54, 5 (September-October 1959): 418-428.
[11] Interviewed in Stephen Liggins, 'Reaching Out in a "Christ-Conscious" World', *Southern Cross Quarterly* (Winter 1999): 2.

Spirituality', and his insights will form a base for later discussion. However, for a comprehensive understanding of the world of 'New Spirituality' we should also look to other sources and authorities.

'New Spirituality' is a movement better known in Christian circles by titles that incorporate the words 'New Age'. In the mood of this spiritual expression an appropriate start would be to hear the global reflections of some of its devotees. The English novelist Phil Rickman in his 'spiritual thriller', *The Midwinter of the Spirit* neatly sums up, through a young character Jane, what New Age spirituality means to so many of her peers:

> The New Age is about ... it's about millions of people saying: I want to know more ... I want an inner life ... I want to commune with nature and the cosmos and things, find out about what we're really doing here and who's running the show, and like what part I can play in the Great Scheme of Things.[12]

Marty Kaplan, a former speech writer for Vice-President Walter Mondale and a Hollywood screenwriter and producer, states how he thought he would spend his life as, 'a cultural Jew, an agnostic, a closet nihilist. Of course I didn't like it. Who wants to face death without God? But the alternative – faith – was unavailable to me.' Then he took up meditation and was awakened. Now he says, 'The God I have found is common to Moses and Mohammad, to Buddha and Jesus ... I used to think of psychic phenomena as New Age flim-flam ... Now I know there is a God.[13] Australian journalist Ruth Ostrow puts it this way:

> At the recent Metaphysical Mastery conference I find 8000 people just like me, gathered at the Entertainment Centre in Sydney, having paid up to $500 a head to believe in 'this sort of nonsense'.
>
> Visiting members of New Age royalty – Louise Hay, Wayne Dyer, an austere looking Deepak Chopra – confirm what people sitting in the audience have come to hear: that magic exists. That the soul never dies ...
>
> I don't know if there really are fairies and gnomes at the bottom of my garden. I don't know if I should be spending up big on New Age rhetoric. I don't know where my aunt, my father or those poor souls washed away in Switzerland have really gone.

---

[12] Phil Rickman, *Midwinter of the Spirit* (London: Pan, 2000), 39.
[13] Marty Kaplan, 'Ambushed by Spirituality', *Time* (24 June 1996), 92.

But faced with the prospect of my mother's prognosis – 'worms' – well, call me a child, a sucker, a disgrace to my profession, but I'll stretch my imagination and wallet in the direction of magical possibilities any day.[14]

Characteristics of 'New Spirituality'
To date a number of descriptions have been used, 'New Spirituality', 'Postmodern Spirituality' and 'New Age'. The term New Age is not currently favoured. The preferred expressions include: 'New Consciousness', 'New Sense', 'New Edge', 'Next Age', 'Aquarian Age', 'Postmodern Spirituality' and 'New Spirituality'.[15] The numerous 'name tags' point to the evolving nature of this spirituality that for some has already taken us to a 'post New Age' movement which phenomenologically describes the larger field of 'modern religious experimentation' and in turn embraces many forms of 'alternative' spirituality.[16] What one can say for certain is that many in the West 'do' religion differently today. They follow a connected spirituality that because of its eclectic, evolving nature is very difficult to define.[17] This is partly because within it there are few empirical marks as is the case with Christianity such as a founder-figure, a Church, an authoritative text, and a Nicene creed. However, even though this work cannot be a thesis on 'New Spirituality' as such, it is important to have some approximate 'definition' of a philosophy before considering one's apologetic response to it.

One mark of 'New Spirituality' that meets with common agreement is its *eclectic* nature. Neville Drury, an occultist and authority on occultism, sees this as one of its major tenets.[18] The leading consumer-predictor Faith Popcorn, states that people will continue to develop personalised faiths by blending parts of belief systems and rituals; and concludes, 'Customised bibles will be created merging passages from Animism to Zen'.[19] Johannes Aagaard speaks of a 'Pacific paradigm', a trans-syncretism that fuses eastern mysticism and western capitalism. This paradigm places no limitations on human capacity and therefore it fits well with

---

[14] Ruth Ostrow, 'Call Me Cosmic Any Day', *The Weekend Australian* (21-22 August 1999), 30.
[15] John A. Saliba, *Christian Responses to the New Age Movement* (London: Geoffrey Chapman, 1999), vii-ix.
[16] Saliba, *Christian Responses*, viii; Steven Sutcliffe and Marion Bowman, eds., *Beyond New Age: Exploring Alternative Spirituality* (Edinburgh: Edinburgh University Press, 2000), 1-11.
[17] Ross Clifford and Philip Johnson, *Jesus and the Gods of the New Age* (Oxford: Lion, 2001), 18. See also Gordon Lewis, 'The Church and the New Spirituality', *Journal of the Evangelical Theological Society* 36, 4 (December 1993): 434.
[18] See interview of Neville Drury, 'New Age Journey', *Compass ABC Television* (10 June 2001).
[19] Clarissa Bye, 'The Future of Popcorn – An Interview', *The Sun-Herald – Tempo* (21 January 2001), 5.

capitalism.[20] And researchers describe Australia's 'religious institution' as 'postmodern' since people's spiritual expectations do not require a single religious identification or affiliation, and some see no conflict among, 'consulting the stars, praying, meditating, wearing a cross along with a crystal'.[21] Whilst such eclecticism is particularly attracted to eastern religion and concepts, for the sake of this thesis it is important to note that on the whole it is not divorced from the person of Jesus. Trenoweth in her feminist embracing of the Goddess and Neo-Paganism recounts her love of the 'myth' of Jesus, even if Christianity is too big a leap of faith.[22]

With Philip Johnson I document similar 'testimonies' to Trenoweth's in *Jesus and the Gods of the New Age*.[23] Some ten years ago we founded an apologetic ministry at Sydney's twice yearly Mind·Body·Spirit festival. It is arguably the largest such festival in the world.[24] In a recent survey we conducted with 'New Spirituality' seekers who were exploring with us the biblical and gospel implications of the tarot,[25] we found that 76% of respondents believed Jesus could truly empower their lives and only 1% was in anyway dismissive.[26] This openness to the person and work of Jesus is confirmed by the thousands of pamphlets we freely distribute. They include: 'The tarot's message', 'Learning from the magi astrologers', 'It's true for you, but not true for me', 'Did Jesus go to India?'. This last pamphlet has uniformly been the most popular choice of those passing our stall.[27] James Sire reports that this quasi openness to Jesus is not a new phenomenon:.

---

[20] Johannes Aagaard, 'Conversion, Religious Change, and the Challenge of New Religious Movements', *Cultic Studies Journal* 8, 2 (1991): 91-103.

[21] Philip Hughes, Craig Thompson, Rohan Pryor and Gary D. Bouma, *Believe it or Not: Australian Spirituality and the Churches in the 90's* (Hawthorn, Victoria: Christian Research Association, 1995), 10.

[22] Trenoweth, *The Future,* x–xi.

[23] Clifford and Johnson, *Jesus and the Gods*, especially 'Vicky's Story', 196-200: 'I have never actually given up on the idea that Jesus died for my sins ... But I would also pray with Buddhists and Pagans and Hindus and Muslims if they let me ... I like Wicca-style paganism. I find its whole life-affirming, non-bigoted, self-empowering, spirit-in-everything ... I will leave the question as to whether I am a Christian or not up to God for s/he alone can judge that one.'

[24] For an assessment of the Mind-Body-Spirit festival in London see Malcolm Hamilton, 'An Analysis of the Festival for Mind-Body-Spirit', *Beyond New Age*, Sutcliffe and Bowman eds., 188-200.

[25] For further details see John Drane, Ross Clifford and Philip Johnson, *Beyond Prediction: The Tarot and Your Spirituality* (Oxford: Lion, 2001).

[26] Survey results held by Global Apologetics and Mission, PO Box 367 Hurstville, Australia 1481.

[27] For an expanded version of our apologetic response on Jesus and his alleged travels during his missing years (13-29) see Clifford and Johnson, *Jesus and the Gods*, 149-169.

> To Eastern-oriented religious groups, Jesus is an avatar – one of many incarnations of God; to Christian Scientists, he is the Great Healer; to political revolutionaries, he is the Great Liberator; to Spiritualists, he is a first-rate medium; to one new consciousness philosopher, he is the prototype of Carlos Castaneda's Don Juan, a sorcerer who can restructure events in the world by mental exercise. Everyone, it seems, wants Jesus for themselves.[28]

The other commonly agreed mark of 'New Spirituality' is *'self-spirituality'*. Drury states it remains a truism with 'New Spirituality' that 'one should transform oneself before endeavouring to transform others.'[29] In a popularist sense it is found in the self-help emphasis of media giants like Oprah Winfrey.[30] Paul Heelas connects 'self-spirituality' with the 'detraditionalization' of the person, implying a move away from hierarchical religions and institutions. Heelas suggests widespread beliefs, '— in the value of the self, in there being an inner domain, in the importance of self-discovery, progress and growth, in the notion that the individual is the primary locus of agency, authority, responsibility and judgement – point in the direction of the New Age teachings'.[31] The task remains to ascertain why only some of those who have moved beyond the 'tradition-informed', gravitate to 'New Spirituality'. Heelas notes that when 'cultural trajectories' exist, namely 'internalized and perennialized views of religion' alongside the doctrine of human kindness, the New Age quest is rendered plausible and attractive.[32] Heelas characterises the autonomous spiritual journey as follows:

> Typically presented as beyond belief, beyond belonging, beyond externally-imposed moral commandments, a major factor in the appeal of the New Age – it is now clear – is that it does not require any great leap of faith. Basically, all that one has to do is *participate*, in order, that is, to *experience* one's barriers, one's potential, or the inner wisdom of Buddhism (for example). Rather than having to convert, in the sense of coming to 'believe' in a set of claims, what matters is seeking within by engaging in *effective* practices; by going with what is 'sensed' as working. As a number

---

[28] James W. Sire, *Scripture Twisting* (Downers Grove: InterVarsity, 1986), 22.
[29] Neville Drury, *Exploring the Labyrinth* (St. Leonards: Allen & Unwin, 1999), 98.
[30] Kate Maver, 'Oprah Winfrey and her Self-Help Saviours: Making the New Age Normal', *Christian Research Journal* 23, 4 (2001): 12-21.
[31] Paul Heelas, *The New Age Movement: The Celebration of the Self and the Sacralization of Modernity* (Oxford and Malden, Massachusetts: Blackwell, 1996), 159.
[32] ibid., 159-174.

of my students (for instance) insist, 'you don't have to make any truth-commitments or judgements; just try it out – see what it does for you'.[33]

Apart from the two marks of eclecticism and self-spirituality there is a diversity of opinion as to what other elements should be emphasised. This is due to the eclectic and evolving nature of 'New Spirituality'. Gordon Lewis typifies *evangelical* apologetic responses when he claims that generally a 'New Spirituality' presupposes, '(1) a pantheistic or panentheistic worldview, (2) a noncognitive, mystical view of spiritual experiences, (3) an occult (magical) approach to spiritual knowledge and power, and (4) a vision of future world peace'.[34] Irving Hexham is critical of such evangelical assessments of the New Age asserting that there is a tendency towards reductionism in boiling the movement down to 'monism, pantheism, relativism, and evolutionary philosophy'.[35] John Drane expresses a similar concern about categorising the New Age in a way that represents it as a monolithic movement. He points out there are different nuances that expose at least two different philosophies, one monistic and the other strongly dualistic. He finds, 'These two strands do not share the same heritage: the one has historical roots to a creation-based spirituality which is either pantheistic or panentheistic, which can be traced through Romantic poets such as Shelley, Blake, and Wordsworth, while the other has more in common with people like Swedenborg, Mesmer, Blavatsky, Bailey and Cayce.'[36]

---

[33] ibid., 173.

[34] Gordon Lewis, 'The Church and the New Spirituality', 434. Similar, if at times more extensive lists, are found in other evangelical tomes. For example Douglas R. Groothuis, *Unmasking the New Age* (Downers Grove: InterVarsity, 1986), 18-31. Groothuis marks are: '(1) All is One', '(2) All is God', '(3) Humanity is God', '(4) A Change in Consciousness', '(5) All Religions are One', '(6) Cosmic Evolutionary Optimism'. See also Elliot Miller, *A Crash Course on the New Age Movement* (Grand Rapids: Baker, 1989), 17-18; David McDowell, *West of Eden* (Shippensburg, Pennsylvania: Companion Press, 1993), 7-13; Kerry D. McRoberts, *New Age or Old Lie*? (Peabody, Massachusetts: Hendrickson, 1989), 3-21; Mary Ann Lind, *From Nirvana to the New Age* (Tarrytown, New York: Fleming H. Revell, 1991), 18-30.

[35] Irving Hexham, 'The Evangelical Response to the New Age' in *Perspectives on the New Age*, James R. Lewis and J. Gordon Melton, eds. (Albany, New York: State University of New York Press, 1992), 159. Hexham also accuses the more sensational evangelical texts of being unscholarly in their methods of research, of accepting uncritically fantastic claims and creating guilt by association. Texts that warrant this critique include Dave Hunt and T.A. McMahon, *America the Sorcerer's New Apprentice: The Rise of New Age Shamanism* (Eugene, Oregon: Harvest House, 1988).

[36] John W. Drane, 'Methods and Perspectives in Understanding the New Age', *Themelios* 23, 2 (February 1998): 30.

A critical response

In light of the concerns of Hexham and Drane one could be led to believe that there are no valid markers of this nebulous spirituality outside of its eclecticism and self orientated nature. This is not so. Although 'New Spirituality' is not a unified system or Weltanschauung, there are indicators. The evangelical markers have some validity, provided one is honest in stating that this is not a uniform movement, and in ensuring that beliefs are not caricatured. As well there are other interconnected categories that assist in understanding 'New Spirituality's' epistemological framework. Drane's proposal is to speak of four dominant polarities through which transformational philosophies and experiences are pursued though the New Age. These are: 'Non-western worldviews' i.e. 'First-nation beliefs', including aboriginal; 'environmentally-friendly' lifestyles; 'Creation-centredness'; and 'Person-centredness'.[37] The 'Creation-centred' focus is important for the 'father' of New Age, David Spangler, who in his definition of the movement highlights global awareness and 'inner relationships with the cosmos'.[38] Matthew Fox's summary of the 'issues at stake' in the paradigm shift to postmodern spirituality is likewise insightful:

> From theistic (and deistic and atheistic) to panentheistic (God is in all creation).
> From left brain (analytic) to (both) left brain *and* right brain (synthetic).
> From rationalistic to mystical.
> From patriarchal to feminist.
> From the quest for the historical Jesus to the quest for the cosmic Christ.
> From knowledge to wisdom ...
> From dualism (either/or) to dialectic (both-and).
> From sentimentalism to a passionate embrace of awe at our existence.
> From a flight from the world to a commitment to social and personal transformation.

---

[37] ibid., 24-26.
[38] David Spangler and William Irwin Thompson, *Reimagination of the World: A Critique of the New Age, Science and Popular Culture* (Sante Fe: Bear, 1991), 57.

> From Eurocentrism to a celebration of the wisdom of ancient and primordial peoples' spiritualities of micro/macrocosm.
> From worship as words—read, preached, and sung—to worship as a nonelitist celebration of our shared existence.
> From Divinity in the sky to Divinity of Mother Earth crucified.[39]

However, although it is clear that 'New Spirituality' is in a state of flux, there are several strands or visions about life and the cosmos that are *often* apparent apart from its eclecticism and self-spirituality. The first is 'Monist holism' and New Age monism has several subtle nuances to it. Some espouse a form of pantheism where seekers discover their own inner divinity.[40] Others adopt a monist outlook grounded in a Western form of neo-Buddhism. Here the quest is not inner divinity but the experience of Nirvana's nothingness.[41] Still others are panentheists and they chart their spiritual life so as to develop as God evolves. In these nuances spiritual evolution is a positive process where we progress into divinity ourselves, or connect with the divine source of the universe.[42] In case studies Johnson and I illustrate the difference in outlook in 'New Spirituality' between those attracted to 'substantive monism' (there is only one real substance or thing) and 'attributive monism' (there is one type or category, for example wind or spirit, but many different things exist within this one category).[43] A second strand is 'Neo-gnostic holism' and this concept suggests that spiritual knowledge is embedded symbolically within the human psyche. Carl Jung and ancient gnostic writings can be significant here. A third strand is 'Neo-pagan/Wiccan holism' and here spirituality is framed around natural magic and, for some, the presence of the Goddess in the world. Another strand is 'Hermetic holism' which is used here in a broad sense to refer to western esoteric and magical traditions such as astrology, alchemy and the tarot.[44] Yet, one should not assume that those exploring 'New Spirituality' articulate their search by using these terms or that they embrace the 'whole package'. New Age is remarkably a 'bits and pieces' thing.

---

[39] Matthew Fox, 'Spirituality for a New Era' in *New Age Spirituality: An Assessment*, Duncan S. Ferguson, ed. (Louisville, Kentucky: Westminster/John Knox Press, 1993), 206. For a list of the issues in the paradigm shift in western cultures see David Tacey, *Reenchantment: The New Australian Spirituality* (Sydney: Harper Collins, 2000), 229.
[40] Redfield, *The Celestine Prophecy*.
[41] Thich Nhat Hanh, *Being Peace* (London: Rider, 1987).
[42] Clifford and Johnson, *Jesus and the Gods*, 19-20.
[43] ibid., 105-112.
[44] ibid., 19-21.

Background to 'New Spirituality'

Influences bearing upon 'New Spirituality'[45]
Another way to envisage 'New Spirituality' is to map out the influential sources of the New Age movement. A chart is offered here which is mainly self-explanatory and is broadly representative of other such mapping.[46] The chart is a guide, not an absolute statement on origins:[47]

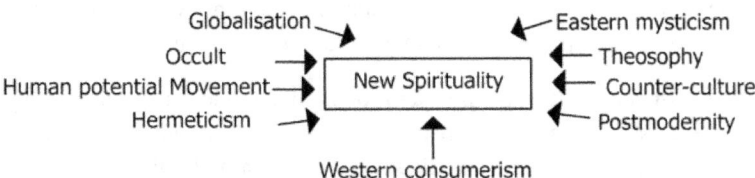

Globalisation appears in the map since the 'global village' character of the world is a major factor in current Western consciousness of Eastern Mysticism and the other influences. It involves a challenge to a universalism that has the idea of a single religion.[48] Whilst one cannot limit the word 'globalisation' to a 'proper meaning' it does embrace the fact that technology and communication have reduced the significance of geographical space.[49] Two other influences require consideration.

One of the finest analyses of New Age religion has been provided by Dutch scholar Wouter Hanegraaff. He agrees that the movement is the heir to the 'counterculture' of the 1960's. As a consequence he sees one of the major tenets as a culture criticism and concludes:

---

[45] For a discussion of the influential figures in the history of the development of 'New Spirituality' (for example Swedenborg, Helen Blavatsky, Annie Besant, and Charles Leadbeater) see Clifford and Johnson, *Jesus and the Gods*, 14-18.

[46] For example see Groothuis, *Unmasking*, 37-56; Russell Chandler, *Understanding the New Age* (Dallas: Word, 1988), 43-79; Robert C. Fuller, *Spiritual but not Religious: Understanding Unchurched America* (New York: Oxford University Press, 2001), 13-100.

[47] For more details see Clifford and Johnson, *Jesus and the Gods*, 21. One for example, could place more emphasis on the role of gnosticism. See John Drane, *What is the New Age Still Saying to the Church?* rev. ed. (London: Marshall Pickering, 1999), 67-80.

[48] Malcolm Waters, *Globalization* (London: Routledge, 1995), 64.

[49] For discussion see Christopher Shiel, 'Globalisation is ...' in *Globalisation: Australian Impacts*, Christopher Shiel, ed. (Sydney: University of New South Wales Press, 2001), 1-16; Harold Netland, *Encountering Religious Pluralism: The Challenge to Christian Faith and Mission* (Downers Grove: InterVarsity; Leicester: Apollos, 2001), 80-89.

> It (New Age) claims that the two trends which have hitherto dominated western culture (dogmatic Christianity and an equally dogmatic rationalistic/scientific ideology) have been responsible for the current world crisis, and that the latter will only be resolved if and when this third option (New Age) becomes dominant in society.[50]

Wuthnow also describes how our contemporary changing world order is the kind of watershed that is a portent for change in religious movements.[51]

The other influence requiring consideration is 'postmodernity'. There is a plethora of evangelical responses to this. Roger Olson's argument that the responses can be divided between 'traditionalists' who see postmodernism as the 'enemy' and the 'reformists' who see it as a 'dialogue partner' is admittedly a generalisation but nevertheless a helpful one. It is not a derogatory commentary as such, but a way of understanding evangelical emphases.[52] In the traditionalist camp he cites Gene Veith[53] and in the reformist camp Stanley Grenz.[54]

The extent of the postmodern condition and whether it means the end of 'modernity' is beyond these pages to debate.[55] Suffice it to note for apologetic purposes that Zygmunt Bauman describes the postmodern condition as 'modernity without illusions', in other words it is much more modest than 'here is the truth – believe it!' It acknowledges that the 'messiness' of the human world remains whatever we do and that our orders and systems are brittle.[56] In a similar vein the international architect Charles Jencks states that it means '"a war on totality", a resistance to single explanations, and a respect for difference ... and is always hybrid,

---

[50] Wouter J. Hanegraaff, *New Age Religion and Western Culture: Esotericism in the Mirror of Secular Thought* (Albany, New York: State University of New York Press, 1998), 517.

[51] Robert Wuthnow, 'World Order and Religious Movements' in *New Religious Movements: A Perspective for Understanding Society*, Eileen Baker, ed. (New York and Toronto: Edwin Mellen, 1982), 61-65.

[52] Roger E. Olson, 'The Future of Evangelical Theology', *Christianity Today* 42, 2 (9 February 1998): 40-48.

[53] Gene Edward Veith, *Postmodern Times: A Christian Guide to Contemporary Thought and Culture* (Wheaton: Crossway, 1994). Other examples one could suggest include Dennis McCallum, ed., *The Death of Truth* (Minneapolis: Bethany, 1996); Millard J. Erickson, *Postmodernizing the Faith: Evangelical Responses to the Challenge of Postmodernism* (Grand Rapids: Baker, 1998); D.A. Carson, *The Gagging of God: Christianity Confronts Pluralism* (Grand Rapids: Zondervan, 1996).

[54] Stanley J. Grenz, *A Primer on Postmodernism* (Grand Rapids: William B. Eerdmans, 1996). See also Brian Walsh and Richard Middleton, *Truth is Stranger than it used to Be* (Downers Grove: InterVarsity, 1995); Timothy R. Phillips and Dennis L. Okholm, eds., *Christian Apologetics in the Postmodern World* (Downers Grove: InterVarsity, 1995); Leonard Sweet, *Post-Modern Pilgrims* (Nashville: Broadman & Holman, 2000).

mixed, ambiguous, or what I have called "doubly-coded".[57] Further, John Drane speaks in terms of 'post-modernity' with a 'hyphen' drawing attention to the fact that it is not a self contained philosophy or ideological position. He finds that whilst the values and attitudes of 'modernity' face rejection, we still 'live happily with the products and personal trappings of modernity'. He asks whether in this dialectical process the journey itself is not more important than the destination.[58]

Unquestionably 'New Spirituality' is on a journey with trappings of 'postmodernity'. It sees the stories of 'modernity', of science and technology as limiting and is looking to myth, if not the supernatural, for stories that transcend materialistic expectations.[59] It does therefore see 'modernity' as a war against mystery and magic. It is in the context of such a world that 'New Spirituality's' re-enchantment is aimed.[60] Also at times 'New Spirituality' is prepared to deconstruct other worldviews by holding that truth in ideologies is socially constructed, can be a matter of pragmatic expression and can lead to the oppression of minority points of view. It can therefore be cautious of the metanarrative and metadiscourse, and can find in language, according to David Wells, 'that a literary text is far less interesting than the subtext'.[61] However, as will be stated in the later section on

---

[55] Lyon argues that the idea of 'postmodernity' may turn out to be a figment of academic imagination or popular hype but it is worth pursuing as it alerts one to a series of important questions about 'modernity'. Above all it refers to the 'exhaustion of modernity'. See David Lyon, *Postmodernity* (Buckingham: Open University Press, 1994), 4-18. For some evangelical assessments of the alleged shift to the postmodern paradigm see David S. Dockery, ed., *The Challenge of Postmodernism: An Evangelical Engagement* (Grand Rapids: Baker, 1995); Winifred Wing Han Lamb, 'Fundamentalism, Modernity and Postmodernity', *Zadok Paper*, S73 (March 1995); Dan R. Stiver, 'Much Ado about Athens and Jerusalem: the implications of postmodernism for faith' 91, 1 *Review and Expositor* (Winter 1994): 83-102; Philip Hughes, 'Christian Faith in a Postmodern Age', *Zadok Paper*, S74 (July 1995).
[56] Zygmunt Bauman, *Postmodern Ethics* (Oxford: Blackwell, 1993), 32. Cf. Bruce who states that 'postmodernity' is 'tendentious theological baggage' when assessing religious change and that the major patterns of change can be regarded as essences of 'modernity'. Steve Bruce, 'Cathedrals to Cults: The Evolving Forms of the Religious Life' in *Religion, Modernity and Postmodernity*, Paul Heelas, ed. (Oxford and Malden, Massachusetts: Blackwell, 1998), 19-35.
[57] Charles Jencks, ed., *The Post-Modern Reader* (London: Academy Editions; New York: St Martins, 1992), 11.
[58] John Drane, *The McDonaldization of the Church* (London: Darton, Longman and Todd, 2000), 6.
[59] Loren Wilkinson, 'Circles and the Cross: Reflections on Neo-paganism, Postmodernity and Celtic Christianity', *Evangelical Review of Theology* 22, 1 (January 1998): 28-30.
[60] Bauman, *Postmodern Ethics*, 33-36.
[61] David F. Wells, 'Living Tradition' in *Where Shall My Wond'ring Soul Begin? The Landscape of Evangelical Piety and Thought*, Mark A. Noll and Ronald F. Thiemann, eds. (Grand Rapids and Cambridge: William B. Eerdmans, 2000), 93.

'Refracting the resurrection narrative' this caution towards metanarratives in 'New Spirituality' has often been misunderstood and overstated by Christian apologists.[62]

It is in a culture of 'modernity without illusions' that scholars like Drane and Garrett correctly see New Age as the religion of the postmodern spirit.[63]

Emergent Methodological Issues

Although 'New Spirituality's' belief pattern is elusive, for positive apologetic purposes the elements that surface for consideration following the above survey, are its eclecticism, its self-spirituality, its cosmic view, its openness to occult or 'Hermetic holism' technologies and its hope of the divine.[64] In the next two sections there will be a brief discussion of apologetic models, and it will there be affirmed that the aim is not to dismantle 'New Spirituality', but rather to engage with it. Hence, in methodology there should be a sensitivity to women's issues[65] as unresolved gender issues are a major criticism given of the church by those exploring alternative spirituality.[66] Further in the following pages it will be stressed that there needs to be an acknowledgment of the place of wisdom and story; an understanding that the average seeker holds personal empowerment and transformation[67] to be the initial journeying point, rather than truth; and a treatment of 'religious others' with respect and dignity (Acts 17:22, 1 Peter 3:15).[68] As McGrath states 'experience is a vital "point of contact" for Christian

---

[62] In support of this assertion see Irving Hexham, 'Evangelical Illusions' in *No Other Gods Before Me?*, John G. Stackhouse, ed. (Grand Rapids: Baker, 2001), 155-160. Hexham also strongly criticises evangelicals who in their apologetic feel the need to embrace 'evangelical postmodernism'. See also James K.A. Smith, 'A Little Story about Metanarratives: Lyotard, Religion and Postmodernism Revisited', *Faith and Philosophy* 18, 3 (July 2001), 353-368. Smith argues postmodernism's incredulity toward metanarratives is not a rejection of grand stories in terms of scope or in the sense of epic claims, but represents 'a displacement of the notion of autonomous reason as itself a myth' (360-362).

[63] Drane, 'Methods and Perspectives', 24; Duane A. Garrett, *Angels and the New Spirituality* (Nashville: Broadman & Holman, 1995), 236-240.

[64] Douglas Groothuis, *Confronting the New Age* (Downers Grove: InterVarsity, 1988), 70: look for apologetic common ground, 'such as the reality of the spiritual realm, life after death, and the need for spiritual growth and social change'. See also McGrath, *Bridge-Building*, 51-75.

[65] 81 percent of visitors to our stand at the Mind•Body•Spirit festival are women, see Clifford and Johnson, *Jesus and the Gods*, 182.

[66] David Burnett, *Dawning of the Pagan Moon* (Eastbourne: Monarch, 1991), 235-238.

[67] See Neville Drury in David Millikan and Neville Drury, *Worlds Apart?: Christianity and the New Age* (Crows Nest, NSW: ABC Enterprises, 1991), 39-43.

[68] Netland, *Encountering Religious Pluralism*, 281-283.

apologetics in a postmodern world'.[69] This does not mean the truth question is irrelevant. And as we look at how the legal apologetic interacts with this spiritual smorgasbord, other apologetic issues will continue to surface.

Apologetic Models in Relation to 'New Spirituality'

Before considering an apologetic model based on Montgomery's work, it is important to note that the majority of evangelical responses to date towards 'New Spirituality' have focused on 'heresy', 'end times conspiracies', 'spiritual warfare' or 'apostate testimony' models.[70] Massimo Introvigne, an Italian lawyer who lectures in the Sociology of Religion at the Theological University of Southern Italy, has another way of describing some of these models. He establishes that there are two basic responses to cults or new religious movements. One is from a secular group made up of lawyers and members of mental health groups, whilst the other is from a group comprising Christian theologians and apologists. This latter group he names 'counter-cult'. He notes that in each group there are two sub-groups, the rationalists and the post-rationalists. The rationalist apologists adopt the 'heresy' model where the New Age is contrasted with Christian doctrine. The post-rationalists operate in the 'spiritual warfare' model where what is in contention is not a matter of knowledge but experience and demons. Often the testimony and 'end-times' models have a similar emphasis.[71] Langone prefers to call Introvigne's two categories 'content focused' (the truth value) and 'process focused' (how inner change in worldview is produced).[72] Undoubtedly the real strength of these 'heresy' and 'spiritual warfare' writings lies in their being a negative apologetic that can helpfully equip or warn the Church.[73]

---

[69] Alister E. McGrath, *A Passion for Truth: The Intellectual Coherence of Evangelicalism* (Leicester: Apollos, 1996), 87.

[70] For example of 'heresy' see Walter Martin, *The New Age Cult* (Minneapolis: Bethany, 1989); 'end times conspiracies' see Constance Cumbey, *The Hidden Dangers of the Rainbow* (Shreveport: Huntington, 1983); 'spiritual warfare' see Frank E. Peretti, *This Present Darkness* (Westchester, Illinois: Crossway, 1986); 'apostate testimony' see Michael Graham, *The Experience of Ultimate Truth* (Melbourne: U-Turn, 2001).

[71] Massimo Introvigne, 'Strange Bedfellows or Future Enemies', *Update and Dialog*, 4 (October 1993): 13-22. Cf. Anson Shupe and David G. Bromley, 'The Modern North American Anti-Cult Movement 1971-1991' in *Anti-Cult Movements in Cross-Cultural Perspectives*, Anson Shupe and David G. Bromley, eds. (New York and London: Garland, 1994), 3-31.

[72] Michael D. Langone, 'Secular and Religious Critiques of Cults: Complementary Visions, not Irresolvable Conflicts', *Cultic Studies Journal* 12, 2 (1995): 166-186.

[73] Two good examples in this regard are Groothuis, *Unmasking* and Miller, *A Crash Course*. Although both authors include a positive apologetic element (see also Groothuis, *Confronting*) their strength lies in being a descriptive, negative apologetic.

However the merits of these evangelical responses is disputed, as for some Christian apologists they typify, on the whole, a great 'anti-cult' crusade and they have been largely ineffective, if not offensive.[74] In this context Saliba remarks that these evangelical models, whilst often containing some valuable critique, simply constitute a soliloquy within the church. He finds,

> At best, it is a process of self-affirmation and self-assurance, providing comfort and solace to confused Christians; it contrasts the teachings of the New Age with those of the Bible; and it discovers, to nobody's surprise, that the movement's religious ideology deviates from biblical texts and from orthodox Christian teachings. At its worst, it degenerates into a senseless diatribe or an emotional harangue.
>
> Moreover, this kind of response is likely to have very limited results because it consists largely of repetitive and boring catalogues of Christian doctrines and New Age heresies. Since it appeals largely to those who are already committed Christians, it cannot engage New Agers in a fruitful exchange of ideas or in a constructive discussion on ideological standpoints, spiritual goals, and practical agendas.[75]

Such a criticism cannot be made of Montgomery's negative or positive apologetic with respect to the occult or the disciplines of 'New Spirituality'. Montgomery's position is that he refuses to 'damn', *a priori*, any occult practice as if it is part of some monolithic evil entity, and that a biblical and fair judgement must be applied to each particular occult phenomenon or psychotechnology.[76] An illustration of his objectivity is his explanation as to why astrological analyses can come so close to the mark at times:

> Let me suggest a possibility. The underlying assumption of astrology is the same as that of alchemy, namely, the unity of the cosmos. For the alchemist, the inorganic and the organic—the impersonal and the personal—operate by the same fundamental laws. For the astrologer, this correlation is focused on the relation

---

[74] Irving Hexham and Karla Poewe, *New Religions as Global Cultures: Making the Human Sacred* (Boulder, Colorado: Westview, 1997), 1-25.

[75] Saliba, *Christian Responses*, 72-78. See also Douglas E. Cowan, *Bearing False Witness: Propaganda, Reality-Maintenance, and Christian Anticult Apologetics* (Ph.D. Thesis, University of Calgary, 1999).

[76] Montgomery, *Principalities*, 20-21.

between planetary positions and human life. In both cases, the Macrocosm (the universe extrinsic to man) and the Microcosm (man himself) are united in a single harmonic relationship. Now such a description would well apply to the *unfallen* cosmos—the Garden in which Adam lived in perfect harmony with nature and walked with the Lord God in the cool of the day. But as a result of man's self-centred fall, modeled on Lucifer's own passion to 'exalt his throne above the stars of God' (Is. 14:12-15), the perfect relation between man and the cosmos was fractured: man had to leave the Garden, and now 'the whole creation groans and travails in pain, waiting for redemption' (Rom. 8:22-23). This does not mean that every trace of the Macrocosmic-Microcosmic harmony has disappeared, but it does mean that, if you will, the monkey wrench of sin has been thrown into the cosmic machinery, so that the original harmony is disrupted on a very wide scale.[77]

Montgomery's 'Incarnational' Model

The 'applied apologetic' model that I have adopted for the rest of this chapter is a positive apologetic that I have labelled the 'incarnational' model.[78] Rob Frost maintains evangelism today must be 'incarnational'.[79] An incarnational paradigm is not to be confused with the principle of contextualization which is a concept with wider ramifications.[80] It is premised on Paul in Athens at the Areopagus (Acts 17:16-34) and on Paul's call to be all things to all people (1 Corinthians 9:22).[81] It searches for common ground and for interaction with the symbols of the 'unknown God' of 'New Spirituality' and it climaxes in the proclamation of

---

[77] John Warwick Montgomery, *Occult Revival*, audiotape (Edmonton: Canadian Institute for Law, Theology and Public Policy, 1997). Montgomery in this address acknowledges the occult includes a lot of 'humbug', but states there is also a great deal of reality in the occult. See also Montgomery, *Principalities*, 119.

[78] An incarnational apologetic is not to be connected with the doctrine espoused by some that the church is another incarnation of God and Christ. See Anthony Petterson, 'The Blasphemy of "Incarnational Ministry"', *Baptist Evangelicals Today*, (November 2001): 15.

[79] Rob Frost, *Sharing Jesus in a New Millennium* (Bletchley, England: Scripture Union, 2000), 63-64. See also David Wilkinson, 'The Art of Apologetics in the Twenty-first Century', *Anvil* 19, 1 (2002): 5-17.

[80] David J. Hesselgrave and Edward Rommen, *Contextualization: Meanings, Methods, and Models* (Grand Rapids: Baker, 1989), 200: 'Contextualization is both verbal and nonverbal and has to do with theologizing; Bible translation, interpretation and application; incarnational lifestyle; evangelism; Christian instruction; church planting and growth; church organisation; worship style – indeed with all of those activities involved in carrying out the Great Commission.'

the kerygma.[82] As Netland argues, it is a culture-specific apologetic; however space does not allow a specific treatment of sub-cultures within 'New Spirituality' such as Wicca and Neo-Paganism.[83] It is the missionary principle of understanding another culture and its religious beliefs, and sharing Christ from within these frameworks.[84] Charles puts it, 'In sum, Acts 17:16-34 mirrors apologetic Christian contact with pagan culture. It begins with the epistemological assumptions of its hearers, it builds on a common understanding of the cosmos, yet it climaxes in the fullest self-disclosure of the Creator—the resurrection of the God-man.'[85] In this spirit Hesselgrave reminds us that the most effective cross-cultural communication is not asking the listener and reader to abandon their sense of the world and to look at ours, but to temporarily adopt the worldview of the people who are targeted.[86] Missiologists use the term 'interpathy' to describe the strong sense of affinity that one should have with another people group.[87] Such a model has a long and revered history in evangelical missionary enterprise, even if it has been neglected in western world apologetics.[88]

Whilst such a positive apologetic holds there is some truth in the cultural Zeitgeist it is penetrating, and may well assert that the symbols it is connecting with reflect universal archetypes as a provision of divine common grace, the apologetic is not primarily about the affirmation or critique of the religion in question. However, unlike Küng, this 'cross-cultural' apologetic model does not detract

---

[81] For a justification of the legal 'incarnational' paradigm, not just in Acts 17:16-34 and 1 Corinthians 9:22, but in Luke-Acts and other parts of the New Testament, see the section 'Scriptural Support' in chapter 5 of this thesis.

[82] See Clifford and Johnson, *Jesus and the Gods*, 26-31.

[83] Harold Netland, 'Toward Contextualized Apologetics', *Missiology* 16, 3 (July 1988): 289-303.

[84] In this context it could be said it has as a foundation the incarnation of Christ. For support of such a model and a critique of other evangelism models that are unconcerned about wrestling with issues of context see H.L. Richard, 'Evangelical Approaches to Hindus', *Missiology* 29, 3 (July 2001): 307-315.

[85] J. Daryl Charles, 'Engaging the (Neo) Pagan Mind: Paul's Encounter with Athenian Culture as a Model for Cultural Apologetics (Acts 17:16-34)' in *The Gospel and Contemporary Perspectives*, Douglas Moo, ed. (Grand Rapids: Kregel, 1997), 133. See also Dean Flemming, 'Contextualizing the Gospel in Athens: Paul's Areopagus Address as a Paradigm for Missionary Communication', *Missiology* 30, 2 (April 2002): 199-214 (for an extensive bibliography see 211-214). These articles are excellent overviews of Acts 17 as a missionary model.

[86] David J. Hesselgrave, *Communicating Christ Cross-Culturally*, 2nd ed. (Grand Rapids: Zondervan, 1991), 209-212.

[87] A good example of this approach with new religious movements is Mark J. Cares, *Speaking the Truth in Love to Mormons* (Milwaukee: Northwestern, 1993), 196-205.

[88] See H.L. Richard, *Following Jesus in the Hindu Context: The Intriguing Implications of N.V. Tilak's Life and Thought* (Pasadena: William Carey library, 1998); Don Richardson, *Peace Child* (Glendale: Regal, 1974); Charles, 'Engaging the (Neo) Pagan', 128-137; David Fetcho, 'Disclosing the Unknown God: Evangelism in the New Religions', *Update* 6,4 (December 1982): 7-16.

from a 'standpoint of superiority' with respect to the Christian worldview and a 'standpoint of exclusivity' with regard to soteriology.[89] So ultimately in the incarnational apologetic there is more than a 'presence' in a culture since the proclamation will challenge the listener's or reader's philosophy of life, and will argue that there is an epistemic duty on the part of the listener or reader to consider whether the challenge allows him or her to retain all his or her truth claims. However the order of contact is, 'perception, engagement and confrontation'.[90] The Asian theologian Ken Gnanakan asserts that this approach builds on the biblical teaching of commonality and continuity (Genesis 1-2, Romans 1-2, Acts 17:16-32) rather than from a foundation of confrontation.[91] Such a missionary model of initial accommodation has real justification in a western world where in most countries attendances at churches are in substantial decline, where any growth is almost totally biological, or by transfer, and yet where the numbers in the community seeking a non-Christian spiritual encounter continue to surge.[92]

Most significant for this thesis is the fact that whilst Montgomery is a strong supporter of the role of negative apologetics,[93] this 'incarnational' paradigm is also consistent with his apologetic model, as he holds that the most important apologetic principle is, 'to be all things to all people'. It is Montgomery who shaped an apologetic into a legal-conscious world; it is Montgomery who decades ago advocated the use of the biblical images on the tarot card pack for reaching the

---

[89] Hans Küng, 'Toward Dialogue' in *Christianity and the World Religions*, Hans Küng, Josef van Ess, Heinrich von Stietencorn and Heinz Bechert, trans. Peter Heinegg (Maryknoll, New York: Orbis, 1993), xiv – xx. This is clearly seen in Montgomery's latest work where whilst acknowledging and apologetically interacting with Jung's insight into 'The universal needs of mankind and necessary conditions for meeting them' he highlights the incompatability of the religions of the world and the 'superiority' of Christianity. Montgomery, *Tractatus*, 6 and 1 – 2.194.
[90] Charles, 'Engaging the (Neo) Pagan', 136.
[91] Ken Gnanakan, 'The Bible and Salvation in Asia', in *Salvation: Some Asian Perspectives*, Ken Gnanakan, ed. (Bangalore: Asia Theological Association, 1992), 1-16.
[92] For research papers on the decline in church attendance, conversion figures and spiritual growth see Kevin Ward, 'Religion in a PostAquarian Age', *Stimulus* 9, 1 (February 2001): 12-21 and 'Christendom, Clericalism, Church and Context: Finding Categories of Connexion in a Culture without a Christian Memory', *Mosaic: The Quarterly Journal of the NSW Baptist Ministers Association* 3, 3 (Spring 2001). Ward teaches at the Bible College of New Zealand and is on the pastoral staff of New Zealand's largest church, Spreydon Baptist. He argues in part that the church growth movement has not in itself answered the failure of the church to reach those who are without church contacts.
[93] Elliot Miller and Kerry McRoberts (see footnote 34) are graduates of his apologetic programme of Simon Greenleaf School of Law where both negative and positive approaches were emphasised. See also Montgomery's 'negative' apologetic critique of Islam and other religions when it comes to ethical issues in *Human Rights*, 113-124. Further on Nietzche, Marx and Freud see John Warwick Montgomery, 'Letter from England: Christianity's Unique Intellectual Opportunity', *New Oxford Review* (March 1995): 21-22. And on world religions see Montgomery, *Tractatus*, 1 - 2.194.

new pagan;[94] and it is Montgomery who supported a linguistic apologetic that sought to draw out the relationship between 'biblical truth' and the meaning of the characters in the ancient Chinese script.[95] These incarnational apologetic methods of Montgomery are in harmony with his theological doctorate, where he verified that the seventeenth century German Lutheran pastor Andreae in his treatise *The Chemical Wedding of Christian Rosenkreutz*, was not a heretic or guilty of syncreticism in his dealings with Rosicrucianism, but that he was an incarnational apologist who created an alchemical allegory of the gospel story.[96] Andreae is a precursor to Montgomery, an insight that is missed in most assessments of Montgomery's apologetic. Like Montgomery, Andreae was incarnational, and was eclectic in that he produced an apologetic based on Hugo Grotius as well as myth and fairytale. In addition he applied the gospel to all phases of life; he held that the sole surpassing 'philosophy' is not any particular philosophy, but the theology of the gospel of Jesus Christ; he had a theological framework which could be held to include the 'Theologian as Artist'.[97]

Further, the concept of being able to project an incarnational emphasis into a worldview, without necessarily owning all of its premises, is found in Montgomery's work. For example, in his apologetic response to a person who is 'tough-minded' about evolution and cannot move beyond a scientific objection to God, he cites theistic evolution and more significantly the writings of Pierre Teihhard de Chardin. Personally Montgomery is not convinced of de Chardin's adaptation of the evolutionary process to a cosmic Christology,[98] yet he is prepared to refer listeners or readers to him in order that they can consider embracing the abiding essential premises of the gospel message within an evolutionary construct.[99] In this context it is important to note that Montgomery views apologetics

---

[94] Montgomery, *Principalities*, 129-132.

[95] John Warwick Montgomery, *Giant in Chains: China Today and Tomorrow* (Milton Keynes, England: Nelson Word, 1994), 173-177.

[96] John Warwick Montgomery, *Cross and Crucible: Johann Valentin Andreae (1586-1654), Phoenix of the Theologians,* 2 vols. (The Hague: Martinus Nijhoff, 1973). For a hostile critique of Montgomery's thesis that establishes Andreae as an orthodox Lutheran, rather than seeing *The Chemical Wedding* as a published work of the Rosicrucian movement, see Adam McLean, *The Chemical Wedding of Christian Rosenkreutz: Introduction and Commentary*, trans. Joscelyn Godwin (Grand Rapids: Phanes Press, 1991), 10, 108. In response to McLean it can be said Montgomery's thesis on Andreae has received strong academic support. For example see the review of former University of California, Berkeley historian William J. Bouwsma in *The Journal of Modern History* 48,1 (March 1976): 160-161. 'Montgomery demonstrates convincingly that, far from advocating Rosicrucianism, his (Andreae) *Chymische Hochzeit* sought to counteract its dangers by reinterpreting the story of Christian Rosencreutz in terms of orthodox Lutheranism' (160).

[97] Montgomery, *Cross and Crucible*, 1: 91-148.

[98] Montgomery, *Tractatus*, 2.464.

as a tool for filling in 'potholes' of uncertainty in the listener's or reader's mind as they journey to the household of faith.[100] However, as a conservative evangelical, Montgomery would agree with Erickson's limitation that a positive apologetic paradigm is not about deconstructing the *apologia* to the relativity of 'New Spirituality', but that it does mean that the style and emphasis of presentation are changed. It is about translating the *kerygma* into a culture, not transforming the *kerygma*.[101]

Montgomery and the Apologist's Craft

It was claimed at the beginning of this chapter that not all of 'New Spirituality' is divorced from the possibility of some factual grounding. However as we come to consider the legal apologetic model in relation to this movement, it is important to balance this assertion with the premise that in apologetic discourse with 'New Spirituality' one cannot simply rely on listing historical or evidential data, as the listener or reader will wish to be involved in more than a mere assent to fact.[102] This is true of all apologetic discourse, but is especially so in a New Age context. Montgomery's seminal essay, 'The Theologian's Craft', can be applied to today's apologetic task and in so doing offers direction and balance to the legal apologist engaged with the world of 'New Spirituality'.[103] His essay includes a defence of the important issues of inerrancy and theological theorizing, all of which lie beyond the boundaries of this thesis, but its implications for the work of an apologist for the Christian faith is of interest. And its application to the apologetic task is appropriate as Montgomery acknowledges that the defence of the faith is one of the tasks of systematic theology, even if it is not 'the center of it'.[104]

---

[99] John Warwick Montgomery, *What About Evolution? Sensible Christianity*, retaped (Edmonton: Canadian Institute for Law, Theology and Public Policy, 2000). See David Gareth Jones, *Teilhard de Chardin: An Analysis and Assessment* (Grand Rapids: William B. Eerdmans, 1970).

[100] See Montgomery, *Defending the Biblical Gospel*, Study Guide, 9-10.

[101] See Millard J. Erickson, 'Postmodern Apologetics: Can Deconstructed Horses Even be Led to Water?', in *Evangelical Apologetics*, Bauman, Hall and Newman, eds., 322-326; John Warwick Montgomery, 'Defending the Hope that is in Us: Apologetics for the 21st Century', <http://www.bucer.de/theologyconsultation/Docs/JWMENGLISH.pdf>: 1-11 at 3.

[102] Also in the whole apologetic process Montgomery never denigrates the work of the Holy Spirit. Conversion is for Montgomery Spirit produced and he avoids any possibility of synergism by holding that everything is done by God, not by human beings. 'The evidential facts are God's work, and the sinner's personal acceptance of them, and the Person on whom they centre is entirely the work of the Holy Spirit'. Montgomery, *Faith Founded*, 150. See also evidentialist Gary R. Habermas 'The Personal Testimony of the Holy Spirit to the Believer and Christian Apologetics', *Journal of Christian Apologetics* 1, 1 (Summer 1997), 49-64.

[103] John Warwick Montgomery, 'The Theologian's Craft: A Discussion of Theory Formation and Theory Testing in Theology' in Montgomery, *The Suicide*, 267-313.

Montgomery's premise is that in theology one interacts at three different levels. The first is 'Scientific', and throughout this thesis it has been apparent that Montgomery places great significance on the data – the facts – for Jesus' life, death and resurrection. Whilst operating out of his evidential and legal/historical model, Montgomery asks, how is one to draw a hypothesis from the facts? He argues that the theologian 'will endeavour to formulate conceptual Gestalts – "networks" of ideas capable of rendering his data intelligible. He will employ "models" to achieve epistemological vividness.'[105] The theologian is looking here for an empirical fit, i.e. which theory best fits the facts. So, for Montgomery, the theologian is engaged in forming and testing theories concerning the divine.[106] Montgomery is here drawing on a comparison between scientific and theological methodologies and is relying heavily on Popper's work on models and 'conceptual fabrics'.[107] Montgomery's process of interpreting the data is therefore not one of 'static, formalistic induction' as he views deduction and what Pierce calls 'retroduction' as complementary with induction. Retroduction is the imaginative formation of theories and the network of ideas which renders the data intelligible, and for Montgomery it has an essential place. This is also highlighted in chapter five of this thesis.[108]

Yet for Montgomery, drawing doctrinal 'theories' such as the Trinity from the facts, is not the end of the task. Again relying on his theological mentors, Luther and Andreae, Montgomery also considers the theologian at 'The Artistic' level.[109] He affirms that theorizing demands the language of experience. The theologian or apologist must relive the past Christ events in imagination – re-enact them by entering into their very heart. So, for example, the resurrection should be presented as happening yesterday and to the apologist it must have a personal inner quality. The third level is 'The Theologian and the Holy'. This aspect, like the second level, has particular appeal to 'New Spirituality'. It is the acknowledgment of the limited character of the doctrines we draw from revelation and also our limited understanding of them. There is a numinous quality to theology and there should be an awareness of the unfathomable nature of God. Montgomery concludes by drawing on a Wittgenstein premise, that one must transcend one's proposition and then one 'will see the world aright'.[110]

---

[104] ibid., 269.
[105] ibid., 277.
[106] ibid., 268.
[107] ibid., 271-276.
[108] ibid., 274-276. For a detailed discussion of the relationship between deduction, induction and retroduction see also Montgomery, *Tractatus*, 2.2 – 2.377.
[109] ibid., 288-292; Montgomery, *Cross and Crucible*, 1: 131-147.

Montgomery and the Apologist's Craft

Montgomery creatively presents the following spiral model of theological explanation which can be applied, with some adjustment, to the theological subset of apologetics:

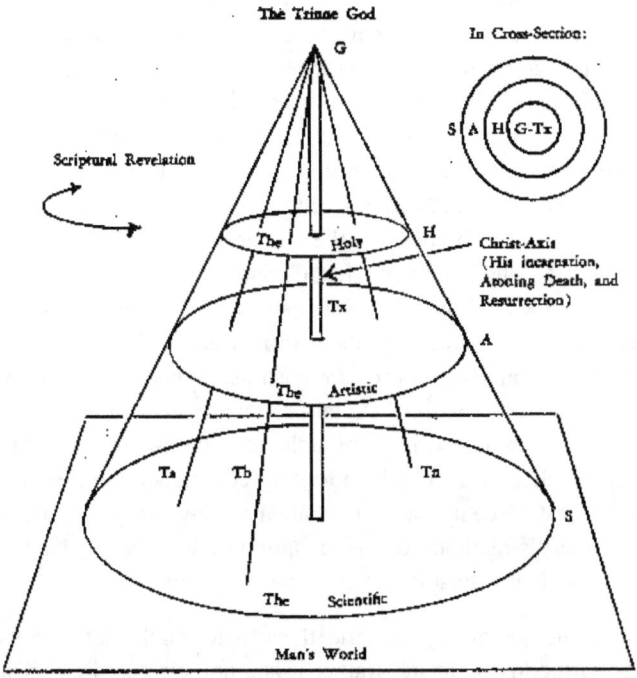

For Montgomery, the cone represents God's special revelation. In our apologetic context it represents the New Testament documentary evidence. For the legal apologetic, one could broaden the parameter to include the narrow band of circumstantial evidence for the resurrection which is not in the special revelation category (for example, the tomb of Christ not being subjected to early pilgrimages of worship). The truths (T) of the revelation are numerous and the task is to discover their proper relation to the focal centre and to each other, and to construct doctrinal formulations that fit the 'truths' in their mutual relations. The focal centre is the person of Christ; however, since this is apologetic theorizing, his incarnation, atoning death and resurrection are not assumed, *a priori*. For Montgomery, the theological theorist builds his theories from bottom to top, but

---

[110] ibid., 299-300.

as he climbs he inevitably reaches a point where, 'he must involve himself subjectively in his material in order to get at the heart of it', and then he steps into the realm of the sacred.[111]

The application of Montgomery's structural theological model to the legal apologetic for the resurrection provides a guide for the apologetic model that follows. The resurrection of Jesus is an hypothesis as to why the tomb was empty. There is no direct evidence for the actual resurrection itself. In formulating this explanation, the legal apologist commences by objectively analysing the direct evidence and circumstantial evidence (Ta, Th, ... Tn). The 'inference', 'interpretation' or 'imagination' of the legal apologist is that Christ arose. It is the 'shoe' that best fits the facts, the idea that best renders the data intelligible. The apologist again subordinates his hypothesis to the numerous facts of varying strengths to justify the finding. The statement that Christ arose is intensely personal and touches the life of the apologist at its very centre. Christ arose *for me*. As the apologist contemplates the character of the resurrection, its Trinitarian implications, and the astonishing ramification for the cosmos, he is caught up in wonder and amazement and does not seek to explain rationally all that it means, or how it could be. The legal apologist, in communicating the finding that Christ arose to the 'New Spirituality' seeker, will normally commence the discourse at level two, before a spiral descent to level one, always conversing with a sense of level three. Montgomery's methodology is an appropriate model for New Age apologetics, albeit it with an adjustment to the starting point.

His theological method of the scientific, the artistic and the holy is not an attempt at some Neo-Orthodox dialectic. Rather it is a holistic paradigm of interaction. Yet, as an evidentialist, there remains the primacy of the data, while 'the objective provides an epistemological check on the artistic, and the artistic serves as an entrée to the sacral'.[112]

Trembath in his well known critique of 'The Theologian's Craft' takes issue on a number of points which lie outside this thesis, as they are related primarily to Montgomery's argument for the inerrancy of scripture. However there is one matter that warrants consideration here. Trembath asserts that Montgomery's

---

[111] ibid., 296-297.

[112] ibid., 296. See also Montgomery, *Tractatus*: 'Assuming (as we must) that truth claims are to be tested by the twin criteria of logical soundness (deduction) and empirical facticity, what if a claim proves genuinely factual but logically problematic, i.e., suppose only the factual test is met?' (2.8). In such instances, one wishes it were otherwise, and every effort is of course made to resolve the contradiction, but if it cannot be solved, the facts nonetheless remain (2.822).

position is little more than a mere assent to fact, and that Montgomery believes historical accuracy alone can elicit an appropriate confession of faith.[113] Trembath evidences here a limited reading of Montgomery's work. Whilst for Montgomery facts are primary in epistemology, such a reductionism applied to his evidentialism is not appropriate in light of his understanding of the sovereignty of God the Holy Spirit in apologetics and salvation,[114] his commitment to the place of the experiential and sacred in argument, life and faith, his openness to other apologetic models, and his application of the Christian calling to ethical and human rights issues.

In conclusion Montgomery's 'The Theologian's Craft' articulates three levels of interaction that are applicable to the methodology of contemporary apologists. They are (i) the 'Scientific'; (ii) the 'Artistic'; and (iii) the 'Holy'.

The Legal Apologetic Model of Montgomery in Relation to New Spirituality

The Resurrection and Circumstantial Evidence

The resurrection of Jesus, which is the focus of Montgomery's apologetic, remains a primary apologetic point of interchange even with 'New Spirituality'. In fact scholars like Charles argue that in view of Paul's Areopagus address to a 'Pagan' audience,[115] where the Lukan narrative mentions the resurrection three times (Acts 17:18,31 and 32), one would have to ask if it is not the central focus.[116] Alister McGrath puts it this way:

> In the end, the debate with the New Age movement will not be won through philosophy, but through the proclamation of Christ. The New Testament offers us invaluable guidance here, which we ought to feel confident about accepting. Paul's Areopagus sermon sets before us a crisp, concise and convincing approach, ideally

---

[113] Kern Robert Trembath, *Evangelical Theories of Biblical Inspiration: A Review and Proposal* (New York and Oxford: Oxford University Press, 1987), 27-37.

[114] John Warwick Montgomery, 'Some Comments on Paul's Use of Genesis in his Epistle to the Romans', *Bulletin of the Evangelical Theological Society* 4, 1 (April 1961): 8-11.

[115] 'Pagan' is used here in a more general sense and not in the context of the specific sub-culture of 'Neo-Paganism' with its 'eco-spirituality' or nature religion foundation.

[116] Charles, 'Engaging the (Neo) Pagan', 135. Beasley-Murray agrees that the resurrection is the central focus of the Christian gospel in a global village. See Paul Beasley-Murray, *The Message of the Resurrection, the Bible Speaks Today* (Leicester: Inter-Varsity, 2000), 258.

suited to the New Age challenge — both in terms of the movement's ideas, and the opportunities available for confronting it. As for the Athenians the resurrection of Christ may hold the key to engagement with New Agers.[117]

With respect to the resurrection of Jesus, Gaffin claims that in the history of doctrine, especially in soteriology, it has been 'relatively eclipsed' by the atonement. As a consequence the soteriological significance of the resurrection 'has been largely overlooked'.[118] Whilst the bodily resurrection of Jesus is central, it is the soteriological character of the resurrection, its existential warrant, that the apologists to 'New Spirituality' need to discover.[119] And McGrath contends evangelicalism has yet to complete 'the apologetic and theological adjustment to the decline of modernity'.[120] Elsewhere I have sought to demonstrate apologetically the powerful nature of the message of Jesus' resurrection in transformation of one's 'soul sorrow', a transformation that is both spiritually self orientated and cosmic. It is a transformation which exhibits the holistic nature of our relationship with the truth.[121] In the resurrection of Jesus the listener or reader discovers: forgiveness (1 Corinthians 15:17); hope (1 Corinthians 15:20-21); a relationship with the Divine (John 2:19, 20:28); values for living as the risen Christ brings new meaning to earthly wisdom. The bodily resurrection of Jesus, seen as the 'firstfruits', demonstrates God's concern not just for one's 'spirit' but the totality of 'New Spirituality's' concept of humanness - mind, body, spirit: an aquarian new world order of cosmic dimensions (1 Corinthians 15:22-28).[122] These resurrection warrants justify Montgomery's findings that whilst persons are 'grounded in the clay of the contingent world', they transcend it. He asserts 'human personhood warrants the designation "semi-transcendent"', i.e. more than 'clay' but not divine.[123] And in the course of this apologetic one may also raise moral arguments as to why the total message of the resurrection is more compatible with

---

[117] Alister McGrath, 'Building Bridges to ...' in *Springboard for Faith*, Alister McGrath and Michael Green (London: Hodder and Stoughton, 1993), 78.
[118] Richard B. Gaffin, 'Redemption and Resurrection: An Exercise in Biblical-Systematic Theology' in *A Confessing Theology for Postmodern Times*, Michael S. Horton, ed. (Wheaton: Crossway, 2000), 230-231.
[119] Ray S. Anderson, *The New Age of Soul* (Eugene: Wipf and Stock, 2001), 116-126
[120] McGrath, *Passion*, 200.
[121] Peter Hicks, *Evangelicals and Truth: A Creative Proposal for a Postmodern Age* (Leicester: Apollos, 1998), 191-195.
[122] See Clifford and Johnson, *Riding the Rollercoaster*. This book is based on a number of addresses or sermons shared in 'market place' environments where the audience comprised seekers and those exploring 'New Spirituality'.
[123] Montgomery, *The Suicide*, 258.

human experience than reincarnation, with its denial of the body. As evangelist Kim Hawtrey remarks, the challenge is to act as a 'broker of meaning' in a world struggling for meaning.[124]

Montgomery in his apologetic debate always brings his presentation to an end at the point of existential need[125] and he holds that good legal advocacy appeals to the 'heart' as well as to the intellect.[126] As stated in the previous section I am advocating that this is a matter of reversing Montgomery's order since with postmodern spirituality one commences with the human predicament of existential anxiety and then is prepared to address the truth question.[127] In a recent lecture Montgomery himself embraced just such a procedure. In responding to how 'we can achieve a vigorous, sound Apologetic for the 21st century' he declared: 'First ... We need to employ the writings of the existentialists (Sartre-and especially Camus) and of the depth psychologists and psychoanalysts to point out the misery of the human condition apart from a relationship with Christ.'[128]

Martin Robinson notes that in our emerging postsecular culture the question of whether something like faith works, appears to be more important than whether it is true.[129] In the case of Montgomery's legal apologetic, all this requires is a reframing so that the commencement point is the circumstantial evidence, rather than the direct, documentary evidence. The relevant strand in the circumstantial evidence is the 'unbroken chain of testimony of changed lives that find their new meaning in the resurrection'.[130] It is one's testimony or story of how the resurrection meets our existential longing. Montgomery is personally open to resurrection focussed testimony as an apologetic strand. In fact he notes how the Apostle Paul, at times, began his defence that way (Acts 26:9-29).[131] Whilst in the

---

[124] Kim Hawtrey, 'The New Apologist', *Impact Bulletin*, 24 (October – December 1996): 1.
[125] For example, Montgomery and Plummer, 'Humanism'. See also, Montgomery, *History and Christianity*, 79-80; Montgomery, *Tracatus*, 6.
[126] John Warwick Montgomery, 'Legal Novels', RealPlayer[(Montgomery 3] jwm6.ram..ram.<http://www.spr-consilio.com/soundarchive.html>.
[127] McGrath, *Bridge-Building*, 11: 'Christianity must commend itself in terms of its relevance to life, not just its inherent rationality'; Fuller, *Spiritual but not Religious*, 173-174.
[128] Montgomery, 'Defending the Hope', 7. This was an invitational lecture at a conference of the Evangelical Alliance, held in Budapest, Hungary (27 April – 1 May 2002).
[129] Martin Robinson, *To Win the West* (Crowborough, East Sussex: Monarch, 1996), 216-217.
[130] Clinton advises that one begin with lived reality, real needs and then personal testimonies before evidence is introduced. See Stephen M. Clinton, 'Apologetic Methods and Post-Modernism' *Philosophia Christi* 19, 1 (Spring 1996): 16-18.
[131] Montgomery, *Defending the Biblical Gospel, Study Guide*, 84.

previous chapter we have acknowledged this strand as one of two 'weak links', it is only one aspect of a cumulative case and is strengthened by the subjective evidential element of the resurrection which is to be discussed shortly.[132]

As previously mentioned, and Barnett concurs, the fact that one starts by presenting one's testimony to the reality of the resurrection to a postmodern seeker does not imply failing to equip oneself mentally for the other questions that will arise about the actuality of the resurrection.[133] And Cole cautions that whilst it is appropriate for evangelicals to share their testimonies in postmodern apologetics these should not be 'manufactured', and the Christological story should still be the primary one.[134] The stress on the empowerment of the resurrection in the testimony of the apologists assists in avoiding the 'danger' of de-emphasising Christ. Also, Cole's second rider ensures that this person-centred apologetic remains faithful to the evangelical apologetic obligation to proclaim the objective nature of the gospel kerygma and not simply to address human needs, even though one begins there.[135] Montgomery in his essay on the constructive religious empiricism of William James enunciates similar cautions to those of Barnett and Cole.[136]

Although the presentation of this chord of circumstantial evidence is submitted within the legal analogy, this does not mean it must be purely oral testimony. For the Argentinean Christian psychologist Carlos Raimundo, 'the play of life' has been personally adapted to such a scenario. The listener or reader is invited to create on a small board a sculpture of how they feel about themselves, others and the world around them by using small plastic figures. After further dialogue about the significance of the resurrection in the apologist's life the listener or reader is then encouraged to create on another board a positive sculpture of how they now feel about themselves, relationships and the world around them as a result of this

---

[132] On the limitation of testimony and its place in a cumulative case see Netland, *Encountering Religious Pluralism*, 247-283.

[133] Paul Barnett, *Southern Cross* (December 2000 to January 2001), 25.

[134] Graham A. Cole, 'Religious Experience and Discernment Today', *Reformed Theological Journal* 56, 1 (January – April 1997): 3-6.

[135] Alister McGrath, 'Why Evangelicalism is the Future of Protestantism', *Christianity Today* 39, 7 (19 June 1995): 21-22.

[136] Montgomery, *The Shape*, 257-295. See also Montgomery, *Defending the Biblical Gospel, Study Guide*, 84; Montgomery, 'The Apologists of Eucatastrophe', 19; Montgomery, 'Defending the Hope', 10: 'We must not reduce the faith once delivered to the saints to a cultic matter of inner experience and personal testimony'.

information. The boards constitute a 'before' and 'after' portrait and the model resonates with the 'New Spirituality' seeker and leads into the evidence that follows.[137]

Refracting the resurrection narrative: testimony and metanarrative.
The limitations of this thesis do not allow the exploration at a theoretical level, of 'New Spirituality's' concerns about how some religious metanarratives[138] spawn 'wars of religion' over the earth and work against minorities and the powerless.[139] Yet in apologetic discourse on the impact of the resurrection of Jesus on one's belief system, one must take cognisance of this possible 'pothole' to faith.[140] Brueggemann's thought of the 'finding of the postmodern imagination' is helpful here. It implies that rather than constructing truth in a mega doctrinal scheme, we share 'the voicing of a lot of little pieces out of which people can put life together in fresh configurations'.[141] Sutcliffe and Bowman write persuasively about the folklorists *refracting* the grand narrative through many little, everyday, not-so-grand narratives which include 'aetiological legends' and 'personal experience narratives'. These insights they relate to 'vernacular religion' and view as applicable to alternative spirituality.[142] For apologetic discourse this points to a considered dialogue that does not seek to address 'the life, the universe and everything'; that varies the dialogue from testimony, to story, to aetiological narratives, for example how the church came into being, or how the gospels found their final form; that shows how the resurrection narratives help put life together, rather than disempowering it. In such an apologetic one does not just churn out arguments for general consumption, for there is a commitment to paying attention to the issues of the listener and the various sub-cultures of 'New Spirituality'.

As well it is argued in this chapter that the evangelical tendency to categorise 'New Spirituality' as having a total aversion to metanarratives is overstated. Just because it is eclectic does not mean that 'New Spirituality' is adverse to all metadiscourse. For example, as will be discussed shortly, 'New Spirituality' places a strong emphasis on myth. The three major influences here are Jung, Eliade and

---

[137] <http://www.playoflife.com>.
[138] For discussion and interaction see Dave Tomlinson, *The Post-Evangelical* (London: Triangle, 1995), 75-83, 139-145.
[139] Jacques Derrida, 'Faith and Knowledge: The Two Sources of "Religion" at the Limits of Reason Alone' in *Religion*, Jacques Derrida and Gianni Vattimo, eds. (Cambridge: Polity, 1998), 24.
[140] J. Richard Middleton and Brian J. Walsh, 'Facing the Postmodern Scalpel: Can the Christian Faith Withstand Deconstruction?' in *Christian Apologetics in a Postmodern World*, Phillips and Okholm, eds., 138-145.
[141] Walter Brueggemann, *The Bible and Postmodern Imagination* (London: SCM, 1993), 19-20.
[142] Sutcliffe and Bowman, *Beyond New Age: Exploring Alternative Spirituality*, 5-7.

Campbell, who all espouse some form of universalism. Ellwood comments that the essential 'point of Jung's archetypes, Eliade's structuralism, and Campbell's one message behind all myths' is that all myths are one, and that behind their 'thousand faces they had in effect one message, based on the psychic unity of humanity, and proclaimed one intrapsychic path to salvation'.[143] Such universalism is found in Drury's tale of four occult shamans from different corners of the globe who come together at the mythic 'centre of the world', to witness a healing of the earth. The healing is based on a common story from the 'ancient ones'. These 'ancient ones' know 'that all beings had come from an ancient and timeless place which had always existed even before the creation of the world'.[144]

So rather than opposing metanarratives *per se*, 'New Spirituality' is a reaction to *disempowering* metanarratives. And, because of its eclectic nature, it also struggles with those who do not see good in beliefs other than their own, and/or who show a lack of respect for the religious traditions of others.[145] However in its reliance on myth 'New Spirituality' clearly shows an appreciation of common psychic life and a common human condition. John Drane puts it this way:

> All this is just another way of saying that the Gospel needs to be people-centred and not predominantly idea-centred. We need to listen to what ordinary people are saying, and recognize that in many ways it is not the same as the ideologies of intellectual post-modernity ... philosophers of the post-modern have invested much time and energy in the effort to convince us that people today no longer believe in truth and values, and have no place for metanarratives in their worldview. Christian apologists, for their part, have largely accepted this position. But why, if this is true, did no one respond to those terrorist atrocities (September 11, 2001) in this post-modern way?[146]

In rejoinder, to the call for caution at least in the use of religious metanarratives in apologetics, one could argue that Paul's Areopagus address that has been relied

---

[143] Robert Ellwood, *The Politics of Myth: A Study of C.G. Jung, Mircea Eliade and Joseph Campbell* (Albany, New York: State University of New York Press, 1999), 174.

[144] Neville Drury, *The Shaman's Quest* (Rose Bay, NSW: Bandl and Schlesinger, 2001), 188.

[145] 1 Peter 3:15-16. For a discussion on whether 1 Peter 3:16 refers to a humility or gentleness in relation to one's curious non-Christian neighbours see J. Ramsay Michaels, *1 Peter, Word Commentary* (Waco: Word, 1988), 189-190.

[146] Drane, 'Unknown Gods, Declining Churches, and the Spiritual Search of Contemporary Culture', *200th Annual C.M.S. Sermon* (delivered Westminster College, Cambridge, St. Andrews-by-the Wardrobe, Blackfriars, London and Fulford Parish Church, York, 2000).

on in this chapter, contains a metanarrative (Acts 17:23-31). Carson appears to support this, and holds that the apologetic implication for proclamation to paganism is that the brief should include a 'worldview' or 'meta-narrative', otherwise the gospel message about the resurrection of Jesus lacks context and it will not make 'sense' to 'postmodern biblical illiterates'.[147] One could debate this position as the brief Lucan account is not an extensive theological overview. Yet this appears not to be Carson's major premise. He is suggesting by a worldview a biblical 'plot-line' that traces out the 'rudiments' of biblical teaching. In fact he is calling for an evangelistic model that is a 'subset' of biblical theology, not systematic theology.[148] This call is consistent with Montgomery's theological method as revealed in his affirmation of Andreae's work. Montgomery observes:

> Certainly Andreae never produced a *Loci theologici* of systematics based upon an original theme. But neither did Luther! – and probably for the same reason: the conviction that true theology reaches too high and plumbs too low to be exhausted in any single system; because the holy God is the author, theology is better expressed in mystery than in dogmatic finality, and at its best does not extend beyond the living kerygmatic witness of Holy Writ. Luther, however, though he was no systematist in the traditional sense formulated a magnificently 'original' theology. And so in fact did Andreae; for him, theology forever describes, in its multifarious facets, a 'pilgrim journeying to a wedding'.[149]

My apologetic framework for the resurrection mentioned in this section seeks to be consistent with Acts 17 and places the message of the resurrection including the evidence of testimony, in the context of basic biblical teachings such as the nature of God (personal creator as against a pantheistic view), humanity (fallen), the provision of forgiveness and principles for living. This is not a doctrinal metanarrative on the Trinity, atonement and the like, nor is it oppressive. It is a theological narrative for a 'pilgrim journeying to a wedding'.[150] Such a biblical 'plot-line' that gives the resurrection proclamation a context is warranted, and, as has been indicated above, it can be established by the *circumstantial* evidence of testimony.

---

[147] Carson, *The Gagging*, 501-505.
[148] ibid., 496-505.
[149] Montgomery, *Cross and Crucible*, 1: 131.
[150] See Montgomery, 'Defending the Hope' where he states that in apologetics one begins with where the believer is, not a simple expounding of dogmatics (2).

However, as Drane and Tomlinson affirm, it needs to be remembered that 'conversion' for 'New Spirituality' seekers is usually a process, not an event.[151] This is certainly true for teachings like the *uniqueness* of Christ.[152] Johnston insightfully comments that the postmodern listener or reader will want to 'test' the teaching of the uniqueness of Christ before making a commitment to it. In other words, the listener or reader says, 'Let me understand this and see how it works before I accept this is right.' A further response may be, 'For now it sits right with me.' So the preaching or apologetic exercise becomes like a journey.[153] The implication is that the biblical 'plot-line' may be presented over a number of apologetic discourses and encounters. And whilst Paul's address appears to be an 'event' this is balanced with the fact that his speech perhaps went on for hours[154] and that there was at least one precursor in the Athenian marketplace (Acts 17:16-18). This concept of 'conversion' as a process is consistent with the Engel 'scale' on religious behaviour, which indicates that maturity in faith is a gradual process. Engel's widely accepted chart has 'Awareness of Supreme Being' at – 8, 'Some Knowledge of Gospel' at – 7, 'Positive Attitude Toward Act of Becoming a Christian' at – 4, 'Decision to Act' at – 2, 'Repentance and Faith in Christ' at – 1 followed by regeneration.[155] The evangelical apologetic task to 'New Spirituality' is to assist the seeker in this spiritual decision process in moving from – 8 to 0, and to do so at whatever entry point one finds the listener or reader.[156] And not all listeners or readers will move in Engel's precise order.

Another circumstantial evidence strand: Montgomery's common subjective experiences
Apart from personal testimony Montgomery, in his literary apologetic, projects another subjective evidential option in his case for Christianity and the resurrection. *It is an argument relying on common myths, folklore and archetypes.* Here it is important to note that Montgomery has always acknowledged that apologetic

---

[151] John Drane, *Evangelism for a New Age* (London: Marshall Pickering, 1994), 111-114; Tomlinson, *The Post-Evangelical*, 142-145. See also Hicks, *Evangelicals and Truth*, 171-178.
[152] A matter for further apologetic research into 'New Spirituality' is the relationship of the doctrine of the uniqueness of Christ to an Engel scale on religious behaviour; and as to whether the effect of the doctrine is not fully comprehended by some until after 'conversion'.
[153] Graham Johnston, *Preaching to a Postmodern World* (Grand Rapids: Baker, 2001), 106-107.
[154] Carson, *The Gagging*, 501.
[155] James F. Engel, *Contemporary Christian Communication: Its Theory and Practice* (Nashville and New York: Thomas Nelson, 1979), 225.
[156] For the relationship between conversion in the early Church and the Jewish or pagan world see Charles H. Talbert, 'Conversion in the Acts of the Apostles: Ancient Auditor's' in *Luke-Acts*, Richard P. Thompson and Thomas E. Phillips, eds. (Marcon, Georgia: Mercer University Press, 1998), 141-153.

arguments normally fall into one of two categories – the rational or the empirical. And empirical arguments can be, 'objective or subjective in nature, depending upon whether harmony with external experience (history, physical and natural science) or conformity with internal (psychological) experience is stressed'.[157] The aim here is to consider this further subjective argument of Montgomery and suggest that it can be incorporated into the legal circumstantial case for the resurrection as the strand of common subjective experiences. This is a step that Montgomery himself has not initiated. If this premise is correct then there are two significant benefits for the legal apologetic. The first is that there is a valid increasing of one's common ground with a listener or reader in the area of personal testimony. This alone justifies this argument for the evidentialist. The second benefit is its strengthening of the 'weaker' strand of circumstantial evidence. Such a subjective apologetic is not without precedent as the lawyer Thomas Erskine[158] maintained an apologetic based on the evidence of inner life. This further subjective evidential argument of Montgomery one could also categorise as mutual revelation between the apologist and the listener or reader.

Kilby suggests that in a broad sense myth, like poetry, is indefinable. It is a cosmic pattern that penetrates us.[159] Hexham and Poewe, who find cosmic mythological fragments in a New Age world, have provided this useful definition of myth that is applicable to a 'New Spirituality' context:

> Probably the most useful definition of 'myth' is: *a story with culturally formative power.* This definition emphasizes that a myth is essentially a story – any story – that affects the way people live. Contrary to many writers, we do not believe that a myth is necessarily unhistorical. In itself a story that becomes a myth can be true or false, historical or unhistorical, fact or fiction. What is important is not the story itself but the *function* it serves in the life of an individual, a group, or a whole society.[160]

---

[157] Montgomery, *Faith Founded*, 92.
[158] See Erskine, *Remarks on the Internal Evidence.* See also Montgomery, ed., *Jurisprudence,* 451-459.
[159] Clyde S. Kilby, 'Mythic and Christian Elements in Tolkien' in *Myth, Allegory and Gospel,* Montgomery, ed., 119-123.
[160] Hexham and Poewe, *New Religions,* 81. The authors also critique Eliade's broad understanding of myth, and such critique will be discussed later in this section. Cf. Campbell's four functions of a myth with its primary emphasis on individual significance, guidance and social function – Joseph Campbell, *Myths to Live By* (New York: Viking, 1972), 214-215.

In folklore there are found common motifs, such as the trickster and the witchtype figure,[161] which Montgomery connects to myths and archetypes.[162] By 'archetypes' Montgomery is referring to the Jungian belief in universal symbolic patterns in the subconscious life of humanity. Jung saw these archetypes as 'universal mental structures or cognitive principles that give shape to human psychic experience'. These 'archetypes of the collective consciousness' or primordial images disclose universal needs for healing and transformation and manifest themselves symbolically in religions, myths, fairytales and fantasies.[163]

This further subjective evidential argument of Montgomery is most succinctly set out in one of his latest essays, 'Neglected Apologetic Styles'.[164] It varies little in substance from his much earlier presentation in the essay on 'The Apologists of Eucatastrophe'.[165] Montgomery also cogently presents this subjective apologetic argument in propositional form.[166]

Montgomery creatively appropriates his argument to the literary apologetic, but, as mentioned, the premise herein is that it is also applicable to the legal apologetic, especially in a New Age world. It is another strand of evidence. Montgomery's apologetic is along the following lines. The 'tender minded' who frown on rational and objective arguments can perhaps find an answer in the subjective depths of their own souls.[167] The literary apologetic may well unlock this 'hidden treasure' of such seekers if it focuses on the supposition that the fallen race had a primordial realisation of its separation, sinfulness and need for redemption. Montgomery continues:

> Under these circumstances, redemptive knowledge would surface not in a direct fashion but by way of symbolic patterns—visible not only to the sensitive psychoanalyst, but also to the folklorist whose material 'bubbles up' collectively from the subconscious of

---

[161] See Stith Thompson, *Motif-Index of Folk Literature* (Indiana: Indiana University Press, 1994).

[162] Cf. Bettelheim who argues that whilst there are essential similarities between myths and fairytales there are also differences, such as the fairytale extending more to the ordinary: something that is unusual but could happen to the person next door on a walk in the woods. Fairytales are more everyday ways than what occurs in the drama of myth. See Bruno Bettleheim, *The Users of Enchantment: The Meaning and Importance of Fairytales* (New York: Penguin, 1978), 36-37.

[163] Stanton L. Jones and Richard E. Butman, *Modern Psycho-Therapies* (Downers Grove: InterVarsity, 1991), 123.

[164] Montgomery, 'Neglected Apologetic', 126-133. See also Montgomery, *Tractatus*, 6.322 – 6.45.

[165] Montgomery, 'The Apologists of Eucatastrophe'. See also Montgomery, *Defending the Biblical Gospel, Study Guide*, 77-80.

[166] Montgomery, *Tractatus*, 6.3 – 6.45.

[167] Montgomery, *Defending the Biblical Gospel, Study Guide*, 75-80.

> the race. Literature in this special sense could therefore reflect the Christian story in an objective sense and trigger conscious acceptance of it. Is this perhaps the background of Paul's literary appeal on the Areopagus: 'As some of your own poets have said, "We are his offspring"' (Acts 17:28)?
>
> Jungian analytical psychotherapy has indeed identified such redemptive 'archetypes', or fundamental and universal symbolic patterns, which appear equally in the physical liturgies of ancient alchemists and in the dreams of contemporary business men. Religious phenomenologists—the greatest being Mircea Eliade—have discovered these motifs in the most widely diversified primitive and sophisticated religions.[168]

Montgomery's connecting of Eliade and Jung is not unwarranted as Eliade certainly appreciated Jung's seminal influence.[169] Montgomery's reliance on Jung and Eliade is also appropriate as together with Joseph Campbell they are primarily associated with the development of today's popular and academic interest in mythology.[170] And in support of Montgomery's case, drawing from Eliade and Jung, one can argue that most cultures offer a filter or matrix in which the archetypes emerge and are passed through stories and folklore from person to person and across generations. Montgomery himself invokes scholars and anthropologists such as Kluckhohn and Levi-Strauss.[171] These scholars find similarities between myths collected in the different regions of our world and discover that there are recurrent themes such as the 'slaying the monster' and the redemptive hero. Eliade's essay on 'The Good Savage, the Yogi and the Psychoanalyst' (Jung and Freud) is also of particular interest in this regard.[172] Montgomery argues that C.S. Lewis and Tolkien have in some ways in their literary works played on such myths and archetypes and he challenges today's apologist to reignite and develop such a literary apologetic.[173] This is appropriate as Lewis includes Jung in his overall theory on the place of archetype in fairytales in stories.[174] Montgomery typically concludes his case citing Tolkien and C.S. Lewis:

---

[168] Montgomery, 'Neglected Apologetic', 127.
[169] See Eric J. Sharpe, *Comparative Religion: A History* (London: Duckworth, 1975), 210-212; Mircea Eliade, *Myths, Dreams and Mysteries*, trans. Philip Mairet (London and Glasgow: Collins, 1968), 54-55.
[170] Ellwood, *The Politics*, vii.
[171] Montgomery, 'The Apologists of Eucatastrophe', 26-29.
[172] Eliade, *Myths, Dreams*, 43-56.
[173] Montgomery, 'Neglected Apologetic, 127-131; Montgomery, *Tractatus*, 6.4.

> The gospels contain...a story of a larger kind which embraces all the essence of fairy stories...The birth of Christ is the eucatastrophe of man's history. The resurrection is the eucatastrophe of the story of the incarnation. This story begins and ends in joy. It has pre-eminently the 'inner consistency of reality'. There is no tale ever told that men would rather find was true, and none which so many sceptical men have accepted as true on its own merits. For the art of it has the supremely convincing tone of primary art, that is of creation. To reject it leads either to sadness or to wrath...
>
> God is the Lord, of angels, and of men—and of elves. Legend and history have met and fused.[175]
>
> We must not be ashamed of the mythical radiance resting on our theology. We must not be nervous about 'parallels' and 'Pagan Christs': they *ought* to be there—it would be a stumbling block if they weren't. We must not, in false spirituality, withhold our imaginative welcome. If God chooses to be mythopoeic—and is not the sky itself a myth?—shall we refuse to be *mythopathic*? For this is the marriage of heaven and earth: Perfect Myth and Perfect Fact: claiming not only our love and our obedience, but also our wonder and delight, addressed to the savage, the child and the poet in each one of us no less than to the moralist, the scholar and the philosopher.[176]

R.C. Sproul presents a profile of humanity, based on Romans 1:18-23, which brings a biblical justification to Montgomery's subjective apologetic model. Sproul, who belongs to the 'classical method' apologetic school, is committed to evidences. Paul in the Romans 1 pericope argues that our universal sinful condition before God leads us to suppress our natural knowledge of God and to replace it with idolatry. Sproul outlines three phases that explain the process of our

---

[174] Lewis also suggests that to Jung's 'Know thyself' precept found in archetypes can be added the role of non human beings in telling our human story. C.S. Lewis, *Of Other Worlds: Essays and Stories*, Walter Hooper, ed. (New York and London: Harcourt, Brace and Jovanovich, 1996), 26-28.

[175] J.R.R. Tolkien, 'On Fairy-Stories' in *Essays Presented to Charles Williams*, C.S. Lewis, ed., rpt. ed. (Grand Rapids: William B. Eerdmans, 1981), 83-84. Cited in Montgomery, *Defending the Biblical Gospel, Study Guide*, 79. Montgomery illustrates the truth of this fusing in Christ of legend and history, via the common folktale of 'Sleeping Beauty'. See Montgomery, *Tractatus*, 6.42 – 6.421.

[176] C.S. Lewis, *God in the Dock: Essays on Theology*, Walter Hooper, ed. (London: Fount, 1979), 45. Cited in Montgomery, 'Neglected Apologetic', 130-131.

response to God's self-revelation. The first phase is personal 'trauma' as in our fallenness we are threatened by God's presence and his moral holiness, and further He is a threat to our quest for autonomy. The second phase to our profile is 'repression'. Repression is the consequence of trauma and as a result our knowledge of God, and our state before Him, is 'put down' or 'held' in the unconscious. The final phase is 'substitution'. As the repressed knowledge is not destroyed it is manifested outwardly in veiled and less threatening concepts. Montgomery's subjective empirical argument is seeking to unearth this repressed and substituted primordial knowledge of God and ourselves.[177]

It would be fair to say that in some quarters Montgomery is misunderstood and represented as a purely rational 'hardnosed' apologist. Montgomery's writings on the subjective empirical defence indicate that for most of his apologetic life, whilst his focus has been on historical and legal arguments, his methodology has been eclectic and broad. Again, the link to Montgomery's subjective evidential argument is Andreae. In his study on Andreae he wrote, 'Myth is the literary genre in which Andreae particularly excelled ... allegorical-parabolic myth is the vehicle for showing how the various realms of human existence and knowledge both reflect the gospel and are reflected in it.' Montgomery quotes one of Andreae's mythical figures, 'Clothe your form in myth and fairy tale, and you will be able to do your duty to God and man.' Montgomery continues in a Jungian vein, 'true myth presents images and concepts which correspond to the fundamental and universal symbols ("archetypes") in man's unconscious mind. Thus myths offer one of the most powerful avenues to self-understanding and physical wholeness'.[178] Throughout his apologetic years Montgomery has not deviated from this position. For him, apologetically whether one looks at psycho-analytical theory, religious phenomenology or folklore, individually or collectively, these portray a portrait of humanity's psychic life.

Justification of the use of myth and archetypes.
As was the case with Montgomery's own doctorate, the focus of this thesis precludes a detailed analysis of whether the archetypal and mythological premises that Jung, Eliade and others rely on here are totally justified, and in a real sense this is not essential to Montgomery's *apologetic* method. As will be shown, the

---

[177] R.C. Sproul, *If there is a God, Why are there Atheists?* (Minneapolis: Bethany, 1978), 73-78. See also Philip Johnson, 'Apologetics and Myths: Signs of Salvation and Postmodernity', *Lutheran Theological Journal* 32, 2 (July 1998), 67. Cf. John Murray, *The Epistle to the Romans, the New International Commentary on the New Testament* (Grand Rapids: William B. Eerdmans, 1968), 34-43.
[178] Montgomery, *Cross and Crucible*, 1: 148-149.

concepts he refers to from Jung and Eliade are consistent with a biblical 'plot-line', and 'New Spirituality' strongly affirms and relies on the findings of Jung and the process of myth. So Montgomery's subjective evidential arguments find true common ground here and are consistent with his understanding of truth. And one could argue that this is consistent with the Apostle Paul, who when citing 'some of your own poets' at the Areopagus, was surely relying on common ground and consistency of the poets' verse with biblical teaching, rather than endorsing the foundational premises of their poetry as such (Acts 17:28). Further Montgomery's positive apologetic is not far removed from the ideas of redemption analogy and concept fulfilment that are strategies adopted by missiologists. In his missionary evangelism Don Richardson found a redemptive analogy of a crucified Christ, and, as a consequence, a concept fulfilment, in a 'Peace Child' of the Sawi tribe. He documents many other instances of redemptive analogies and concludes, 'When conversion is facilitated by redemptive analogy people are made aware of spiritual meaning dormant within their own culture'.[179] This is not to say that all missiologists are as supportive as Richardson is of the common nature of redemptive analogies.[180]

In a negative apologetic one may find some basis for criticising 'New Spirituality's' reliance on myth[181] and Jung, but that is not the focus of this apologetic endeavour.[182] And it should be noted that Montgomery does comment on the 'dangers' of Jung's work, including his hostility towards reason and history[183] and his psychological reductionism. An illustration of the latter is found in his thesis on Andreae and the Alchemist's interpretation of the Philosopher's Stone:

---

[179] Don Richardson, 'Redemptive Analogy' in *Perspectives on the World Christian Movement, a Reader,* Ralph D. Winter and Stephen C. Hawthorne, eds. (Passadena: William Carey Library; Carlisle: Paternoster, 1999), 398.

[180] For example Hesselgrave whilst acknowledging that the culture, folklore and belief systems of people groups is important, holds that communicating the gospel message is more important from redemptive analogies in the Old Testament than trying to discover redemptive analogies in a culture. See David J. Hesselgrave, *Scripture and Strategy: The Use of the Bible in Postmodern Church and Mission* (Passadena: William Carey Library, 1994), 101-111.

[181] For example see Tom Snyder, *Myth Conceptions: Joseph Campbell and the New Age* (Grand Rapids: Baker, 1995). Cf. Loren Wilkinson, 'The Bewitching Charms of Neo-Paganism', *Christianity Today* 43, 13 (15 November 1999): 54-63.

[182] For a critique of Jung see J. Budziszewski, 'C.G. Jung's War on the Christian Faith', *Christian Research Journal* 21, 3 (1999): 28-33. Also Noll suggests that the foundation for Jung's thought lies as much in occultism, Nietzscheanism and social Darwinism as it does in the natural sciences. See Richard Noll, *The Jung Cult* (Hammersmith, London: Fontana, 1995), 9, 137. Ellwood in his more moderate assessment of the origins of Jung's ideas, raises similar concerns as Noll, not only with respect to Jung, but also to the right-wing influences on Eliade and mythologist Joseph Campbell. See Ellwood, *The Politics,* 37-169.

[183] For example see Montgomery, *The Suicide,* 136-137.

> (But) when Jung reduces Christian and esoteric alchemy to a single psychological process—by regarding the Christian alchemist's identification of the Philosopher's Stone with Christ as no more than an ideogram of the self—Andreae would raise the strongest objection. For Andreae, alchemy does properly represent the psychological process of 'individuation' (he would call it 'conversion'!), but this is not something that can happen in the psyche apart from the transcendent action of the personal, living Christ. We can be sure that Andreae, while accepting Jung's psychological insights into the alchemical process, would never condone the psychological reductionism by which he absorbs theocentric Christian theology into anthropocentric psychotherapy.[184]

Montgomery here is not suggesting that Jung is at fault for suggesting one should know oneself but rather that his '"sacred" egoism', 'individuation'[185] or 'God-images'[186] are a fixation on self rather than glorifying an objective God.[187] However, Montgomery's accusation of reductionism in the sense of bringing down the Christ and the transcendent God to become a mere factor in the human psyche would be answered by some Jungians on the basis that we can never experience anything except through the psyche, and our images of God do reflect such conditioning. So the Jungian question is, who knows what God is objectively?[188] Montgomery would still assert here his charge of a psychological and theological reductionism. Kenneth Becker who positively encourages the mutual sharing between Jungian and Ignatian interests would support Montgomery. He concludes that Jung in principle excludes the gospel message of the incarnation of God's and Jesus' love into our lives. He states:

---

[184] Montgomery, *Cross and Crucible*, 1: 253. See Carl Gustav Jung, *Psychology and Religion* (New Haven: Yale University Press, 1938), 108-114.

[185] C.G. Jung, 'Psychotherapists or the Clergy' in *Modern Man in Search of a Soul*, trans. W.S. Dell and Cary F. Baynes (London and Henley-on-Thames: Routledge and Kegan Paul, 1962), 273-276.

[186] For Jung 'God-images' cannot be clinically (empirically) differentiated from 'self-images' and therefore from a Jungian psychological viewpoint the Trinity is an archetypal symbol of the individual's Father-stage, a Son-stage and a Holy Ghost-stage. See for discussion Michael Palmer, *Freud and Jung on Religion* (London and New York: Routledge, 1997), 156-165.

[187] See C.G. Jung, 'The Mana-Personality' in *The Collected Works of C.G. Jung*, trans. R.F.C. Hull, Vol. 7, 2nd ed. (London: Routledge and Kegal Paul, 1953), 237-241; Jeffrey Satinover, *The Empty Self: Gnostic and Jungian Foundations of Modern Identity*, Grove Series (Bramcote: Nottingham, 1995), 9-10.

[188] See Ann Ulanov, 'Jung and Religion: The Opposing Self' in *The Cambridge Companion to Jung*, Polly Young-Eisendrath and Terence Dawson, eds. (Cambridge: Cambridge University Press, 1997), 299-301.

The problem with Jung's psychology is not that he talks about religion in archetypal terms, but that he takes as natural, essential, and autonomous the roles and dynamics of the particular archetypes as they are twisted by the psychic wounds.[189]

Irrespective of one's view on the place of God in Jung's thought, Jones and Butman note that in Jungian tradition this knowing of truth is a matter of individual discernment, and that the complete trust in the guidance of the unconscious, means one does not fully address the limitations of self awareness, including our capacities for self-serving biases and self deception. This subjective epistemology leads to an exaggerated individualism and a self-salvation.[190] Loder summarises the problem well,

> Jung tends to see human wholeness as the ultimate reality. As a result, he confuses the orders of being and knowing. The archetype, as a structural reality, is on a par with grammar in speech and logic in intelligence. As a result, it is a structure by which one comes to know one's personal wholeness; it is not a structure of being.[191]

In short, while finding value in Jung's insights Montgomery holds that care must be exercised to employ these insights 'within Andreae's Christian framework'.[192]

Whilst Eliade's work is foundational to the study of the nature of religion, he is criticised today for placing his findings in 'far-flung contexts'. The academic concerns include: the 'over-applying' of the Shaman motifs found in some cultures;[193] the extrapolation of conclusions too frequently from the common

---

[189] Kenneth L. Becker, *Unlikely Companions: C.G. Jung on the Spiritual Exercises of Ignatius of Loyola* (Leominster, Herefordshire: Gracewing; New Malden, Surrey: Inigo Enterprises, 2001), 322.

[190] Jones and Butman, *Modern Psycho-Therapies*, 131-132. For a positive interaction of Jungian theory in a Christian gospel context see Steve Price and David Haynes, *Dreamworks: A Meeting of the Spiritual and Psychology* (Blackburn, Victoria: HarperCollins, 1997), 111-119; W. Harold Grant, Magdala Thompson and Thomas E. Clarke, *From Image to Likeness: A Jungian Path in the Gospel Journey* (New York and Ramsey, New Jersey: Paulist Press, 1983), 5-28.

[191] James E. Loder, *The Logic of the Spirit: Human Development in Theological Perspective* (San Francisco: Jossey-Bass, 1998), 307. Loder identifies other substantive theological issues that are at stake in considering Jung including the following: (1) it is through developing human wholeness (not grace) that one draws closer to God; (2) the transformation of the ego does not take sufficient account of the role of the mediator; and (3) the existence of a gnostic doctrine of evil (306-309). Cf. Ann Belford Ulanov, *Religion and the Spiritual in Carl Jung* (New York and Mahwah, New Jersey: Paulist Press, 1999), 9-15.

[192] Montgomery, *Cross and Crucible*, 1: 271.

[193] Garry Trompf, *In Search of Origins* (London: Oriental University Press, 1990), 137-139.

cultural concern with renewal of yearly and millennium cycles;[194] the over expansive work on cargo cults.[195] Ellwood also claims that, like Jung and Campbell, Eliade did little fieldwork on myth; rather he depended heavily 'on the labours of others'.[196] However, Eliade's scholarship in religious studies remains significant with respect to the relating of myth and time to cosmic salvation. In this context Montgomery is on sure ground.[197]

Biblical 'plot line'.
From Montgomery's writings on a literary apologetic one can outline a subjective evidential apologetic that is consistent with biblical teaching. There is a 'plot-line' that builds a case for a universal Christ figure. In a contemporary 'myth' context the archetypal connections for Montgomery can be illustrated by the *via negativa*. He states, 'Here an effort is made to show that secular literary classics (1) depict the sinful, fallen human condition in exact accord with biblical anthropology, and (2) demonstrate that all contemporary secular ways of salvation are deceptive and unable to solve man's dilemma. By process of elimination, then, the reader is brought to a consideration of the Christian answer as the only, or at very least the most meaningful solution to his fallen condition.'[198]

Our common frailty and angst is reflected in Albert Camus' *The Plague*, which depicts a city in the grip of disease, and for which there is no prospect, hope or cure. Montgomery writes that Camus used that imagery to portray the human condition, as 'mortally diseased' and not capable of being cured. He notes George Orwell's novel *1984* uses a similar kind of imagery to depict the consequences of the human capacity for nasty and brutish life. Also Franz Kafka's *The Trial*, depicts the universal human being judged for the human condition. The false solutions to this human dilemma, which reflects biblical teaching, are found for Montgomery in such works as William Golding's, *Lord of the Flies*, Samuel Beckett's, *Waiting for Godot* and John Updike's, *Rabbit, Run*[199] Updike indirectly acknowledges Montgomery's first point about secular literary classics in stating: 'Fiction holds the mirror up to the world' and in his belief that his

---

[194] G.W. Trompf, 'Millenarism: History, Sociology, and Cross-Cultural Analysis', *Journal of Religious History* 24, 2 (February 2000): 115-116.
[195] G.W. Trompf, 'Mircea Eliade and the Interpretation of Cargo Cults', *Religious Traditions*, 12 (1989): 31-64.
[196] Ellwood, *The Politics*, xii.
[197] Philip Johnson, 'Apologetics and Myths', 62-72.
[198] Montgomery, 'The Apologetics of Eucatastrophe', 21.
[199] ibid., 20-22.

characters show that all men and women are both 'radically valuable and radically imperfect.' However, he admits that there are different angles at which to hold the mirror.[200] Yet he connects with Montgomery's basic idea when he states:

> ... the hero of *Rabbit, Run* was meant to be a representative Kierkegaardian man, as his name, Angstrom, hints. Man in a state of fear and trembling, separated from God, haunted by dread, twisted by the conflicting demands of his animal biology and human intelligence, of the social contract and the inner imperatives, condemned as if by otherworldly origins to perpetual restlessness—such was, and to some extent remains, my conception. The modern Christian inherits an intellectual tradition of faulty cosmology and shrewd psychology.
>
> St. Augustine was not the first Christian writer nor the last to give us the human soul with its shadows, its Rembrandtesque blacks and whites, its chiaroscuro; this sense of ourselves, as creatures caught in the light, whose decisions and recognitions have a majestic significance, remains to haunt non-Christians as well, and to form, as far as I can see, the raison d'être of fiction.[201]
>
> Fiction is rooted in an act of faith: a presumption of an inherent significance in human activity, that makes daily life worth dramatizing and particularizing. There is even a shadowy cosmic presumption that the universe — the totality of what is, which includes our subjective impressions as well as objective data — composes a narrative and contains a poem, which our own stories and poems echo.[202]

Outside of a literary context Montgomery illustrates a number of archetypal connections. For example, in *The Quest for Noah's Ark* he discusses Eliade's stress on the place of a 'Cosmic Mountain' and a 'Cosmic Tree' in universal religious symbolism.[203] The 'Cosmic Tree', as a 'Tree of Life', is an image found in the enactment of the Tree of Life in the Garden of Eden as well as the Cross, and the

---

[200] John Updike, 'Remarks Upon Receiving the Campion Medal' in *John Updike and Religion: The Sense of the Sacred and Notions of Grace*, James Yerkes, ed. (Grand Rapids and Cambridge: William B. Eerdmans, 1999), 4-5.
[201] ibid., 5-6.
[202] ibid., flyleaf.
[203] John Warwick Montgomery, *The Quest for Noah's Ark*, 2nd ed. (Minneapolis: Bethany, 1974), 284.

cosmic mountain motif, where amongst other things humans ascend to meet with the gods, is a reminder of the stories of Noah, Moses and Jesus.[204] Eliade claims that these common archaic stories betray the 'desire to recover the state of freedom and beatitude before "the Fall", and the will to restore communication between Earth and Heaven; in a word, to abolish all the changes made in the very structure of the cosmos and in the human mode of being by that primordial disruption'.[205]

In *Principalities and Powers* Montgomery shows how Eliade's and Jung's observations on the actual 'scientific' laboratory operations of the alchemist, whose symbols and motifs still appear in dreams today, indicated how alchemy also served as a 'physical liturgy'. Alchemy was a ritual of transmutation 'whereby the adept (alchemist) searched for the means to overcome the disjunction in himself (expressed as the opposing principles of "Sulphur and Mercury")'.[206] It is a short step from this foundation to argue apologetically that Jesus is the alchemist's Philosopher's Stone, the precious element, the Elixir of Life, who turns into reality the universal longing to refine spiritual dross into gold.[207] Also the motif of Faerie brings the sensitive seeker to face spiritual reality: '... archetypically in their own souls and factually in terms of the "existence of an invisible world"'.[208]

From Montgomery's subjective evidential apologetic a biblical 'plot-line' is evident that is consistent with basic biblical teaching of creation, fall and the ache for redemption. It requires no modification. This 'plot-line' is both 'truthful' and apologetically attractive to the world of 'New Spirituality'.

Christ figure.
Montgomery's subjective evidential apologetic is not limited to the *via negativa* and he positively looks for the 'Christ-figure'. Whilst he relies on archetypal images from sources like alchemy, the archetypal thrust is from literature and myth. He cautions that no literary figure can be the actual historic Christ. However, he asserts few would have difficulty in recognising a Christ figure in Condrad's *Lord Jim* or Dostoyevsky's *The Idiot*.[209] Michael Frost, who was influenced on this issue by Montgomery, lists classics that portray a character

---

[204] See for example Eliade, *Myths, Dreams*, 57-71.
[205] ibid., 64.
[206] Montgomery, *Principalities*, 101; Montgomery, *Tractatus*, 6.32-6.36. Also see Jung, *Psychology and Religion*, 109-110.
[207] ibid., 101-103.
[208] Montgomery, *Principalities*, 132-136.

with an aspect of the Christ image. He reflects on Jerzy Kosinski's *Being There*, Scott Fitzgerald's *The Great Gatsby*, John Steinbeck's *Grapes of Wrath* and Ernest Hemingway's *The Old Man and the Sea*.[210]

In Sherlock Holmes, Montgomery also finds a limited 'Christ-figure' analogous to Dickens' Sidney Carton or Melville's Billy Budd.[211] Although he has most apparent weaknesses, Holmes shows that evil can be conquered, and displays a willingness even to sacrifice himself in the struggle.[212] With respect to myth, the common Sleeping Beauty tale with its motifs of a prince who comes in accordance with prophecy to conquer the evil spell, is only fully comprehended in the light of the Redeemer of humankind, as is the myth of a gift bearing ubiquitous Santa Clause.[213] In the case of Santa Clause, Montgomery contends that Christmas calls not for a liberal theology of demythologizing but for remythologizing.[214]

In this positive apologetic Montgomery does not want to enter the realm of the bizarre in the search for Christ images. By way of caution he refers to Crews' 'tongue in cheek' discovery of the Christ figure in *Winnie-the-Pooh*.[215] Ultimately, the best protection for a sensible apologetic for Montgomery is to ensure that the argument for a Christ figure in literature, myth and archetypes is connected to the broader redemptive analogies that reflect the biblical 'plot-line' outlined above. The Christ figure therefore for Montgomery must be centred in humanity's yearning for paradise and transformation, a yearning from the 'beginning' as well as at the 'end' of our religious history.[216] Eliade, who incidentally served on the faculty of the University of Chicago with Montgomery,[217] affirms

---

[209] Montgomery, 'The Apologists of Eucatastrophe', 23-24. Montgomery cites here Moseley's work on Christ image guises in secular literature. See Edwin M. Moseley, *Pseudonyms of Christ in the Modern Novel* (Pittsburg: University of Pittsburg Press, 1962).

[210] Michael Frost, *Seeing God in the Ordinary: A Theology of the Everyday*, rev. ed. (Peabody, Massachusetts: Hendrickson, 2000), 92-93. This book won the Australian Christian book of the year in 1999 and is further evidence of Montgomery's continuing influence. For a critique of the 'superhero' myth in film and comics see John Shelton Lawrence and Robert Jewett, *The Myth of the American Superhero* (Grand Rapids and Cambridge: William B. Eerdmans, 2002), 338-364. The authors argue that the 'superhero' is the antidemocratic counterpart of Joseph Campbell's classical 'monomyth'.

[211] Montgomery, *The Transcendent Holmes*, 116.

[212] ibid.

[213] Montgomery, *The Quest for Noah's Ark*, 283.

[214] Montgomery, *The Suicide*, 493-494.

[215] Montgomery, 'The Apologists of Eucatastrophe, 24-25. See Frederick C. Crews, *The Pooh Perplex* (New York: Dutton, 1965), 58.

[216] Montgomery, 'The Apologists of Eucatastrophe', 25-29.

[217] Montgomery, *The Transcendent Holmes*, 112.

that there are in the human condition, 'nostalgic memories of an "earthly paradise", and some sort of "realizable" eternity to which man still thinks he may have access.'[218] He holds that right across the history of civilisation, including our profane time, there is a longing for a return to 'sacred time' that is expressed in all sorts of rituals, myths, beliefs and sharmanic figures.[219] However, it needs to be acknowledged that for Eliade this 'nostalgia for eternity' is also a longing for a concrete paradise that can be realised in the 'now, in the present moment'.[220]

Montgomery's subjective evidential Christ figure is a resurrected one. He speaks of the 'slaying of a monster' myth as being a myth that can be drawn on as a theme and pattern for this aspect of apologetics. Of this myth Barbara Sproul finds,

> All over the world, in the Babylonians' Enuma Elish and in the earliest creed of the Celts, in the books of Job and Psalms from the Old Testament, in the myths of the Hottentots of Africa and those of the Mandan and of the Huron Indians of North America, valiant defenders of the principles of being and order do fierce battle with the forces of not-being and chaos and finally subdue them so that order and life can be established.[221]

In this regard Montgomery states, 'Gustaf Aulén has demonstrated the centrality of the Christus Victor motif to the entire New Testament message: Jesus, born of a woman, is in fact the Divine Christ who conquers the Evil Power that has brought the race into bondage, and thereby restores mankind'.[222] Vital to the slaying of evil for the Christus Victor motif is the death and resurrection of Jesus. However, as has been previously stressed, Montgomery's apologetic reliance on a particular aspect of someone's thought does not mean he accepts their position uncritically. Whilst appreciative of Aulén's 'dramatic' motif he is critical of his position on the doctrine of the substitutionary atonement.[223]

---

[218] Mircea Eliade, *Patterns in Comparative Religion*, trans. Rosemary Sheed (New York: New American Library, 1958), 407-408.
[219] Mircea Eliade, *The Sacred and the Profane: The Nature of Religion*, trans. William R. Trask (New York and Evanston: Harper & Row, 1961), 68-113; Mircea Eliade, *Cosmos and History: The Myth of the Eternal Return*, trans. William R. Trask (New York: Pantheon, 1954), esp. chaps. 2 and 3.
[220] Eliade, *Patterns*, 408.
[221] Barbara C. Sproul, *Primal Myths: Creating the World* (London, Melbourne, Sydney, Auckland and Johannesburg: Rider, 1980), 18.
[222] Montgomery, 'The Apologists of Eucatastrophe', 28. See Gustaf Aulén, *Christus Victor*, trans. A.G. Herbert (London: Society for Promoting Christian Knowledge, 1931), 20-31.

More specifically Montgomery identifies Lewis' Aslan the Lion as a deep 'allegorical thread' that resonates with one's subjective need for a resurrected hero. Kilby would argue one can avoid turning such a story simply into Christian allegory, by ensuring that the story is not just a sermon preached, but has cosmic mythic elements.[224] Aslan dies in the boy Edmund's place and is resurrected through 'deeper magic from before the dawn of time'.[225]

As will be discussed shortly, such a concept of a dying or rising god, a mythical image like the Phoenix who made the journey to Heliopolis, was burnt to ashes and rose again more radiantly wonderful than before, is a concept with which the 'New Spirituality' on the whole interconnects.[226]

In his illuminating study *Pagan Resurrection Myths and the Resurrection of Jesus*, Leon McKenzie opens another possibility for Montgomery's subjective evidential apologetic. He argues that there were two reasons why those who first heard the news of Jesus' resurrection were eventually prepared to receive the announcement favourably. The first was that their conscious familiarity with pagan resurrection myths gave a sense of appropriateness for resurrection in Jesus' case. The second was because of their largely subliminal awareness of resurrection motifs structured in the created world. This in itself explains the origins of pagan resurrection myths. They are not a copying of other religious traditions but they reflect thousands of years of human experience of resonating on resurrection archetypes in the world of nature. McKenzie states, 'The proclamation of Jesus' resurrection resonated in the profound reaches of the unconscious of those who listened to the promptings of the resurrection archetype'.[227] These 'created world' resurrection analogies include sleep and wakefulness, climatic and solar cycles, and the fortunes of tribal families who faced seeming downfall from nature and enemies while yet their mythmakers went on to tell a story of resurrection and survival. McKenzie provides evidence that death and resurrection are part of the natural order.[228] Such a resurrection archetype argument is not far removed apologetically from Butler's *Analogy of Religion*, where he argues that

---

[223] See the appendix in John Warwick Montgomery, *Chytraeus on Sacrifice* (Saint Louis: Concordia, 1962), 139-146.
[224] Kilby, 'Mythic and Christian Elements', 119-143.
[225] Montgomery, 'The Chronicles of Narnia', 109-110. See C.S. Lewis, *The Lion, the Witch and the Wardrobe* (Hammondsworth, Middlesex: Penguin, 1959), 147-148.
[226] Clifford and Johnson, *Riding the Rollercoaster*, 39.
[227] Leon McKenzie, *Pagan Resurrection Myths and the Resurrection of Jesus* (Charlotteville, Virginia: Bookwrights, 1997), 138.
[228] ibid., 137-145. See also Wilkinson, 'Circles and the Cross', 38-40. Cf. Thomas F. Torrance, *Space, Time and Incarnation* (London: Oxford University Press, 1969), 27.

the revelational claim that we exist hereafter in a different and more wonderful state, is evidenced in the order of nature.[229] It is the argument that before the butterfly can emerge, the caterpillar must form a cocoon and die.

Summary

The unique and creative subjective evidential argument of Montgomery has a resurrection focus and places Jesus' death and resurrection within a biblical 'plotline' context. It is therefore an apologetic that is not without warrant as it is biblically consistent, and as will be discussed, it is in line with the aspirations and beliefs of 'New Spirituality'. It is therefore a highly relevant strand of circumstantial evidence. Furthermore, in the next section it will be shown how this strand actually forms part of the circumstantial case for the resurrection. It is, of course, based on an argument that there is epistemological common ground.[230]

Reframing the Circumstantial Apologetic

In a legal apologetic discourse with 'New Spirituality' seekers the legal case, or in fact any case for the Christ, is often not the starting point. The discourse, with its initial focus on one's existential needs, is normally more informal than that. This does not mean that one cannot present the circumstantial evidence in the informal discourse with the aim of connecting it to a legal case analogy in conclusion. However, there are times when it is appropriate to commence the apologetic discourse in a legal setting. This may simply be in response to questions like those raised by Deepak Chopra, as to whether there are facts about the Almighty which would hold up in a court of law or the court of human experience. In either case it is argued that the legal apologist should normally follow this kind of structure whilst being aware that the listener or reader may jump stages, revisiting them at a later time.

What follows is a dynamic, not a static model. It is based on Montgomery's subjective evidential case, but the reframing is a substantial development and reshaping of Montgomery's general argument which, to date, he has only applied to a literary apologetic.

---

[229] Butler, *The Analogy*, esp. part 1, chap. 1.
[230] Mouw, relying on Calvin, would want to stress that the pagans' awareness of God and his created order is more like a 'momentary lightning flash' in the dark. See Richard J. Mouw, *He Shines in All That's Fair: Culture and Common Grace, The 2000 Stob Lectures* (Grand Rapids and Cambridge: William B. Eerdmans, 2001), 67-68.

The setting and The question of proof is as set out in 'The Technical Apologetic' in the previous chapter. It is a *primary facie* case where the question is, is there a case to answer? The standard of proof is a civil standard.

The brief. Firstly, is set out the 'unbroken chain of testimony, from the (first) disciples to today, of changed lives that find their new meaning in the resurrection'. Such a discourse will normally focus on the apologist's experience with the appropriate brief historical connections establishing a chain from the disciples to the present time. Elsewhere, I have published a legal apologetic that includes brief testimonies of lawyers over four centuries, with a final chapter on 'It may be true, but does it work?' This chapter is a short biography of Lionel Luckhoo whom *Guinness Book of Records* lists as the world's 'most successful' lawyer.[231] Sir Lionel, whose testimony and apologetic is based on the resurrection of Christ,[232] found that despite all his accomplishment he was not satisfied. Then on a day in 1978:

> I had no peace. Peace comes from God and belongs to him. I never went to the Prince of peace, to Jesus to seek peace, until one day ... I invited Jesus to come into my life as my Lord and Saviour. It was the first time I have ever so invited him. That was it! It was in a hotel! The transformation was immediate. From that day my life changed — I moved from death to life, from darkness to light. I was born again. My life took a 180° change. I found real peace and happiness and joy and righteousness and holiness.[233]

In the appendix to this work there are other examples of legal personal testimonies listed. Of course, the testimonial circumstantial evidence does not have to be from lawyers. However such illustrations are consistent with this legal apologetic genre.

Secondly, the apologist will interact with 'New Spirituality' seekers on archetypes and myths that may then naturally lead to the third step of a subjective evidential apologetic. By this process of mutual revelation one is potentially increasing the common ground. As previously mentioned much of 'New Spirituality' strongly affirms the insights of Jung and Jungian archetypes.[234] This can be substantiated from a number of sources. Jung critic, Richard Noll, speaks of the

---

[231] Clifford, *The Case for the Empty Tomb*, 109-119.
[232] See chapter one.
[233] Lionel Luckhoo, *What is Your Verdict?* (Surrey, British Columbia: Fellowship Press, 1984), 19.
[234] For the influence of Jung on Joseph Campbell see Ellwood, *The Politics*, 163-164.

'Jungian movement and its merger with the New Age Spirituality' and asks as a consequence are we 'witnessing the birth of another religious movement ...?'[235] Margot Adler, a leading writer on 'Neo-Paganism', records that many in this religious movement see 'the gods' in Jungian terms.[236] This 'New Spirituality' connection with Jungian theory is particularly evident in its psychotechnologies, such as the tarot. Sallie Nichols says 'The Trumps' (major arcana), represent symbolically those instinctual forces operating autonomously in the depths of the human psyche which Jung called archetypes'.[237] Sheldon Kopp sees the tarot as the means of unlocking distorting cultural factors that obscure the timeless and universal meanings of the archetypal themes.[238] In accordance with Montgomery's apologetic in 'New Spirituality' one also finds common links between Jungian archetypes and mythology.[239]

The reliance of 'New Spirituality' on myth is common knowledge. Drane argues that story or myth is as central to the contemporary quest for meaning as 'abstract analysis was central to the outlook of modernity'.[240] Robert Bly, in his influential book *Iron John* says that stories, be they 'fairy stories, legends, myths, hearth stories – amount to a reservoir where we can keep new ways of responding that we can adopt when the conventional and current ways wear out'.[241] And Dr George Miller, the director of the *Mad Max* movies and co-producer and co-writer of *Babe,* tells that for him Jung 'described the terrain', but the guru of myth Joseph Campbell, was the 'consummate guide'.[242] Miller challenges Christianity with the thought:

> The cinema storytellers have become the new priests. They're doing a lot of the work of our religious institutions, which have so

---

[235] Noll, *The Jung Cult*, 297.
[236] Margot Adler, *Drawing Down the Moon*, rev. ed. (New York: Penguin/Arkana, 1997), 30-34. On the relationship between Jung's thought and modern witchcraft see Vivianne Crowley, *Wicca: The Old Religion of the New Millennium* (London: Thorsons, 1996), 79-80.
[237] Sallie Nichols, *Jung and Tarot: An Archetypal Journal* (York Beach, Maine: Samuel Weiser, 1980), 9. See also Carl Sargent, *Personality, Divination, and the Tarot* (Rochester, New York: Destiny, 1988); Edward A. Aviza, *Thinking Tarot* (New York: Simon and Schuster, 1997); Irene Gad, *Tarot and Individuation: Correspondences with Cabala and Alchemy* (York Beach, Maine: Nicolas – Hays, 1994), xxvi – xxviii.
[238] Sheldon Kopp, *The Hanged Man* (Palo Alto, California: Science and Behaviour, 1974), 3-5.
[239] Carol S. Pearson, *The Hero Within: Six Archetypes We Live By* (San Francisco: HarperSanFrancisco, 1989), 13-24.
[240] Drane, *The McDonaldization*, 133-138.
[241] Robert Bly, *Iron John* (Shaftesbury, Dorset; Rockport, Massachusetts; Brisbane: Element, 1990), xi.
[242] George Miller, 'The Apocalypse and the Pig: or the Hazards of Storytelling', *The Sydney Papers* 8, 4 (Spring 1996): 40.

concretized the metaphors in their stories, taken so much of the poetry, mystery and mysticism out of religious belief, that people look for other places to question their spirituality.[243]

Joseph Campbell, who has propagated this modern dependence on myth, holds all myths deal with, 'The maturation of the individual, from dependency through adulthood, through maturity, and then to exit, and then how to relate to this society and how to relate this society to the world of nature and the cosmos.'[244] Bill Moyers' interview of the *Star Wars trilogy* director George Lucas shows the power and place of myth today. Lucas stated of the trilogy, 'I consciously set out to re-create myths and the classic mythological motifs. I wanted to use these motifs to deal with issues that exist today. The more research I did, the more I realised that the issues are the same that existed 3,000 years ago.'[245]

Thirdly, the apologist should outline the subjective apologetic that ties itself to archetypes and myths. This is a circumstantial strand of common subjective experiences. As Montgomery avers: '... when I tell you my story, you are listening to your own story'.[246] It is 'proving' that one's testimony of transformation is part of the human search and condition and that Jesus is the fulfilment of myth. Apologetic illustrations of an archetype and myth discourse that makes links with the Christ event, and in particular the resurrection, have been outlined above in Montgomery's references to common motifs in literature, and in symbols like alchemy. As stated, this apologetic methodology has a strong pedigree. It was Andreae who in the seventeenth century employed the hermeneutic symbolism of alchemy and the founding myth of Rosicrucianism to prove that the risen Christ is the philosopher's stone.[247] This apologetic is consistent with alchemy which understands that, 'the transmutation of base metals into gold is tantamount to a miraculously rapid maturation'.[248] An apologetic discourse along these subjective evidential lines is not one of manipulation as naturally the discussion on testimony leads to our universal search and ache for fulfilment.

---

[243] George Miller quoted in Janet Hawley, 'The Hero's Journey', *Sydney Morning Herald*, *Good Weekend Supplement* (14 October 1995), 57.
[244] Joseph Campbell with Bill Moyers, *The Power of Myth* (New York, London, Toronto, Sydney and Auckland: Doubleday, 1988), 32.
[245] Bill Moyers' interview with George Lucas *Time* (3 May 1999), 71-74. Lucas states he wanted people to think about God in the process of his myth.
[246] Montgomery, *Tractatus*, 6.361.
[247] Montgomery, *Cross and Crucible*.
[248] Mircea Eliade, 'What is Alchemy?' in *Hidden Truths: Magic, Alchemy and the Occult*, Lawrence E. Sullivan, ed. (New York: MacMillian; London: Collier MacMillian, 1987), 246.

With Drane and Johnson I have set out a framework of how this apologetic interaction among Jungian archetypes, Eliade, and myth and the risen Christ, naturally occurs in the classic Rider Waite tarot pack.[249] It is a paradigm we have taken from Montgomery and whilst it is consistent with his basic presentation of the tarot, we have developed it.[250] It is a model we use in tarot 'readings' at Mind•Body•Spirit festivals.[251] Many of the images on the cards are taken from the bible.[252] The framework incorporates spiritual exercises, based on the major arcana, for transformation and healing. The 'Lovers' card (Genesis 1-2) depicts Adam and Eve before the 'Cosmic Mountain' and 'Cosmic Tree' in harmony with themselves, the world and the numinous. Montgomery states, 'The fairy tales of the world attest our deepest desire to "live happily ever after"'.[253] The 'Devil' card is where one confronts the dark lord in Tolkien's *Lord of the Rings* or *Star Wars*' Darth Vader or Jung's Shadow, and it shows the same couple now in bondage to the devil[254] but still with fruits of the 'Cosmic Tree' (image of God) though removed from the 'Cosmic Mountain' (God's presence). It is the 'Death' card which shows that, whether king, pope or child, we will confront the Grim Reaper, and that there appears to be no path to the eternal celestial city depicted on the card. The 'Judgement' card portrays the archangel blowing the trumpet at the end of time and people being resurrected (not reincarnated) from their tombs; and on the pennant connected to the angel's trumpet is a red cross which is a universal symbol of hope and healing.

---

[249] Drane, Clifford and Johnson, *Beyond Prediction*. A similar apologetic can connect to the Neo-Pagan cosmic myth of the 'Wheel of the Year', and according to this seasonal cyclical myth a virgin goddess conceives a child, who does battle with a dark lord and dies and rises again. See Clifford and Johnson, *Jesus and the Gods*, 43-54. For the world of fairytales and the tarot see Dorothy Morrison, *The Whimsical Tarot* (Stanford: U.S. Games Systems, 2000), 4-5.

[250] See the earlier section 'Montgomery's "Incarnational" Model'.

[251] Taylor criticises this apologetic method. However, he fails to acknowledge scholarship that points to the strong possibility of the Christian origins of the Tarot (see endnote 251); the apologetic interaction of writers such as Charles Williams with the Tarot (see endnote 261); and that, apart from Waite, others in 'New Spirituality' assert there is a strong Tarot connection between the Fool and the dying and resurrected sun-god (see for example endnote 255). One senses Taylor's concern, apart from his personal fears of the occult, is that the Rider-Waite Tarot pack 'mixes truth with serious error'. However, that assertion could be made of any non-Christian paradigm or world view that positive apologists interact with. See Mike Taylor, 'Illegitimate Evangelism?', *Evangelicals Now* (November 2001): 23.

[252] Timothy Betts, *Tarot and the Millennium* (Rancho Palos Verdes: New Perspective Media, 1998).

[253] Montgomery, *Tractatus*, 6.901.

[254] Joseph Campbell and Richard Roberts, *Tarot Revelations* (San Anselmo: Vernal Equinox, 1987), 74: The Devil, presents an image of the underworld or winter solstice, with the sovereign Lord of the abyss, Saturn/Capricorn. The serpent is of course a form of this so called Devil ...'.

The 'Magician's' card is more than the Jungian archetype of the wise man, for above his head is the symbol of infinity which shows we need help from one beyond us; while the dual sign of the wand in the magician's hand raised towards heaven with the left hand pointing to the earth is known as a source of grace drawn from above.[255] The key card is the 'Fool' which Campbell and Roberts observe clearly symbolizes the dying and resurrected sun-god.[256] The 'Fool' is also an archetype for the sage or medieval jester who is not a 'natural' fool but an 'artificial' fool who by his antics disturbs 'the court of human arrogance and self-interest'.[257] So, it is by the dying and rising Christ-'Fool' that one returns to the 'Lover's' paradise. [258] Such a model and message is consistent with Liz Greene's words in the foreword to Waite's, *The Key to the Tarot*, that the tarot maps the human condition and is 'fundamentally a description of the human journey from birth to death'.[259] It is our common story that is readily shared with the listener or reader. It calls for the positive apologetic, as Waite himself says, of the

---

[255] See A.E. Waite, *The Key to the Tarot*, rev. ed. (London: Rider, 1993), 67-68. Waite also sees the card signifying the divine motive in humanity, reflecting God.

[256] Campbell and Roberts, *Tarot*, 253-254.

[257] Michael Frost, *Jesus the Fool* (Sutherland, NSW: Albatross, 1994), 51. See also Elizabeth-Anne Stewart, *Jesus the Holy Fool* (Franklin, Wisconsin: Sheed & Ward, 1999), 45-54.

[258] In the circumstantial apologetic one may face a rejoinder as to the uniqueness and character of the dying and rising god, the 'Fool'. Why should this mythological figure be Jesus? Nash has apologetically shown the strength of Jesus' claim in contrast to competing pagan saviours. He lists six strengths: 1. None of the pagan gods died for someone else. 2. Only Jesus died for sin. 3. Jesus died once and for all. (In contrast the mystery gods die repeatedly.) 4. Jesus' death was an actual event in history, but the deaths of the other gods appear in mythical dramas. 5. Unlike the mystery gods, Jesus died voluntarily. 6. Jesus' death stands entirely apart from the pagan mysteries in that the report of his death is one of triumph. See Ronald H. Nash, *Christianity and the Hellenistic World* (Grand Rapids: Zondervan; Dallas: Probe, 1984), 171-172. One can also refer to Habermas' work on the alleged claims for historical persons, other than Jesus, being raised from the dead. Unlike he resurrection of Jesus they remain unsubstantiated. See Gary R. Habermas, 'Resurrection Claims in Non-Christian Religions', *Religious Studies*, 25 (June 1989): 167-177. If the rejoinder was provoked by a listener or reader having pursued Freke and Gandy's popular postmodern tome, *The Jesus Mysteries*, a further response may be that the church borrowed its ideas from the taurobolium, or full-sacrifice rites, of the mystery religion Mithraism. See Timothy Freke and Peter Gandy, *The Jesus Mysteries: Was the Original Jesus a Pagan God?* (London: Thorsons, 1999), 65-66. Edwin Yamauchi has shown that the taurobolium is only attested around 160AD and became a fully fledged bull sacrifice in the fourth century A.D. It is thus more likely that Christianity influenced Mithraism. In this context, Licona has argued that as the vast majority of the pagan religions which teach a resurrection of their deity do not document this in written form until years after Jesus' resurrection account, one could therefore make the counter claim that pagan religions borrowed the idea of resurrection of deity from Christianity. See Edwin Yamauchi, *Persia and the Bible* (Grand Rapids: Baker, 1990), 513; Licona, *Cross Examined*, 33-36.

[259] Liz Greene, 'Foreword' in Waite, *The Key*, 6.

'Strength' card that it 'has nothing to do with self-confidence in the ordinary sense, though this has been suggested, but it concerns the confidence of those whose strength is God, who have found their refuge in Him'.[260]

Charles William, playwright, novelist and member of 'The Inklings' circle with Lewis and Tolkien, wrote a story based on the actual original tarot deck. Williams also had a friendship with Waite and did join Waite's order, the Fellowship of the Rosy Cross.[261] Williams' novel incorporated dancing figurines that appear to be in perpetual motion, and which turn out to be sculptures depicting the symbols of the major arcana. The central archetype of this tale is the Fool. Williams uses the motif of the dancing figures as a metaphor for our journey through life. There is a divine dance and the key is to move in rhythm with the Fool.[262]

Montgomery charts the positive role that Williams' 'numinous novels' have in the mythic Christian apologetic.[263] The tarot journey is just one method of exploring subjective empirical facts. One can do so by simply exploring common archetypes found in myths such as the magician, the hanged man, and the hero and their connection to the risen Christ.[264] In any event, 'the combined weight of psychology and mythopoeic confirms Augustine's declaration that "Thou has made us for thyself, O Lord, and our hearts are restless until they rest in thee"!'[265]

Fourthly, the apologist will present the other four circumstantial strands of evidence outlined in the previous chapter.

The Resurrection and Direct Evidence – Montgomery and the Place of Story

In our discussion on circumstantial evidence and the subjective empirical argument, we have already mentioned the place of the literary apologetic in 'New Spirituality'. For Montgomery it is a much neglected apologetic paradigm today.[266] In this section the aim is to show that Montgomery's literary apologetic

---

[260] Arthur Edward Waite, *The Pictorial Key to the Tarot* (Stamford: U.S. Games Systems, 1991), 103.
[261] See R.A. Gilbert, *Revelations of the Golden Dawn: Rise and Fall of the Magical Order* (London: Quantum, 1997), 183-185.
[262] Charles Williams, *The Greater Trumps* (Grand Rapids: William B. Eerdmans, 1976).
[263] Montgomery, 'The Apologists of Euctastrophe', 29.
[264] Montgomery, *Tractatus*, 6.3222. For background on the archetypes see Pearson, *The Hero Within*; Fraser Boa, with Marie Louise von Franz, *The Way of the Dream: Conversations on Jungian Dream Interpretations* (Boston and London: Shambhala, 1994).
[265] Montgomery, *Tractatus*, 6.45.

has a place in the apologetic argument for the documentary evidence that was assessed in the two previous chapters. Again, Montgomery's insights given in the context of another apologetic model can be directly applied to his legal apologetic. As much of what is said builds on the previous discussions on the subjective evidential evidence and literature, this section, whilst of some significance for the future of the legal apologetic, can be brief.

It is the premise of this section that there is a real benefit in the placing of the direct evidence arguments for the resurrection, i.e. proof from testimony and documents, into a narrative. James Sire reiterates 'stories are indeed a major postmodern way of communicating'.[267] Certainly 'New Spirituality' gurus Deepak Chopra and James Redfield have chosen at times to communicate their philosophy on life through narrative rather than propositional argument.[268]

However, the Lutheran scholar Richard Jensen highlights a benefit to storytelling that goes beyond the 'New Spirituality' connection. He notes that nearly all scholars in the communications field agree that there have been only two major shifts in the communication culture in the entire history of humankind. The first shift is from oral to script (with the invention of the alphabet and then later of alphabetic movable type). The second stage is the shift occurring now – from script to electronic.[269] This means that the task of communicating must be re-examined in our day. His premise is that the electronic age is a 'secondarily oral' world that, like the first oral age, massages the ear and many of our senses simultaneously, not just the eye. It is an age of participation in communication, not just a response to proposition. In this kind of 'back to the future' world, story telling is paramount in preaching and all gospel proclamation.[270] He reminds us that consistently one of the best-selling theologians is C.S. Lewis who is oftimes a consummate story-

---

[266] Montgomery, 'Neglected Apologetic', 126-133.
[267] James Sire, 'On Being a Fool for Christ and an Idiot for Nobody', *Christian Apologetics in the Postmodern World*, Phillips and Okholm, eds., 112.
[268] Deepak Chopra, *The Return of Merlin: A Novel* (New York: Harmony, 1995); Redfield, *The Celestine Prophecy*.
[269] Richard A. Jensen, *Thinking in Story: Preaching in a Post-Literate Age* (Lima, Ohio: C.S.S., 1993), 17-18.
[270] ibid., 45-66. See also Tony Schwartz, *Media: the Second God* (New York: Random, 1981), 11-13; Drane, *The McDonaldization*, 133-154.

teller.²⁷¹ Fellow Lutheran, Montgomery, has shown his willingness to adapt to such a communications' shift, and actually predict edits coming.²⁷²

There are precedents and models for placing the direct factual testimony and documentary evidence into a story genre. There is for example Andreae's allegorical novel, *The Chemical Wedding*.²⁷³ Then currently Australian broadcaster and journalist Kel Richards has successfully placed the testimonial and documentary evidence for Christ's resurrection into a detective novel genre. The setting is the first century, but it is a world of telephones, cars and pizzas. A history in modern dress. His central character, detective Ben Bartholomew, in his final report concludes, 'Everything else has been eliminated. Hence, we must accept the improbable truth – that God brought Jesus back to life, and brought him out of the tomb.'²⁷⁴ In short story form Montgomery, through the character of Sherlock Holmes, has also placed Christ's resurrection within the detective genre.²⁷⁵ Licona and Luckhoo both create a novel-moot trial genre where the emphasis is the transcript of a modern day trial over whether Jesus historically rose from the dead.²⁷⁶ In Licona's story a professor is fired for teaching the resurrection as fact, and he sues the college for wrongful termination. Whilst the novel, or novel-moot trial, is of a different genre from the classical legal apologetic it should not distort the legal case and it should keep within the epistemological and legal categories discussed in the previous three chapters. Good secular legal fiction evidences an understanding of the laws of evidence. Hence whilst Licona and Luckhoo are to be commended for their apologetic creativity, they do infringe at times the foregoing caution. For example, Licona, whilst advocating a burden of proof 'beyond a reasonable doubt', speaks of his historical evidence in terms of probabilities.²⁷⁷ And although he endeavours to avoid in depth questions on the reliability of the New Testament gospels, by focusing on the secondary historical evidence for the resurrection in the accounts of Josephus and Phlegon, he does mention the eye-

---

²⁷¹ Richard A. Jensen, *Telling the Story: Variety and Imagination in Preaching* (Minneapolis: Augsburg, 1980), 117.
²⁷² Montgomery, *Cross and Crucible*, 1: 147-149. For a discussion of the characteristics of successful storytelling such as provoking curiosity, repetition, binding one to all humankind, evoking right-brain imagination, promoting healing and hope see Walter J. Bausch, *Storytelling: Imagination and Faith* (Mystic, Connecticut: Twenty third Publications, 1984), 29-63.
²⁷³ Montgomery, *Cross and Crucible*, Vol. 2.
²⁷⁴ Kel Richards, *The Case of the Vanishing Corpse* (Sydney, Auckland, London and Toronto: Hodder & Stoughton, 1990), 258. This is the first book of a series.
²⁷⁵ Montgomery, 'The Search for Ultimates', 2-10. Reprinted in Montgomery, *The Transcendent Holmes*, 119-135.
²⁷⁶ Licona, *Cross Examined*; Luckhoo and Thompson, *The Silent Witness*.
²⁷⁷ Licona, *Cross Examined*, 16, 28, 140.

witness nature of the disciples' evidence without ever addressing the hearsay issues raised in this thesis.[278] Also, Licona may, in an historical apologetic, have some justification for not dealing at length with the gospel eyewitness testimony, but, as his is a legal apologetic, it is hard to imagine a court being satisfied with the secondary evidence while not delving into the primary eyewitness documentary accounts, which are the best evidence. Further, it is the premise of this thesis that the legal apologetic, even in story form, should frame its case so that the evidence admits a hearing, not a verdict.

This placing of the resurrection debate into legal fiction is consistent with a 'long tradition of English writers, including Daniel Defoe, Samuel Richardson, Henry Fielding, Charles Dickens, and George Eliot, who felt the need to ground their fictional endeavours in the conditions or sanctions which govern the telling of truthful tales in a court of law'.[279] It is also consistent with the work of the legal novel writers, who often use this genre for more than mere storytelling as their tales provide a forum for life's questions, such as the ethical issues of abortion and human rights.[280] Furthermore, legal novelist Buffa suggests that court trials are stories, stories about people's lives; and that is why legal novels are so appealing today.[281] Certainly trial lawyer John Martel says that juries see cases as stories.[282] So a people-centred legal literary apologetic is an appropriate structure within which to confront ultimate questions.

There is another strength to a literary apologetic that is worth noting. John Drane claims that in the past the Church has been committed to 'high culture'. It has engaged with philosophers and sceptics often at a high intellectual level. And whilst acknowledging that there is nothing wrong with that he provocatively asks:

> I often wonder where we might be today if, instead of listening to the voices of those few theologians who spoke of the 'death of God' back then, we had paid more attention to the icons of popu-

---

[278] ibid., 39, 51-52, 140, 146.

[279] Schramm, *Testimony*, 2.

[280] For example see Richard North Patterson, *Protect and Defend* (London: Hutchinson, 2000); Alan M. Dershowitz, *Just Revenge* (London: Headline, 1999).

[281] Buffa, *The Judgement*, 402. For a comprehensive study on the profound impact of the changing nature of evidence in law (legislation enabled barristers to address the jury on behalf of prisoners) on the literary narrative in the nineteenth century; where as a result the authors of fiction created a style of literary advocacy which both imitated, and reacted against their counterparts at the Bar see Schramm, *Testimony*, 174-192.

[282] John Martel, *The Alternate* (New York: Signet, 2000), 241.

lar culture – people like the Beatles, who never had any problem at all with transcendence, but inspired a whole generation to head off in new directions to search for spiritual meaning in some unexpected places. The people of that generation are now the cultural and business leaders, and their understanding of popular spirituality has been one of the major forces facilitating the rise of today's alternative faiths.[283]

A literary legal apologetic in the legal fiction mould, which communicates with the mass public, addresses some of Drane's concerns and ensures that one's polemic is more than a demanding apologetic textbook.

This argument for telling by story the case for the Resurrection is not meant to imply that story is the only communication possible to 'New Spirituality'. In discourse, if one begins with the reframed circumstantial case, a more traditional legal apologetic still has a place, as the following case study will suggest. And 'New Spirituality' advocates certainly do not limit their apologetic to story as witnessed by the bountiful self help literature. However, in proclamation and writing, the legal apologetic would benefit, at times, from an integration of its arguments into the literary apologetic. Whilst Montgomery has not directly advocated such a step it is consistent with his literary apologetic and his writings on Sherlock Holmes.[284]

The resurrection and the direct evidence – the legal apologist as a legitimate witness
In the next chapter I draw upon the insights of Allison Trites as to the forensic aspect of the Old and New Testaments. Whilst not wanting to overstate the juridical nature of the bible, Trites has documented the numerous lawcourt scenes of the Old Testament and the prominent idea of eyewitness in the New Testament.[285] In particular, in chapter five it is argued that the sustained metaphor of witness in the New Testament gospels and the book of Acts is a relevant biblical support for the legal apologetic.

In his conclusion Trites supports the argument that our age is a sceptical, questioning and pluralistic one, which is not dissimilar to the one in which the early

---

[283] John Drane, 'Unknown Gods, Declining Churches'.
[284] Montgomery, *The Transcendent Holmes*, 119-135.
[285] Allison A. Trites, *The New Testament Concept of Witness* (Cambridge: Cambridge University Press, 1977). Trites asserts, 'The New Testament use of witness rests squarely on the Old Testament concept of justice in the gate. In the Old Testament the lawsuit or controversy theme grows out of the legal assembly and plays an important part' (223).

followers of Christ shared their message.[286] He presses the point that the witness motif in such times has a direct implication for apologists, not only in the context of their message, but also in their method of communication. Trites then draws upon three features from the concept of witness that he relates to the apologist's communication of direct evidence. These three features can be directly related to the apologetic interacting with 'New Spirituality'. As the technical and non-technical legal apologetic relies heavily on the idea of witness and eyewitness testimony, these three features are a timely reminder.

Firstly, Trites asserts that biblical witnesses, like many witnesses, are passionately involved in the case they seek to represent. Secondly, the biblical witnesses, like all witnesses, are held accountable for the truthfulness of their testimony (1 Corinthians 15:14-15). Thirdly, the biblical witnesses must be faithful not only to the bare facts, in this case of the Christ-event, but also to their meaning (John 3:28-30).[287] Trites states, 'modern witnesses are summoned to speak of the life, death and resurrection of Christ in such a way that the intrinsic divine significance of these events is brought to life'.[288] The ramifications for the legal apologist, who espouses the direct evidence route for the resurrection to 'New Spirituality', is evident. The message of witness is more than the citing of facts: it is passionate; yet it does not overstate or understate its case;[289] it relates the resurrection to ultimate issues and questions.

There is another important angle to Trites' first reflection on the apologist as a witness. The biblical witnesses are bystanders. In a non-theological context they are not the ones responsible for the deed, i.e. the death and resurrection of Christ, nor are they the ones upon whom the deed was brought to bear. As they are neither the agent nor the object of the deed, nor both agent and object there could be a sense of their removal from the event – a 'detached' testimony. However in the gospel bystander testimony you hear the experiences of the witnesses in the first person, and the person of the witness also appears (for example, John 21). In the apologetic of direct evidence to 'New Spirituality', it is essential to let the listener or reader hear the 'I' of the New Testament witnesses. This is affirmed by Montgomery in his stress on the 'The Artistic' level. This is not to deny the elu-

---

[286] ibid., 225.
[287] ibid., 229-230. Cf. Derrida, 'Faith and Knowledge', 63-65.
[288] ibid.
[289] This is not unrelated to Montgomery's call for the advocate to be of good character. See Montgomery, *Christ our Advocate*, 267-281.

siveness of a traumatic experience such as Christ's passion and resurrection, and a gulf between what was witnessed and the recorded written testimony on which we rely.[290]

The focus on witness in the process of communicating the direct testimony has another significant role. I have advocated that the legal apologists can consider a 'story' apologetic. Sociolinguists advise that stories by their nature are complex multigeneric texts that comprise different types of talk.[291] When a legal fiction writer tells a story, we the reader get much more than a legal narrative. The legal apologist as a novelist will do likewise in character development and descriptions. The focus on this literary genre as 'witness testimony' of the fact of the resurrection will ensure that a legal literary apologetic has a frame that delivers more than a narrative with a moral twist.

In summary as apologists enter into an actual discourse, of whatever form it be, not only is it important that they allow the evidence to be heard as witness testimony, but that as apologists they enact the features of the biblical witnesses themselves. It is the voices of witnesses, and the voices of those who tell their stories, which are not the voices of a detached bystander, that will find legitimacy in 'New Spirituality'.[292] As Montgomery avers, 'Christ arose for *me*'.

Reframing the Direct Evidence

The brief. Firstly, the apologist will consider at times placing the arguments based on the proof from testimony and documents into a narrative form. This consideration would apply to an oral, written or cyberspace apologetic.[293] In so doing the apologist, in both a technical and non-technical legal apologetic, will avoid overstating the case for the resurrection. He or she will stay within the legal parameters as to the admissibility of documents and hearsay evidence that have been outlined in the previous two chapters. Ideally this apologetic will not take

---

[290] For a discussion on the witness and testimony in the context of traumatic events see Michael Bernard-Donals and Richard Glejzer, *Between Witness and Testimony: The Holocaust and the Limits of Representation* (Albany: State University of New York Press, 2001), 49-78.

[291] For sociolinguistic perspective on the structure of biblical discourse see Eugene A. Nida, 'Sociolinguistics and Translating' in *Sociolinguistics and Communication*, Johannes P. Louw, ed. (London, New York and Stuttgart: United Bible Societies, 1986), 28-46.

[292] Drane, *The McDonalization*, 141-145.

[293] On the attraction of Neo-Pagans ('techno-paganism') to the Internet and web especially for story telling and role-plays see Neville Drury, *The History of Magic in the Modern Age* (London: Constable, 2000), 234-250.

the story to trial but will centre on a preliminary hearing or a preparation for trial. The evidence admits a hearing, not a verdict.[294]

Secondly, the apologist in presenting the accounts of the biblical witnesses will himself act in the spirit of such witnesses. He is more than a bystander and, in sharing the testimony of the biblical witnesses, something of their passion, integrity and application of the fact of the resurrection to life itself will be evident.

Thirdly, as is argued in chapter five in the section 'A Legal Formalist Approach', the legal apologist will be open to a 'conciliation' model as well. In many jurisdictions Christian lawyers have been at the forefront of developing non-adversarial arbitration models.[295] In this apologetic framework, a dialogical, person-centred model is paramount. The legal factual argument is subsequent to discussion about the values grid of the parties present, and the possible obstacles to faith and outcomes hoped for. The legal case is presented conversationally in the context of the dialogue taking place. Clark in his work on dialogical apologetics affirms that one must still use evidence, but likewise highlights the power of a story in this process.[296] He also advocates requesting a response from those involved.[297] This reframing along a more non-adversarial line has a real place in a small group environment.

Faddishness

One can imagine a response to this apologetic discussion on 'New Spirituality' being: 'Will it survive current waves of faddishness?' John Newport has no doubt of its survival and concludes that when one judges the Christian and New Age sections of most bookstores one can note its popular appeal and see that its influence is pervasive.[298] This appeal stretches across the broad spectrum of the book reading public.[299] Jay Kinney, editor of *Gnosis* magazine, does acknowledge however that New Age is evolving like the civil rights and women's movements. Movements like these begin on the fringes and then spill from the avante-garde

---

[294] See 'Epistemological Concerns' in chapter one where I list as an example legal novels that don't take their story to an actual trial.
[295] Lynn Buzzard, *With Liberty and Justice* (Wheaton: Victor, 1984), 138; Lynn Buzzard, *Tell it to the Church* (Elgin, Illinois and Weston, Ontario: David C. Cook, 1982).
[296] David K. Clark, *Dialogical Apologetics* (Grand Rapids: Baker, 1993), 221-223.
[297] ibid., 223-224.
[298] John P. Newport, *The New Age Movement and the Biblical Worldview* (Grand Rapids and Cambridge: William B. Eerdmans, 1998), 46.
[299] See Andrew West, 'Meet Mr Westie, the Man Who Put Howard in Power', *The Sun Herald* (18 November 2001), 21.

Faddishness 225

into the main fabric of mainstream social discourse.[300] So, the faddishness may have levelled out, but its spiritual influence flourishes. Surely its immediate survival is ensured in a western world that appears to be 'becoming more and more religious but less and less Christian'.[301] Or as iconoclastic comedian Lenny Bruce cheekily puts it, 'everyday people are straying away from church and going back to God'.[302] It is clearly an era where people are looking beyond the limited 'stories' of science and technology to understand things.[303] Dennis Kenny poignantly outlines the task confronting the church:

> Never have so many people been so involved in talk of, and discovery of, spirituality. The country is immersed in it, even to the fiction best seller lists. Traditional religion, and more importantly, traditional religion ministers are not a major part of the movement. It is being led by physicians, social workers, psychologists, and shamans. Most often mainline churches and their representatives are speaking out against it. Workshop announcements and conference advertisements for spirituality events come across my desk by the dozens. Rarely are traditionally trained ministers a part of these faculties.' [304]

Also academic David Tacey has aptly captured the social indicators of 'New Spirituality' and the apologetic task:

> As the masculinist pubs, churches, convents, and barber shops go broke or close down in Australian cities, New Age bookshops and 'awareness centres' are popping up everywhere, offering the pub-

---

[300] Jay Kinney, 'Dissecting the New Age', *Gnosis*, 49 (1998): 14-17.
[301] Martin Robinson, *To Win the West*, 238. See also James R. Lewis and J. Gordon Melton, eds., *Perspectives on the New Age* (Albany, New York: State University of New York Press, 1992), ix–xii; Richard Guilliatt, 'The Spiritual on Tap: A Prayer, a Chant and a Chakra Chart are Proving Mightier than the Pub', *The Sydney Morning Herald Weekend Magazine* (17 November 2001), 73; Leonard Sweet, *Carpe Mañana* (Grand Rapids: Zondervan, 2001), 141-146.
[302] Empirical research indicates that whilst church attendance in England has fallen by 20% between 1987-1999, reports of people having a 'spiritual experience' increased by some 60% in the same period. See David Hay and Kate Hunt, 'Is Britain's Soul Waking Up?', *The Tablet* (24 June 2000). See also Fuller, *Spiritual but Religious*, 98-100.
[303] John Carroll, *The Western Dreaming: The Western World is Dying for Want of a Story* (Sydney: HarperCollins, 2001), 6-18. For a discussion of other possible reasons for the growth of 'New Spirituality' such as 'life is difficult', 'generalised angst', 'identification with meaninglessness', materialism see Clifford and Johnson, *Riding the Rollercoaster*, 1-15. For a questioning of the significance of such functional arguments that stress primarily 'unsatisfied needs' see Colin Campbell, 'Some Comments on the New Religious Movements, the New Spirituality and Post-Industrial Society', in *New Religious Movements*, Eileen Baker, ed., 232-242.

lic a broad range of largely non-Christian, non-patriarchal esoteric arts and sciences, such as astrology, tarot, I Ching, karma sutra, sacred sex, herbalism, naturopathy, meditation, yoga, psychic massage, channelling, neo-paganism and wicca, martial arts, reincarnation, Eastern religions and philosophies, Native American vision quests and goddess spirituality.[305]

Conclusion: An Apologetic Case Study Approach

The format of this case study is of a narrative style which is consistent with the approach of 'New Spirituality'.

Sharon approached our 'Community of Hope' stall at the Mind·Body·Spirit festival.[306] The stall was located opposite the 'Kirlian Photographic Diagnosis' booth and alongside the 'Vegetarian and Vegan Societies' stand. The 'Community of Hope' stall featured as a backdrop, a large size picture poster of the famous 'Face in the Snow' and overhead the words, 'Life is a puzzle. He (Jesus) can make sense of it'.[307] The picture in the snow had proved to be a highly successful way of attracting people, which created numerous opportunities for conversation. There was free literature available including a postcard size replica of the 'Face in the Snow'.

A conversation began with Sharon who shared something of her own spiritual journey from fairly normal Catholicism to a commitment to Wicca. We discussed how upbringing, education, and external spiritual experiences had influenced her views on life and faith. Sharon, during the telling of the story, indicated that she appreciated Jesus, but her understanding of life was centred on reincarnation. She then briefly outlined some of her concerns about the church. She asked me, 'Do you believe in reincarnation?' I said, 'I believe in its understanding that there is more to life than death, but I find the message of the resurrection more empowering.' I then shared the strand of circumstantial evidence for the resurrection based on the testimony of changed lives. She listened to my story and other sto-

---

[304] Dennis E. Kenny, 'Editorial: Pastoral Care for the Twenty-first Century', *Journal of Pastoral Care* 52, 3 (Fall 1998): 215.
[305] David Tacey, *The Edge of the Sacred* (Blackburn, Victoria: Harper Collins, 1995), 192.
[306] Interview by the author drawn from field notes taken at the time (Darling Harbour, NSW, 3 December 1997). Sharon is just one of many similar apologetic interactions that are verified by New Age Mission, P.O. Box 367, Hurstville, 1481, Australia.
[307] The picture is based on a photograph of some burnt coals in the snow that, when developed, appeared to contain the shape of a face that resembles church art portraits of Jesus' face. Some claim the picture was the work of a well known Japanese photographer.

ries including those of Lionel Luckhoo, Anglican deacon Geneive Blackwell (who worked on the stand) and the Apostle Paul, that linked the transformation to the resurrection of Christ. In the course of this apologetic discourse Sharon indicated an openness to the holistic character of the resurrection. Unlike reincarnation's denial of the body, the resurrection of Jesus was truly mind, body and spirit.

At the 'community of Hope' stall we were also doing tarot 'readings' and Sharon and I discussed for some time how the cards mimic archetypes and symbols that reveal our common search for meaning. I specifically asked Sharon if she was aware of the message of the resurrection in the cards. I explained the Judgment card (card XX) is full of hope and life in its apocalyptic symbolism. Attached to the angel's trumpet is a pennant which features a red cross, the universal symbol of healing. Sharon noticed in the foreground of the card that people are rising from their graves in joy, and I pointed out the contrast with the Death card (card XIII) where the people have succumbed to the agent of death. I said, 'Sharon the image on the card is one of resurrection, not reincarnation. The cards testify to a universal resurrection hope.' At Sharon's request I then gave a 'reading' of the cards that covered our universal bliss as seen in the Lovers' card, our fall (Death and Tower card), our universal search for transformation (Hermit card) and the one who restores the Lovers' Utopia (Fool card). I shared with Sharon that Jesus did not remain dead. The Chariot card (card VII) signifies that he arose triumphantly and shattered the hold of death forever, a shattering that the Judgement card illustrates awaits all those who know and love his name.[308]

In this process the circumstantial strand of the subjective evidential apologetic unfolded which focused on the universal character of our own individual journeys and that the resurrected Jesus is the fulfilment of the myths and fairytales that express this.

After a pause in the conversation there was a short dialogue about the other circumstantial evidence, in particular the fact of the empty tomb and Sharon quizzed me about the 'swoon' theory based on her reading of Barbara Thiering.[309] Sharon then stated, 'But the account of the resurrection of Jesus is in your New Testa-

---

[308] For a full description of this tarot exercise and other exercises for healing, purpose and direction see Drane, Clifford and Johnson, *Beyond Prediction*, 108-132.

[309] Thiering holds Jesus lost consciousness on the cross and the aloes revived him in the tomb with the assistance of Mary Magdalene and other friends. For discussion and background on Thiering's view see Leonie Star, *The Dead Sea Scrolls and the Riddle Debated* (Crows Nest, NSW: ABC Books, 1991), 69-82.

ment gospels that are really pretty average stuff. Haven't Barbara Thiering and Bishop Spong basically shown that?' I replied, 'Sharon, you are not meant to ask such a cognitive question.' She laughed. The discourse then turned to the evidence for the resurrection including whether it had any legal standing and whether the New Testament narratives could be trusted. The 'stories', testimonies of the Apostles John and Paul were highlighted. A basic legal apologetic for the direct evidence was outlined that set out the case for a brief for trial and that reiterated the chords of the circumstantial evidence. Sharon was particularly interested in the role of the women in the resurrection brief. She also asked what was the evidence for Jesus being in Tibet during his missing years (13-29 years).[310]

Sharon's response was to share again something of her own personal hurts. She asked for prayer for faith and healing and for further information on Jesus. She took a pamphlet that set out a list of churches that we would recommend. Not an atypical apologetic discourse had taken place.[311]

---

[310] For apologetic discussion see Clifford and Johnson, *Jesus and the Gods,* 149-169.
[311] ibid.

Chapter 5

Is Montgomery's Legal Apologetic an Appropriate Analogy?

In chapters two to four, the strengths and perceived limitations of Montgomery's legal apologetic for the resurrection was outlined. These chapters consider this model's appeal to the evidence and the criteria used to assess it. The reason for this emphasis is that if Montgomery can convince us that the evidence is admissible, credible and material and to some degree that the facts in issue speak for themselves, there is a significant foundation for the Christian truth claims.[1] However, it is also important to ask, at a broader level, whether Montgomery and the legal apologists are justified in employing the legal analogy at all. Apart from Montgomery, this is a fundamental issue that juridical apologists have scarcely addressed.

Strenghts of the Legal Paradigm

Scriptural Support

Montgomery as an Evangelical Lutheran would not adopt an apologetic analogy that he believed was contrary to scripture.[2] Most legal apologists would hold to that position. Montgomery goes further and actually finds a biblical warrant in support of it. His argument is based on 1 Peter 3:15. The etymology of the concept 'to give an answer' is traced to the legal system. In a number of places Montgomery specifically refers to the legal 'flavour' of the text, and points out: 'the apostle consciously employed a technical term (apologia) of ancient Greek law, having reference to the answer given by a defendant before a tribunal'.[3]

---

[1] As to the facts in issue see also the 'Perceived Limitations' section in this chapter.
[2] John Warwick Montgomery, 'A Normative Approach to the Acquisition Problem in the Theological Seminary Library', *American Theological Library Association Summary of Proceedings*, 16 (12-15 June 1962): 75-78. For Montgomery's biblical justification of offering evidence for faith, and for apologetics generally see *Defending the Gospel*, especially the tapes on 'The Scriptural Approach to Apologetics' and 'The Validity of Offering Evidence'. See also Montgomery, *Faith Founded*, ix-42.
[3] Montgomery, 'Neglected Apologetic', 120; Montgomery, *Faith Founded*, ix-x. In support see L. Joseph Rosas, 'Evangelism and Apologetics' in *Evangelism in the Twenty-first Century*, T. Rainer, ed. (Wheaton: Harold Shaw, 1989), 113-114; Bernard Ramm, *Varieties of Christian Apologetics* (Grand Rapids: Baker, 1961), 11. Cf. Peter H. Davies, *The First Epistle of Peter, the New International Commentary on the New Testament* (Grand Rapids: William B. Eerdmans, 1990), 131. Davies states 'make a defence' can indicate formal legal or judicial settings, but it was 'also used for informal and personal situations'.

He comments that the Apostle Paul was a rabbinic lawyer and in his address to the Stoic philosophers at Athens he offered the gospel as the verifiable fulfilment of the natural law tradition, articulated by the Stoic poets, that human life is the product of divine creation.[4] He also expends much effort illustrating ways law can appropriately aid our interpretation and understanding of theology, hermeneutics and ethics.[5]

Montgomery and other contemporary apologists could, if they desired, capitalize more on the biblical data in support of the legal metaphor.[6] Biblical justification is of primary importance for evangelical apologists. In this regard we refer to the significant work of Allison Trites. Trites stresses the witness motif in the New Testament as being a very live metaphor. Specifically he argues that Luke's gospel conceptually at times draws from a legal paradigm. For example, Trites notes the disciples will be forced to stand before hostile tribunals and authorities.[7] This will be a time for the disciples to bear testimony (μαρτψρινγ).[8] He observes, 'Luke has taken the original notion of bearing witness before a court of law and adapted it to the conditions of the Messianic Age.'[9]

With respect to the Book of Acts he states it actually offers legally acceptable evidence for Christ.[10] This is seen in the 'convincing proofs' of Acts chapter 1, and the eyewitness testimony to the resurrection as claimed in speeches like Paul's at the Areopagus.[11] As well there are the courtroom scenes before magistrates and the like. In fact Barnes presents the possibility that Paul's Areopagus speech (Acts 17:22-31) is not a missionary speech as such, but a legal defence before the

---

[4] Montgomery, *Human Rights*, 133-134.
[5] For example Montgomery, *Law and Gospel*.
[6] One exception is Dean Davis who uses the legal analogies in the Old and New Testaments as a model of a courtroom apologetic by putting humanity in the dock whilst facing God's judgement on submitting to today's idols. See Dean Davis, 'Man in the Dock: Courtroom Evangelism in an Age of Idolatry', *Christian Research Journal* 23, 2 (2000): 10-11, 57.
[7] Trites, *The New Testament*, 130-133. Cf. Allison A. Trites, 'The Idea of Witness in the Synoptic Gospels – Some Juridical Considerations', *Themelios*, 5 (1968): 18-26. See Luke 12:11, 21:12. See also Alexandru Neagoe, *The Trial of the Gospel: An Apologetic Reading of Luke's Trial Narratives* (Cambridge: Cambridge University Press, 2002), 219-227.
[8] Luke 21:13. Paul Barnett notes the dominant idea of witness in the New Testament is an 'onlooker who could "bear witness" in a court hearing for or against an accused person'. See Barnett, *Is the New Testament History?*, 50-55.
[9] Trites, *The New Testament*, 133. Cf. Joel B. Green, *The Gospel of Luke* (Grand Rapids: William B. Eerdmans, 1997). Green says the term witness in Luke – Acts applies not just to the apostles who have been with Jesus from the beginning, but its emphasis is on those empowered by the Spirit who cannot keep from speaking about what they have seen and heard. Green also notes Luke's use of eyewitness in his prologue is not a claim to any personal observation of events describe (40-42).
[10] ibid., 133-135.

Strenghts of the Legal Paradigm

Council of the Areopagus to the charge of introducing a new religion to Athens (Acts 17:16-20). Luke has written this defence in a way to suit his apologetic purposes.[12] Further, Trites draws attention to the actual juridical character of the testimony. It is twofold: proof from prophecy and proof from eyewitness testimony. The Jewish rules of evidence laid down in Deuteronomy 19:15 called for double testimony, and this rule would be known by those who had a good knowledge of the Jewish scriptures, whether they were Jew or Gentile. William Lane Craig observes that this double testimony is not incidental and is fresh evidence which, as it were, 'serves to re-open his (Jesus) trial'.[13] Trites concludes,

> ... the only testimony Luke means to offer is that which would satisfy a court of law, and this demands twofold or threefold testimony; this is the significance of his repeated use of the principle of twofoldness. By this device Luke seeks to provide evidence for the truth of the events which have transpired, thereby giving Theophilus 'authentic knowledge' (ἀσφάλεια, Lk. 1:4, N.E.B.; the same word is used by Thucydides in the preface to his historical work, I.22) and vindicating his own name as an historian. His whole book is meant as a witness to the truth. He uses the historical material for the Book of Acts according to the standards of his time as they are expressed by such ancient historians as Herodotus, Polybius, Thucydides and Josephus, and certainly intends to offer evidence that will stand the test of the closest scrutiny; after all, he has 'investigated' all the pertinent facts 'carefully' (παρακο λουθηκότι πᾶσιν ἀκριβῶς, Lk. 1:3).[14]

Montgomery writes that Markus Barth likewise finds that in Acts the resurrection fits within a juridical setting. Barth asserts Luke has a literary device of depicting the early church as being in confrontation with judges, courts and accusations, and involves the Apostles at times reversing the order and actually being the prosecutors, 'You have murdered!' The context is a legal process. Barth proceeds in

---

[11] ibid., 129. Cf. Allison A. Trites, 'The Importance of Legal Scenes and Language in the Book of Acts', *Novum Testamentum*, 16 (1974): 278-284. Trites concludes, 'In other words, the frequent use of legal language in connection with real courts of law is germane to Luke's presentation and part of his theological intention. The claims of Christ are being debated, and Luke intends by the use of law court scenes and legal language to draw attention to this fact ... An important part of his task is the presentation of the courtroom evidence in such a way that it will bear witness to Christ.' (284).

[12] Timothy D. Barnes, 'An Apostle on Trial', *The Journal of Theological Studies* 20, 2 (October 1969): 417-419. See also Mauck, *Paul on Trial*, 131-132.

[13] Craig, *The Historical*, 13.

[14] Trites, *The New Testament*, 135.

this legal view, by creatively comparing the infamous American Leopold – Loeb murder trial with the Lucan and broad New Testament principles of confession of guilt, forgiveness and new life.[15] Alexander also finds that the language of forensic *apologia*, of charge and counter-charge, 'is a prominent feature of the textual surface of Acts'. However he argues that Luke's vehicle of narrative, where the narrator does not intervene in the text to explain how it is to be construed, points to Acts being closer to the world of novels and pamphlets, than to the 'higher' forms of rhetorical discourse.[16]

As has been previously stated in chapter one, this forensic nature of Acts is also most evident in Paul's Roman apologetic. In Acts 24-26 Paul not only appeals to Roman rules of evidence (24:19-20) but McGrath, Winter and others maintain his apologetic here is based on the Roman legal custom of speeches which contained four or five standard components with the defence answering specific accusations.[17] This form critical analysis also points to Luke's redactional hand, not necessarily as the composer, but as one who has ensured the editing of the forensic reports and has captured the legal nature of Paul's speeches. This was vital for the Roman reader.

Another reason for the legal nature of Luke-Acts is found in the suggestion that Theophilus (Luke 1:1-4, Acts 1:1) was himself a judge, magistrate or Roman official with judicial powers in view of his being referred to as 'you, most excellent'.[18] R.E.O. White argues that Luke's careful and full defence may be in part a result of Theophilus' being a judicial official involved, 'in assessing the legality of Christianity, as a new religion, a new moral force, a new political group'.[19] White's position is supported by the lawyer John Mauck's analysis of Luke-Acts

---

[15] See Markus Barth's contribution in Markus Barth and Verne H. Fletcher, *Acquittal by Resurrection* (New York: Holt, Rinehart and Winston, 1964), 72-84. 'An amazing crime and trial that took place in our time appears to be a suitable illustration that can show what logical connection may exist between crime, due legal process, confession of guilt, forgiveness – and resurrection' (73). Montgomery notes this emphasis of Barth in *Law and Gospel*, 46.

[16] Loveday Alexander, 'The Acts of the Apostles as an Apologetic Text' in *Apologetics in the Roman Empire: Pagans, Jews and Christians*, Mark Edwards, Martin Goodman and Simon Price, eds. (Oxford: Oxford University Press, 1999), 28-29, 44.

[17] McGrath, 'Apologetics to the Romans', 390-391; Bruce W. Winter, 'Official Proceedings and the Forensic Speeches in Acts 24-26' in *The Book of Acts in its Ancient Literary Settings*, Vol 1, Bruce W. Winter and Andrew D. Clarke, eds. (Grand Rapids: William B. Eerdmans, 1994), 333-336. See also C. Clifton Black, *The Rhetoric of the Gospel: Theological Artistry in the Gospels and Acts* (St. Louis: Chalice, 2001), 115-133.

[18] For a discussion see Mauck, *Paul on Trial*, 21-22.

[19] R.E.O. White, *Luke's Case for Christianity* (London: The Bible Reading Fellowship, 1987), 23-24.

from both the intrinsic evidence and what was known of Roman legal custom in that day. In fact he takes it a step further and holds Luke's defence is in response to specific charges laid against Paul of inciting riots and establishing a new religion. Mauck argues that probably Theophilus held the office of a cognitionibus (investigator) for Nero's consilium.[20] Whilst Mauck's hypothesis is not the most likely in light of the material included in Luke-Acts that would not have been useful for the legal brief purpose (for example, Paul's shipwreck in chapter 27)[21], it highlights that Luke-Acts is filled with legal material that was recorded for a purpose and which is often slanted towards the apologetic purposes of the author.

In John's gospel Trites finds a different lawsuit model from that employed in Luke-Acts. His conclusion is supported by more recent scholarship.[22] He finds that the fourth gospel presents a controversy very similar to the one in Isaiah 40-55. The apologist William Edgar says the prophet Isaiah, 'is asking for a courtroom debate where the truth will be tested.'[23] Whereas, in Isaiah it is Yahweh and the false gods, in John it is a lawsuit between God and the world.[24] Isaiah 40-55 is not the only Old Testament text to adopt this legal genre format. For example scholars find the legal challenge process in the book of Jeremiah,[25] and the Yahweh speeches in Job 38-41.[26] Scholnich holds the Yahweh speeches as being God in the dock, responding to the lawsuit brought by Job:

> As many scholars have recognized, the poet chooses the court of justice as the setting for the dialogue between Job and his friends. He dramatizes the hero's search for an acceptable definition of the

---

[20] Mauck, *Paul on Trial*, 25-32.
[21] Bruce, *The Book of the Acts*, 23-24; Alexander, 'The Acts of the Apostles', 33-38.
[22] For discussion see Lincoln, *Truth on Trial*. Lincoln holds a Johannine community lies behind the gospel. He concludes the fourth gospel, 'is a narrative that asserts the truth about God, Christ, and life is to be seen in terms of the metaphor of a cosmic lawsuit, and it displays this assertion by making its discourse and plot have Jesus on trial, a trial in which the other characters (and, by extension the readers) have to come to a verdict and are invited to become witnesses' (169-170).
[23] William Edgar, *Reasons of the Heart: Recovering Christian Persuasion* (Grand Rapids: Baker, 1996), 44.
[24] Trites, *The New Testament*, 78-124.
[25] William H. Holladay, 'Jeremiah's Lawsuit with God', *Interpretation*, (July 1963): 280-287. In Jeremiah Holladay finds the clear image of 'man and God as legal adversaries' which 'brings to mind the book of Job' (285). For example see Jeremiah 12:1.
[26] See Eugene J. Mayhew, 'God's Use of General Revelation in His Response to Job', *Journal of Christian Apologetics* 2, 1 (Summer 1998): 94-104. See also Michael Brennan Dick 'The Legal Metaphor in Job 31', *The Catholic Biblical Quarterly* 41, 1 (January 1979): 37 –50. Dick further notes the reliance of the prophets on juridical language (37).

meaning of divine justice by structuring the work around a lawsuit which the man from Uz initiates against God. The case is comprised of several interwoven complaints.[27]

Whilst Yahweh 'wins' the lawsuit without a traditional apologetic defence, he certainly relies on the insights of General Revelation as to the enormity and majesty of his creation in the making of his case.[28] This reliance on general revelation lends weight to Montgomery's latest apologetic that sees benefit, at times, of 'interlocking' the historical-legal evidence with natural theology.[29]

Let us now return to the gospel of John lawsuit. The witnesses God calls include, 'John the Baptist, the scriptures, the words and works of Christ, and later the witness of the Apostles and the Holy Spirit'.[30] In the first twelve chapters the 'lawsuit' is between Jesus and the Jews. In the battle Satan himself is legally cast out and condemned.[31] Johan Ferreira, who holds to a compositional history behind the fourth gospel, argues the genre of the 'High Priestly prayer' of chapter 17 is the Jewish 'law-court' petitions. It reflects the early prayers of the Johannine community as it sought God's vindication for its Christological beliefs and incorporates, 'strong apologetic motifs for the legitimacy of the Johannine community within a Jewish context …'.[32] The gospel concludes its case with the apostles being eyewitnesses. Trites holds, 'Like witnesses to the fact in Greek and Hebrew

---

[27] Sylvia Huberman Scholnick, 'Poetry in the Courtroom: Job 38-41', in *Directions in Hebrew Poetry*, Elaine Follis, ed. (Sheffield: JSOT, 1987), 185. See also Peter C. Craigie, *The Old Testament* (Nashville: Abingdon, 1986), 227; Claus Westermann, *The Structure of the Book of Job*, trans. Charles A. Muenchow (Philadelphia: Fortress Press, 1981). Westermann notes, together with Lament the legal nature of the book of Job: 'In line with the legal proceedings, Job was accused by the friends of being a transgressor (chapter 22), appeals to that higher court which is at the same time, however, the very opponent he summons to a lawsuit.' Yet, Job is reproved in the Yahweh speeches for thinking 'he can talk to God on an equal footing, summon him to a lawsuit, confront him as a legal opponent.' (106).

[28] Mayhew, 'God's Use', 123-124. Mayhew asserts General Revelation was used in part, 'To spread a panorama of evidence for unbelievers/believers to interact with the Designer.' (123).

[29] Montgomery, *Tractatus*, 3.87. See for discussion in chapter three 'Conformity of the testimony with experience'.

[30] Trites, *The New Testament*, 79.

[31] ibid., 113; John 12:31, 16:11.

[32] Johan Ferreira, 'The So-called "High Priestly prayer" of John 17 and Ecclesiology: The Concerns of an Early Christian Community' in *Prayer and Spirituality in the Early Church*, Vol. 1, Pauline Allen, Raymond Canning, Lawrence Cross and B. Janelle Craiger, eds. (Everton Park, Queensland: Centre for Early Christian Studies, 1988), 31. Ferreira holds to a Johannine school authorship, see Johan Ferreira, *Johannine Ecclesiology, Journal for the Study of New Testament Supplementary Series 160* (Sheffield: Sheffield Press, 1998), 29-35.

courts of law, they can give firsthand information on some disputed matter; in their case, they can attest both the words and works of Jesus'.[33] Geisler similarly documents this legal apologetic nature of John's gospel. He avers:

> Johannine apologetics takes place in a courtroom. The eyewitness, confirmed, sealed, sworn, last-will-and testament evidence is offered to the unbelieving jury; but by the very nature of the case, it is evidence that demands a verdict![34]

It may be argued that the theological tone of John's gospel stops one speaking of witness in a juridical sense. Paul Ricoeur holds however that John's shift from a narrational pole to a confessional pole does not mean the narration framework is lost. Whilst Luke and John are different he maintains they agree on this point, 'Testimony – confession cannot be separated from testimony – narration without the risk of turning toward gnosticism ... John designates his work in terms which would be possible for Luke (John 19:35)'.[35]

Trites supports his case for an emphasis upon the juridical nature and witness of the New Testament by referring first to Paul's being a *bona fide* witness as recorded in 1 Corinthians 15, and also to the law court setting of texts like 1 Peter 3:15 and 1 Peter 5:8.[36] Support for a legal genre in the Epistles and Letters of the New Testament is found in an unexpected quarter. The critical scholar Hans Dieter Betz likewise asserts a New Testament 'legal' apologetic genre in the New Testament letters. He holds that apologetic letters such as Galatians 'presuppose

---

[33] Trites, *The New Testament*, 114; John 20:25, 21:24. See also Barnett, *Is the New Testament History?* 61, 'The author (John's gospel), therefore is using these miracles, and what Jesus says about them to argue a case as a lawyer might, to persuade the readers of the rightness of what he is saying'.
[34] Norman L. Geisler 'Johannine Apologetics', *Bibliotheca Sacra* 136, 544 (October – December, 1979): 338.
[35] Paul Ricoeur, 'The Hermeneutics of Testimony', *Anglican Theological Review* 61, 4 (October 1979): 450. Ricoeur discusses the juridical nature of Luke-Acts and John (438-444).
[36] Trites, *The New Testament*, 199-221. In 1 Peter 5:8 the devil is described as an 'adversary' which Trites notes elsewhere in scripture as having a juridical context. For a discussion on whether Paul was trying to prove the resurrection historically in 1 Corinthians 15 see Fee, *The First Epistle*, 713-760; Craig, *The Historical*, 19-25. Both Fee and Craig find the text holds to the objective reality of the resurrection. Craig interacts with the positions of Pannenberg (thesis supervisor), Conzelmann, Barth and Bultmann. Also see John T. Moen, 'A Lawyer's Logical and Syllogistic Look at the Facts of the Resurrection', *Simon Greenleaf Law Review*, VIII (1987-88), 81-110. Lawyer Moen critiques Tillich's non-historical restitution approach and makes a case for the historical eyewitness structure of 1 Corinthians 15. Cf. Stephen Davis who discusses whether the resurrection of Jesus in 1 Corinthians 15 and elsewhere is to be seen as 'ordinary/normal vision' or 'objective vision' (see-er has an inspired ability to see what others lack). Davis, '"Seeing" the Risen Jesus', 127-147. And for the case for uncertain historical roots and a preferred focus on the theological significance of the resurrection see Lorenzen, *Resurrection*, 174-181.

the real or fictitious situation of the court of law, with jury, accuser and defendant. In the case of Galatians, the addressees are identical with the jury, with Paul being the defendant, and his opponents the accusers'.[37] There are weaknesses in Betz's critical findings on Galatians. He admits chapters 3 to 4 are 'extremely difficult' to analyse in terms of rhetoric.[38] Also, because of Galatians' blessings and cursings, he concedes there is more than rhetoric here and it is a 'magical letter' as well.[39] This supports the fact that for Paul his writings are more than human logic and are instruments of the Spirit. These concessions do not override Betz's case for Paul's apparent openness to a legal format.[40] However, this is not to imply that Paul limited himself to forensic rhetoric, since he also used 'deliberative' rhetoric whose typical venue was the public assembly.[41]

Whilst the seminal work of Trites may have been lost on the legal apologists, the contribution of the apologist William Lane Craig is another story. In one of his published doctorates he interacts with Trites and examines the double testimony of Acts. Although his work is primarily on historical apologetics his conclusions connect with the legal apologetic:

> In Luke-Acts then we have a sophisticated example of early Christian argument for the resurrection. Indeed, in a sense Luke stands like a rock far out at sea, as the first systematic attempt to establish the resurrection through historical evidence; for with Luke's lengthy and close scrutiny of the facts, his research into eyewitness reports, his descriptions of unmistakable appearances of Jesus alive from the dead, and his repeated emphasis on the

---

[37] Hans Dieter Betz, *Galatians* (Philadelphia: Fortress Press, 1979), 24. An example of Betz's argument is: 'the addressees of the letter, that is, the hearers of the arguments, are also the eye-witnesses of the evidence (3:1). This situation provides the writer of the letter with the possibility of proceeding as if the eye-witnesses are "in court". Paul makes full use of this opportunity in 3:1-5; by applying the inductive method, which rhetoricians traced back to Socrates, he enters into his first argument by an *interrogatio* of these witnesses. In every case the answers to the questions are self-evident and need not be recorded. Paul is not only fortunate in being able to question the eye-witnesses themselves, but he also compels them to produce the strongest of all possible defense arguments – undeniable evidence. This undeniable evidence is the gift of the Spirit, which the Galatians themselves have experienced. The gift of the Spirit was an ecstatic experience. Together with the miracles which are being performed at present among the Galatians, this constitutes evidence of supernatural origin and character which is, for ancient rhetoric, evidence of the highest order.' (129-130).
[38] ibid., 129.
[39] ibid., 25. Galatians 1:8-9, 6:16.
[40] For critique of Betz, see Heikke Raisanen, *Paul and the Law* (Philadelphia: Fortress Press, 1983), 266-269.
[41] See Collins, *First Corinthians*, 18-20.

first-hand testimony of the apostolic preachers, a historical proof for the resurrection, among other things, is exactly what he is about.[42]

If this is the case then Craig gives support to Trites' juridical, apologetic framework for much of Luke-Acts, John's gospel and other sections of the New Testament. The framework also is found in the Old Testament.

It is believed that it has been shown here that the legal apologist can mount a strong argument that their paradigm is a continuum of apostolic proclamation. It has a biblical warrant.[43]

Resurrection focus
To what has been said there could be added another biblical justification for the legal apologetic. As Montgomery argues the case, Christ's resurrection was the foundational and fundamental apologetic for Christianity.[44] This is seen in the book of Acts where the apostolic speeches have a primary focus on the resurrection.[45] This resurrection emphasis in the sermons of Paul and Peter is not inconsistent with the more theologically developed and atonement centred Pauline epistles. The sermons represent the first word to Jewish and Gentile seekers, the epistles the second word to a believing church. The 'first word' takes the form of the apologetic model.[46]

---

[42] Craig, *The Historical*, 15-16. Justice Ken Handley argues from a legal perspective that both Luke and Paul appeal to actual eyewitness evidence. Handley, 'A Lawyer', 11-12.

[43] Cornelius Trimp, 'The Witness of the Scriptures' in *Jerusalem and Athens*, E.R. Geehan, ed. (n.p.: Presbyterian and Reformed, 1971), 172-174. A further argument in support is the fact that in the gospel parables the teller often seeks a verdict from his hearers on the story he has told. See Humphrey Palmer, 'Seeking Verdicts for Parables', *The Expository Times* 111, 8 (May 2000): 262-265.

[44] Montgomery, *Faith Founded*, xii.

[45] See for example, Acts 2:29-39, 10:39-41, 13:26-41, 17:31-32. David Peterson states the proclamation of the resurrection in Acts shows it, 'links together a whole complex of biblical hopes and is a key to their fulfilment'. 'Resurrection Apologetics and the Theology of Luke-Acts' in *Proclaiming the Resurrection*, Peter M. Head, ed. (Carlisle: Paternoster, 1998), 56.

[46] See Dodd, *The Apostolic Preaching*, 9; Paul Barnett, *Move in for Action* (Sydney: Anzea, 1971), 64. Cf. E. Haenchen, *The Acts of the Apostles*, trans. B. Blackwell (Oxford: Blackwell, 1971), 528-530. Haenchen sees the Paul of Athens as inconsistent with the Paul of the epistles. For refutation of Haenchen see C.J. Hemer, 'The Speeches of Acts 11. The Areopagus address', *Tyndale Bulletin*, 40.2 (November 1989), 248-255.

Margueritte Shuster has documented how the centrality of the resurrection as articulated by Paul has been the continuing thrust of major preacher-theologians from Augustine through to Luther, Barth and Thielicke.[47] As the legal apologetic normally focuses on the resurrection it is consistent with the biblical paradigm for evangelism.

Historical Precedent

In chapter one the prominent place of the legal apologetic in the early Church has been established so our discussions here need only be brief. Whilst for the most part the thinkers who have used this argument have come to prominence since the time of Hugo Grotius and the development of Protestant apologetics and legal systems, they were indebted to earlier disputants for the role of legal method in argumentation. This historical lineage, which is often drawn on by Montgomery and other legal apologists,[48] is a strength as it establishes that this apologetic is tested, and has a rich heritage within the church. The last point is of particular importance for those from traditional and confessional denominations.

Apart from the embryonic findings of Montgomery a weakness in the work of the legal apologetic advocates to date has been their failure to really evaluate the history of the school and the diversity of approach within it. In chapter one, and appendix one, there is an attempt to correct this anomaly.

Other Factors Supporting the Application of the Legal Method to Ultimate Questions

Law and history
Christian orthodoxy claims that the Christ event occurred in 'objective' history. Law is a craft that tackles the past. Supreme Court Justice K.R. Handley notes that in 1974 the Australian High Court, in a significant case had to decide what happened in Port Moresby in 1886, and in the process the judges did not hesitate to rely on historical evidence. He stated, 'The tools of trade of the judge in such a case, and of the historian in every case, are historical evidence – what people wrote about the events, the evidence from archaeology, and circumstantial evi-

---

[47] Margueritte Shuster, 'The Preaching of the Resurrection of Christ in Augustine, Luther, Barth and Thielicke' in *The Resurrection*, Davis, Kendall and O'Collins, eds., 308-338.
[48] Montgomery, *The Law Above*, 84-87; Ankerberg and Weldon, *Ready*, 99-109.

Strenghts of the Legal Paradigm

dence ... The Christian approach to the evidence for the resurrection is no different.'[49] Thus, the appeal to historical fact is a plea lawyers are held to understand and can assess.

Law and documents

Montgomery asserts, 'law is necessitarian, coloring all aspects of societal life; so its solutions to fundamental problems carry powerful weight. On the interpretation of contracts, wills, statutes and constitutions hang the lives and property of us all'.[50] Law works with documents, including ancient documents and we have seen that it has developed its own hermeneutical methodology. Robert Anderson takes it further and favourably contrasts the skills of the legally trained with a 'Professor of Theology or of Hebrew'.[51] A strength of the legal apologetic is law's familiarity with documents and the criteria developed as to their admissibility, interpretation and credibility. These criteria were addressed in the previous chapters.

Law, facts and inductions

It was William Paley who declared, 'the truth of Christianity depends upon its leading facts, and them alone'.[52] This assertion is obviously reductionist but is not without some biblical justification. The apostle Paul summarises the gospel factually (1 Cor 15:3-9). The fact or otherwise of the resurrection for Paul, determines the efficacy of Christianity (1 Cor 15:17). Chapter 20 of John's gospel concludes by appealing to Jesus' signs as a foundation of belief. Paul and John write as if there are facts they must prove. Clearly in the New Testament the main fact at issue is the resurrection, with collateral other facts or signs.

A legal apologetic is appropriate to a fact based religion. It is an apologetic that by its nature is accustomed to sifting evidence to find the principle items, that can clearly discriminate between issues and sources, and that can weigh the significance of subordinate facts; such as a relationship that would tend to make a witness biased, and the competency of a witness. It also offers criteria to evaluate oral testimony, hearsay and circumstantial evidence in determining the facts.[53]

Yet, as we have discussed in this thesis, legal science is not just about facts it is concerned with drawing warranted inferences or interpretations.[54] And at the

---

[49] Handley, 'A Lawyer', 11.
[50] Montgomery, 'Legal Hermeneutics', 18.
[51] Robert Anderson, *A Doubter's*, 154-155.
[52] Paley, *A View*, 364. (This presumably includes interpretation of the facts.)
[53] See chapters two and three herein.
[54] G. Abrahams, *The Legal Mind* (London: H.F.L., 1954), 20.

heart of the Christian tradition is not just the fact of the empty tomb, but the inferences that can be drawn from it. Francis Beckwith puts it, '... the attorney in order to have a sound case, must demonstrate that his premises are true and that his conclusion logically follows from these premises'.[55] A warranted inference in law is an interpretation that fits the facts to the exclusion of any other hypothesis. Shaw illustrates with homicide. He states the evidence must establish the offence committed as charged and must not only prove a death by violence, but must to a reasonable extent, exclude the hypothesis of suicide or death by the act of some other person.[56] In chapter three it has been argued that a legal methodological rigour does not *per se* exclude an unlikely hypothesis, if it alone fits the facts.[57] In this regard we have Montgomery's reliance on his fictional mentor Sherlock Holmes[58] who holds, 'When you have eliminated the impossible, whatever remains, however improbable, must be the truth.'[59] In fact the nearest the master detective ever came to advancing an argument for the existence of God was in *The Adventure of the Naval Treaty*. Here Holmes, falling into 'reverie' goes further and informs Watson, 'There is nothing in which deduction is so necessary as in religion.'[60] This Sherlockian spirit Montgomery, Davis and Swinburne specifically evoke in endorsing the traditional understanding of the resurrection: Christ is Risen, after elimination of the other hypothesis as to what happened to his body.[61]

The Christian truth claims warrant assessment by a legal apologetic.

Difficult to jettison
Montgomery advocates that the advantage of a jurisprudential approach lies in the difficulty of jettisoning it, 'legal standards of evidence develop an essential means of resolving the most intractable disputes in society... thus one cannot very well throw out legal reasoning merely because its application to Christianity results in a verdict for the Christian faith and its approach to human rights!'.[62]

---

[55] Beckwith, *David Hume's*, 126.
[56] Cited in Montgomery, ed., *Jurisprudence*, 258.
[57] G. Abrahams states that the only claim that can be placed on a jury's sympathy is that they should seek to understand the defendant's case and appreciate the possibility of the defendant's story, even if improbable, as they consider the facts. G. Abrahams, *The Legal Mind*, 20.
[58] Montgomery, 'The Search for Ultimates', 6-7.
[59] Arthur Conan Doyle, *The Sign of the Four, Sherlock Holmes the Complete Illustrated Novels* (London: Chancellor, 1987), 114.
[60] Arthur Conan Doyle, *Naval Treaty, Complete Sherlock Holmes* (London: Penguin, 1981), 445-456. Holmes also argues here that religion could be built up as an exact science by the reasoner.
[61] Davis, Kendall and O'Collins, eds., *The Resurrection*, 146-147, 198-201.
[62] Montgomery, *Human Rights*, 134-135.

Strengths of the Legal Paradigm

Whilst Montgomery's observation does not enthrone the law as infallible, it does point to its usefulness in our daily lives. The law has come under scrutiny over time and hence endured in significant ways, and therefore it is a model society knows and accepts for adjudicating life and death issues. It is appropriate for a sceptical, questioning age.[63] Beckwith, in support of the legal analogy, cites Windes and Hindes: '... evidential law imposes a rigidity seldom encountered in other disciplines'.[64]

Montgomery develops his argument with respect to jettisoning by citing the universal nature of the Law of Evidence:

> And here, in contact with Greco-Roman jurisprudence, we see that the Law of Evidence is not a self-serving technique developed by common-law jurists in subtle support of Christian theology! The fundamental canons of evidence which we have employed in defense of biblical faith are found with remarkable consistency in all legal systems — from primitive to civilized, from ancient to modern. Max Gluckman writes of the Lozi people of Northern Rhodesia: The Lozi distinguish between different kinds of evidence as hearsay, circumstantial, and direct, and attach different degrees of cogency to these and different degrees of credibility to various witnesses... In the words of the pre-Christian Roman dramatist Plautus, 'One eyewitness is worth more than ten purveyors of hearsay; Those who only hear about things say what they've heard, but those who see know the score!'[65]

Could it be argued that Montgomery here has overstated his case as the technical legal apologetic is primarily based on rules of evidence in common law countries? The laws of evidence and systems of proof of countries not beholden to common law, indicate there is not international uniformity on questions such as hearsay, admissibility of evidence and onus of proof.

---

[63] Montgomery acknowledges that lawyers are the butt of legal jokes which is often deserved. However he says it is still one of the three 'historic, great, classical professions': law, theology, medicine. His point is there is still a strong respect for, and reliance on, the process of the law. John Warwick Montgomery, 'An Interview', by Craig Parton (University of California Santa Barbara, *Veritas Forum*, 1999).
[64] Beckwith, *David Hume's*, 123.
[65] Montgomery, 'Neglected Apologetic', 123-125.

Yet, it is fair to say there are universal issues that most legal systems address:

(1) what is to be proved (the object of proof);

(2) who is to prove it (the burden of proof);

(3) how it must or may be proved (the means of proof, including capacity to give evidence);

(4) how the evidence is to be assessed (the weight of evidence); and

(5) what degree of proof is required (the quantum of proof).[66]

These 'universals' guide the topics to be addressed in any just legal system. The principles of evidence enacted on the basis of such in any just legal system could arguably form the shape of a culturally sensitive legal apologetic.

Most important however, is that any paradigm for assessing truth claims whether it be philosophical, historical or legal, whilst relying on 'universals', will have various schools, factions and procedures.

Montgomery's claim that a legal apologetic is difficult to jettison has real merit, even though the question as to whether there are universal laws of evidence may need some qualification to avoid creating conceptual difficulties in the mind of some hearers.[67]

Common usage
Montgomery does not succumb to the temptation to find some kind of essentialism, a single positive theory or model that will satisfy everyone and alone will

---

[66] Honoré, 'The Primacy of Oral Evidence?', 176. Cf. Keith Mason QC, Solicitor General for New South Wales, 'Every legal contest (civil or criminal) involves the interaction of three matters: (1) the (true) facts as they occurred in the past; (2) the evidence or means whereby the judge or jury gets a window through which to search for the facts; and (3) a verdict, which represents a decision about the impact of the facts as found. So too with much of life. In both great and small matters we are constantly confronted with these three aspects of decision-making. For example, my decision about where to go on holidays this year may be based on how I recall and perceive the actuality of last year's holiday. There is nothing unusual about this exercise. Only the human ostrich avoids it in the contemplation of the larger issues of life's purpose and death significance'. Barnett, *The Truth*, iv. For the problematic status of universal principles in legal and moral philosophy see Stanley Fish, *The Trouble with Principles* (Cambridge, Massachusetts: Harvard University Press, 1999), 1-15.

[67] For further discussion on Montgomery's position that the processes of induction, deduction and retroduction are always the same as there is only one human reasoning faculty, see John Warwick Montgomery, 'Good and Bad Legal Reasoning', RealPlayer[Montgomery 1] jwm4.ram..ram. .<http://www.spr-consilio.com/soundarchive.html>.

lead one to truth. He quotes favourably Edward John Carnell, 'there are as many apologetics as there are facts in the world.'[68] So, his evidence-based legal apologetic is not the standard currency, against which other apologetics systems are devalued. However, in his historical overview of apologetics he gives a test to determine the appropriateness of a particular apologetic method. It is not simply whether the model will have, or has had, a long term application, but whether it assists in answering questions actually being asked.[69] Or, to put it another way, it is what Montgomery calls 'the fundamental technique'. It is using a paradigm that challenges the unbeliever to apply the same kind of reasoning used in non-religious life to the issue of Christian truth.[70] Montgomery by this approach is not suggesting epistemological questions are irrelevant, nor has he drifted into pragmatism. He is affirming that the choice of apologetic method cannot be divorced from the *sitz im leben*. Apologetic models must be applicable to the listener or reader.[71]

The appeal of the legal apologetic is the common usage of the legal paradigm. People encounter daily the juridical process. As a consequence Wharton argues, 'what jurisprudence declares to be a true mode of proof, the community is apt to accept as such; what jurisprudence declares to be an incompetent instrument of proof, the community is apt to regard as incompetent.'[72] As well, legal fiction dominates the secular and Christian best seller lists.[73] For Montgomery the legal apologetic undeniably meets Paul's injunction to be all things to all people, which he views as the highest apologetic call.[74]

Philosophical apologetics and other models
Montgomery is not known for his philosophical apologetic even though much of his other work focuses on the history of ideas. However, a philosophical apologetic is not entirely absent from his writings.[75] In his brief but neglected eclectic apologetic *in Christianity for the Tough Minded*, he argues from: the historical resurrection; Peter Berger's sociological experiences of death, judgement, order, honour, and play as a signpost to the transcendental;[76] the philosophical theologian, Ian Ramsay's partial transcendence of the human subject as pointing to the possibility of metaphysical assertions and God-language; and from the traditional proofs argument of contingency.[77] This eclectic cumulative case method of Montgomery is also open to the legal apologetic. Paul D. Feinberg views his own

---

[68] Montgomery, 'Neglected Apologetic', 119.
[69] Montgomery, *Defending the Gospel*, Anslem tape.
[70] Montgomery, *Faith Founded*, 125-127.
[71] McGrath, *Bridge-Building*, 9-14; Montgomery, 'Defending the Hope', 2.
[72] Wharton, 'Recent Changes in Jurisprudence', 149. See also Montgomery, *Tractatus*, 3.1252

cumulative case apologetic as one that does not conform to the ordinary patterns of deductive or inductive reasoning, rather it is 'more like the brief that a lawyer brings'.[78]

In his case Montgomery admittedly rebuts the ontological argument for its lack of empirical grounding, and refutes the causal argument for gratuitously presupposing an unalterable cause and effect structure in the universe.[79] Yet on occasions, a philosophical apologetic based on the contingency argument and intelligent design, has underpinned his case.[80] And elsewhere he acknowledges the historical basis for philosophical apologetics citing Augustine's heavy dependence on Plato and Aquinas on Aristotle.[81]

One reason for Montgomery's resistance to embracing the use of a more philosophical apologetic is its apparent lack of common usage.[82] International apologist Ravi Zacharias affirms in practice the limited role of the philosophical apolo-

---

[73] For examples of lawyers who have written legal fiction see Steve Martini, *The Attorney* (London: Headline, 2000); John Grisham, *The Testament* (London: Century, 1999); Scott Turrow, *Personal Injuries* (New York: Michael Joseph, 1999); Perri O'Shaughnessy [Pamela and Mary O'Shaughnessy], *Acts of Malice* (New York: Island, 2000); Buffa, *The Legacy*; Martel, *The Alternate*; Dershowitz, *Just Revenge*; Chris Nyst, *Cop This!* (Sydney: HarperCollins, 1999); Lisa Scottoline, *Moment of Truth* (London: Harper Collins, 2000). For a more 'twenty something' readership see Brad Meltzer, *The Tenth Justice* (London: Hodder and Stoughton, 1977). Legal fiction by non-lawyers includes John Lescroat, *The Mercy Rule* (London: Headline, 1988). For details of legal fiction writers who have published novels in the small press and stories in magazines see Michael Hemmingson, ed., *The Mammoth Book of Legal Thrillers* (London: Robinson, 2001). For Christian legal fiction see: Blackstock who has moved from romance to a Christian romance legal drama genre, Terry Blackstock, *Evidence of Mercy* (Grand Rapids: Zondervan, 1995); the spiritual legal genre of Robert Whitlow, *The Trial* (Nashville: Word, 2001); T. Dovis Bunn, *The Great Divide* (New York: Doubleday; Colorado Springs: Waterbook, 2000) and Grisham's, *The Testament* is bordering on Christian legal fiction. See also John Grisham, *The Chamber* (London: Arrow, 1994), 497-499. Grisham has a chaplain sharing with a condemned man and the conversation includes, 'How many murders will he forgive?' 'All of them. If you sincerely ask forgiveness, then he'll wipe the slate clean. It's in the Scriptures.' (499). Montgomery discusses how the legal novel has a place and can assist in the ethical practice of law in 'Legal Novels'.
[74] Montgomery, *Cross and Crucible*, 1: 240.
[75] For example Montgomery, *Tractatus*, 3.8 – 3.8732.
[76] For a critical discussion see William Edward Gordon, 'A Contemporary Apologetics: The Concept of Christian Apologetics in the Writings of Peter L. Berger and Hans Küng' (Th.D. Thesis, New Orleans Baptist Theological Seminary, 1987), 170-210.
[77] Montgomery, *Christianity for the Tough Minded*, 21-34.
[78] Paul D. Feinberg, 'The Cumulative Case Method' in *Five Views on Apologetics*, Cowan, ed., 151.
[79] Montgomery, *Christianity for the Tough Minded*, 26; Montgomery, *Tractatus*, 3.83 – 3.84212.
[80] Reference has already been made to his latest work, *Tractatus* which provides for the 'interlocking' of 'natural theology' with historical legal evidence.
[81] Montgomery, *Law and Gospel*, 34.
[82] ibid, 34-35; Montgomery, *Myth, Allegory*, 17-21.

Strenghts of the Legal Paradigm 245

getic today, even on university campuses.[83] As a result Montgomery asserts, that whilst in no way undervaluing the contribution of philosophical apologetics, 'the interminable attempts to baptize and rehabilitate Aristotle's traditional proofs for God's existence, justify Anslem's ontological argument and refute Kant's critical philosophy have led many moderns to conclude that apologetics as such is an arid and irrelevant activity.'[84]

C. Stephen Evans concurs in suggesting that philosophical 'proofs' for most today are complicated, technical, and hard to follow. Such reasoning he asserts is suitable for the professional philosopher, but offers little for the ordinary person. He states that a legal approach to 'proof' is therefore more personable, accessible and relevant, even for those disenchanted with 'modernity'.[85] Further, it could be argued that a legal apologetic is not inconsistent with philosophy that developed in ancient Athens out of techniques of cross-examination and debate.[86] Montgomery's summary is: 'What if a revelational truth-claim did not turn on questions of theology and religious philosophy... but on the very questions employed in the law to determine questions of fact?'.[87] In this context,

---

[83] Ravi Zacharias, 'The Touch of Truth' in *Telling the Truth*, D.A. Carson, ed. (Grand Rapids: Zondervan, 2000), 30-43. For a different perspective see Michael S. Hamilton and Johann G. Yngvason, 'Patrons of the Evangelical Mind', *Christianity Today* 46, 8 (July 2002): 42-47.

[84] Montgomery, 'Neglected Apologetic',119. For a personal 'testimony' in this regard see Bryan Magee, *Confessions of a Philosopher* (New York: Random, 1997), 346-349.

[85] Evans, *Why Believe?*, 10-21. In the same spirit Coady argues the place of testimony, including formal (legal) testimony, 'is an absolutely fundamental epistemological attitude which is far more pervasive in ordinary life and in specialized theory than we normally recognize ...'. Coady, *Testimony*, 262-263. Further Dan Story advocates the legal paradigm on the basis that other religions require the acceptance of their tenets on authoritarian grounds (testimony of leaders) or one's personal experience. In contrast, Christianity is a religion whose truth claims can be tested and legal reasoning provides a way for same. Dan Story, *Christianity on the Offensive* (Grand Rapids: Kregel, 1998), 81-83. See also Stephen Toulmin, *Cosmopolis: The Hidden Agenda of Modernity* (New York: Free Press, 1990), 31-32, 188; Stephen Toulmin, *The Uses of Argument* (Cambridge: Cambridge University Press, 1958), 7. Toulmin holds we need to move from a deductive model and seek another, for example the legal paradigm. For Montgomery's use of Toulmin see Montgomery, *Human Rights*, 135. For a critique of Toulmin see C.F. Presley, 'Review of the Uses of Argument', *Australasian Journal of Philosophy* 37, 2 (August 1959): 168-176. Jerome Hall is another to advocate the application of legal reasoning to pertinent questions about faith. See Jerome Hall, 'Religion, Law and Ethics – A Call for Dialogue', *Hastings Law Journal*, 29 (July 1978): 1273, cited in Montgomery, *Human Rights*, 136. For a stronger role for philosophical argument see Don R. Stiver, 'Much Ado About Athens and Jerusalem: The Implications of Postmodernism for Faith', *Review and Expositor* 91, 1 (Winter, 1994): 96-97.

[86] Byrskog, *Story*, 205-223. For a discussion on this point and a Van Til style of critique of the Socratic jury approach as it applies to apologetics see Greg L. Bahnsen, 'Socrates or Christ (?)' in *Foundations of Christian Scholarship*, ed., Gary North (Vallecito, California: Ross House, 1979), 191-240.

[87] Montgomery, 'The Jury Returns', 319.

Montgomery is in part highlighting the presumption of law that the senses do 'function as instruments of finding out how the world is' and the apparent advantage of this position in advocacy.[88] Whilst one in rejoinder may suggest that there is plenty of philosophy carried out on a popular level,[89] Montgomery still has a strong case for the legal apologetic being a more applicable paradigm, or at least being acknowledged today as one of the most appropriate models.

Montgomery's holding to the limitation of philosophy in apologetics is not just on cultural grounds. For Montgomery, the traditional proofs lead at best to a generic god and to the view that belief in God is basic.[90] Graham Phillips, an ABC science producer, presents a theistic case from the 'string' and the 'big bang' theories, and concedes, 'It's still a long way from claiming there is a personal God ... but it's a start.'[91] As a positive apologist Montgomery finds philosophy's other main contribution operates in the area of negative apologetics as it assesses the logical inconsistencies of worldviews such as pantheism, humanism and agnosticism.[92] Here philosophy makes a valuable contribution to apologetics, 'Philosophy has served its purpose when it has shown the logical errors in attempting to reach absolutes by analysing the human situation ...'.[93] Montgomery maintains that if one uses philosophy in this negative sense, the case for Christianity should then be established positively by legal-historical evidence.

Whilst Montgomery is completely justified in asserting the role of evidence in a positive apologetic not all would argue that facts alone are the answer. Some would also point to better theorising and argument.[94] Montgomery states:

---

[88] Stephen Toulmin, *Knowing and Acting* (New York: Macmillan, 1976), 106-112. Also see the limitation of this position in the following discussion on 'A Legal Formalist Approach'.

[89] For example Jostein Gaarder, *Sophie's World: A Novel about the History of Philosophy*, trans. Paulette Moller (London: Phoenix House, 1995). See also Douglas Groothuis, 'Are Theistic Arguments Religiously Useless? A Pascalian Objection Examined' in *The Gospel and Contemporary Perspectives*, Douglas Moo, ed. (Grand Rapids: Kregel, 1997), 116-127. Groothuis concludes with respect to the theistic proofs, 'The argumentative procedures may be more complex than what is used in the common operations of life, but this in no way diminishes a proof's probative force or its possible existential impact' (127).

[90] ibid. Cf. Boa and Moody, *I'm Glad*, 17-39.

[91] Graham Phillips, 'God Makes a Comeback', *The West Australian* (23 October 2000), 14.

[92] Montgomery, *Christianity for the Tough Minded*, 21-25. For a more detailed, but general, discussion on the understanding of many evidentialists that the primary task of philosophy is in the examination and clarification of the knowledge claims of other worldviews and disciplines, rather than advocating a 'constructive' view that sees philosophy as a means of developing a comprehensive world-and-life view see Boa and Bowman, *Faith*, 188-192.

[93] John Warwick Montgomery, 'The Quest for Absolutes: An Historical Argument' in *Jurisprudence*, Montgomery, ed., 523.

> And even if it were possible in some fashion to destroy all existent alternative world-views but that of orthodox Christianity, the end result would still not be the necessary truth of Christianity; for in a contingent universe, there are an infinite number of possible philosophical positions, and even the fallaciousness of infinity-minus-one positions would not establish the validity of the one that remained (unless we were to introduce the gratuitous assumption that at least one had to be right!).
>
> When world-views collide, an appeal to common facts is the only preservative against philosophical solipsism and religious anarchy.[95]

Foundational to Montgomery's philosophical delimitation is his commitment to his theological mentor, Martin Luther.[96] Luther had little time for philosophy in divine matters.[97] More significant was Luther's focus on the incarnation.[98] For Montgomery in light of the Lutheran Confessions, apologetics is about the gospel and providing a case for the deity of Christ.[99] Such an apologetic, in contrast to the 'theology from above' of much of contemporary 'Reformed epistemology', is a 'theology from below', from specific to general. Its point of departure is concrete particularity.[100] For Montgomery the Lutheran, it is noteworthy that, at least until the Enlightenment, such an incarnational, historical apologetic paradigm was supported by the tradition of the church.[101]

Law and the bible

Another factor in support of the legal analogy is the strategic place law plays in scripture. The Torah is divinely given and foundational to the Old Testament. Within Old Testament law are found legal criteria such as the place played by

---

[94] For an example of this see C.S. Lewis, *Mere Christianity* (London and Glasgow: Fontana, 1964).
[95] Montgomery, *Faith Founded*, 119.
[96] Like Luther you cannot divorce Montgomery the apologist from Montgomery the theologian. See Montgomery, *Christ our Advocate*, 61.
[97] William J. Abraham, *An Introduction to the Philosophy of Religion* (Englewood Clifts, New Jersey: Prentice-Hall, 1985), 1-6. Abrahams adds 'Luther would not have worried if philosophers had agreed to embark on an eternal strike' (1).
[98] Montgomery, *Faith Founded*, 142-143.
[99] John Warwick Montgomery, 'Christian Apologetics in Light of the Lutheran Confessions', *Concordia Theological Quarterly* 42, 3 (July 1978): 272; John Warwick Montgomery, 'The Incarnate Christ: The Apologetic Thrust of Lutheran Theology',
<http://www.alliancenet.org/pub/mr/mr98/1998.01.JanFeb/mr9801.jwm.incarnate.html>.
[100] Montgomery, *Giant in Chains*, 176-177.
[101] Montgomery, *Faith Founded*, ix-iv.

witnesses. The Sermon on the Mount reveals Jesus' fulfilment of the law, his interpretative deepening of it, and his commitment to it. And Markus Barth does not leave the matter there but pleads that Jesus in the New Testament is portrayed as an advocate, pleader or defence attorney.[102] The Epistles are rich in legal metaphor.[103] Montgomery concurs that the legal apologetic is clearly not without scriptural parallels.[104]

Law and ultimate questions
The appropriateness of the legal apologetic to religious truth claims is held by Philip Johnson to be evident in its already established artistic role of tackling ultimate questions in the public arena. He notes the following examples: Kafka's *The Trial* employs the legal paradigm as a backdrop for expressing his agnostic metaphysic; in the 1957 motion picture *The Story of Mankind*, the human race was on trial before the heavenly court for centuries of evil deeds; *Star Trek: The Next Generation* has used the legal paradigm to debate ultimate questions in the episodes *Encounter at Farpoint* and *Justice*; and human rights specialist Geoffrey Robertson has employed it in his televised hypotheticals.[105]

Summary
There are then, strong arguments in support of the appropriateness of the legal apologetic paradigm. And as already indicated, some arguments could be further developed. From an evangelical perspective one looks firstly to scripture, then to tradition and finally to other factors or sources.[106] In all three categories there are bases for justifying Montgomery's legal analogy.

Perceived Limitations of the Legal Paradigm Analogy

Whilst Montgomery is to a large extent responsible for the current popularity and development of the legal model, he has not seen it as his brief to substantially justify it via a written thesis.[107] The warrant for it has been a pithy case that interacts with appropriate citations from scripture, lawyers and philosophers in support.[108]

---

[102] Markus Barth, *Justification* (Grand Rapids: William B. Eerdmans, 1971), 1931. For example see 1 John 2:1. Barth also finds a sense of glory in the law. See Markus Barth 'Christ and Law', *Oklahoma Law Review* 12, 1 (February 1959): 67-85.

[103] Francis Lyall, *Slaves, Citizens, Sons: Legal Metaphors in the Epistles* (Grand Rapids: Zondervan, 1984), 10.

[104] Montgomery, *Human Rights*, 164-170.

[105] Philip Johnson, 'Judicial Apologetics; Origins, Epistemology and Application', intended publication <http://www.sacredtribes.com>. See Montgomery, *The Law Above*, 89.

[106] Millard J. Erickson, *Christian Theology* (Grand Rapids: Baker, 1985), 66-79.

[107] Interview by the author (Strasbourg, France, 26 July 1996).

Perceived Limitations of the Legal Paradigm Analogy

As a consequence, the appropriateness of the legal apologetic has not been fully assessed *from within the boundaries of law itself*. And whilst the legal case for Christ' resurrection is strong, there are potential and perceived limitations that some lawyers, and others, have raised with me.

Law and Astonishing Events

A question to address is whether law would see itself entering the realm of the supernatural? As the legal realist would claim, should not law be concerned with observable relations between definite tangibles? Certainly in this context, many beholden to a rationalist-materialist 'modernity' worldview, would have no doubt that differentiation has taken place and therefore one now works by distinguishing between the natural world and 'the numinous'.[109] On a popular level, the lawyer and legal fiction writer Phillip Margolin concurs, in that one of his characters had been 'weaned on logic and had the overtly rational mind of the contract lawyer, which has no cubbyhole where the supernatural can dwell comfortably'.[110]

Montgomery in his Sherlockian apologetic counters this mechanistic reductionism by applying the previously mentioned 'Holmes' dictum' from *The Sign of the Four* to Christ: 'The great miracle of the Resurrection may be a hard metaphysical pill to swallow, but swallow we can and must when the facts require it. Eliminate the factually impossible, and "whatever remains, however improbable, must be the truth."'[111] As previously mentioned, both Stephen Davis and Richard Swinburne rely on this Holmes statement in their defences of the resurrection.

The improbable in this case is the truth of the resurrection of Christ based on sound historical evidence, as all other hypotheses for the empty tomb are impossible.[112]

---

[108] Montgomery, *Human Rights*, 132-137; Montgomery, *Tractatus*, 3.12-3.14.
[109] John W. Drane, 'Christians, New Agers and Changing Cultural Paradigms', *The Expository Times* 106, 6 (March 1995): 172-176. Drane addresses the evident dissatisfaction with this worldview.
[110] Phillip M. Margolin, *The Undertaker's Widow* (London: Warner, 1998), 136.
[111] Montgomery, 'The Search for Ultimates', 8.
[112] Davis, Kendall and O'Collins, eds., *The Resurrection*, 147. For a discussion of Sir Arthur Conan Doyle's openness to Spiritualism and psychic phenomena and the impact this had on the character of Holmes see Robert S. Ellwood, *Islands of the Dawn* (Honolulu: University of Hawaii Press, 1993), 53-57; Stephen Kendrick, *Holy Clues: The Gospel According to Sherlock Holmes* (New York: Random, 1999).

However, this reliance on the mythical Holmes to justify an hypothesis based on an empirical investigation of a supernatural event is not fully supported by Holmes himself. In the *Hound of the Baskervilles* it is Holmes who indicates he has confined his investigations to this world, and if there are forces outside of the ordinary laws of nature then this would be perhaps too ambitious a task. For Sherlock Holmes there are cases for the policeman (lawyer), others for a clergyman.[113]

There is legal precedent to support Holmes' reservation. In the Australian High Court case that considered whether Scientology was a religious institution and therefore exempt from pay-roll tax wages, Justices Mason and Brennan observed:

> Under our law, the State has no prophetic role in relation to religious belief; the State can neither declare supernatural truth nor determine the paths through which the human mind must search in a quest for supernatural truth. The courts are constrained to accord freedom to faith in the supernatural, for there are no means of finding upon evidence whether a postulated tenet or supernatural truth is erroneous or whether a supernatural revelation of truth has been made.[114]

It needs to be remembered that this case was not about what is truth in religion, but what are the factual *indicia* of whether a group, for taxation purposes, constitutes a religion.

Also the view of the two justices that a supernatural truth is beyond a finding upon the evidence, and is surely the stuff of faith, is refuted by the distinguished legal apologists referred to herein after their own examination of the evidence for the resurrection of Jesus.

However, there are possible further precedents which relate to what is called 'incredible evidence', i.e. something that does not appear to fit with what we know about our world. In *Haw Tau Tau v Public Prosecutor* the Privy Council,

---

[113] Arthur Conan Doyle, *The Hound of the Baskervilles, Sherlock Holmes the Complete Illustrated Novels,* 221-234. See also Arthur Conan Doyle, *The Adventure of the Sussex Vampire, The Case-Book of Sherlock Holmes* (Harmondsworth, Middlesex: Penguin, 1977), 98-115 esp. 99: 'Rubbish, Watson, rubbish! What have we to do with walking corpses who can only be held in their grave by stakes driven through their hearts? It's pure lunacy.' Cf. *Naval Treaty,* 455-456.
[114] *The Church of the New Faith v The Commissioner for Pay-Roll Tax (Victoria)* (1983) 154 CLR 120 at 134.

Perceived Limitations of the Legal Paradigm Analogy 251

in considering whether the prosecution at the conclusion of its argument had made out a case against the accused that had to be answered, stated the prosecution case must be taken at its highest with this one exception: '... unless (evidence of the primary fact) it is inherently so incredible that no reasonable person would accept it as being true'. Lord Diplock further stated: '... if there is no evidence (or only evidence that is so inherently incredible that no reasonable person could accept it as true) to prove any or more of those essential elements, it is the judges' duty to direct an acquittal.' [115] Is this not a limitation of Montgomery's view? Could a case be made for the post resurrection appearances to be evidence of material facts that is 'inherently incredible'?

In *Briginshaw v Briginshaw* the exception with respect to 'incredible' evidence is more problematic. Dixon J. of the Australian High Court stated,

> ... the truth is that, when the law requires the proof of any fact, the tribunal must feel an actual persuasion of its occurrence or existence before it can be found. It cannot be found as a result of a mere mechanical comparison of probabilities independently of any belief in its reality... The seriousness of an allegation made, the inherent unlikelihood of an occurrence of a given description, or the gravity of the consequences flowing from a particular finding are considerations which most affect the answer to the question whether the issue has been proved to the reasonable satisfaction of the tribunal. [116]

Whilst Montgomery does not directly address the issue of whether the legal analogy has a restricted role in apologetics, because the resurrection enters the category of astonishing events, a response can be drawn from his work. Firstly, he relies considerably on Simon Greenleaf, who in his classic work on the credit due to the testimony of witnesses acknowledged the issue and pleaded the criteria, 'The conformity of their testimony with experience'[117] Greenleaf points out that the evidence for the miracles of Jesus was of the kind that was plain and simple in nature, 'easily seen and fully comprehended by persons of common capacity and observation'.[118] It can also be argued that one can investigate the evidence

---

[115] *Haw Tau Tau v Public Prosecturor (P.C.)* 1982 AC 136 at 150-151.
[116] *Briginshaw v Briginshaw* at 361-362. See Heydon, *Cross*, 259-261; Colin Howard, *Criminal Law* (Sydney: The Law Book Company, 1982), 20: 'Nevertheless it should not be forgotten that nothing is established in court unless the tribunal itself is persuaded to believe it. The rules of proof are not mere ciphers for skilful manipulation'.
[117] Simon Greenleaf, *The Testimony*, 36. See Montgomery, *The Law Above*, 125-131.

surrounding the resurrection without *a priori* addressing its supernatural agency. In this regard Beckwith states that even opponents of miracles are unlikely to give up the possibility of disproving the historicity of a miracle.[119] Without assessing here the weight to be given to the evidence Greenleaf's argument is useful in showing that much of the evidence for Jesus' resurrection is of an 'ordinary' kind, and straightforward, that is likely to draw the attention of the believer and sceptic alike. One wonders if Justices Mason and Brennan were aware of this kind of evidence for the resurrection before they made their comments.

Secondly, in defence of the legal analogy being applied to the resurrection is the fact that law and religion have worked closely together. In fact in many legal systems the 'Divine' has been a source of its law. Montgomery himself places great weight on the sacred roots of the law. The foundational common law of Blackstone and others is based on divine Judaic-Christian revelation.[120] Further Montgomery notes that the major author of the Universal Declaration of Human Rights, René Cassin locates its ideological roots in the Ten Commandments.[121]

The interconnection between the origin of legal systems and divine relation is not restricted to common law jurisdictions. Esser comments on *nomos*:

> The legal, ethical and religious meanings of *nomos* are inseparable in antiquity, for all goods were believed to come from the gods, who upheld order in the universe and in relations between men. Hence the universal conviction, found throughout history, that law is linked to the divine – an idea which has persisted subconsciously even in periods when the purely human aspects of law have been emphasized... Philosophy (even that of the Sophists), kept alive the awareness that, since human laws are so fallible, man cannot exist unless he conforms to cosmic, universal law. [122]

---

[118] Simon Greenleaf, *The Testimony*, 42. For development of the same argument see Russell, *A Lawyer's*, 123-127.

[119] Francis J. Beckwith, 'History and Miracles' in *In Defense of Miracles*, Geivett and Habermas, eds., 87-88.

[120] John Warwick Montgomery, *The Shaping of America* (Minneapolis: Bethany, 1976), 136-140; Montgomery, *Human Rights*, 54; Montgomery, *The Law Above*, 67-70.

[121] Montgomery, *Human Rights*, 30.

[122] Hans-Helmet Esser, 'Law, Customs, Elements' in *The New International Dictionary of the New Testament*, Vol. 2, Colin Brown, ed. (Exeter: Paternoster, 1976), 439. See also Derek H. Davis, 'Competing Notions of Law in American Civil Religion', *Law, Text, Culture* 5, 1 (2000): 275, 'In the scope of human history, revealed law has more often than not been the source of civil and criminal codes.'

Perceived Limitations of the Legal Paradigm Analogy 253

It could be argued that to apply the legal apologetic to questions of God's existence and character is consistent with the very establishment of the law itself.

Thirdly, fundamental to Montgomery's apologetic is his commitment to a monistic view of knowledge. His empirical method precedes any critical study and is foundational to all his interdisciplinary work: theology, jurisprudence, historiography, library science, apologetics.[123] Just as the legal paradigm helps us justify on the evidence whether an ordinary statement is true, so it can claim to justify whether Christ arose. And as Christianity is an historical religion Montgomery, unlike many modern Protestant theologians, sees no justification in detaching the gospel from the structure of an historical referent.[124] As Torrance suggests, 'Theological formulations cannot be without their empirical correlates... the Christian doctrine of the resurrection cannot do without its empirical correlate in the empty tomb; cut that away and it becomes nonsensical.' [125]

For Montgomery to place the resurrection beyond the legal metaphor because it is 'incredible' would be to create a false dichotomy between the natural and the metaphysical.[126] This is a legal fiction that the legal apologists as a class would dismiss. The resurrection either happened in time or space, or it did not.[127] This position has been affirmed throughout this thesis. And, as mentioned in chapter three, Beckwith also argues in this vein.

He asserts one should not use the concept of probability in such a way to disallow any amount of evidence to establish the reality of a particular event. Therefore if there is sufficient evidence for an astonishing event it should not be ruled out *a priori*.[128]

Fourthly, there is legal precedent for giving attention to matters beyond the experience of our senses. For example, the legal concept of the corporation which the

---

[123] Montgomery, ed., *God's Inerrant*, 25-28. Winifred Fallers Sullivan, argues for the using of legal materials in teaching religion in undergraduate courses. He indicates that in the community there is clear interaction between law, religious ideas and cultural forms. Legal materials help students understand this interaction which is true irrespective of one's religious background. See 'Using Legal Materials in Teaching Religion', *Teaching Theology and Religion* 3, 1 (2000): 33-41. Also *Theological Education* dedicates an entire volume to the case study method, X, 3 (Spring 1974).
[124] For full analysis of the issues and a questioning of the role of historiography with respect to the resurrection see Peter Carnley, *The Structure of Resurrection Belief* (Oxford: Clarendon Press, 1987), with an extensive bibliography.
[125] Torrance, *Space, Time*, 89-90.
[126] Montgomery, *Where is History Going?*, 116-117.
[127] Norman Anderson, *A Lawyer Among*, 29-105.
[128] Beckwith, *David Hume's*, 94-97.

former United States Chief Justice, John Marshall described as 'an artificial being, invisible, intangible, and exciting only in contemplation of law'.[129]

Relying on Montgomery's insights, it has been argued here that the legal paradigm is an appropriate model for assessing the supernatural resurrection of Jesus. Yet one can imagine that for some it raises questions whether the metaphor reaches beyond its proper boundaries. Here Coady points to a way forward. He asserts that openness to what is completely novel (testimonies to astonishing events), 'whether directly encountered or as subject to report, is certainly a virtue ... but the wholly "open mind" is not only unattainable in fact but undesirable in theory'. To ask that it be a 'lethargic bias' in the doubter's basic framework of belief is an appropriate starting point.[130]

Eternal Facts in Issue

Robert Cavin raises a number of issues with respect to the historical apologetic, two of which his school of thought would no doubt see as particularly applicable here. The first is that the resurrection claims of Christ should include his being unable to die, be sick, move from place to place; not just his defeat of the grave. Relying on a principle of inductive logic, he argues that all aspects of the eternal dimension of the resurrection require independent verifications. In their absence the traditional historical evidence for the resurrection proves little more than resuscitation. General speculations like Thomas' cry, 'My Lord and my God' do not prove eternal revivification.[131] In other words there are facts in issue relating to the dispositional properties of the resurrection body that go beyond the resurrection event itself. In the context of the legal apologetic it would appear the Cavin style critique has raised a crucial question. In order to succeed in a legal tribunal *all* the facts in issue must be supported by the evidence.[132] The legal apologetic traditionally closes with the evidence for the empty tomb and offers little or no evidence of the facts for eternal revivification that Cavin requires. Is this an evaluation of ambiguous and incomplete data?

---

[129] Montgomery, *Law and Gospel*, 28; Margaret Davies, *Asking*, 126; Peter Fitzpatrick, *The Mythology of Modern Law* (London: Routledge, 1992), x. For Fitzpatrick's discussion on the relationship between the law, the sacred and Freud's legacy of law in *Totem and Taboo* see, 'Being Original: Law and the Insistence of the Sacred', *Law, Text, Culture* 5, 1 (2000): 63-95. See also Adam Gearey, 'Law in the Gospel of the Female Messiah: Myth, Gnosticism and Finnegans Wake', *Australian Feminist Law Journal*, 10 (March 1998): 61-83.

[130] Coady, *Testimony*, 196.

[131] Robert Greg Cavin, 'Is there Sufficient Historical Evidence to Establish the Resurrection of Jesus', *Faith and Philosophy* 12, 3 (July 1995): 361 – 379.

[132] Heydon, *Cross*, 13.

Perceived Limitations of the Legal Paradigm Analogy 255

The response of Montgomery and the legal apologists as a whole would be dismissive. They seek to establish only the actual resurrection of Christ. This is expressed in language like 'What is needed to prove the resurrection of Jesus? Simply that a person (Jesus) was A. alive, B. then dead, and C. subsequently alive again'.[133] They no doubt would argue that the central issues in a judicial setting do emerge and Jesus' resurrection would become the single question of fact. If this fact is proved, then the legal apologist would have completed his or her task. The 'jury' having found that Christ arose is left with no option but to admit the eternal nature of same.

This is so for Montgomery for two reasons. The first is the empirical value of the event which scholars like Cavin understate. The resurrection deals with the most fundamental human need: the conquest of death. If death is indeed that significant then not to worship the one who defeats it and offers the same gift to others is to hopelessly misread, i.e. misinterpret the resurrection.[134] The second, and more persuasive, is with respect to Christ's own understanding. He saw his resurrection justifying responses like 'My Lord and my God' and justifying his own teaching 'I and my Father are one.' Montgomery quips, If Jesus has been raised 'he is in a far better position (indeed in the only position!) to interpret or explain it.'[135]

It is also interesting to note Montgomery's reliance on a legal hermeneutic when defending scripture. This hermeneutic was considered in chapter two but suffice to say by relying on legal principles, adopted by courts for the interpretation of documents, such as the 'parol evidence rule', Montgomery seeks to establish the historical trustworthiness of the gospels and their accurate recording of Christ's words which assert his own understanding of himself.

The British criminal lawyer, Gerard Chrispin is representative of the legal apologetic school in stating:

> The resurrection suffices!... If Jesus Christ really did rise again from the dead then His claim to be God would be fulfilled both in logic and in the power of an endless life. The sealed tomb could not be conquered by a mere prophet, a simple or sincere religious leader, a well meaning martyr, or even a super angel. Only the One Who is both perfect Man and perfect God, as Jesus claimed

---

[133] Bauer, 'The Logician's Model, 113-116, 126; Montgomery, *Human Rights*, 155.
[134] Montgomery, *Human Rights*, 158.
[135] ibid.

to be, could rise from the dead in His resurrected body. If it happened then Christ's claim was vindicated. If that, the hardest of the miraculous to achieve, were really a fact, then all doubts must flee... Thomas was right, as his scepticism gave way to reality, 'My Lord and my God!' The resurrection shows He is God, and He can be trusted fully in every way. [136]

It also seems clearly to have been the Apostle Paul's and the gospel writers' view that the whole interconnected system of Christian beliefs about the nature of Jesus' resurrection, and what it established, hinged on the empty tomb and the resurrection appearances. Like the legal apologists they felt they could rest their case on such facts.[137] Pannenberg concurs:

> Jesus' claim to authority, through which he put himself in God's place, was ... blasphemous for Jewish ears. Because of this, Jesus was then also slandered by the Jews before the Roman governor as a rebel. If Jesus really has been raised, this claim has been visibly and unambiguously confirmed by the God of Israel, who was allegedly blasphemed by Jesus ... That the primitive Christian proclamation in fact understood Jesus' resurrection from the dead as the confirmation of his pre-Easter claim emerges above all in the speeches in Acts, and perhaps also in the old expression that Jesus was shown to be justified in the Spirit.[138]

So whilst technically it may be argued that the legal apologist has only established by the evidence a resurrection and not eternal revivification, the apologists would be confident they have made their case. In their defence, in law one argues from the strongest evidence to the real issues.[139] And in fact Cavin's arguments fail to give due weight to the place of interpretation, imagination and common sense in reaching an hypothesis both in law and history. The legal academic Marcus Stone iterates 'It is a universal tendency in the mind to derive meanings from the facts which go beyond them.'[140] The lawyer and legal fiction writer

---

[136] Chrispin, *The Resurrection*, 56.

[137] 1Cor. 15:1-11. With respect to the gospels, whilst John records Jesus having new freedom in movement he does not establish what Cavin asked for.

[138] Wolfhart Pannenberg, *Jesus-God and Man*, trans. Lewis L. Wilkins and Duane A. Priebe, 2nd ed. (Philadelphia: Westminster Press, 1977), 67-68.

[139] See Morrison, *The Proofs*, 3: 'The best evidence of which the subject admits, is all that is required in the courts.'.

[140] Marcus Stone, *Proof of Fact in Criminal Trials* (Edinburgh: W. Green and Son, 1984), 379.

Scott Turrow pleads 'The law's truth never ends strictly with the evidence. It depends as well on what attorneys call "inference" and what less-restricted souls refer to as "imagination".'[141]

In light of the above discussion it might be thought there is no direct evidence of the 'eternal' facts in issue. This is not so. The gospel narratives record eyewitness testimony of Jesus' ability to move from place to place, and Luke records in Acts 1 that Jesus, for forty days after his resurrection, gave other convincing proofs in the presence of the same eyewitnesses. Luke also said some witnessed his ascension which was both an historical and symbolical event.[142] This evidence adds considerable weight to Thomas' finding even though Gain would hold the evidence is not an 'adequate sample' upon which to base findings of such scope.[143]

Then there is the teaching and life of Christ prior to his crucifixion. The timelessness of his teaching, its universal acceptance and the authority claimed, are consistent with Christ being God. Norman Anderson opens his case with, 'The Teaching of Jesus Stands on an Everest above.'[144] Chrispin is of a similar mind to Anderson, and in his taking a sceptic through the gospel story of Jesus he points out that only an eternal resurrection fits the perfect life, peerless teaching, and fully attested miracles of Christ and that as a consequence Jesus was clearly God with us.[145] The case for the eternal nature of the resurrection in part precedes the actual event. So, in response to Cavin's concerns one can argue that there is direct evidence of Jesus' resurrection being more than resuscitation.

With respect to circumstantial evidence for the 'eternal' facts in issue there is the point that lives have been confronted and transformed by the risen Christ from the Apostle Paul to this date. Further circumstantial evidence that answers Cavin's argument is the twofold nature of a Jewish burial. N.T. Wright observes the first stage was laying the body on a slab, wrapped in cloth with spices. A year or so later the decomposed body would be collected by relatives and friends and the bones placed in an ossuary. If the disciples thought the resurrection was just a spiritual or temporary event sooner or later they would have had to return for the body. The fact they never returned, asserts Wright, establishes 'this wasn't a

---

[141] Turrow, *Personal Injuries*, 27.
[142] Norman Anderson, *The Teaching*, 168
[143] Cavin, 'Is there Sufficient Historical Evidence?', 371.
[144] Norman Anderson, *The Teaching*, 7. See also Scott Peck, *Further Along the Road Less Travelled* (New York: Simon & Schuster, 1993), 160-161.
[145] Chrispin, *The Resurrection*, 27-32. See also Wharton, 'Recent Changes in Jurisprudence', 150-153.

resuscitation, a journey back into the present life; it was a resurrection, a going on through death and out the other side into a new mode of physicality, the beginning of God's new creation'.[146]

In defence of Cavin, there is no reason why in future the legal apologetic could not offer some of the evidence mentioned above for the 'eternal' facts in issue. It could do so whilst still pleading primarily its strongest case – the resurrection event.

Cavin's second critique is that even if there is historical 'admissible' evidence for the 'eternal' facts in issue, and there may be some brief, insufficient evidence, we lack the requisite experience necessary for establishing general hypotheses that would link the information we have with an eternal resurrected body.[147] The legal apologists as a class would simply not admit this. Montgomery would rely on his previous twofold argument: the interpretation of the event is basically self evident; but if one does concede that an interpretation is beyond our experience and knowledge, the one who was raised interprets for us.[148]

The explanation of Jesus is enhanced if it is linked to the principle of his being an expert witness. This is an argument Lionel Luckhoo briefly pursues.[149] This special pleading would have to operate in a non-technical framework as the event in issue relates to the person of the witness – Jesus. Expert witnesses should be heard where the subject matter is such that a person without instruction or experience in the area of knowledge would not be able to form a sound judgement. The expert is recognised as having a special acquaintance with the experience in question that would aid the tribunal.[150] If the Cavin assertion of a normal person's lack of requisite experience and knowledge was held, clearly a tribunal could direct that Jesus Christ's explanation would satisfy such. The factual basis of Jesus' opinion is his own firsthand observation, experience and knowledge. He could give evidence as to the conclusions that can be drawn. It may be argued that common law provides that one should avoid asking of an expert witness ultimate questions which the court alone should decide, for example 'Is this an eternal resurrected body?'. However, there is willingness to allow medical experts to express opinion as to both the physical and psychological state of the person.[151]

---

[146] N.T. Wright, 'Grave Matters', *Christianity Today* 4, 2 (April 6 1998): 52.
[147] Cavin, 'Is there Sufficient Historical Evidence?', 371-375.
[148] Montgomery, *Human Rights*, 158-159.
[149] Luckhoo, *What is Your Verdict?*, 11-12.
[150] Heydon, *Cross*, 785-790.
[151] ibid., 801-805.

Jesus' own testimony in this regard strongly links the eternal resurrection hypothesis with the facts.

Ultimately, one would sense that Montgomery's prime objection to the detailed logical critique of Cavin would be that its stringent demands with respect to proof [152] renders it ineffective in assessing the historicity, at any rate, of the resurrection.[153]

A Legal Formalist Approach

It could well be argued that the legal apologists approach legal theory from a formalist perspective.[154] Their traditional legal epistemology holds the law is coherent and rational with fairly precise rules that can be applied to particular disputes: a 'modernity' type paradigm. As the legal authority Wigmore states, law does not attempt to consider the subjectivity of knowledge and it presumes the objectivity of external nature.[155] In such a legal epistemology a correspondence theory of truth is normally preferred to a coherence theory of truth.[156]

It is true that the legal apologetic rarely addresses the questions of modern jurisprudence. There are a plethora of voices over fact positivism.[157] The realist

---

[152] 'In criminal trials, what is vital is that the beliefs which are formed about the facts should correspond to reality and not that one statement of belief should be related with perfect logic to another.' Stone, *Proof of Fact*, 378. This does not mean the life of the law is just experience. Law is rational. It should draw on logic. Syllogistic reasoning may make an evidential fallacy clear. Yet it would be a fallacy to see certain aspects of law, such as testimony before a judge and jury simply as a science. For discussion see K.H. Bailey, 'Law and Logic', "*The Australasian Journal of Psychology and Philosophy* ix, 2 (June 1931): 103-119; Spiros Simotis, 'The Problem of Legal Logic', *Ratio* iii, 1 (1960): 60-94.

[153] Montgomery, *Tractatus*, 6.9611: 'Verification can be analogised to the construction of a building: one does not need, and it would be irrational to demand, supports under every position of the roof; what is required is sufficient support, e.g. under each of the roof's four corners.' Sufficient proof here is evidence for the death and resurrection of Jesus.

[154] Here we are not considering the questionable argument that formalists blind themselves to the real needs of litigants and society by binding themselves to a traditional understanding of the separation of powers between the judiciary and legislators, but whether a formalist perspective lacks an appreciation of the societal influences upon evidence. It is the second issue that relates specifically to the legal apologetic. The first issue is addressed by John Warwick Montgomery, 'Whose Life Anyway? A Re-examination of Suicide and Assisted Suicide', *Christian Perspectives on Law Reform*, Paul R. Beaumont, ed. (Carlisle: Paternoster, 1998), 83-103.

[155] Wigmore, *Evidence*, 4: 322.

[156] Twining, *Rethinking*, 71-76; Montgomery, *Tractatus*, 3.122.

[157] Davies, *Asking*, 94-259. For general discussion see Twining, *Rethinking*, 32-91, 341-372; David Nicolson, 'Truth, reason and justice: epistemology and politics in evidence discourse', *The Modern Law Review* 57, 5 (September 1994): 726-744.

claims law is political, the more radical Critical Legal Studies School conceives that a legal paradigm cannot be divorced from its social and political moorings.[158] Feminism points to the patriarchal make-up of the theorising and decision making group as well as the domination of the cognitive, left brain advocacy model. The postmodernists are amongst those who plead that before the brief is considered there are conventions, language games, social, political and sexual influences that not only shape presentation of the facts on issue but also their interpretation.[159] William Pencak noted at the Eleventh Round Table on Law and Semiotics that even though the signs indicate a perfectly regulated trial, 'yet hidden or perjured evidence may convict the wrong person'.[160] The argument of these critical legal theorists is summarised by Richard Matasar:

> Legal scholarship that relies on this pseudo-objective and falsely scientific rhetoric double distorts: it abstracts legal problems from the real people who have those problems and it pretends that law provides answers to problems without reference to the particular social context in which any given legal problem arises.
>
> The language of neutral principles, rationales, and holdings may be perceived as a cover for actual reasoning, the influence of culture, and the hold of ideology. Thus, today, many legal scholars are searching for a new rhetoric that more candidly reveals the way that law is a reflection of very personal matters.[161]

These 'outsider' voices are not always nihilistic, but are a cry to demystify and deconstruct a simple, objective understanding of the legal paradigm. It's the issue of whether one can trust the system. And their scepticism towards the legal process, judges and juries is not without warrant. Lori B. Andrews documents the advantage of linguistic style. One study of thirty-eight criminal cases found that

---

[158] The Critical Legal Studies Movement has roots to legal realism and postmodernism. For an understanding of the CLS see Duncan Kennedy, *A Critique of Adjudication {fin de siècle}* (Cambridge, Massachusetts: Harvard University Press, 1997), 8-20, 280-296; Davies, *Asking,* 143-276; Mark Kelman, *A Guide to Critical Legal Studies* (Cambridge, Massachusetts: Harvard University Press, 1987). For critique see J.W. Harris, 'Legal Doctrine and Interests in Land' in *Oxford Essays in Jurisprudence,* 3rd series, John Eekelaar and John Bell, eds. (Oxford: Clarendon Press, 1987) 167-197.

[159] Nicholson, 'Truth, Reason and Justice', 734-742.

[160] William Pencak, 'Is a Fair Trial Possible? The Collapse of the Jury System in Revolutionary America' in *Revolutions, Institutions and the Law: Eleventh Round Table on Law and Semiotics,* Joel Levin and Roberta Kevelson, eds. (New York: Peter Lang, 1998), 167.

[161] Richard A. Matasar, 'Storytelling and Legal Scholarship', *Chicago – Kent Law Review* 68, 1 (1992): 355.

successful prosecutors and defence attorneys had distinct speech patterns. And the significance of speech applies to other parties: 'analysis of actual criminal trials in which the defendant's native tongue was not English suggests that language constraints leave the jury with an unwarranted poor impression of the defendant.'[162] As well, matters as insignificant as the defendant's dress can influence a verdict.[163] The litigation lawyer Julie Hamblin highlighted the bias of some judges, 'You have good judges and you have bad judges and if you have a judge... who has a particular empathy with the issues before the court, or a particular prejudice, then very often that as much as any set of legal principles is what determines the outcome.'[164] Margaret Beazley JA in her opening address to the Australian Association for Quality in Health Care warned: '... there can be no doubt, in my view, that the outcome in cases can be due, not to the hard analysis of medical and other evidence, but to the life experiences and philosophies of the judges who decide the case'.[165]

In fact one would have to ask what chance the resurrected Christ would have of a fair trial today in light of his questionable human pedigree, his minority status, his ethnic origins, his radical teachings, and his disdain of authority as seen in his vague answers before Pilate. Certainly his blasphemy trial was complete with wrong findings in law and prejudicial adjudicators.[166] Today's jurisprudence 'outsiders' could well argue their position from the marginalised life of Christ.

In the context of the appropriateness of a formalist legal metaphor to questions of 'truth', a significant argument in favour at this stage ought to be raised. Twining who refuses to totally reject fact positivism concludes that whilst social, political construction and relativity of knowledge is widely accepted, theorists who deny the existence of objective truth are 'rare birds'.[167] Further, few practitioners would accept that all we have is data and language games. As a consequence in tribunals, sociological factors and the role of the interpreter may play a part, but

---

[162] Lori B. Andrews, 'You the Jury, Exhibit A: Language', *Psychology Today* 18, 2 (February 1984): 30.
[163] ibid., 33.
[164] Julie Hamblin, 'Discussion' in *Ethics Fatigue Symposium: The Fracturing of Medical Ethics* (Sydney: University of Sydney, Centre for Values, Ethics and the Law in Medicine, 1998), 83-84.
[165] J.A. Beazley, 'Evidence or Intuition: The Autonomy of a Medico – Legal Trial', Paper delivered to the annual conference of the Australasian Association for Quality in Health Care (Hotel Niko, Darling Harbour, NSW, 19 June 1998), 1. See also Kennedy, *A Critique*, 69: 'Adjudication (legal) is a forum of ideology ...'. Lawyer and legal fiction writer Barry Reed portrays the prejudices and idiosyncrasies of trial judges in *The Indictment*, 286.
[166] See list of the advocates of this position in Appendix one.
[167] Twining, *Rethinking*, esp. chap. 4.

the party with the most credible evidentiary support generally wins.[168] Whilst Pencak concedes a prejudicial world ensures there is no such thing as a fair trial he pleads, 'we will retain the humility to treat the fairness of jury trials as a valuable experience and require those who would replace them to prove the higher justice of their cause beyond a reasonable doubt'.[169] However, even allowing for the fact that the more reasonable radical voices would allow considerable objectivity, they are still suggesting a more sceptical legal epistemology and an appreciation of the sociology of evidence.

In response to the alternate voices the traditional legal apologetic school should make some constructive response. Apart from Montgomery its advocates have been mainly silent.

Firstly, a negative apologetic critique of this postmodern theory is really called for. If there is no truth out there because all is relative and contingent, then why give credence to the arguments of the 'outsider' voices in the first place?[170]

Ironically at its worst deconstructionism uses its own words as proof that there is no absolute. In Christian terms instead of the Word made flesh it shows flesh (its own arguments) being made Word.

Further, in a legal context, as Montgomery points out the impact of these critical theorists on day to day judicial activity is virtually nil.[171] As we have seen, it's 'rare birds' that insist even in law, that there is no objective truth. One can therefore argue they turn a 'blind eye' to the epistemic status of the normative in order to preserve their own particular theory of knowledge. Yet their own epistemology cannot make sense of the legal experience proving it is inadequate.[172] Also, their fusion of the object/subject distinction can lead one to solipsism.[173] Finally, as Montgomery argues, it is not true that law is one set of values against another. The place of precedent in law establishes that there is an objective base. Law is a developing paradigm, but within a framework that in part is already present. Montgomery likens the law to a novel where chapters are written that build on chapters (values) already built in.[174]

---

[168] Mark Cooney, 'Evidence as Partisanship', *Law and Society* 28, 4 (1994): 834.

[169] Pencak, 'Is a Fair Trial Possible?', 182-183.

[170] Montgomery, 'Defending the Hope', 5-6. See Andrew Phang, Associate Professor National University of Singapore, 'Critical Legal Studies, Economic Development and Human Rights', Paper delivered to the School of Oriental and African Studies (London University, 17 May 1999), 10-18. For an abbreviated version of the paper see 'Critical Legal Studies, Economic Development and Human Rights', *Law and Justice*, 142-143 (Trinity Michaelmas 1999): 122-139.

[171] Montgomery, 'Legal Hermeneutics', 15-29.

Perceived Limitations of the Legal Paradigm Analogy 263

Secondly, there needs to be an acknowledgment of some of the issues being raised in modern jurisprudence about the quality of consciousness. Few practising lawyers accept a value free environment and hold that principles of ideology impact the adjudicator as well as the legislator.[175] There is a human agent factor. Who would dispute Tur's advice: 'He who would study law would profit from an awareness of his (and his teacher's) theory of (legal) knowledge.'?[176] The infamous Chamberlain case also bears witness to the social, religious and political factors that can at times shape judgement. It resulted in an erroneous 'finding' for the dingo not taking the baby as a result of the influence of a number of non factual sources: over zealous crown, sensational media, a jury's identification with one barrister, sectarianism.[177] Further, it can be argued that the gradual appearance of defence counsel in felony trials throughout the eighteenth century was as a challenge to the then held proposition that a defendant should represent themselves as 'plain facts' speak for themselves, and therefore a defendant could speak as if he were the best lawyer.[178]

Whilst Montgomery holds it is the very nature of legal argument for facts to speak for themselves,[179] he acknowledges that a party may misunderstand the text (or fact) for any number of personal, societal or cultural reasons.[180] He is not adverse to pointing out that in ethical issues courts have bowed to societal pressures. In particular he rightly pleads that radical feminism and self-centrism have strongly influenced the United States Supreme Court justices in their interpreting of the facts in the matter of abortion.[181] And in a recent publication he accepts

---

[172] Montgomery, *Tractatus*, 2.552. Further Montgomery notes that jurisprudence professor Ronald Dworkin is yet another who whilst open to constructive interpretation of a text 'nonetheless shows that he is at heart an objectivist who refuses to sacrifice the integrity of the legal documentary tradition to the subjective whims of the interpreter'. See Montgomery, 'Legal Hermeneutics', 22. Dworkin advocates a distinction between 'internal scepticism' which he supports and 'external scepticism'. With respect to 'internal scepticism' there is an acceptance that whilst there may be uncertainty as to the objectively correct position all parties agree there is an objectively correct answer. See R.M. Dworkin, *Law's Empire* (Cambridge, Massachusetts: Harvard University Press, 1986), 78-85.
[173] Montgomery, *Tractatus*, 2.322 – 2.32212.
[174] John Warwick Montgomery, 'Critical Legal Studies: Postmodern Deconstruction and the Law', RealPlayer [Montgomery 4] jwm2.ram..ram..<http://www.spr-consilio.com/soundarchive.html>.
[175] Kennedy, *A Critique*, 26-38; Costas Douzinas, Ronnie Warrington and Shaun McVeigh, *Postmodern Jurisprudence* (London and New York: Routledge, 1991), IX-51.
[176] R.H.S. Tur, 'What is Jurisprudence?' *The Philosophical Quarterly* 28, 111, (April 1978): 157.
[177] See Ken Crispin, *The Crown versus Chamberlain* (Sutherland, NSW: Albatross, 1987) 346-371; Keith Mason, *Constancy and Change* (Sydney: Federation Press, 1990), 132-140.
[178] Schramm, *Testimony*, 101.
[179] Montgomery, *Human Rights*, 157.
[180] Montgomery, 'Legal Hermeneutics', 105.

that the interpreter brings his prejudices and presuppositions to a factual argument and it is a 'poor apologist who disregards where a non-Christian is coming from' as one's worldview and biases can and do 'colour one's receptivity of the message presented'.[182] In light of this Habermas asserts, 'Montgomery is fully aware that the human subject of experience has proclivities, presuppositions, hopes, fears, and a long list of dreams and apprehensions that can, in some measure, affect even one's perceptions to a significant, and sometimes even telling, extent.'[183] It is from this vantage point that Montgomery calls on his theological method (craft), that is outlined in the previous chapter, to shift through conflicting interpretations. 'Thus the most sophisticated academic analysis of legal interpretation would appear to focus on the Wittgenstein-Popper approach; the analogy of the shoe and the foot. Interpretation is like a shoe and the text (data/ facts) like the foot. One endeavours to find the interpretation that best fits the text...'[184] Montgomery's 'key insight' is the various kinds of interpretations (shoes) that can exist.[185]

Therefore, to assist the postmodern enquirer in examining the objective evidences for the resurrection via the legal apologetic the notion of external influences should at least be raised. This occurred in the 'Case Study' in the previous chapter. And Habermas, in a valid criticism notes, that while such a 'subjective' element is emphasised by Montgomery, his focus on the objective nature of the case for the resurrection, means that sometimes this balance between external influences and 'brute' facts is not readily perceived in his writings.[186] Further, the apologist is also part of the audience and has her own story that interconnects

---

[181] John Warwick Montgomery, *Slaughter of the Innocents* (Westchester, Illinois: Cornerstone, 1981), 12-13, 50-51, 104-109.
[182] John Warwick Montgomery, 'Rejoinder to Professor Millard', *Faith and Thought*, 26 (October 1999): 7-8.
[183] Habermas, 'Bahnsen, Montgomery', 1-3. As indicated in the Introduction to this thesis it is beyond the scope of this work to consider in detail Montgomery's historical apologia and its relationship to facts. For our purposes Habermas' assessment of Montgomery's position being one that also allows for presuppositions to affect one's perception is where this brief discussion should rest. It acknowledges some of the concerns of modern jurisprudence, but the practice of law today is still basically committed to a traditional legal epistemology. Habermas' article is found in a recent journal edition that has the primary purpose of setting out and defending Montgomery's thought. Montgomery is the general editor of the journal and assisted in the selection of the contributors.
[184] Montgomery, 'Legal Hermeneutics', 105. See Montgomery's 'The Theologian's Craft', in *The Suicide*, 267-313. This essay explores the place of data, interpretation, imagination and the model of retroduction and is discussed in the previous chapter when considering the apologist's craft. For Montgomery's latest essay on this issue see John Warwick Montgomery, 'A Critique of Certain Uncritical Assumptions in Modern Historiography', *Global Journal of Classical Theology* 2, 1 (December 1999): 1-10, <http://www.trinitysem.edu/journal/toc_v3n1.html>.
[185] Habermas, 'Bahnsen, Montgomery', 2.

Perceived Limitations of the Legal Paradigm Analogy 265

with the 'facts' of the resurrection. In using the helpful model of the 'shoe that fits the facts' one should be aware of one's own prejudices as to colour and style. That concession the history of law and theory warrants. [187]

Thirdly, as Montgomery's apologetic involves being all things to all people, there is a place for pleading the 'powerlessness' of Christ. As previously mentioned, in an 'earthly' trial Jesus would be seen as one of the legally marginalised. This in itself is an attractive premise for the radical jurists who would struggle with the technical confidence of the traditional legal apologetic. Those like Kim Scheppele, for example, assert judges or courts find those experiences of other people, their ways of 'imagining the real', that are not similar to their own, largely incomprehensible.[188] The case to radical jurists in part should focus on what stops us from finding out the 'truth' about Christ, including our own personal prejudices and lack of trust in those who espouse such truth claims. This incarnational apologetic model to 'outsider voices' should be added to the repertoire of the legal apologist.

Fourthly, as outlined in the previous chapter in the section 'Reframing the Direct Evidence', the legal apologetic should consider the conciliation model. In particular postmodern feminism would be more receptive to the non-adversarial approach. The focus would be a problem, related to the resurrection, that is formulated as clearly and consequentially as possible. Whilst the traditional model will appeal to most, this arbitration model which is widely recognised, understood and appreciated has a place.[189]

In such a paradigm one could engage in dialogical apologetics.[190] In this discourse the question of fact and legal argument would be subsequent to a discussion about the grid of interpretation of the parties present, the possible obstacles

---

[186] ibid. In my conversations with Montgomery his rejoinder is always that such critics should read all his texts and that is possible as he cross-references in his books.

[187] 'Lawyers must be encouraged to pay as much attention to the morality and politics of the issues before them as to what they consider to be the factual truth and the best ways of discovering the factual truth'. Nicholson, 'Truth, Reason', 741. See also Pamela Ewen who in her legal apologetic includes a paragraph that makes the reader aware of their philosophical and other predispositions, *Faith*, 16.

[188] Kim Lane Scheppele, 'Manners of Imagining the Real', *Law and Social Enquiry* 19, 4 (Fall 1994): 995-1022.

[189] An example of this is that the medical profession has on occasions combined with consumers of health care and the legal profession to explore problematic areas of law and fact and to find possible solutions. L. Waller, 'Patients and Their Doctors', *Issues Paper 4*, Canberra, Australian Institute of Health, Law and Ethics (1997).

[190] See Clark, *Dialogical Apologetics*, 205-232. Clark argues evidence should be 'need-based' and 'person-relative' (220).

to faith, and outcomes hoped for. The legal case would still be present but conversationally so and shaped by the dialogue.[191]

Summary

The legal analogy's perceived limitations of not addressing eternal facts in issue and being restricted to a legal formalist method, are found not to be so, especially if the legal apologetic takes note of the potential concerns. The more significant potential limitation is whether the law should address astonishing events. Here the fact that the evidence for the death and resurrection is of the 'ordinary' kind is most significant. To those who may still have concerns, there is the call for the doubter at least to start from a 'lethargic bias'.

In assessing truth claims it would be fair to say that most paradigms relied on will raise perceived and potential difficulties. It is no different for the legal model. However, it has evident strengths and the perceived limitations do not outweigh them.

---

[191] ibid., 206-211.

Conclusion

No doubt the critic of the legal apologetic for the resurrection of Jesus would claim that the late nineteenth century was its end-point, particularly if its case was a pleading of the testimony and evidences. Powell even speaks of a protestant obsession with proofs in support of faith.[192] Yet, the legal apologetic still flourishes. The tide of biblical higher criticism has not been able to stop its momentum. As we have endeavoured to show in chapter one, it has had many protagonists who have ensured it has a strong, if not fully appreciated place, in evangelical apologetics.

Of these advocates John Warwick Montgomery has had a profound influence. He rightly argues, as has been indicated in this study, that his juridical paradigm is part of the Christian heritage. It is hard to escape in the New Testament scriptures and in particular from the time of Greenleaf it has been most evident.

The reason for the legal apologetic method's ongoing significance can be related to humanity's eternal search for truth and meaning and their appreciation of the role of law, testimony and evidences in any such quest. The legal paradigm is one of common usage. As well the central tenet of the Christian truth claim, i.e. the resurrection of Jesus, is one that is often presented factually in the New Testament. Material facts are what legal evidence is all about.

The central issues raised in this study are: epistemological concerns over the quantum of proof, the amount of evidence required, and whether the evidence admits a hearing, rather than a verdict; the appropriateness of the legal analogy; the adequacy of Montgomery's legal apologetic paradigm; its relevance for 'New Spirituality'. The latter two issues have involved a progressive assessment of Montgomery's approach to the New Testament documents and testimony, and other evidence. Further, the connecting of the legal apologetic to 'New Spirituality' is a direction that Montgomery has not directly taken, but it is consistent with his apologetic ethos.

This study has established that there is credible and relevant evidence for the resurrection of Jesus that admits a hearing, at a technical and non-technical apologetic level. The conclusion reached is that the 'best' and most reliable documentary evidence is the admissible first-hand hearsay. Realistically the quantum of proof is a preponderance of the evidence. I believe the case of Montgomery, and

---

[192] Baden Powell, *The Order of Nature Considered in Reference to the Claims of Revelation* (London: Longman, Bowman, Green, Longmans & Roberts, 1859), 145.

the legal apologetic in general, requires some reframing as it continues to interact with legal epistemology, the legal criteria of proof, and in particular the aspirations of 'New Spirituality'.

My response has been to endeavour to reframe the legal apologetic for the technical, non-technical and 'New Spirituality' paradigms. By relying on Montgomery's apologetic material and remaining within the structure of the juridical model I have sought to show that Montgomery's legal apologetic is truly an *apologetic for all seasons*. It is a gift to all those who take seriously the command: 'Always be willing, to give a reason for the hope that is within you'.

Appendix 1 Table of Lawyers' Apologetic Writings

Resurrection and Reliable Gospels[1]

Sir Norman Anderson, Sir Robert Anderson, Clarence Bartlett, Edward Bennett, Clarrie Briese, Herbert C. Casteel, Walter M. Chandler, Gerard Chrispin, Ross Clifford, Charles Colson, Thomas Erskine, Pamela Binning Ewen, Dale Foreman, Simon Greenleaf, Val Grieve, Nicky Gumbel, Don Gutteridge, Lord Hailsham, K.R. Handley, Frank Hanft, Roger Himes, Erwin H. Linton, Sir Lionel Luckhoo, Jeffrey C. Martin, John Warwick Montgomery, Charles Carrol Morgan, Charles Robert Morrison, Oliver Mowat, Albert L. Roper, Howard Hyde Russell, Joseph Sagebeer, Britton H. Tabor, John Ford Whitworth, Stephen Williams.

Bible (not just the gospels) Reliability

Sir Norman Anderson,[2] Sir Robert Anderson,[3] Gleason C. Archer,[4] Clarence Bartlett, Hugo Grotius, Irwin H. Linton, John Warwick Montgomery,[5] William Warburton,[6] Francis Wharton, Phineas Bacon Wilcox, Stephen Williams.

---

[1] To avoid unnecessary repetition lawyers' works that have already been cited in the fourfold classification in chapter one are not cited in these endnotes. Only new lawyers or new works are cited, unless there is a need to distinguish between more than one text by one lawyer. Some editorial comments are made on leading lawyers who are not mentioned in the fourfold classification. For a further detailed listing of legal apologists see Philip Johnson, 'Juridical Apologetics 1600-2000 AD: A Bio-Bibliographical Essay', *Global Journal of Classical Theology* 3, 1 (March 2002): 1-25, <http://www.trinitysem.edu/journal/toc_v3n1.html>.
[2] Norman Anderson, *A Lawyer Among*.
[3] Robert Anderson, *The Bible and Modern Criticism*.
[4] Archer, *Encyclopedia*. Archer holds a law degree.
[5] For example, Montgomery, *Human Rights*, 136-137; Montgomery, *The Shape*, 138-140.
[6] See Arthur William Evans, *Warburton and the Warburtonians* (London and Oxford: Oxford University Press, 1932).

Creation and Evolution

Sir Robert Anderson,[7] Clarrie Briese, Henry Lord Brougham (Lord Chancellor of England),[8] William Jennings Bryan (known for his prosecution of John T. Scopes),[9] Phillip E. Johnson,[10] Charles Lyell,[11] Norman Macbeth,[12] Philip Mauro (a contributor to the seminal work, *The Fundamentals*),[13] St. George Mivat.[14]

Trial of Jesus

Andrew Bevins,[15] David K. Breed,[16] Walter M. Chandler, Charles Edmund De Land,[17] Andre Marie Jean Dupin,[18] Dale Foreman, Val Grieve,[19] Edward Wingate Hatch,[20] Sir Leslie Herron (former Chief Justice of NSW),[21] Jean Imbert (Professor of Law, University of Paris),[22] Joseph Edward Ingram,[23] A. Taylor

---

[7] Robert Anderson, *A Doubter's*.

[8] Henry Lord Brougham, *A Discourse on Natural Theology Showing the Nature of the Evidence and Advantages of the Study* (London: Charles Knight; New York: William Jackson, 1835), esp. 164-175 which speaks of proofs, testimony and eyewitnesses in the context of natural revelation.

[9] William Jennings Bryan, *The Last Message of William Jennings Bryan* (New York: Fleming Revell, 1925).

[10] Johnson, *Darwin on Trial*.

[11] For the details of the roles played by Charles Lyell, St. George Mivat (both who trained at Lincoln's Inn) Robert Anderson, Philip Mauro and William Jennings Bryan see James R. Moore, *The Post-Darwinian Controversies* (Cambridge: Cambridge University Press, 1979), 380.

[12] Norman Macbeth, *Darwin Retried: An Appeal to Reason* (Ipswich, Massachusetts: Gambit, 1971). This text has no theological apologetic however Macbeth was an influence on Phillip E. Johnson.

[13] Philip Mauro, *Evolution at the Bar* (Boston: Hamilton Brothers, 1922).

[14] St. George Jackson Mivat, *Contemporary Evolution: An Essay on Some Recent Social Changes* (New York: D. Appleton, 1876).

[15] Andrew Bevins, *The Trial and Conviction of Jesus Christ from a Legal Standpoint* (Omaha, Nebraska: Douglas Printing, 1898).

[16] David K. Breed, *The Trial of Christ from a Legal and Scriptural Standpoint* (Grand Rapids: Baker, 1982).

[17] Charles Edmund De Land, *The Mis-Trials of Jesus* (Boston: R.G. Badger, 1914).

[18] Andre Marie Jean Dupin, *The Trial of Jesus Before Caiaphas and Pilate Being a Refutation of Mr. Salvador's Chapter Entitled 'The Trial and Condemnation of Jesus'*, trans. John Pickering (Boston: C.C. Little & J. Brown, 1839). Dupin was a French lawyer who is cited by Chandler and reprinted in part in Baker's reprint of Greenleaf's, *The Testimony*.

[19] Val Grieve, *The Trial of Jesus* (Bromley, Kent: STL, 1990).

[20] Edward Wingate Hatch, *The Trial and Condemnation of Christ as a Legal Question* (New York: Knickerbocker, 1892).

[21] Herron, *The Trial of Jesus*.

[22] Jean Imbert, *Le Proces de Jesus* (Paris: Presses Universitaries de France, 1980). For a positive review of this text see John Warwick Montgomery, 'The trial of Christ defended: Jean Lambert's Le procès de Jèsus' in Montgomery, *Christ our Advocate*, 309-312.

Innes,[24] Irwin H. Linton[25], J.C. Mabry,[26] James C. McRuer (former Chief Justice of the High Court of Ontario),[27] Frank J. Powell,[28] James M. Rollins,[29] George W. Thompson,[30] Dee Wampler,[31] W.D. Webb,[32] Thomas Frew Wilson,[33] Earl L. Wingo.[34]

Miracles, Historico-Philosophical Attacks

Sir Robert Anderson,[35] Simon Greenleaf (Greenleaf and most of those who model their apologetic on him include a brief defence when considering his fourth test for the gospel testimony being reliable – 'conformity of their testimony with experience'),[36] Francis Lamb, John Warwick Montgomery.[37]

Citing Fulfilled Prophecy

Sir Robert Anderson (his work is primarily focussed on Daniel 9 and has been used by many popular apologists),[38] Herbert C. Casteel, Irwin H. Linton,[39] Sir Lionel Luckhoo,[40] John Warwick Montgomery,[41] Howard Hyde Russell.

---

[23] Joseph Edward Ingram, *On the Witness Stand, He Who Was Now Is* (Los Angeles: Hoffman Press, 1931). Also released as *Criminal and Illegal Trial of the Nazarene Peasant* (Fort Worth: World, 1924).
[24] A. Taylor Innes, *The Trial of Jesus Christ: A Legal Monograph* (Edinburgh: Oliphant, 1905).
[25] Irwin H. Linton, *The Sanhedrin Verdict* (New York: Loizeaux Brothers, 1943).
[26] J.C. Mabry, *A Legal View of the Trial of Christ* (Cincinatti, Ohio: Standard, 1895).
[27] James C. McRuer, *This Man was Innocent* (Toronto & Vancouver: Clarke Irwin, 1978).
[28] Frank J. Powell, *The Trial of Jesus Christ* (Exeter: Paternoster, 1952).
[29] James M. Rollins, *The Arrest, Trial and Conviction of Jesus Christ from a Lawyer's Standpoint* (St. Louis: Hughes Printing, 1910).
[30] Thompson, *The Trial of Jesus*.
[31] Dee Wampler, *The Trial of Christ: A Criminal Lawyer Defends Jesus* (Springfield, Missouri: Dee Wampler, n.d.).
[32] W.D. Webb, *The Trial of Jesus Christ* (Atchison, Kansas: Schauer & Burbank, 1907).
[33] Thomas Frew Wilson, *The Trial of Jesus of Nazareth from an Historical and Legal Standpoint* (New York: T. Whittaker, 1906).
[34] Earl L. Wingo, *The Illegal Trial of Jesus* (Indianapolis & New York: Bobbs-Merrill, 1962).
[35] Robert Anderson, *The Bible and Modern Criticism*.
[36] Greenleaf, *The Testimony*, 36-42; for example Russell, *A Lawyer's*, 101-133.
[37] In his legal apologetic Montgomery includes a defence in *Human Rights*, 150-151. For an example of his defence outside of his legal apologetic see *Faith Founded*, 43-74.
[38] Sir Robert Anderson, *The Coming Prince*, 19th ed. (Grand Rapids: Kregal, 1975). For example see Josh McDowell, *Evidence that Demands a Verdict* (n.p.: Campus Crusade, 1973), 178-181.
[39] Linton, *A Lawyer Examines*.
[40] Lionel Luckhoo, *Prophecy* (Dallas: Luckhoo Ministries, n.d.).

Apologetic Ethics (the focus is on ethics in an apologetic format)

Sir Norman Anderson,[42] Charles Colson,[43] John Warwick Montgomery.[44]

Worldview and Culture

Sir Norman Anderson,[45] Ross Clifford,[46] Constance Cumbey (her 'sensational' assessment of the New Age Movement was the forerunner for the evangelical apologetic industry on this religion),[47] Jacques Ellul,[48] John Gilchrist,[49] Hugo Grotius, Sir Lionel Luckhoo,[50] John Warwick Montgomery,[51] Francis Wharton.

Legal Forms (for example wills and contracts) to Apologetically Explain Theological Motifs

Roger Himes, John Warwick Montgomery.[52]

Theodicy

Sir Robert Anderson,[53] Jeffrey C. Martin, John Warwick Montgomery.[54]

---

[41] Montgomery cites Sir Robert Anderson and reproduces his treatise on Daniel in *The Transcendent Holmes*, 129-139. See also Montgomery, ed., *Jurisprudence*, 494-497. Montgomery's two latest publications develop his argument on the fulfilled biblical prophecies to the point of a 'product rule' calculation on the probability of the Old Testament prophecies of Christ occurring. See Montgomery, *Tractatus*, 4.1 – 4.15; Montgomery, *Christ our Advocate*, 255-265.

[42] Norman Anderson, *The Teaching*, 79-148.

[43] Charles Colson and Ellen Vaughn, *Gideon's Torch* (Dallas: Word, 1995).

[44] Montgomery, *Human Rights*.

[45] Sir Norman Anderson, *Christianity and World Religions: The Challenge of Pluralism*, rev. ed. (Leicester: Inter-Varsity, 1984).

[46] Clifford and Johnson, *Jesus and the Gods*.

[47] Constance Cumbey, *Hidden Dangers of the Rainbow* (Shreveport: Huntington House, 1983).

[48] For example, Jaques Ellul, *The New Demons* (Oxford: Mowbray, 1975).

[49] Josh McDowell and John Gilchrist, *The Islam Debate* (San Bernardino: Here's Life Publishers, 1983), 13-139.

[50] Lionel Luckhoo, *The Quran is not the Word of God* (Dallas: Luckhoo Ministries, n.d.); Lionel Luckhoo, *Christianity or Islam, You Decide!* (Madison: Power Press, n.d.).

[51] See Montgomery, 'The Marxist Approach'. Another example is Montgomery, *Principalities*.

[52] Montgomery, *Law and Gospel*.

[53] Sir Robert Anderson, *The Silence of God*, 8th ed. (London: Hodder & Stoughton, 1907).

[54] Montgomery, *Tractatus*, 4.8 – 4.893.

Appendix 1 Table of Lawyers' Apologetic Writings

Personal Testimony

Sir Norman Anderson,[55] Charles Colson,[56] Sir Matthew Hale (former Lord Justice of England),[57] Allen W. Harrell,[58] Reginald L. Hine,[59] Sir Lionel Luckhoo,[60] Jeffrey C. Martin, Sir Hendrik Rutgers.[61]

---

[55] Sir Norman Anderson, *An Adopted Son: The Story of my Life* (Leicester: Inter-Varsity, 1985).
[56] Charles Colson, *Born Again* (London: Hodder & Stoughton, 1977).
[57] Sir Matthew Hale, *A Letter of Advice to his Grandchildren*, 2nd ed. (London: Taylor & Hessey, 1823).
[58] Allen W. Harrell, *Splinters from my Gavel: Confessions of a Judge* (Grand Rapids: Zondervan, 1970).
[59] Reginald L. Hine, *Confessions of an Un-Common Attorney* (London: J.M. Dent & Sons, 1946).
[60] Luckhoo, *What is Your verdict?*
[61] Sir Hendrik Rutgers, *Testimony of a Lawyer* (Blacktown, Sydney: Hexagon Press, 1990).

Bibliography

Primary Sources

articles, essays and interviews

Montgomery, John Warwick and James R. Moore. 'The Speck in Butterfield's Eye: A Reply to William A. Speck'. *Fides et Historia* 4, 1 (Fall 1971): 71-77.

Montgomery, John Warwick. 'A Critique of Certain Uncritical Assumptions in Modern Historiography'. *Global Journal of Classical Theology* 2, 1 (December 1999): 1-10. <http://www.trinitysem.edu/journal/toc_v3n1.html>.

----------------------------------. 'A Lawyer's Case for Christianity'. *Christian Legal Journal* 2, 3 (Spring 1993): 10-16.

----------------------------------. 'A Lively Exchange on Evidentialism and Presuppositionalism'. *Philosophia* 1, 4 (8 April 1999). <http://www.trinitysem.edu/philosophia.html>.

----------------------------------. 'A Normative Approach to the Acquisition Problem in the Theological Seminary Library'. *American Theological Library Association Summary of Proceedings*, 16 (12-15 June 1962): 65-95.

----------------------------------. 'An Interview with John Warwick Montgomery'. Interview by Craig Parton. University of California, Santa Barbara. *Veritas Forum*, 1999.

----------------------------------. 'Christian Apologetics in Light of the Lutheran Confessions'. *Concordia Theological Quarterly* 42, 3 (July 1978): 258-275.

----------------------------------. 'Critical Legal Studies: Postmodern Deconstruction and the Law'. RealPlayer[4] jwm2.ram..ram. <http://www.spr-consilio.com/soundarchive.html>

----------------------------------. 'Defending the Hope that is in Us: Apologetics for the 21st Century'. <http://www.bucer.de/theologyconsultation/Docs/JWMENGLISH.pdf: 1-11>.

----------------------------------. 'Editor's Introduction'. *Global Journal of Classical Theology* 3, 1 (March 2002): 1. <http://www.trinitysem.edu/journal/toc_v3n1.html>.

----------------------------------. 'God & Other Law-Makers'. *Beyond Culture Wars* (May/June 1993). <http://www.alliancenet.org/pub/mr/mr93/1993.03.MayJun/mr9303.jwm.lawmakers.html>.

----------------------------------. 'Good and Bad Legal Reasoning'. RealPlayer[1] jwm4.ram..ram. <http://www.spr-consilio.com/soundarchive.html>.

----------------------------------. Interview by the author. Strasbourg, France. 26 July 1996.

----------------------------------. 'Is Man his own God?'. In *Christianity for the Tough Minded*. Ed. John Warwick Montgomery. Minneapolis: Bethany, 1973, 21-34.

----------------------------------. 'Legal Hermeneutics and the Interpretation of Scripture'. In *Evangelical Hermeneutics*. Eds. Michael Bauman and David Hall. Camp Hill, Pennsylvania: Christian Publications, 1995, 15-29.

----------------------------------. 'Legal Novels', RealPlayer[3] jwm6.ram..ram. <http://www.spr-consilio.com/soundarchive.html>.

----------------------------------. 'Legal Reasoning and Christian Apologetics'. *Christianity Today* XIX, 10 (14 February 1975): 71-72.

----------------------------------. 'Letter from England: Christianity's Unique Intellectual Opportunity'. *New Oxford Review* (March 1995): 21-22.

----------------------------------. 'Neglected Apologetic Styles: The Juridical and the Literary'. In *Evangelical Apologetics*. Eds. Michael Bauman, David Hall and Robert Newman. Camp Hill, Pennsylvania: Christian Publications, 1996, 119-133.

----------------------------------. 'Rejoinder to Professor Millard'. *Faith and Thought*, 26 (October 1999): 7-8.

----------------------------------. 'Some Comments on Paul's Use of Genesis in his Epistle to the Romans'. *Bulletin of the Evangelical Theological Society* 4, 1 (April 1961): 4-11.

----------. 'The Apologetics of Eucatastrophe'. In *Myth, Allegory and Gospel*. Ed. John Warwick Montgomery. Minneapolis: Bethany, 1974, 11-31.

----------. 'The Chronicles of Narnia and the Adolescent Reader'. In *Myth, Allegory and Gospel*. Ed. John Warwick Montgomery. Minneapolis: Bethany, 1974, 97-118.

----------. 'The Criminal Standard of Proof'. *New Law Journal* 148, 6837 (24 April 1998): 582 – 585.

----------. 'The Incarnate Christ: The Apologetic Thrust of Lutheran Theology'. <http://www.alliancenet.org/pub/mr/mr98/1998.01.JanFeb/mr9801.jwm.incarnate.html>.

----------. 'The Jury Returns: A Juridical Defense of Christianity'. In *Christians in the Public Square*, C E B Cranfield, David Kilgour and John Warwick Montgomery. Edmonton: Canadian Institute for Law, Theology, and Public Policy, 1996, 223-250.

----------. 'The Marxist Approach to Human Rights: Analysis and Critique'. *Simon Greenleaf Law Review*, III (1983-1984): 3-202.

----------. 'The Quest for Absolutes: An Historical Argument'. In *Jurisprudence: A Book of Readings*. Ed. John Warwick Montgomery. Strasbourg: International Scholarly Publishers, 1974.

----------. 'The Reasonable Reality of the Resurrection'. *Christianity Today* 24, 7 (4 April 1980): 16-19.

----------. 'The Search for Ultimates: A Sherlockian Inquiry'. *Christian Legal Journal* 2, 3 (Spring 1993): 2-10.

----------. 'The Theologian's Craft: A Discussion of Theory Formation and Theory Testing in Theology'. In *The Suicide of Christian Theology*. John Warwick Montgomery. Minneapolis: Bethany, 1970, 267-313.

----------. 'Whose Life Anyway? A Re-examination of Suicide and Assisted Suicide'. *Christian Perspectives on Law Reform*. Ed. Paul R. Beaumont. Carlisle: Paternoster, 1998, 83-103.

----------------------------------. 'Why has God Incarnate Suddenly Become Mythical?'. In *Christians in the Public Square*. C.E.B. Cranfield, David Kilgour and John Warwick Montgomery. Edmonton: Canadian Institute for Law, Theology and Public Policy, 1996, 307-316.

books, debates and audiotapes

Montgomery, John Warwick and Mark Plummer. 'Humanism or Christianity?'. Debate. 17 February 1986, Randwick, Sydney. Report. *The Sydney Morning Herald*, 19 February 1986, 23. Audiotape held by Canadian Institute for Law, Theology, and Public Policy.

Montgomery, John Warwick. 'A Lawyer's Case for Christianity'. Lecture. University of Calgary, 15 November 1991. Audiotape held by Canadian Institute for Law, Theology, and Public Policy.

----------------------------------. *Christ our Advocate*. Bonn: Verlag für Kultur und Wissenschaft, Culture and Science, 2002.

----------------------------------. *Chytraeus on Sacrifice*. Saint Louis: Concordia, 1962.

----------------------------------. *Crisis in Lutheran Theology*. Minneapolis: Bethany, 1967.

----------------------------------. *Cross and Crucible: Johann Valentin Andreae (1586-1654), Phoenix of the Theologians*. Vols. 2. The Hague: Martinus Nijhoff, 1973.

----------------------------------. *Defending the Biblical Gospel, Study Guide*. Prepared by Joseph P. Gudel. Edmonton: Canadian Institute for Law, Theology and Public Policy, 1997.

----------------------------------. *Defending the Gospel Through the Centuries: A History of Christian Apologetics*. Audiotape. Newport: Institute for Law and Theology, 1980.

----------------------------------. (ed.). *Evidence for Faith*. Dallas: Probe, 1991.

----------------------------------. *Faith Founded on Fact*. Nashville: Thomas Nelson, 1978.

----------. (ed.). *God's Inerrant Word.* Minneapolis: Bethany, 1974.

----------. *Giant in Chains: China Today and Tomorrow.* Milton Keynes, England: Nelson Word, 1994.

----------. *History and Christianity.* Downers Grove: InterVarsity, 1971.

----------. *How do we Know there is a God?* Minneapolis: Bethany, 1973.

----------. *Human Rights and Human Dignity.* Grand Rapids: Zondervan, 1986.

----------. (ed.). *Jurisprudence: A Book of Readings.* Strasbourg: International Scholarly Publishers, 1974.

----------. *Law and Gospel: A Study in Jurisprudence.* Oak Park, Illinois: Christian Legal Society, 1978.

----------. (ed.). *Myth, Allegory and Gospel.* Minneapolis: Bethany, 1974.

----------. *Occult Revival.* Audiotape. Edmonton: Canadian Institute for Law, Theology and Public Policy, 1997.

----------. *Principalities and Powers.* Minneapolis: Bethany, 1981.

----------. *Slaughter of the Innocents.* Westchester, Illinois: Cornerstone, 1981.

----------. *The Law Above the Law.* Minneapolis: Bethany, 1975.

----------. *The Quest for Noah's Ark.* 2nd ed. Minneapolis: Bethany, 1974.

----------------------------------. *The Repression of Evangelism in Greece: European Litigation vis-à-vis a Closed Religious System*. Lanham, Maryland and Oxford: University Press of America, 2001.

----------------------------------. *The Shape of the Past: A Christian Response to Secular Philosophies of History*. Rev.ed. Minneapolis: Bethany, 1975.

----------------------------------. *The Shaping of America*. Minneapolis: Bethany, 1976.

----------------------------------. *The Suicide of Christian Theology*. Minneapolis: Bethany, 1970.

----------------------------------. *The Transcendent Holmes*. Seacraft, British Columbia: Calabash Press, 2000.

----------------------------------. *Tractatus Logico – Theologicus*. Bonn: Verlag für Kultur und Wissenschaft, Culture and Science, 2002.

----------------------------------. 'What about Evolution?' *Sensible Christianity*. Retaped. Edmonton: Canadian Institute for Law, Theology and Public Policy, 2000.

----------------------------------. *Where is History Going? A Christian Response to Secular Philosophies of History*. Minneapolis: Bethany, 1972.

Cases

Administration of Papua and New Guinea v Daera Guba (1972-1974) 130 CLR 353.

Anchor Products Ltd. v Hughes (1966) 115 CLR 493.

William Henry Bailey v Charles Lindsay Bailey (1924) 34 CLR. 558.

Baker v Elcona Homes Corp. 588 F.2d 551 (6th Cir. 1978).

Briginshaw v Briginshaw (1938) CLR 60.

Carter v Wood 103 Va 68, 48 S.E. 553.

Dallas County v Commercial Union Assurance Co. 286 F.2d 388 (5th Cir. 1961).

Deeks v Wells et al (1930) 4 D.L.R. 513.

Dickson v Smith 134 Wis. 6, 114 N.W. 133.

Fontaine v British Columbia (Official Administrator) 1998 1 SCR 424.

Haw Tau Tau v Public Prosecutor (P.C.) 1982 AC 136.

R. v Exall (1866) 4 F & F 922 (176 ER 850).

R. v Turnbull and Others (1976) 3 All ER 549.

Reardon Smith Line Ltd. v Yngvar Hansen-Tangen (1976) 1 W.L.R. 989.

Schellenberg v Tunnel Holdings Pty. Ltd. (2000) HCA 18 (13 April 2000) 2.

Sherrill v Estate of Plumley 514 SWR 2d 286.

The Church of the New Faith v The Commissioner for Pay-Roll Tax (Victoria) (1983) 154 CLR 120.

Town of Ninety Six v Southern Ry 67 F.2d 579 (4th Cir. 1959).

United States v Tellier 255 F.2d 441 (2d Cir. 1958).

West v Houston Oil Co. 56 Tex. Civ. App. 341, 120 S.W. 228.

General Bibliography

Aagaard, Johannes. 'Conversion, Religious Change, and the Challenge of New Religious Movements'. *Cultic Studies Journal* 8, 2 (1991): 91-103.

Abraham, William J. *An Introduction to the Philosophy of Religion*. Englewood Clifts, New Jersey: Prentice-Hall, 1985.

Abrahams, G. *The Legal Mind*. London: H.F.L., 1954.

Ackland, Richard. 'There's Life in the Marsden Monster Yet'. *Sydney Morning Herald*. 29 June 2001, 14.

Adamson, James B. *James: The Man and his Message*. Grand Rapids: William B. Eerdmans, 1989.

Adler, Margot. *Drawing Down the Moon*. Rev. ed. New York: Penguin/Arkana, 1997.

Albright, William F. 'Interview, Toward a More Conservative View'. *Christianity Today*, 7, 8 (18 January 1963): 3.

Alexander, Loveday. 'The Acts of the Apostles as an Apologetic Text'. In *Apologetics in the Roman Empire: Pagans, Jews and Christians*. Eds. Mark Edwards, Martin Goodman and Simon Price. Oxford: Oxford University Press, 1999, 15-44.

Anderson, J.N.D. *The Evidence for the Resurrection*. London: InterVarsity, 1966.

Anderson, Norman. *A Lawyer Among the Theologians*. London: Hodder & Stoughton, 1973.

----------------------. *An Adopted Son: The Story of my Life*. Leicester: Inter-Varsity, 1985.

----------------------. *Christianity and World Religions: The Challenge of Pluralism*. Rev. ed. Leicester: Inter-Varsity, 1984.

----------------------. *Jesus Christ: The Witness of History*. Leicester: Inter-Varsity, 1985.

----------------------. *The Fact of Christ: Some of the Evidence*. Leicester: Inter-Varsity, 1979.

----------------------. *The Teaching of Jesus*. Downers Grove: InterVarsity, 1983.

Anderson, Ray S. *The New Age of Soul*. Eugene: Wipf and Stock, 2001.

Anderson, Robert. *A Doubter's Doubts about Science and Religion*. 3rd edn. Glasgow: Pickering & Inglis, 1924.

---------------------. *The Bible and Modern Criticism*. 5th ed. London: Hodder & Stoughton, 1905.

---------------------. *The Coming Prince*. 19th ed. Grand Rapids: Kregal, 1975.

---------------------. *The Silence of God*. 8th ed. London: Hodder & Stoughton, 1907.

Andrews, Lori B. 'You the Jury, Exhibit A: Language'. *Psychology Today* 18, 2 (February 1984): 28-33.

Ankerberg, John and John Weldon. *Ready with an Answer*. Eugene: Harvest House, 1997.

Anonymous. *A Quaint Old Nova Scotian Judge's View of the Roman Governor's Question, 'What is Truth?'*. London: William Ridgway, 1878.

Archer, Gleason C. *Encyclopedia of Bible Difficulties*. Grand Rapids: Zondervan, 1982.

Arnolds, Edward B, William K. Carroll, Melvin B. Lewis and Michael P. Seng. *Eyewitness Testimony: Strategies and Tactics*. New York: McGraw Hill, 1984.

Ascough, Richard S. 'Matthew and Community Formation'. In *The Gospel of Matthew in Current Study*. Ed. David E. Aune. Grand Rapids: William B. Eerdmans, 2001, 96-126.

Aulén, Gustaf. *Christus Victor*. Trans. A.G. Herbert. London: Society for Promoting Christian Knowledge, 1931.

Aviza, Edward A. *Thinking Tarot*. New York: Simon and Schuster, 1997.

Bahnsen, Greg L. 'Socrates or Christ (?)'. In *Foundations of Christian Scholarship*. Ed. Gary North. Vallecito, California: Ross House, 1979, 191-240.

Bahnsen, Greg. 'A Critique of the Evidentialist Apologetical Method of John Warwick Montgomery'. *Covenant Media Foundation*. <http://www.cmfnow.com/cgi-bin/nextpg?cmd=NextPg!1172&dir=s7!articles&tpl=PA016.htm>.

Baignet, Michael, Richard Leigh and Henry Lincoln. *The Holy Blood and the Holy Grail*. London: Jonathan Cape, 1982.

Bailey, K.H. 'Law and Logic'. *The Australasian Journal of Psychology and Philosophy* IX, 2 (June 1931): 103-119.

Baker, David. *Introduction to Torts*. North Ryde, NSW: The Law Book Company, 1985.

Barna, George. *Evangelism that Works*. Ventura, California: Regel, 1995.

Barnes, Timothy D. 'An Apostle on Trial'. *The Journal of Theological Studies* 20, 2 (October 1969): 407-419.

Barnett, Paul. *1 Corinthians*. Ross-shire, Great Britain: Christian Focus, 2000.

----------------. Interview by the author. Radio station 2CH. 8 April 2001.

----------------. *Is the New Testament History?* Sydney: Hodder and Stoughton, 1986.

----------------. *Jesus and the Logic of History*. Grand Rapids: William B. Eerdmans, 1997.

----------------. *Jesus and the Rise of Early Christianity*. Downers Grove: InterVarsity, 1999.

----------------. *Move in for Action*. Sydney: Anzea, 1971.

----------------. 'Risen Christ is Historical Reality'. *Sydney Morning Herald*. 5 April 1994, 12.

----------------. *Southern Cross*. December 2000 to January 2001, 25.

----------------. *The Truth about Jesus*. Sydney South: Aquila, 1994.

Barr, Allan. *A Diagram of Synoptic Relationships*. Edinburgh: T & T Clark, 1938.

Barth, Markus and Verne H. Fletcher. *Acquittal by Resurrection*. New York: Holt, Rinehart and Winston, 1964.

Barth, Markus. 'Christ and Law'. *Oklahoma Law Review* 12, 1 (February 1959): 67-85.

----------------. *Justification*. Grand Rapids: William B. Eerdmans, 1971.

Bartlett, Clarence. *As a Lawyer Sees Jesus: A Logical Analysis of the Scriptural and Historical Record*. New York: Greenwich, 1960.

Batts, Martin. 'A Summary and Critique of the Historical Apologetic of John Warwick Montgomery'. Thesis (Th.M.). Dallas Theological Seminary, 1977.

Bauckham, Richard. 'James and Jesus'. In *The Brother of Jesus: James the Just and his Mission*. Eds. Bruce Chilton and Jacob Neusner. Louisville: Westminster/John Knox Press, 2001, 100-137.

Bauer, Jeffrey E. 'The Logician's Model of Judgment and the Resurrection of Christ'. *Simon Greenleaf Law Review*, VII (1987-1988): 113-116, 126.

Bauman, Zygmunt. *Postmodern Ethics*. Oxford: Blackwell, 1993.

Bausch, Walter J. *Storytelling: Imagination and Faith*. Mystic, Connecticut: Twenty third Publications, 1984.

Beasley-Murray, George R. *John, Word Biblical Commentary*. 2nd ed. Nashville: Thomas Nelson, 1999.

Beasley-Murray, Paul. *The Message of the Resurrection, the Bible Speaks Today*. Leicester: Inter-Varsity, 2000.

Beazley, Margaret. 'Evidence or Intuition: The Autonomy of a Medico – Legal Trial'. Paper. Annual Conference of the Australasian Association for Quality in Health Care, Hotel Niko, Darling Harbour, Sydney. 19 June 1998.

Bebbington, David. *Patterns in History*. Leicester: InterVarsity, 1979.

Becker, Kenneth L. *Unlikely Companions: C.G. Jung on the Spiritual Exercises of Ignatius of Loyola*. Leominster, Herefordshire: Gracewing; New Malden, Surrey: Inigo Enterprises, 2001.

Beckwith, Francis J. 'History and Miracles'. In *Defense of Miracles*. Eds. R. Douglas Geivett and Gary R. Habermas. Downers Grove: InterVarsity, 1997, 86-98.

----------------------. *David Humes' Argument against Miracles: A Critical Analysis*. New York: University Press of America, 1989.

Benke, Patricia D. *Cruel Justice*. New York: Avon, 1999.

Bennett, Edmund H. *The Four Gospels from a Lawyer's Standpoint*. Boston: Houghton, Mifflin, 1899.

Bernard-Donals, Michael and Richard Glejzer. *Between Witness and Testimony: The Holocaust and the Limits of Representation*. Albany: State University of New York Press, 2001.

Bettleheim, Bruno. *The Users of Enchantment: The Meaning and Importance of Fairytales*. New York: Penguin, 1978.

Betts, Timothy. *Tarot and the Millennium*. Rancho Palos Verdes: New Perspective Media, 1998.

Betz, Hans Dieter. *Galatians*. Philadelphia: Fortress Press, 1979.

Bevins, Andrew. *The Trial and Conviction of Jesus Christ from a Legal Standpoint*. Omaha, Nebraska: Douglas Printing, 1898.

Bibliography of Dr John Warwick Montgomery's Writings. 3rd ed. Edmonton: Canadian Institute for Law, Theology and Public Policy, 2000.

Binder, F.W. *Hearsay Handbook*. 2nd ed. Colorado Springs: Shepard's/McGraw-Hill, 1983.

Black, C. Clifton. *The Rhetoric of the Gospel: Theological Artistry in the Gospels and Acts*. St. Louis: Chalice, 2001.

Blackford, Alice. Assistant Keeper of the Archives of Oxford University. Email received by the author. 19 March 2001.

Blackstock, Terry. *Evidence of Mercy*. Grand Rapids: Zondervan, 1995.

Blaiklock, E.M. *Jesus Christ: Man or Myth?* Nashville: Thomas Nelson, 1974.

------------------. *The Archaeology of the New Testament*. Grand Rapids: Zondervan, 1970.

Blanchard, John. *Will the Real Jesus Please Stand Up?* Darlington, Durham: Evangelical Press, 1989.

Bloch, Marc. *The Historian's Craft*. Trans. Peter Putman. Manchester: Manchester University Press, 1954.

Bly, Robert. *Iron John*. Shaftesbury, Dorset; Rockport, Massachusetts; Brisbane: Element, 1990.

Boa, Fraser. *The Way of the Dream: Conversations on Jungian Dream Interpretations*. With Marie Louise von Franz. Boston, London: Shambhala, 1994.

Boa, Kenneth and Larry Moody. *I'm Glad You Asked*. Wheaton: Victor, 1982.

Boa, Kenneth D. and Robert M. Bowman. *Faith Has its Reasons: An Integrative Approach to Defending Christianity*. Colorado Springs: NavPress, 2001.

Boa, Kenneth Dale. 'A Comparative Study of Four Christian Apologetic Systems'. Thesis (Ph.D.). New York University, 1985.

Booth, Roger P. *The Bedrock Gospel: Sifting the Sources, with Commentary*. N.p., England: Paget, 2001.

Bouwsma, William J. Review of *Cross and Crucible*, by John Warwick Montgomery. In *The Journal of Modern History* 48,1 (March 1976): 160-161.

Bozeman, Theodore Dwight. *Protestants in an Age of Science*: *The Baconian Ideal and Antebellum American Religious Thought*. Chapel Hill: University of North Carolina Press, 1977.

Bracht, John. *Let's Talk about it: A Letter to the Members of the Church of Jesus Christ of Latter-day Saints*. Mortdale, NSW: n.p., 1993.

Breed, David K. *The Trial of Christ from a Legal and Scriptural Standpoint*. Grand Rapids: Baker, 1982.

Briese, Clarrie. 'The Verdict'. *Australian Presbyterian* (April 2000): 5-8.

----------------. 'Witnesses to the Resurrection – Credible or Not?'. Lawyers' Christian Fellowship. <http://www.lcf.pnc.com.au/Resurrection.htm>.

Brougham, Henry Lord. *A Discourse on Natural Theology Showing the Nature of the Evidence and Advantages of the Study*. London: Charles Knight; New York: William Jackson, 1835.

Brown, Colin. *Jesus in European Protestant Thought 1778-1860*. Grand Rapids: Baker, 1985.

----------------. *Miracles and the Critical Mind*. Grand Rapids: William B. Eerdmans; Devon: Paternoster, 1984.

----------------. *Philosophy and the Christian Faith*. London: Inter-Varsity, 1969.

Brown, R.A. *Documentary Evidence in Australia.* 2nd ed. North Ryde, NSW: LBC Information Services, 1996.

Brown, Raymond E. 'A Between-the-Lines Look at Jesus'. *U.S. Catholic* 53, 3 (March 1998): 6-14.

------------------------. 'The Burial of Jesus (Mark 15:14-47)'. *Catholic Biblical Quarterly* 50 (April 1988): 233-245.

------------------------. *The Death of the Messiah: A Commentary on the Passion Narratives in the Four Gospels, the Anchor Bible Reference Library.* Vol. 2. New York, London, Toronto, Sydney and Auckland: Doubleday, 1994.

Bruce, Alexander Balmain. *Apologetics or, Christianity Defensively Stated.* Edinburgh: T & T Clark, 1911.

Bruce, F.F. *The Book of the Acts, the New International Commentary on the New Testament.* Grand Rapids: William. B. Eerdmans, 1980.

------------. *The New Testament Documents: Are They Reliable?.* 5th ed. London: Inter-Varsity, 1960.

Bruce, Steve. 'Cathedrals to Cults: The Evolving Forms of the Religious Life'. In *Religion, Modernity and Postmodernity.* Ed. Paul Heelas. Oxford and Malden, Massachusetts: Blackwell, 1998, 19-35.

Brueggemann, Walter. *The Bible and Postmodern Imagination.* London: SCM, 1993.

Brunner, Frederick Dale. *Matthew.* Vol. 2. Dallas, London, Vancouver and Melbourne: Word, 1990.

Bryan, William Jennings. *The Last Message of William Jennings Bryan.* New York: Fleming Revell, 1925.

Bryant, Vaughn M. 'Does Pollen Prove the Shroud Authentic?'. *Biblical Archaeology Review* 26, 6 (November/December 2000): 36-44, 75.

Buckhout, Robert. 'Eyewitness Testimony'. *Scientific American* 231, 6 (December 1974): 23-31.

Budziszewski, J. 'C.G. Jung's War on the Christian Faith'. *Christian Research Journal* 21, 3 (1999): 28-33.

Buffa, D.W. *The Judgment*. Crows Nest, NSW: Allen & Unwin, 2001.

--------------. *The Legacy*. Crows Nest, NSW: Allen and Unwin, 2002.

--------------. *The Prosecution*. Crows Nest, NSW: Allen and Unwin, 2001.

Burchard, Christopher. 'Jesus of Nazareth'. In *Christian Beginnings*. Ed. Jünger Becker. Louisville: Westminster/John Knox Press, 1993, 15-72.

Burnett, David. *Dawning of the Pagan Moon*. Eastbourne: Monarch, 1991.

Burridge, R.A. *What are the Gospels*? Cambridge: Cambridge University Press, 1995.

Burrows, Mark S. 'Christianity in the Roman Forum: Tertullian and the Apologetic Use of History'. *Vigilae Christianae* 42, 3 (September 1988): 209-235.

Butler, Joseph. *The Analogy of Religion*. London: Bell and Daldy, 1871.

Buzzard, Lynn Robert. *Law and Theology: An Annotated Bibliography*. Oak Park: Christian Legal Society, 1979.

Buzzard, Lynn. *Tell it to the Church*. Elgin, Illinois and Weston, Ontario: David C. Cook, 1982.

------------------. *With Liberty and Justice*. Wheaton: Victor, 1984.

Bye, Clarissa. 'The Future of Popcorn – An Interview'. *The Sun-Herald – Tempo*, 21 January 2001, 5.

Byrskog, Samuel. *Story as History – History as Story*. Tübingen: Mohr Siebeck, 2001.

Campbell, Colin. 'Some Comments on the New Religious Movements, the New Spirituality and Post-Industrial Society'. In *New Religious Movements: A Perspective for Understanding Society*. Ed. Eileen Baker. New York and Toronto: Edwin Mellen, 1982, 232-242.

Campbell, Joseph and Bill Moyers. *The Power of Myth*. New York, London, Toronto, Sydney and Auckland: Doubleday, 1988.

Campbell, Joseph and Richard Roberts. *Tarot Revelations*. San Anselmo: Vernal Equinox, 1987.

Campbell, Joseph. *Myths to Live By*. New York: Viking, 1972.

Cannata, Raymond. 'History of Apologetics at Princeton Seminary'. In *Unapologetic Apologetics*. Eds. William A. Dembski and Jay Wesley Richards. Downers Grove: InterVarsity, 2001, 57-76.

Cares, Mark J. *Speaking the Truth in Love to Mormons*. Milwaukee: Northwestern, 1993.

Carnley, Peter. *The Structure of Resurrection Belief*. Oxford: Clarendon Press, 1987.

Carroll, John. *The Western Dreaming: The Western World is Dying for Want of a Story*. Sydney: HarperCollins, 2001.

Carson, D.A. *Scripture and Truth*. Grand Rapids: Zondervan, 1983.

---------------. *The Gagging of God: Christianity Confronts Pluralism*. Grand Rapids: Zondervan, 1996.

---------------. *The Gospel According to John*. Leicester: Inter-Varsity; Grand Rapids: William B. Eerdmans, 1991.

Carter, J.W. *Breach of Contract*. North Ryde, NSW: The Law Book Company, 1984.

Carter, J.W., D.J. Harland and K.E. Lindgren. *Cases and Materials on Contract Law in Australia*. Sydney: Butterworths, 1988.

Cassidy, Michael. *Chasing the Wind*. London: Hodder and Stoughton, 1985.

--------------------. 'The Uniqueness and Divinity of Jesus Christ'. *Theologically Speaking* (November 1996).

Casteel, Herbert C. *Beyond a Reasonable Doubt*. Joplin, Missouri: College Press, 1990.

Cavin, Robert Greg. 'Is there Sufficient Historical Evidence to Establish the Resurrection of Jesus'. *Faith and Philosophy* 12, 3 (July 1995): 361 – 379.

Chandler, Russell. *Understanding the New Age*. Dallas: Word, 1988.

Chandler, Walter M. *The Trial of Jesus from a Lawyer's Standpoint*. 2 vols. New York: Federal Book 1925.

Charles, J. Daryl. 'Engaging the (Neo) Pagan Mind: Paul's Encounter with Athenian Culture as a Model for Cultural Apologetics (Acts 17:16-34)'. In *The Gospel and Contemporary Perspectives*. Ed. Douglas Moo. Grand Rapids: Kregel, 1997, 128-137.

Choo, L-T. Andrew. *Hearsay and Confrontation in Criminal Trials*. Oxford: Clarendon Press, 1996.

Chopra, Deepak. *How to Know God*. London, Sydney, Auckland, Johannesburg: Rider, 2000.

------------------. *The Return of Merlin: A Novel*. New York: Harmony, 1995.

Chrispin, Gerard. *The Resurrection: The Unopened Gift*. Epsom, Surrey: Day One Publications, 1999.

Clark, David K. *Dialogical Apologetics*. Grand Rapids: Baker, 1993.

Clark, George Luther. *A Lawyer Looks at the Bible*. New York: Vantage Press, 1956.

Clarke, M.L. *Paley: Evidences for the Man*. Toronto: University of Toronto Press, 1974.

Cleary, Edward W. (ed.). *McCormick on Evidence*. 3rd ed. St. Paul: West Publishing, 1984.

Clifford, Brian R. and Ray Bull. *The Psychology of Person Identification*. London, Henley and Boston: Routledge & Kegan Paul, 1978.

Clifford, Ross and Philip Johnson. *Jesus and the Gods of the New Age*. Oxford: Lion, 2001.

---------------------------------------. *Riding the Rollercoaster: How the Risen Christ Empowers Life*. Sydney: Strand, 1998.

---------------------------------------. *Sacred Quest*. Rev. ed. Sydney: Albatross, 1993.

Clifford, Ross. 'The Case of Eight Legal Apologists for the Defense of Scripture and the Christ Event'. Thesis (M.A.). Simon Greenleaf School of Law, May 1987.

----------------. *The Case for the Empty Tomb*. 2nd Rev. ed. Sutherland, NSW: Albatross, 1993. Also published as *Leading Lawyers' Case for the Resurrection*. Edmonton: Canadian Institute for Law, Theology and Public Policy, 1996; *Leading Lawyers Look at the Resurrection*. Sutherland, NSW: Albatross, 1991.

Clinton, Stephen M. 'Apologetic Methods and Post-Modernism' *Philosophia Christi* 19, 1 (Spring 1996): 16-18.

Coady, C.A.J. *Testimony: A Philosophical Study*. Oxford: Clarendon Press, 2000.

Cole, Graham A. 'Religious Experience and Discernment Today'. *Reformed Theological Journal* 56, 1 (January – April 1997): 1-13.

Collins, Raymond F. *First Corinthians, Sacra Pagina Series*. Vol. 7. Collegeville, Minnesota: The Liturgical Press, 1999.

Colson, Charles and Ellen Vaughn. *Gideon's Torch*. Dallas: Word, 1995.

Colson, Charles. *Born Again*. London: Hodder & Stoughton, 1977.

----------------. *Loving God*. Basingtoke: Marshalls, 1983.

Cooney, Mark. 'Evidence as Partisanship'. *Law and Society* 28, 4 (1994): 833-858.

Copan, Paul and Ronald K. Tacelli. *Jesus' Resurrection Fact or Fiction? A Debate Between William Lane Craig and Gerd Lüdemann*. Downers Grove: InterVarsity, 2000.

Copleston, Frederick. *A History of Philosophy*. Vol. 6. New York: Doubleday, 1985.

Corduan, Winfried. 'Recognizing a Miracle'. In *Defense of Miracles*. Eds. R. Douglas Geivett and Gary Habermas. Downers Grove: InterVarsity, 1997, 99-111.

Cowan, Douglas E. *Bearing False Witness: Propaganda, Reality-Maintenance, and Christian Anticult Apologetics*. Thesis (Ph.D.). University of Calgary, 1999.

Cox, A. Cleveland. 'Introducing Note'. In *The Ante-Nicene Fathers*. Vol. III. Ed. Alexander Roberts and James Donaldson. Grand Rapids: William B. Eerdmans, 1968, 3-15.

Craig, Samuel G. 'Benjamin B.Warfield'. In *B.B. Warfield, Biblical and Theological Studies*. Ed. Samuel G. Craig. Philadelphia: Presbyterian and Reformed, 1968, xv.

Craig, William Lane. *Apologetics: An Introduction*. Chicago: Moody, 1984.

------------------------. *The Historical Argument for the Resurrection of Jesus During the Deist Controversy*. Lewiston: Edwin Mellen, 1985.

------------------------. 'John Dominic Crossan and the Resurrection'. In *The Resurrection*. Eds. Davis, Kendall and O'Collins, 249-271.

------------------------. 'The Empty Tomb of Jesus'. In *Defense of Miracles*. Eds. R. Douglas Geivett and Gary Habermas. Downers Grove: InterVarsity, 1997, 247-261.

Craigie, Peter C. *The Old Testament*. Nashville: Abingdon, 1986.

Crews, Frederick C. *The Pooh Perplex*. New York: Dutton, 1965.

Crispin, Ken. *The Crown versus Chamberlain*. Sutherland, New South Wales: Albatross, 1987.

Cross, Rupert and Nancy Wilkins. *An Outline of the Law of Evidence*. 3rd ed. London: Butterworths, 1971.

Crossan, John Dominic. *Jesus: A Revolutionary Biography*. San Francisco: Harper San Francisco: 1994.

Crowley, Vivianne. *Wicca: The Old Religion of the New Millennium*. London: Thorsons, 1996.

Culpepper, R. Alan. *John*. Edinburgh: T. & T. Clark, 2000.

----------------. *The Johannine School: An Examination of the Johannine School Hypothesis Based on an Investigation of the Nature of Ancient Schools*. Missoula: Scholars Press, 1975.

Cumbey, Constance. *The Hidden Dangers of the Rainbow*. Shreveport: Huntington House, 1983.

Danin, Avinoam, Alan D. Whanger, Uri Barueh and Mary Whanger. *Flora of the Shroud of Turin*. St. Louis: Missouri Botanical Garden Press, 1999.

Darrow, Clarence. *Why I am an Agnostic and Other Essays*. Buffalo: Prometheus, 1984.

David, Orville E. *A Harmony of the Four Gospels*. 2nd. ed. Grand Rapids: Baker, 1996.

Davids, Peter. *Commentary on James, New International Greek Testament Commentary*. Exeter: Paternoster, 1982.

Davies, Margaret. *Asking the Law Question*. North Ryde, NSW: The Law Book Company, 1994.

Davies, Peter H. *The First Epistle of Peter, the New International Commentary on the New Testament*. Grand Rapids: William B. Eerdmans, 1990.

Davis, Dean. 'Man in the Dock: Courtroom Evangelism in an Age of Idolatry'. *Christian Research Journal* 23, 2 (2000): 10-11, 57.

Davis, Derek H. 'Competing Notions of Law in American Civil Religion'. *Law, Text, Culture* 5, 1 (2000): 265-290.

Davis, Stephen T. '"Seeing" the Risen Jesus'. In *The Resurrection*. Eds. Davis, Kendall and O'Collins, 126-147.

Davis, Stephen T., Daniel Kendall and Gerald O'Collins (eds.). *The Resurrection*. Oxford: Oxford University Press, 1997.

De Land, Charles Edmund. *The Mis-trials of Jesus*. Boston: R.G. Badger, 1914.

Derrett, J. Duncan M. *Law in the New Testament*. London: Durton, Longman and Todd, 1970.

Derrida, Jacques. 'Faith and Knowledge: The Two Sources of "Religion" at the Limits of Reason Alone'. In *Religion*. Eds. Jacques Derrida and Gianni Vattimo. Cambridge: Polity, 1998, 1-78.

Dershowitz, Alan M. *Just Revenge*. London: Headline, 1999.

Desmond, Adrian. *Huxley: Evolution's High Priest*. London: Michael Joseph, 1997.

Dick, Michael Brennan. 'The Legal Metaphor in Job 31'. *The Catholic Biblical Quarterly* 41, 1 (January 1979): 37–50.

DiZerega, Gus. *Pagans and Christians: The Personal Spiritual Experience*. St. Paul: Llewellyn, 2001.

Docker, E.B. *If Jesus did not Die on the Cross? A Study in Evidence*. London: Robert Scott, 1920.

Dockery, David S. (ed.). *The Challenge of Postmodernism: An Evangelical Engagement*. Grand Rapids: Baker, 1995.

Dodd, C.H. *More New Testament Studies*. Manchester: Manchester University Press, 1968.

-------------. *The Apostolic Preaching and its Developments*. London: Hodder & Stoughton, 1944.

Douglas, J.D. (ed.). *The New International Dictionary of the Christian Church*. Exeter: Paternoster, 1974.

Douzinas, Costas, Ronnie Warrington and Shaun McVeigh. *Postmodern Jurisprudence*. London and New York: Routledge, 1991, ix-51.

Doyle, Arthur Conan. *Naval Treaty, Complete Sherlock Holmes*. London: Penguin, 1981, 447-469.

-------------------------. *The Adventure of the Sussex Vampire, The Case-Book of Sherlock Holmes*. Harmondsworth, Middlesex: Penguin, 1977, 98-115.

-------------------------. *The Hound of the Baskervilles, Sherlock Holmes the Complete Illustrated Novels*. London: Chancellor, 1987, 201-352.

-------------------------. *The Sign of the Four, Sherlock Holmes the Complete Illustrated Novels*. London: Chancellor, 1987, 109-200.

Drane, John, Ross Clifford and Philip Johnson. *Beyond Prediction: The Tarot and your Spirituality*. Oxford: Lion, 2001.

Drane, John. *Evangelism for a New Age*. London: Marshall Pickering, 1994.

--------------. *The Bible Phenomenon*. Oxford: Lion, 1999.

--------------. *The McDonaldization of the Church*. London: Darton, Longman and Todd, 2000.

──────────. 'Unknown Gods, Declining Churches, and the Spiritual Search of Contemporary Culture'. *200th Annual C.M.S. Sermon*. Delivered Westminster College, Cambridge, St. Andrews-by-the Wardrobe, Blackfriars, London and Fulford Parish Church, York, 2000.

──────────. *What is the New Age Still Saying to the Church?* Rev. ed. London: Marshall Pickering, 1999.

Drane, John W. 'Christians, New Agers and Changing Cultural Paradigms'. *The Expository Times* 106, 6 (March 1995): 172-176.

──────────. 'Methods and Perspectives in Understanding the New Age'. *Themelios* 23, 2 (February 1998): 22-34.

──────────. 'The Religious Background'. In *New Testament Interpretation*. Ed. I. Howard Marshall. Exeter, Paternoster, 1977, 117-125.

Drury, Neville. *Exploring the Labyrinth*. St. Leonards: Allen & Unwin, 1999.

──────────. Interview. 'New Age Journey'. *Compass*, ABC Television. 10 June 2001.

──────────. *The History of Magic in the Modern Age*. London: Constable, 2000.

──────────. *The Shaman's Quest*. Rose Bay, NSW: Bandl and Schlesinger, 2001.

Dulles, Avery. *A History of Apologetics*. Philadelphia: Westminster Press, 1972.

Dunn, James D.G. 'Demythologizing – The Problem of Myth in the New Testament'. In *New Testament Interpretation*. Ed. Howard Marshall. Exeter: Paternoster, 1977, 285-307.

──────────. *Romans 1-8*. Dallas: Word, 1988.

──────────. *The Evidence for Jesus*. Louisville: Westminster Press, 1985.

Dupin, Andre Marie Jean. *The Trial of Jesus Before Caiaphas and Pilate Being a Refutation of Mr. Salvador's Chapter Entitled 'The Trial and Condemnation of Jesus'*. Trans. John Pickering. Boston: C.C. Little & J. Brown, 1839.

Dworkin, Gerald. *Odger's Construction of Deeds and Statutes*. 5th ed. London: Sweet & Maxwell, 1967.

Dworkin, R.M. *Law's Empire*. Cambridge, Massachusetts: Harvard University Press, 1986.

Dyer, Wayne W. *There's a Spiritual Solution to Every Problem*. Sydney: HarperCollins, 2001.

Edgar, William. *Reasons of the Heart: Recovering Christian Persuasion*. Grand Rapids: Baker, 1996.

Edwards, Joel. *The Cradle, the Cross and the Empty Tomb*. London, Sydney and Auckland: Hodder & Stoughton, 2000.

Eliade, Mircea. *Cosmos and History: The Myth of the Eternal Return*. Trans. William R. Trask. New York: Pantheon, 1954.

-----------------. *Myths, Dreams and Mysteries*. Trans. Philip Mairet. London and Glasgow: Collins, 1968.

-----------------. *Patterns in Comparative Religion*. Trans. Rosemary Sheed. New York: New American Library, 1958.

-----------------. *The Sacred and the Profane: The Nature of Religion*. Trans. William R. Trask. New York and Evanston: Harper & Row, 1961.

-----------------. 'What is Alchemy?'. In *Hidden Truths: Magic, Alchemy and the Occult*. Ed. Lawrence E. Sullivan. New York: MacMillian; London: Collier MacMillian, 1987, 243-247.

Ellingsen, Mark. 'Common Sense Realism: The Cutting Edge of Evangelical Identity'. *Dialog*, 24 (1985): 197-205

Ellul, Jaques. *The New Demons*. Oxford: Mowbray, 1975.

Ellwood, Robert S. *Islands of the Dawn*. Honolulu: University of Hawaii Press, 1993.

Ellwood, Robert. *The Politics of Myth: A Study of C.G. Jung, Mircea Eliade and Joseph Campbell*. Albany, New York: State University of New York Press, 1999.

Engel, James F. *Contemporary Christian Communication: Its Theory and Practice*. Nashville and New York: Thomas Nelson, 1979.

Erdel, Timothy Paul. 'Stigma and Dogma: A Reply to Earl William Kennedy on Behalf of John Warwick Montgomery'. *Fides et Historia* 6, 1 (Fall 1974): 26-32.

Erickson, Millard J. *Christian Theology*. Grand Rapids: Baker, 1985.

----------------------. 'Postmodern Apologetics: Can Deconstructed Horses Even be Led to Water?'. In *Evangelical Apologetics*. Eds. Michael Bauman, David Hall and Robert Newman. Camp Hill: Christian Publications, 1996, 322-326.

----------------------. *Postmodernizing the Faith: Evangelical Responses to the Challenge of Postmodernism*. Grand Rapids: Baker, 1998.

Erskine, Thomas. *Remarks on the Internal Evidence for the Truth of the Revealed Religion*. 7th ed. Edinburgh: Waugh and Innes, 1823.

Esser, Hans-Helmet. 'Law, Customs, Elements'. In *The New International Dictionary of the New Testament*. Vol. 2. Ed. Colin Brown. Exeter: Paternoster, 1976, 439.

Evans, Arthur William. *Warburton and the Warburtonians*. London and Oxford: Oxford University Press, 1932.

Evans, C. Stephen. *Why Believe?* Leicester: Inter-Varsity, 1996.

Ewen, Pamela Binnings. *Faith on Trial*. Nashville: Broadman and Holman, 1999.

Fairbanks, James D. Review of *Christians in the Public Square*, by C E B Cranfield, David Kilgour, John Warwick Montgomery. In *Fides et Historia* XXIX, 1 (Winter/Spring 1997): 117-119.

Fee, Gordon D. *The First Epistle to the Corinthians, the New International Commentary on the New Testament*. Grand Rapids: William B. Eerdmans, 1987.

Feinberg, Paul D. 'History: Public or Private? A Defence of John Warwick Montgomery's Philosophy of History'. *Christian Scholar's Review* 1, 4 (Summer 1971): 325-331.

--------------------. 'The Cumulative Case Method'. In *Five Views on Apologetics*. Ed. Steven B. Cowan. Grand Rapids: Zondervan, 2000, 147-172.

Ferreira, Johan. *Johannine Ecclesiology, Journal for the Study of New Testament Supplementary Series 160*. Sheffield: Sheffield Press, 1998.

-----------------. 'The So-called "High Priestly Prayer" of John 17 and Ecclesiology: The Concerns of an Early Christian Community'. In *Prayer and Spirituality in the Early Church*. Vol. 1. Eds. Pauline Allen, Raymond Canning, Lawrence Cross and B. Janelle Craiger. Everton Park, Queensland: Centre for Early Christian Studies, 1988, 15-37.

Fetcho, David. 'Disclosing the Unknown God: Evangelism in the New Religions'. *Update* 6,4 (December 1982): 7-16.

Filson, Floyd V. *The Gospel According to Matthew*. London: Adam and Charles Black, 1971.

Finney, Charles G. *An Autobiography*. London: The Salvationist, n.d.

Fish, Stanley. *The Trouble with Principles*. Cambridge, Massachusetts: Harvard University Press, 1999.

Fisher, George Park. *Manual of Christian Evidences*. New York: Charles Scribner's Sons, 1888.

Fitzpatrick, Peter. 'Being Original: Law and the Insistence of the Sacred'. *Law, Text, Culture* 5, 1 (2000): 63-95.

--------------------. *The Mythology of Modern Law*. London: Routledge, 1992.

Fleming, John G. *The Law of Torts*. 7th ed. North Ryde, Sydney: The Law Book Company, 1987.

Flemming, Dean. 'Contexualizing the Gospel in Athens: Paul's Areopagus Address as a Paradigm for Missionary Communication'. *Missiology* 30, 2 (April 2002): 119-214

Flew, Anthony G.N. *God, Freedom and Immortality*. Buffalo: Prometheus, 1984.

Flint, Robert. *Vico*. Edinburgh and London: Blackwood, 1884.

Ford, H.A.J. and W.A. Lee. *Principles of the Law of Trusts*. North Ryde, NSW: The Law Book Company, 1990.

Foreman, Dale. *Crucify Him: A Lawyer Looks at the Trial of Jesus*. Grand Rapids: Zondervan, 1990.

Fox, Matthew. 'Spirituality for a New Era'. In *New Age Spirituality: An Assessment*. Ed. Duncan S. Ferguson. Louisville, Kentucky: Westminster/ John Knox Press, 1993, 196-219.

France, R.T. *Matthew, Tyndale New Testament Commentaries*. Leicester: Inter-Varsity; Grand Rapids: William B. Eerdmans, 1985.

--------------. *The Gospel of Mark, The New International Greek Testament Commentary*. Grand Rapids and Cambridge: William B. Eerdmans; Carlisle: Paternoster, 2002.

Francis Lyall. *Slaves, Citizens, Sons: Legal Metaphors in the Epistles*. Grand Rapids: Zondervan, 1984.

Frederick, Kenyon. *The Bible and Archaeology*. New York & London: Harper, 1940.

Freke, Timothy and Peter Gandy. *The Jesus Mysteries: Was the Original Jesus a Pagan God?* London: Thorsons, 1999.

Frost, Michael. *Jesus the Fool*. Sutherland, NSW: Albatross, 1994.

----------------. *Seeing God in the Ordinary: A Theology of the Everyday*. Rev. ed. Peabody, Massachusetts: Hendrickson, 2000.

Frost, Rob. *Sharing Jesus in a New Millennium*. Bletchley, England: Scripture Union, 2000.

Fuller, Robert C. *Spiritual but not Religious: Understanding Unchurched America*. New York: Oxford University Press, 2001.

Funk, Robert W., Roy W. Hoover and the Jesus Seminar. *The Five Gospels: The Search for the Authentic Words of Jesus*. New York: Macmillan, 1993.

Gaarder, Jostein. *Sophie's World: A Novel about the History of Philosophy*. Trans. Paulette Moller. London: Phoenix House, 1995.

Gad, Irene. *Tarot and Individuation: Correspondences with Cabala and Alchemy*. York Beach, Maine: Nicolas–Hays, 1994.

Gaffin, Richard B. 'Redemption and Resurrection: An Exercise in Biblical-Systematic Theology'. In *A Confessing Theology for Postmodern Times*. Ed. Michael S. Horton. Wheaton: Crossway, 2000, 229-249.

Gard, Spencer, A. *Jones on Evidence*. 6th ed. Rochester: The Lawyers Co-operative; San Francisco: Bancroft–Whitney, 1972.

Garland, David E. *Reading Matthew: A Literary and Theological Commentary on the First Gospel*. New York: Crossroad, 1993.

Garrett, Duane A. *Angels and the New Spirituality*. Nashville: Broadman & Holman, 1995.

Gearey, Adam. 'Law in the Gospel of the Female Messiah: Myth, Gnosticism and Finnegans Wake'. *Australian Feminist Law Journal*, 10 (March 1998): 61-83.

Geisler, Norman L. and Paul K. Hoffman (eds.). *Why I am a Christian*. Grand Rapids: Baker, 2001.

Geisler, Norman L. *Baker Encyclopedia of Christian Apologetics*. Grand Rapids: Baker, 1999.

----------------------. 'Johannine Apologetics'. *Bibliotheca Sacra* 136, 544 (October–December, 1979): 333-343.

Geisler, Norman. *Christian Apologetics*. Grand Rapids: Baker, 1976.

--------------------. *Miracles and Modern Thought*. Grand Rapids: Zondervan, 1982.

--------------------. *Miracles and the Modern Mind*. Rev. ed. Grand Rapids: Baker, 1992.

Gilbert, R.A. *Revelations of the Golden Dawn: Rise and Fall of the Magical Order*. London: Quantum, 1997.

Gill, John. '"Of Miracles", Lord Lyttelton, and Alexander the Miracle Worker'. <http://arts.adelaide.edu.au/philosophy/jgill/miracles.htm>.

Gillies, Peter. *Criminal Law*. 2nd ed. North Ryde, NSW: The Law Book Company, 1990.

Givens, Richard A. *Advocacy: The Art of Pleading a Cause*. Colorado Springs: Shepard's/McGraw Hill, 1980.

Gleeson, Murray. *The Rule of Law and the Constitution, 2000 Boyer Lectures*. Sydney: ABC Books, 2000.

Glissan, J.L. and S.W. Tilmouth. *Advocacy and Practice*. Sydney: Butterworths, 1998.

Gnanakan, Ken. 'The Bible and Salvation in Asia'. In *Salvation: Some Asian Perspectives*. Ed. Ken Gnanakan. Bangalore: Asia Theological Association, 1992, 1-16.

Gordon, William Edward. *A Contemporary Apologetics: The Concept of Christian Apologetics in the Writings of Peter L. Berger and Hans Küng*. Thesis (Th.D.). New Orleans Baptist Theological Seminary, October 1987.

Gorman, Michael. *Elements of Biblical Exegesis*. Peabody, Massachusetts: Hendricksen, 2001.

Gottschalk, Louis. *Understanding History*. New York: Alfred A. Knopf, 1960.

Graham, Michael. *The Experience of Ultimate Truth*. Melbourne: U-Turn, 2001.

Grant, W. Harold, Magdala Thompson and Thomas E. Clarke. *From Image to Likeness: A Jungian Path in the Gospel Journey*. New York and Ramsey, New Jersey: Paulist Press, 1983.

Green, Garrett. *Theology, Hermeneutics, and Imagination*. Cambridge: Cambridge University Press, 2000.

Green, Joel B. *The Gospel of Luke*. Grand Rapids: William B. Eerdmans, 1997.

Green, Michael. *Man Alive!* Downers Grove: InterVarsity, 1967.

Greene, Liz. 'Foreword'. In *The Key to the Tarot*. A.E. Waite. Rev. ed. London: Rider, 1993, 6-13.

Greenleaf, Simon. *A Treatise on the Law of Evidence*. Boston: C.C. Little and J. Brown, 1842.

----------------------. *The Testimony of the Evangelists*. Grand Rapids: Baker, 1984.

Grenz, Stanley J. *A Primer on Postmodernism*. Grand Rapids: William B. Eerdmans, 1996.

Grieg, D.W. and J.L.R. Davis. *The Law of Contract*. North Ryde, NSW: The Law Book Company, 1987.

Grieve, Val. *The Trial of Jesus*. Bromley, Kent: STL, 1990.

---------------. *Verdict on the Empty Tomb*. London: Falcon Booklet, 1970.

---------------. *Your Verdict*. Bromley: STL, 1988.

Grisham, John. *The Chamber*. London: Arrow, 1994.

------------------. *The Testament*. London: Century, 1999.

Groothuis, Douglas R. *Unmasking the New Age*. Downers Grove: InterVarsity, 1986.

Groothuis, Douglas. 'Are Theistic Arguments Religiously Useless? A Pascalian Objection Examined'. In *The Gospel and Contemporary Perspectives*. Ed. Douglas Moo. Grand Rapids: Kregel, 1997, 116-127.

------------------------. *Confronting the New Age*. Downers Grove: InterVarsity, 1988.

Grotius, Hugo. *The Truth of the Christian Religion*. Trans. John Clarke. London: William Baynes, 1825.

Gudel, Joseph P. 'An Examination and Critique of Thomas Paine's *Age of Reason*'. *The Simon Greenleaf Law Review*, 1 (1981-1982): 75-100.

Guelich, Robert. 'The Gospel Genre'. In *The Gospel and the Gospels*. Ed. Peter Stuhlmacher. Grand Rapids: William B. Eerdmans, 1991, 173-208.

Guest, A.A. (gen. ed.). *Chitty on Contracts*. 25th ed. London: Sweet & Maxwell, 1983.

Guilliatt, Richard. 'The Spiritual on Tap: A Prayer, a Chant and a Chakra Chart are Proving Mightier than the Pub'. *The Sydney Morning Herald Weekend Magazine*. 17 November 2001, 73.

Gumbel, Nicky. *Why Jesus*. Eastborne: Kingsway, 1991.

Gundry, Robert H. *Mark: A Commentary on his Apology for the Cross*. Grand Rapids: William B. Eerdmans, 1993.

----------------------. *Matthew*. 2nd ed. Grand Rapids: William B. Eerdmans, 1994.

----------------------. 'The Essential Physicality of Jesus' Resurrection According to the New Testament'. In *Jesus of Nazareth: Lord and Christ*. Eds. Joel B. Green and Max Turner. Grand Rapids: William B. Eerdmans, Carlisle: Paternoster, 1994, 204-219.

Gutteridge, Don. *The Defence Rests its Case*. Nashville: Broadman, 1975.

Gwynne, Paul. 'The Fate of Jesus' Body: Another Decade of Debate'. *Colloquium* 32, 1 (May 2000): 3-21.

Habermas, Gary R. and J.P. Moreland. *Immortality: The Other Side of Death*. Nashville: Thomas Nelson, 1992.

Habermas, Gary R. *Ancient Evidence for the Life of Jesus*. Nashville: Thomas Nelson, 1984.

----------------------. 'Evidential Apologetics'. In *Five Views on Apologetics*. Ed. Steven B. Cowan. Grand Rapids: Zondervan, 2000, 92-121.

----------------------. 'Explaining Away Jesus' Resurrection: The Recent Revival of Hallucination Theories'. *Christian Research Journal* 23, 4 (2001): 26-31, 47-49.

----------------------. 'Greg Bahnsen, John Warwick Montgomery, and Evidential Apologetics'. *Global Journal of Classical Theology* 3, 1 (March 2002): 1-12. <http://www.trinitysem.edu/journal/toc_v3n1.html>.

----------------------. 'Philosophy of History, Historical Relativism and History as Evidence'. In *Evangelical Apologetics*. Eds. Michael Bauman, David Hall and Robert Newman. Camp Hill: Christian Publications, 1996, 91-118.

----------------------. 'Resurrection Claims in Non-Christian Religions'. *Religious Studies*, 25 (June 1989): 167-177.

----------------------. *The Historical Jesus: Ancient Evidence for the Life of Christ*. Joplin, Missouri: College Press, 1996.

----------------------. 'The Personal Testimony of the Holy Spirit to the Believer and Christian Apologetics'. *Journal of Christian Apologetics* 1, 1 (Summer 1997), 49-64.

----------------------. 'The Resurrection Appearances of Jesus'. In *Defense of Miracles*. Eds. R. Douglas Geivett and Gary Habermas. Downers Grove: InterVarsity, 1997, 262-275.

----------------------. 'Why I Believe in Miracles'. In *Why I am a Christian*. Eds. Geisler and Hoffman, 111-124.

Haenchen, E. *The Acts of the Apostles*. Trans. B. Blackwell. Oxford: Blackwell, 1971.

Hale, Matthew. *A Letter of Advice to his Grandchildren*. 2nd ed. London: Taylor & Hessey, 1823.

Hall, Jerome. 'Religion, Law and Ethics – A Call for Dialogue'. *Hastings Law Journal*, 29 (July 1978): 1273.

Hamblin, Julie. 'Discussion'. In *Ethics Fatigue Symposium: The Fracturing of Medical Ethics*. Sydney: University of Sydney, Centre for Values, Ethics and the Law in Medicine, 1998, 83-84.

Hambrick-Stowe, Charles E. *Charles G. Finney and the Spirit of American Evangelicalism*. Grand Rapids: William B Eerdmans, 1996.

Hamer, David. 'The Civil Standard of Proof Uncertainty: Probability, Belief and Justice'. *Sydney Law Review* 16, 4 (December 1994): 506-536.

Hamilton, Malcolm. 'An Analysis of the Festival for Mind-Body-Spirit'. *Beyond New Age*. Eds. Sutcliffe and Bowman, 188-200.

Handley, Ken. 'A Lawyer Looks at the Resurrection'. *Kategoria*, 15 (1999): 11-21.

Hanegraff, Wouter J. *New Age Religion and Western Culture: Esotericism in the Mirror of Secular Thought*. Albany, New York: State University of New York Press, 1998.

Hanft, Frank. *You Can Believe*. Indianapolis: Bobbs-Merrill, 1952.

Harrell, Allen W. *Splinters from my Gavel: Confessions of a Judge*. Grand Rapids: Zondervan, 1970.

Harris, J.W. 'Legal Doctrine and Interests in Land'. In *Oxford Essays in Jurisprudence*, 3rd series. Eds. John Eekelaar and John Bell. Oxford: Clarendon Press, 1987, 167-197.

Hatch, Edward Wingate. *The Trial and Condemnation of Christ as a Legal Question*. New York: Knickerbocker, 1892.

Hawley, Janet. 'The Hero's Journey'. *Sydney Morning Herald, Good Weekend Supplement*. 14 October 1995, 57.

Hawtrey, Kim. 'The New Apologist'. *Impact Bulletin*, 24 (October – December 1996): 1.

Hay, David and Kate Hunt. 'Is Britain's Soul Waking Up?'. *The Tablet*, 24 June 2000.

Hazen, Craig. '"Ever Hearing but Never Understanding": A Response to Mark Hutchin's Critique of John Warwick Montgomery's Historical Apologetics'. *Global Journal of Theology*, 3, 1 (March 2002): 1-10. <http://www.trinitysem.edu/journal/toc_v3n1.html>.

Heelas, Paul. *The New Age Movement: The Celebration of the Self and the Sacralization of Modernity*. Oxford and Malden, Massachusetts: Blackwell, 1996.

Hein, Steven A. 'The Christian Historian: Apologist or Seeker?- A Reply to Ronald J. VanderMolen'. *Fides et Historia* 4, 2 (Spring 1972): 85-93.

Hemer, C.J. 'The Speeches of Acts 11. The Areopagus Address'. *Tyndale Bulletin*, 40.2 (November 1989), 248-255.

Hemer, Colin J. 'Luke the Historian'. *Bulletin of the John Rylands University Library*, 60 (1977): 28-51.

Hemmingson, Michael (ed.). *The Mammoth Book of Legal Thrillers*. London: Robinson, 2001.

Hengel, Martin. *Studies in the Gospel of Mark*. Trans. John Bowden. Philadelphia: Fortress, 1985.

Herron, Leslie. *The Trial of Jesus of Nazareth from a Lawyer's Point of View*. Paper. The Australian Lawyer's Christian Fellowship, Sydney. 22 March 1970.

Hesselgrave, David J. and Edward Rommen. *Contextualization: Meanings, Methods, and Models*. Grand Rapids: Baker, 1989.

Hesselgrave, David J. *Communicating Christ Cross-Culturally*. 2nd ed. Grand Rapids: Zondervan, 1991.

-------------------------. *Scripture and Strategy: The Use of the Bible in Postmodern Church and Mission*. Passadena: William Carey Library, 1994.

Hexham, Irving and Karla Poewe. *New Religions as Global Cultures: Making the Human Sacred*. Boulder, Colorado: Westview, 1997.

Hexham, Irving. 'Evangelical Illusions'. In *No Other Gods Before Me?* Ed. John G. Stackhouse. Grand Rapids: Baker, 2001, 137-160.

------------------. 'The Evangelical Response to the New Age'. In *Perspectives on the New Age*. Eds. James R. Lewis and J. Gordon Melton. Albany, New York: State University of New York Press, 1992, 152-163.

Heydon, J.D. *Cross on Evidence*. 5th Australian ed. Sydney: Butterworths, 1996.

Hicks, Peter. *Evangelicals and Truth: A Creative Proposal for a Postmodern Age*. Leicester: Apollos, 1998.

Hill, David. *The Gospel of Matthew, the New Century Bible Commentary*. Grand Rapids: William B. Eerdmans; London: Marshall, Morgan & Scott, 1972.

Himes, Roger. *Counsellor State Your Case!* Denver: Accent, 1978.

Hine, Reginald L. *Confessions of an Un-Common Attorney*. London: J.M. Dent & Sons, 1946.

Hocker, P.J., Ann Duffy and Peter G. Heffey. *Cases and Materials on Contract*. 5th ed. North Ryde, NSW: The Law Book Company, 1985.

Hoffman, Paul K. 'A Jurisprudential Analysis of Hume's "In Principal" Argument against Miracles'. *Christian Apologetics Journal* 2, 1 (Spring 1999). <http://www.ses.edu/journal/issue2_1/2_hoffman-mn.htm>.

Holding, James Patrick. 'Robert (Richard) Packham Refuted'. <http://www.tektonics.org/JPH_LLL.html>.

Holladay, William H. 'Jeremiah's Lawsuit with God'. *Interpretation*. (July 1963): 280-287.

Holland, R.F. 'The Miraculous'. *American Philosophical Quarterly* 2, 1 (January, 1965): 43-51.

Honoré, Tony. 'The Primacy of Oral Evidence?'. In *Crime Proof and Punishment: Essays in Memory of Sir Rupert Cross*. Ed. C.F.H. Tapper. London: Butterworths, 1981, 172-192.

Hopkins, Mark. *Evidences of Christianity*. Boston: Marvin, 1876.

Horne, Thomas Hartwell. *An Introduction to the Critical Study and Knowledge of the Holy Scriptures*. 4 vols. Philadelphia: E. Littell, 1825.

Howard, Colin. *Criminal Law*. Sydney: The Law Book Company, 1982.

Howard, M.N., Peter Crane and Daniel A. Hochberg. *Phipson on Evidence*. 14th ed. London: Sweet & Maxwell, 1990.

Howe, Frederic R. *Challenge and Response*. Grand Rapids: Zondervan, 1982.

Howson, J.S. 'Preface'. In William Paley, *Horae Pauline*. London: Society for Promoting Christian Knowledge, 1891, xi-xiii.

Hughes, Philip, Craig Thompson, Rohan Pryor and Gary D. Bouma. *Believe it or Not: Australian Spirituality and the Churches in the 90's*. Hawthorn, Victoria: Christian Research Association, 1995.

Hughes, Philip Hughes. 'Christian Faith in a Postmodern Age'. *Zadok Paper*, S74 (July 1995).

Hunt, Dave and T.A. McMahon. *America the Sorcerer's New Apprentice: The Rise of New Age Shamanism*. Eugene, Oregon: Harvest, 1988.

Hutton, Richard A. *Cardinal Newman*. London: Methuen, 1905.

Huxley, Thomas. 'Agnosticism and Christianity'. In *Science in Christian Tradition: Essays*. Thomas Huxley. New York: D. Appleton, 1899, 334-342.

Imbert, Jean. *Le Proces de Jesus*. Paris: Presses Universitaries de France, 1980.

Ingram, Edward Joseph. *On the Witness Stand, He Who was Now Is*. Los Angeles: Hoffman Press, 1931.

Introvigne, Massimo. 'Strange Bedfellows or Future Enemies'. *Update and Dialog*, 4 (October 1993): 13-22.

Irvine, William. *Apes, Angels and Victorians*. London: Weidenfeld and Nicolson, 1956.

Jencks, Charles (ed.). *The Post-Modern Reader*. London: Academy Editions; New York: St Martins, 1992.

Jensen, P.F. 'History and the Resurrection of Jesus Christ – III'. *Colloquium* 3, 4 (May 1970): 343-354.

Jensen, Richard A. *Telling the Story: Variety and Imagination in Preaching*. Minneapolis: Augsburg, 1980.

----------------------. *Thinking in Story: Preaching in a Post-Literate Age*. Lima, Ohio: C.S.S., 1993.

Johnson, Philip. 'Apologetics and Myths: Signs of Salvation and Postmodernity'. *Lutheran Theological Journal* 32, 2 (July 1998), 62-72.

------------------. 'Judicial Apologetics; Origins, Epistemology and Application'. Intended publication <http:// www.sacredtribes.com>.

------------------. 'Juridical Apologetics 1600-2000 AD: A Bio-Bibliographical Essay', *Global Journal of Classical Theology* 3, 1 (March 2002): 1-25. <http://www.trinitysem.edu/journal/toc_v3n1.html>.

Johnson, Phillip E. *Darwin on Trial*. Downers Grove: InterVarsity, 1991.

Johnston, Graham. *Preaching to a Postmodern World*. Grand Rapids: Baker, 2001.

Jones, David Gareth. *Teilhard de Chardin: An Analysis and Assessment*. Grand Rapids: William B. Eerdmans, 1970.

Jones, Stanton L. and Richard E. Butman. *Modern Psycho-Therapies*. Downers Grove: InterVarsity, 1991.

Jung, C.G. 'Psychotherapists or the Clergy'. In *Modern Man in Search of a Soul*. Trans. W.S. Dell and Cary F. Baynes. London and Henley-on-Thames: Routledge and Kegan Paul, 1962, 255-282.

------------. 'The Mana-Personality'. In *The Collected Works of C.G. Jung*. Vol. 7. Trans. R.F.C. Hull. 2nd ed. London: Routledge and Kegal Paul, 1953, 227-241.

Jung, Carl Gustav. *Psychology and Religion* New Haven: Yale University Press, 1938.

Justice Beazley. 'Hearsay and Related Evidence – A New Era?'. *University of New South Wales Law Journal* 18, 1 (1995): 38-66.

Kaplan, Marty. 'Ambushed by Spirituality'. *Time*. 24 June 1996, 92.

Kelly, J.N.D. *Jerome*. Peabody, Massachusetts: Hendrickson, 1998.

Kelman, Mark. *A Guide to Critical Legal Studies*. Cambridge, Massachusetts: Harvard University Press, 1987.

Kendrick, Stephen. *Holy Clues: The Gospel According to Sherlock Holmes*. New York: Random, 1999.

Kennedy, Duncan. *A Critique of Adjudication {fin de siècle}*. Cambridge, Massachusetts: Harvard University Press, 1997.

Kenny, Dennis E. 'Editorial: Pastoral Care for the Twenty-first Century'. *Journal of Pastoral Care* 52, 3 (Fall 1998): 215.

Keon-Cohen, B.A. 'Some Problems of Proof: The Admissibility of Traditional Evidence'. In *Mabo: A Judicial Revolution: The Aboriginal Land Rights Decision and its Impact on Australian Law*. Eds. M.A. Stephenson and Suri Ratnapala. St Lucia: University of Queensland Press, 1993, 185-205.

Ker, Ian. *John Henry Newman*. Oxford: Oxford University Press, 1988.

Kersten, Holger and Elmar R. Gruber. *The Jesus Conspiracy: The Turin Shroud and the Truth about the Resurrection*. Shaftesbury, Dorset; Rockport, Massachusetts; Brisbane: Element, 1994.

Khoury, Daniel and Yvonne S. Yamouni. *Understanding Contract Law*. 2nd ed. Sydney: Butterworths, 1989.

Kilby, Clyde S. 'Mythic and Christian Elements in Tolkien'. In *Myth, Allegory and Gospel*. Ed. John Warwick Montgomery, 119-143.

Kinney, Jay. 'Dissecting the New Age'. *Gnosis*, 49 (1998): 14-17.

Kopp, Sheldon. *The Hanged Man*. Palo Alto, California: Science and Behaviour Books, 1974.

Kreeft, Peter Kreeft and Ronald K. Tacelli. *Handbook of Christian Apologetics*. Downers Grove: Inter-Varsity, 1994.

Küng, Hans. 'Toward Dialogue'. In *Christianity and the World Religions*. Hans Küng, Josef van Ess, Heinrich von Stietencorn and Heinz Bechert. Trans. Peter Heinegg. Maryknoll, New York: Orbis, 1993, xiv – xx.

Lamb, Francis J. *Miracle and Science: Biblical Miracles Examined by the Methods, Rules and Tests of the Science of Jurisprudence as Administered Today in Courts of Justice*. Oberlin, Ohio: Bibliotheca Sacra, 1909.

Lamb, Winifred Wing Han. 'Fundamentalism, Modernity and Postmodernity'. *Zadok Paper*, S73 (March 1995).

Lane, William L. *Commentary on the Gospel of Mark*. Grand Rapids: William B. Eerdmans, 1974.

--------------------. 'Unexpected Light on Hebrews 13:1-6 from a Second Century Source'. *Perspectives in Religious Studies* 9, 3 (Fall 1982): 267-274.

Langone, Michael D. 'Secular and Religious Critiques of Cults: Complementary Visions, not Irresolvable Conflicts'. *Cultic Studies Journal* 12, 2 (1995): 166-186.

Lanham, David, Mark Weinberg, Kenneth E. Brown and George W. Ryan. *Criminal Fraud*. North Ryde, NSW: The Law Book Company, 1987.

Lapide, Pinchas. *The Resurrection of Jesus*. Minneapolis: Augsburg, 1983.

Lescroat, John. *The Mercy Rule*. London: Headline, 1988.

Lewis, C.S. *God in the Dock: Essays on Theology*. Ed. Walter Hooper. London: Fount, 1979.

-------------. *Mere Christianity*. London and Glasgow: Fontana, 1964.

-------------. *Of Other Worlds: Essays and Stories*. Ed. Walter Hooper. New York and London: Harcourt, Brace and Jovanovich, 1996.

-------------. *The Lion, the Witch and the Wardrobe*. Hammondsworth, Middlesex: Penguin, 1959.

Lewis, Gordon. *Testing Christianity's Truth Claims*. Chicago: Moody, 1976.

------------------. 'The Church and the New Spirituality'. *Journal of the Evangelical Theological Society* 36, 4 (December 1993): 433-444.

Lewis, James R.and J. Gordon Melton (eds.). *Perspectives on the New Age*. Albany, New York: State University of New York Press, 1992.

Licona, Michael R. *Cross Examined*. Falls Church, Virginia: Truth Quest, 1998.

Liefeld, David R. 'Lutheran Motifs in the Writings of John Warwick Montgomery'. Thesis (M.Th.). Westminster Theological Seminary, 1986.

Liggins, Stephen. 'Reaching out in a "Christ-Conscious" World'. *Southern Cross Quarterly* (Winter 1999): 1-3.

Lincoln, Andrew T. *Truth on Trial: The Lawsuit Motif in the Fourth Gospel*. Peabody, Massachusetts: Hendricksen, 2000.

Lind, Mary Ann. *From Nirvana to the New Age*. Tarrytown, New York: Fleming H. Revell, 1991.

Linton, Irwin H. *A Lawyer Examines the Bible: An Introduction to Christian Evidences*. 5th edn. Boston: W.A. Wilde, 1943.

Lockwood, Gregory J. *1 Corinthians, Concordia Commentary*. Saint Louis: Concordia, 2000.

Loder, James E. *The Logic of the Spirit: Human Development in Theological Perspective*. San Francisco: Jossey-Bass, 1998.

Loftus, Elizabeth F. 'Eyewitnesses: Essential but Unreliable'. *Psychology Today* 18, 2 (February, 1984): 22-26.

----------------------. *Eyewitness Testimony*. Cambridge, Massachusetts; London: Harvard University Press, 1979.

Longman, Tremper III. 'Literary Approaches to Old Testament Study'. In *The Face of Old Testament Studies*. Eds. David W. Baker and Bill T. Arnold. Grand Rapids: Baker, 1999, 97-115.

Lord Denning. *Landmarks in the Law*. London: Butterworths, 1984.

Lord Hailsham. *The Door Wherein I Went*. London: Collins, 1975.

Lorenzen, Thorwald. *Resurrection and Discipleship*. Maryknoll, New York: Orbis, 1995.

Lucas, Edward Deming. *The Logic and Reason in Christianity: A Brief by a Lawyer*. New York: Fleming Revell, 1945.

Luckhoo, Lionel A. and John R. Thompson. *The Silent Witness*. Nashville: Thomas Nelson, 1995.

Luckhoo, Lionel. *Christianity or Islam, You Decide!* Madison: Power Press, n.d..

--------------------. *Prophecy*. Dallas: Luckhoo Ministries, n.d..

--------------------. *The Quran is not the Word of God*. Dallas: Luckhoo Ministries, n.d..

--------------------. *What is your Verdict*? Surrey, British Columbia: Fellowship Press, 1984.

Lyon, David. *Postmodernity*. Buckingham: Open University Press, 1994.

Mabry, J.C. *A Legal View of the Trial of Christ*. Cincinatti, Ohio: Standard, 1895.

Macbeth, Norman. *Darwin Retried: An Appeal to Reason*. Ipswich, Massachusetts: Gambit, 1971.

Magee, Bryan. *Confessions of a Philosopher*. New York: Random, 1997.

Magner, Eilis S. 'The Best Evidence – Oral Testimony or Documentary Proof?'. *The University of New South Wales Law Journal* 18, 1 (1995): 67-94.

Maier, Gerhard. *Biblical Hermeneutics*. Wheaton: Crossway, 1994.

Maier, Paul L. *First Easter*. New York: Harper & Row, 1973.

Margolin, Phillip M. *The Undertaker's Widow*. London: Warner, 1998.

Marsden, George M. 'Everyone One's Own Interpreter? The Bible, Science and Authority in Mid-Nineteenth Century America'. In *The Bible in America: Essays in Cultural History*. Ed. Nathan O. Hatch and Mark A Noll. New York and Oxford: Oxford University Press, 1982, 79-100.

------------------------. *Fundamentalism and American Culture*. New York and Oxford: Oxford University Press, 1980.

Martel, John. *The Alternate*. New York: Signet, 2000.

Martin, Jeffrey C. *A Lawyer Briefs the Big Questions*. Anderson, Indiana: Bristol House, 2000.

Martin, Michael. *Basic Problems of Evidence*. 6th ed. Philadelphia: American Law Institute – American Bar Association, 1988.

Martin, Roger. 'R.A. Torrey – Defender of the Faith'. *Simon Greenleaf Law Review*, VII (1987-1988):165-197.

Martin, Walter and Jill Martin Rische. *Through the Windows of Heaven*. Nashville: Broadman & Holman, 1998.

Martin, Walter. *The New Age Cult*. Minneapolis: Bethany, 1989.

Martini, Steve. *The Attorney*. London: Headline, 2000.

Mascord, Keith Andrew. *Faith, History and the Morality of Knowledge: The Contrasting Views of J.W. Montgomery and V.A. Harvey*. Thesis (M.Th.). Australian College of Theology, February 1993.

Mason, Keith. *Constancy and Change*. Sydney: Federation Press, 1990.

Matasar, Richard A. 'Storytelling and Legal Scholarship'. *Chicago – Kent Law Review* 68, 1 (1992): 353-361.

Mauck, John W. *Paul on Trial: The Book of Acts as a Defense of Christianity*. Nashville: Thomas Nelson, 2001.

Mauet, Thomas A. *Fundamentals in Trial Techniques*. 2nd ed. Boston & Toronto: Little, Brown and Company, 1988.

Mauro, Philip. *Evolution at the Bar*. Boston: Hamilton Brothers, 1922.

Maver, Kate. 'Oprah Winfrey and her Self-Help Saviours: Making the New Age Normal'. *Christian Research Journal* 23, 4 (2001): 12-21.

Mayhew, Eugene J. 'God's Use of General Revelation in his Response to Job'. *Journal of Christian Apologetics* 2, 1 (Summer 1998): 94-104.

McCallum, Dennis (ed.). *The Death of Truth*. Minneapolis: Bethany, 1996.

McCloskey Patrick L. and Richard L. Schoenberg. *Criminal Law Advocacy*. Vol. 5. New York: Matthew Bender, 1984.

McCormick, Charles T., Frank W. Elliott and John F. Sutton Jr., *Cases and Materials on Evidence*. St. Paul: West Publishing, 1981.

McCrone, Walter C. *Judgement Day for the Shroud*. Chicago: McCrone Research Institute, 1996.

McDowell, David. *West of Eden*. Shippensburg, Pennsylvania: Companion Press, 1993.

McDowell, Josh and John Gilchrist. *The Islam Debate*. San Bernardino: Here's Life Publishers, 1983.

McDowell, Josh. *Evidence that Demands a Verdict*. N.p.: Campus Crusade, 1973.

---------------------. *The Resurrection Factor*. San Bernardino: Here's Life, 1981.

McEwan, Jenny. *Evidence and the Adversarial Process*. Oxford: Blackwell Business, 1992).

McGrath, Alister E. 'Apologetics to the Romans'. *Bibliotheca Sacra*, 155 (October-December 1998): 387-393.

-----------------------. *A Passion for Truth: The Intellectual Coherence of Evangelicalism*. Leicester: Apollos, 1996.

McGrath, Alister. *Bridge-Building: Effective Christian Apologetics*. Leicester: Inter-Varsity, 1992.

----------. 'Building bridges to ...'. In *Springboard for Faith*. Alister McGrath and Michael Green. London: Hodder and Stoughton, 1993, 63-85.

----------. 'Why Evangelicalism is the Future of Protestantism'. *Christianity Today* 39, 7 (19 June 1995): 18-23.

McGuire, Christine. *Until Proven Guilty*. London: Mandarin, 1994.

McKenzie, Leon. *Pagan Resurrection Myths and the Resurrection of Jesus*. Charlotteville, Virginia: Bookwrights, 1997.

McKnight, Edgar V. 'A Defence of a Postmodern Use of the Bible'. In *A Confessing Theology for Postmodern Times*. Ed. Michael S. Horton. Wheaton: Crossway, 2000, 65-90.

----------. *Postmodern Use of the Bible*. Nashville: Abingdon, 1988.

McLean, Adam. *The Chemical Wedding of Christian Rosenkreutz: Introduction and Commentary*. Trans. Joscelyn Godwin. Grand Rapids: Phanes Press, 1991.

McRoberts, Kerry D. *New Age or Old Lie?* Peabody, Massachusetts: Hendrickson, 1989.

McRoberts, Kerry. 'Faith Founded on Fact: The Apologetic Theology of John Warwick Montgomery. Thesis (M.C.S.). Regent College, 2000.

McRuer, James C. *This Man was Innocent*. Toronto & Vancouver: Clarke Irwin, 1978.

Meltzer, Brad. *The Tenth Justice*. London: Hodder and Stoughton, 1977.

Metzger, Bruce M. *The Text of the New Testament*. New York and Oxford: Oxford University Press, 1968.

Michaels, J. Ramsay. *1 Peter, Word Commentary*. Waco: Word, 1988.

Middleton, J. Richard and Brian J. Walsh. 'Facing the Postmodern Scalpel: Can the Christian Faith Withstand Deconstruction?'. In *Christian Apologetics in a Postmodern World*. Eds. Phillips and Okholm, 131-154.

Miethe, Terry and Anthony Flew. *Does God Exist? A Believer and Atheist Debate*. New York: Harper San Francisco, 1991.

Millard, Alan. *Reading and Writing in the Time of Jesus*. Sheffield: Sheffield Academic Press, 2000.

Miller, Elliot. *A Crash Course on the New Age Movement*. Grand Rapids: Baker, 1989.

Miller, George. 'The Apocalypse and the Pig: Or the Hazards of Storytelling'. *The Sydney Papers* 8, 4 (Spring 1996): 39-49.

Millikan, David and Neville Drury. *Worlds Apart?: Christianity and the New Age*. Crows Nest, NSW: ABC Enterprises, 1991.

Mivat, St. George Jackson. *Contemporary Evolution: An Essay on Some Recent Social Changes*. New York: D. Appleton, 1876.

Moen, John T. 'A Lawyer's Logical and Syllogistic Look at the Facts of the Resurrection'. *Simon Greenleaf Law Review*, VIII (1987-88), 81-110.

Mohler, Richard Albert. 'Evangelical Theology and Karl Barth: Representative Models of Response'. Thesis (Ph.D.). The Southern Baptist Theological Seminary, 1989.

Moo, Douglas J. *James, Tyndale New Testament Commentaries*. Leicester: Inter-Varsity; Grand Rapids: William B. Eerdmans, 1985.

Moore, James R. *The Post-Darwinian Controversies*. Cambridge: Cambridge University Press, 1979.

Moreland, J.P. 'The Circumstantial Evidence'. In *The Case for Christ*. Strobel, 244-257.

Morgan, Charles Carrol. *A Lawyer's Brief on the Atonement*. Boston: The Fort Hill Press, 1910.

Morison, Frank. *Who Moved the Stone?* Downers Grove: InterVarsity, 1982.

Morris, Leon. *Luke*. London: Inter-Varsity, 1974.

----------------. *Studies in the Fourth Gospel*. Exeter: Paternoster, 1969.

----------------. *The Gospel According to John*. Grand Rapids: William. B. Eerdmans, 1971.

Morrison, Charles R. *The Proofs of Christ's Resurrection from a Lawyer's Standpoint*. Andover: Warren F. Draper, 1882.

Morrison, Dorothy. *The Whimsical Tarot*. Stanford: U.S. Games Systems, 2000.

Mortimer, John. *The Best of Rumpole*. New York: Penguin, 1994.

Moseley, Edwin M. *Pseudonyms of Christ in the Modern Novel*. Pittsburg: University of Pittsburg Press, 1962.

Mosley, A.W. 'Historical Reporting in the Ancient World'. *New Testament Studies* 12, 1 (October 1965): 10-26.

Mouw, Richard J. *He Shines in all that's Fair: Culture and Common Grace, The 2000 Stob Lectures*. Grand Rapids and Cambridge: William B. Eerdmans, 2001.

Mowat, Oliver. *Christianity and its Evidences*. Toronto: Williamson, 1890.

Moyers, Bill. Interview with George Lucas. *Time*. 3 May 1999, 71-74.

Murray, John. *The Epistle to the Romans, the New International Commentary on the New Testament*. Grand Rapids: William B. Eerdmans, 1968.

Nash, Ronald H. *Christianity and the Hellenistic World*. Grand Rapids: Zondervan; Dallas: Probe, 1984.

Neagoe, Alexandru. *The Trial of the Gospel: An Apologetic Reading of Luke's Trial Narratives*. Cambridge: Cambridge University Press, 2002.

Neill, Stephen. *The Interpretation of the New Testament*. Oxford: Oxford University Press, 1964.

Netland, Harold. *Encountering Religious Pluralism: The Challenge to Christian Faith and Mission*. Downers Grove: InterVarsity; Leicester: Apollos, 2001.

------------------. 'Toward Contextualized Apologetics'. *Missiology* 16, 3 (July 1988): 289-303.

Newport, John P. *The New Age Movement and the Biblical Worldview.* Grand Rapids and Cambridge: William B. Eerdmans, 1998.

Nichols, Sallie. *Jung and Tarot: An Archetypal Journal.* York Beach, Maine: Samuel Weiser, 1980.

Nicolson, David. 'Truth, Reason and Justice: Epistemology and Politics in Evidence Discourse'. *The Modern Law Review* 57, 5 (September 1994): 726-744.

Nida, Eugene A. 'Sociolinguistics and Translating'. In *Sociolinguistics and Communication.* Ed. Johannes P. Louw. London, New York and Stuttgart: United Bible Societies, 1986, 1-49.

Noll, Mark A. 'Common Sense Traditions and American Evangelical Thought'. *American Quarterly*, 37 (1985): 216-238.

Noll, Richard. *The Jung Cult.* Hammersmith, London: Fontana, 1995.

Nyst, Chris. *Cop This!* Sydney: HarperCollins, 1999.

O'Collins, Gerald. *Jesus Risen.* New York/Mahwah: Paulist Press, 1987.

O'Donovan, Oliver and Joan Lockwood O'Donovan (eds.). *From Irenaeus to Grotius: A Sourcebook in Christian Political Thought 100-1625.* Grand Rapids and Cambridge: William B. Eerdmans, 1999.

O'Shaughnessy, Perri [Pamela and Mary O'Shaughnessy]. *Acts of Malice.* New York: Island, 2000.

------. *Presumption of Death.* London: Piatkus, 2003.

Odgers, Stephen. *Uniform Evidence Law.* 3rd ed. North Ryde, NSW: LBC Information Services, 1998.

Olson, Roger E. 'The Future of Evangelical Theology'. *Christianity Today* 42, 2 (9 February 1998): 40-48.

Ostling, Richard N. Clergy/Leader's Mail-list, No 1-059. clergy@pastor-net.net.au.

Ostrow, Ruth. 'Call Me Cosmic Any Day'. *The Weekend Australian.* 21-22 August 1999, 30.

Packel, Leonard and Dolores B. Spina. *Trial Advocacy a Systematic Approach*. Philadelphia: American Law Institute-American Bar Association Committee, 1984.

Packham, Richard. 'Critique of John Warwick Montgomery's Arguments for the Legal Evidence for Christianity'. <http://www.infidels.org/library/modern/richardpackham/montgomery.html>.

----------------------. Email received by the author. 21 March 2000.

Paley, William. *A View of the Evidences of Christianity*. Rev. ed. London: The Religious Tract Society, 1848.

Palmer, Andrew. 'The Reliability-based Approach to Hearsay'. *Sydney Law Review* 17, 4 (December 1995): 522-548.

Palmer, Humphrey. 'Seeking Verdicts for Parables'. *The Expository Times* 111, 8 (May 2000): 262-265.

----------------------. *The Logic of Gospel Criticism*. London: MacMillan, 1968.

Palmer, Michael. *Freud and Jung on Religion*. London and New York: Routledge, 1997.

Pannenberg, Wolfhart. *Jesus-God and Man*. Trans. Lewis L. Wilkins and Duane A. Priebe. 2nd ed. Philadelphia: Westminster Press, 1977.

Parkin-Speer, Diane. 'John Bunyan's Legal Ideas and the Legal Trials in his Analogies'. *The Baptist Quarterly* XXXV, 7 (July 1994): 324-331.

Parton, Craig. *Richard Whately: A Man for all Seasons*. Edmonton: Canadian Institute for Law, Theology and Public Policy, 1997.

Patterson, Richard North. *Protect and Defend*. London: Hutchinson, 2000.

Pearson, Carol S. *The Hero Within: Six Archetypes we Live By*. San Francisco: HarperSanFrancisco, 1989.

Peck, Scott. *Further Along the Road Less Travelled*. New York: Simon & Schuster, 1993.

Pelikan, Jaroslav. *The Christian Tradition: A History of the Development of Doctrine*. Vol. 2. Chicago and London: The University Press, 1974.

Pencak, William. 'Is a Fair Trial Possible? The Collapse of the Jury System in Revolutionary America'. In *Revolutions, Institutions and the Law: Eleventh Round Table on Law and Semiotics*. Eds. Joel Levin and Roberta Kevelson. New York: Peter Lang, 1998, 165-187.

Pendarvis, George H. *The Living Witness: A Lawyer's Brief for Christianity*. St Louis: B. Herder, 1912.

Person, Boyd Pehrson. 'How Not to Critique Legal Apologetics: A Lesson from a Skeptic's Internet Page Objections'. *Global Journal of Classical Theology* 3, 1 (March 2002): 1-9. <http://www.trinitysem.edu/journal/toc_v3n1.html>.

Penter, John. *Circumstantial Evidence*. San Francisco: Faraday Press, 1981.

Peretti, Frank E. *This Present Darkness*. Westchester, Illinois: Crossway, 1986.

Perkins, Pheme. *Peter: Apostle for the Whole Church*. Edinburgh: T. & T. Clarke, 2000.

Perry, Max. *Hampel on Advocacy*. N.p. (Victoria): Leo Cussen Institute, 1996.

Peterson, David. 'Resurrection Apologetics and the Theology of Luke-Acts'. In *Proclaiming the Resurrection*. Ed. Peter M. Head. Carlisle: Paternoster, 1998, 29-57.

Petterson, Anthony. 'The Blasphemy of "Incarnational Ministry"'. *Baptist Evangelicals Today* (November 2001): 15.

Phang, Andrew. 'Critical Legal Studies, Economic Development and Human Rights'. *Law and Justice*, 142-143 (Trinity Michaelmas 1999): 122-139.

------------------. 'Critical Legal Studies, Economic Development and Human Rights'. Paper. School of Oriental and African Studies, London University. 17 May 1999.

Phillips, Graham. 'God Makes a Comeback'. *The West Australian*. 23 October 2000, 14.

Phillips, J.B. *Ring of Truth*. Basingstoke, Hants: Lakeland, 1984.

Phillips, Timothy R. and Dennis L. Okholm (eds.). *Christian Apologetics in the Postmodern World*. Downers Grove: InterVarsity, 1995.

Phillips, W. Gary. *Apologetics and Inerrancy: An Analysis of Select Axiopistic Models*. Thesis (Th.D.). Grace Theological Seminary, May 1985.

Picknett, Lynn and Clive Price. *Turin Shroud in Whose Image?* London: Corgi, 2000.

Pike, James Albert. *What is this Treasure?* New York: Harper & Row, 1966.

Pines, Shlomo. 'Philosophy'. In *Cambridge History of Islam*. Vol. 2B. Eds. P.M. Holt, Ann K.S. Lantern and Bernard Lewis. Cambridge University Press, 1977, 780-823.

Pollard, Ruth. Legal Officer, Public Trustee of NSW. Interview by the author. Darling Harbour, NSW. 3 November, 2000.

Powell, Baden. *The Order of Nature Considered in Reference to the Claims of Revelation*. London: Longman, Bowman, Green, Longmans & Roberts, 1859.

Powell, Frank J. *The Trial of Jesus Christ*. Exeter: Paternoster, 1952.

Prescott, David. 'Anthony Flew's Presumption of Atheism Revisited: A Christian Lawyer's Perspective'. *Simon Greenleaf Law Review*, VII (1987-1988): 139-162.

Presley, C.F. 'Review of The Uses of Argument'. *Australasian Journal of Philosophy* 37, 2 (August 1959): 168-176.

Price, Steve and David Haynes. *Dreamworks: A Meeting of the Spiritual and Psychology*. Blackburn, Victoria: HarperCollins, 1997.

Proctor, William. *The Resurrection Report*. Nashville: Broadman & Holman, 1998.

Raisanen, Heikke. *Paul and the Law*. Philadelphia: Fortress Press, 1983.

Ramm, Bernard. *Varieties of Christian Apologetics*. Grand Rapids: Baker, 1961.

Ramsay, W.M. *The Bearing of Recent Discovery on the Trustworthiness of the New Testament*. Rpt. ed. Grand Rapids: Baker, 1953.

Redfield, James. *The Celestine Prophecy*. Sydney, Auckland, Toronto, New York and London: Bantam, 1993.

Reed, Barry. *The Indictment*. New York: St Martins, 1994.

Rees, Frank D. *Wrestling with Doubt*. Collegeville, Minnesota: Liturgical Press, 2001.

Reid, W. Stanford Reid. 'The Problem of the Christian Interpretation of History'. *Fides et Historia* 5, 1-2 (Spring 1973): 96-106.

Reimarus, H.S. 'Concerning the Intention of Jesus and his Teachings'. In *Reimarus Fragments*. Trans. Ralph S. Fraser. Ed. Charles H. Talbert. London: SCN, 1971), 59-269.

Richard, H.L. 'Evangelical Approaches to Hindus'. *Missiology* 29, 3 (July 2001): 307-315.

----------------. *Following Jesus in the Hindu Context*: *The Intriguing Implications of N.V. Tilak's Life and Thought*. Pasadena: William Carey Library, 1998.

Richards, Kel. *Jesus on Trial*. Kingsford, NSW: Matthias Media, 2001.

----------------. *The Case of the Vanishing Corpse*. Sydney, Auckland, London and Toronto: Hodder & Stoughton, 1990.

Richardson, Don. *Peace Child*. Glendale: Regal, 1974.

--------------------. 'Redemptive Analogy'. In *Perspectives on the World Christian Movement, a Reader*. Eds. Ralph D. Winter and Stephen C. Hawthorne. Passadena: William Carey Library; Carlisle: Paternoster, 1999, 397-403.

Riches, John. 'Matthew'. In *The Synoptic Gospels*. John Riches, William R. Telford and Christopher M. Tuckett. Sheffield: Sheffield Academic Press, 2001, 41-126.

Rickman, Phil. *Midwinter of the Spirit*. London: Pan, 2000.

Ricoeur, Paul. 'The Hermeneutics of Testimony'. *Anglican Theological Review* 61, 4 (October 1979): 435-461.

Rimmer, Harry. *That Lawsuit against the Bible*. Grand Rapids: William B. Eerdmans, 1940.

Riss, Richard. *The Evidence for the Resurrection of Jesus Christ*. Minneapolis: Bethany, 1977.

Roberts, Graham. *Evidence: Proof and Practice*. North Ryde, NSW: LBC Information Services, 1998.

Robertson, W.M. *The Bible at the Bar*. London: Pickering & Inglis, n.d..

Robinson, James M. (ed.). *The Nag Hammadi Library*. Leiden and New York: E.J. Brill, 1998.

Robinson, John A.T. *Redating the New Testament*. London: SCM, 1976.

Robinson, Martin. *To Win the West*. Crowborough, East Sussex: Monarch, 1996.

Roden, Adrian. 'The Place of Individual Rights in Corruption Investigations'. Paper. The Fourth International Anti-Corruption Conference, Sydney. 16 November 1989.

Roe, Jill. 'Challenge and Response: Religious Life in Melbourne 1876-86'. *Journal of Religious History 5,* 2(1968): 149-166

Rollins, James M. *The Arrest, Trial and Conviction of Jesus Christ from a Lawyer's Standpoint*. St. Louis: Hughes Printing, 1910.

Rook, Stephen D. *Historical Objectivism: The Apologetic Methodology of John Warwick Montgomery*. Thesis (M.A.). Harding Graduate School of Religion, November 1985.

Roper, Albert L. *Did Jesus Rise from the Dead?* Grand Rapids: Zondervan, 1965.

Rosas, L. Joseph. 'Evangelism and Apologetics'. In *Evangelism in the Twenty-first Century*. Ed. T. Rainer. Wheaton: Harold Shaw, 1989, 113-120.

Row, C.A. *A Manual of Christian Evidences*. London: Hodder and Stoughton, 1892.

Russell, Howard Hyde. *A Lawyer's Examination of the Bible*. Westerville, Ohio: Bible Bond, 1935.

Rutgers, Hendrik. *Testimony of a Lawyer*. Blacktown, Sydney: Hexagon Press, 1990.

Sagebeer, Joseph Evans. *The Bible in Court*. Philadelphia: Lippincott, 1900.

Saliba, John A. *Christian Responses to the New Age Movement*. London: Geoffrey Chapman, 1999.

Sargent, Carl. *Personality, Divination, and the Tarot*. Rochester, New York: Destiny, 1988.

Satinover, Jeffrey. *The Empty Self: Gnostic and Jungian Foundations of Modern Identity, Grove Series*. Bramcote: Nottingham, 1995.

Saunders, David M., Neil Vidmar and Erin C. Hewitt. 'Eyewitness Testimony and the Discrediting Effect'. In *Evaluating Witness Evidence*. Eds. Sally M.A. Lloyd-Bostock and Brian R. Clifford. Chichester, New York, Brisbane, Toronto and Singapore: John Wiley, 1983, 57-80.

Scheppele, Kim Lane. 'Manners of Imagining the Real'. *Law and Social Enquiry* 19, 4 (Fall 1994): 995-1022.

Scholnick, Sylvia Huberman. 'Poetry in the Courtroom: Job 38-41'. In *Directions in Hebrew Poetry*. Ed. Elaine Follis. Sheffield: JSOT, 1987, 185-204.

Schramm, Jan-Melissa Schramm. *Testimony and Advocacy in Victorian Law, Literature and Theology*. Cambridge: Cambridge University Press, 2000.

Schwartz, Louis E. *Proof, Persuasion and Cross-Examination*. 2 vols. Englewood Cliffs, New Jersey: Executive Reports Corporation, 1976.

Schwartz, Tony. *Media: The Second God*. New York: Random, 1981.

Schweitzer, Albert. *The Quest of the Historical Jesus*. Trans. W. Montgomery. London: A. & C. Black, 1911.

Scottoline, Lisa. *Moment of Truth*. London: Harper Collins, 2000.

Selby, Hugh. *Winning in Court*. Melbourne: Oxford University Press, 2000.

Shafer, Robert. *Christianity and Naturalism*. New Haven: Yale Press, 1926).

Sharpe, Eric J. *Comparative Religion: A History*. London: Duckworth, 1975.

Sherlock, Thomas. *The Tryal of the Witnesses of the Resurrection of Jesus*. Photoreproduced in *Jurisprudence: A Book of Readings*. Ed. John Warwick Montgomery. Strasbourg: International Scholarly Publishers, 1974.

Shiel, Christopher. 'Globalisation is …'. In *Globalisation: Australian Impacts*. Ed. Christopher Shiel. Sydney: University of New South Wales Press, 2001, 1-16.

Shupe, Anson and David G. Bromley. 'The Modern North American Anti-Cult Movement 1971-1991'. In *Anti-Cult Movements in Cross-Cultural Perspectives*. Eds. Anson Shupe and David G. Bromley. New York and London: Garland, 1994, 3-31.

Shuster, Margueritte. 'The Preaching of the Resurrection of Christ in Augustine, Luther, Barth and Thielicke'. In *The Resurrection*. Ed. Davis, Kendall and O'Collins, 308-338.

Simotis, Spiros. 'The Problem of Legal Logic'. *Ratio* III, 1 (1960): 60-94.

Sire, James W. *Scripture Twisting*. Downers Grove: InterVarsity, 1986.

Sire, James. 'On Being a Fool for Christ and an Idiot for Nobody'. In *Christian Apologetics in the Postmodern World*. Eds. Phillips and Okholm, 101-127.

Smalley, Stephen S. *John: Evangelist and Interpreter*. Exeter: Paternoster, 1978.

Smith, James K.A. 'A Little Story about Metanarratives: Lyotard, Religion and Postmodernism Revisited'. *Faith and Philosophy* 18, 3 (July 2001), 353-368.

Smith, Wilbur. *Therefore Stand*. Boston: Wilde, 1945.

Snyder, Tom. *Myth Conceptions: Joseph Campbell and the New Age*. Grand Rapids: Baker, 1995.

Spangler, David and William Irwin Thompson. *Reimagination of the World: A Critique of the New Age, Science and Popular Culture*. Sante Fe: Bear, 1991.

Speck, William A.'Herbert Butterfield on the Christian and Historical Study'. *Fides et Historia* 4, 1 (Fall 1971): 50-70.

Spong, John Shelley. *Resurrection: Myth or Reality?* New York: HarperSan Francisco, 1994.

Sproul, Barbara C. *Primal Myths: Creating the World.* London, Melbourne, Sydney, Auckland and Johannesburg: Rider, 1980.

Sproul, R.C., John Gerstner and Arthur Linsley. *Classical Apologetics.* Grand Rapids: Zondervan, 1984.

Sproul, R.C. *If there is a God, Why are there Atheists?* Minneapolis: Bethany, 1978.

Star, Leonie. *The Dead Sea Scrolls and the Riddle Debated.* Crows Nest, NSW: ABC Books, 1991.

Starkie, Thomas. *A Practical Treatise of Evidence and Digest of Proofs, in Civil and Criminal Proceedings.* Vol. 1. 2nd Rev. ed. London: J and W.T. Clarke, 1833.

Stegemann, Ekkehard W. and Wolfgard Stegemann. *The Jesus Movement: A Social History of its First Century.* Trans. O.C. Dean. Minneapolis: Fortress Press, 1999.

Stephen, Leslie. 'Joseph Butler'. In *The Dictionary of Natural Biography.* Vol. III. Eds. Leslie Stephen and Sidney Lee. London: Oxford University Press, 1917, 519-525.

Stevenson, Kenneth D. and Gary R. Habermas. *Verdict on the Shroud.* Ann Arbor: Servant, 1981.

Stewart, Don. Interview by the author. Eastwood, NSW. 8 August 1997.

---------------. *You be the Judge.* San Bernardino: Here's Life, 1983.

Stewart, Elizabeth-Anne. *Jesus the Holy Fool.* Franklin, Wisconsin: Sheed & Ward, 1999.

Stiver, Don R. 'Much Ado about Athens and Jerusalem: The Implications of Postmodernism for Faith'. *Review and Expositor* 91, 1 (Winter, 1994): 83-102.

Stone, Marcus. *Proof of Fact in Criminal Trials.* Edinburgh: W. Green and Son, 1984.

Story, Dan. *Christianity on the Offensive.* Grand Rapids: Kregel, 1998.

------------. *Defending your Faith*. Grand Rapids: Kregel, 1997.

Strauss, David Friedrich. *The Life of Jesus for the People*. Vol 1. 2nd ed. London: William and Norgate, 1879.

Strobel, Lee. *God's Outrageous Claims*. Grand Rapids: Zondervan, 1997.

------------. *The Case for Christ*. Grand Rapids: Zondervan, 1998.

Summers, Ray. *2 Peter, the Broadman Bible Commentary*. Vol. 12. Nashville: Broadman, 1972.

Sutcliffe, Steven and Marion Bowman (eds.). *Beyond New Age: Exploring Alternative Spirituality*. Edinburgh: Edinburgh University Press, 2000.

Sweet, Leonard. *Carpe Mañana*. Grand Rapids: Zondervan, 2001.

------------. *Post-Modern Pilgrims*. Nashville: Broadman & Holman, 2000.

Swinburne, Richard. 'Evidence for the Resurrection'. In *The Resurrection*. Davis, Kendall, O'Collins, 191-212.

------------. *The Existence of God*. Oxford: Clarendon, 1979.

Tabor, Britton H. *Skepticism Assailed*. Philadelphia: Monarch, 1895.

Tacey, David. *Reenchantment: The New Australian Spirituality*. Sydney: Harper Collins, 2000.

------------. *The Edge of the Sacred*. Blackburn, Victoria: Harper Collins, 1995.

Talbert, Charles H. *Conversion in the Acts of the Apostles*: Ancient Auditor's. In *Luke-Acts*. Eds. Richard P. Thompson and Thomas E. Phillips. Marcon, Georgia: Mercer University Press, 1998, 141-153.

Taylor Innes, A. *The Trial of Jesus Christ: A Legal Monograph*. Edinburgh: Oliphant, 1905.

Taylor, Mike. 'Illegitimate Evangelism?'. *Evangelicals Now* (November 2001): 23.

Taylor, V. *The Gospels*. 4th ed. London: Epworth, 1938.

Telford, William R. 'Mark'. In *The Synoptic Gospels*. John Riches, William R. Telford and Christopher M. Tuckett. Sheffield: Sheffield Academic Press, 2001, 127-149.

Thaxton, Charles B. 'A Dialogue with "Prof" on Christianity and Science'. In *God and Culture: Essays in Honor of Carl F.H. Henry*. Eds. D.A. Carson and John D. Woodbridge. Grand Rapids: William B. Eerdmans, 275-300.

Thich Nhat Hanh. *Being Peace*. London: Rider, 1987.

Thiering, Barbara. *Jesus the Man*. Sydney: Doubleday, 1992.

Thiessen, Gerd. *Sociality, Reality and the Early Christians*. Minneapolis: Fortress Press, 1992.

Thiselton, Anthony C. *The First Epistle to the Corinthians, the New International Greek Testament Commentary*. Grand Rapids, Cambridge: William B. Eerdmans; Carlisle: Paternoster, 2000.

Thompson, George W. *The Trial of Jesus: A Judicial Review of the Law and Facts of the World's Most Tragic Courtroom Trial*. Indianapolis: Bobbs-Merrill, 1927.

Thompson, J.A. *The Bible and Archaeology*. Rev. ed. Exeter: Paternoster, 1973.

Thompson, Stith. *Motif-Index of Folk Literature*. Indiana: Indiana University Press, 1994.

Tippett, A.R. *Verdict Theology in Missionary Theory*. South Pasadena: William Carey Library, 1973.

Tolkien, J.R.R. 'On Fairy-Stories'. In *Essays Presented to Charles Williams*. Ed. C.S. Lewis. Rpt. ed. Grand Rapids: William B. Eerdmans, 1981, 38-89.

Tomlinson, Dave. *The Post-Evangelical*. London: Triangle, 1995.

Torrance, Thomas F. *Space, Time and Incarnation*. London: Oxford University Press, 1969.

Torrey, R.A. 'The Centrality and Importance of the Bodily Resurrection of Christ from the Dead'. In *The Fundamentals for Today*. Vol. 1. Ed. R.A. Torrey. Grand Rapids: Kregel, 1958, 265-279.

──────────. *What the Bible Teaches*. New York: Revell, 1898.

Toulmin, Stephen. *Cosmopolis: The Hidden Agenda of Modernity*. New York: Free Press, 1990.

──────────. *Knowing and Acting*. New York: Macmillan, 1976.

──────────. *The Uses of Argument*. Cambridge: Cambridge University Press, 1958.

Trembath, Kern Robert. *Evangelical Theories of Biblical Inspiration: A Review and Proposal*. New York and Oxford: Oxford University Press, 1987.

Trenoweth, Samantha. *The Future of God*. Alexandria, NSW: Millennium, 1995.

Trimp, Cornelius. 'The Witness of the Scriptures'. In *Jerusalem and Athens*. Ed. E.R. Geehan. N.p.: Presbyterian and Reformed, 1971, 172-184.

Trites, Allison A. 'The Idea of Witness in the Synoptic Gospels – Some Juridical Considerations'. *Themelios*, 5 (1968): 18-26.

──────────. 'The Importance of Legal Scenes and Language in the Book of Acts'. *Novum Testamentum*, 16 (1974): 278-284.

──────────. *The New Testament Concept of Witness*. Cambridge: Cambridge University Press, 1977.

Trompf, G.W. 'Millenarism: History, Sociology, and Cross-Cultural Analysis'. *Journal of Religious History* 24, 2 (February 2000): 103-124.

──────────. 'Mircea Eliade and the Interpretation of Cargo Cults'. *Religious Traditions*, 12 (1989): 31-64.

Trompf, Garry. *In Search of Origins*. London: Oriental University Press, 1990.

Tur, R.H.S. 'What is Jurisprudence?'. *The Philosophical Quarterly* 28, 111 (April 1978): 149-161.

Turrow, Scott. *Personal Injuries*. New York: Michael Joseph, 1999.

Twining, William. 'Identification and Misidentification in the Legal Process: Redefining the Problem'. In *Evaluating Witness Evidence*. Eds. Sally M.A. Lloyd-Bostock and Brian R. Clifford. Chichester, New York, Brisbane, Toronto and Singapore: John Wiley, 1983, 255-283.

----------------------. *Rethinking Evidence: Exploratory Essays*. Oxford: Basil Blackwell, 1990.

Ulanov, Ann Belford. *Religion and the Spiritual in Carl Jung*. New York and Mahwah, New Jersey: Paulist Press, 1999.

Ulanov, Ann. 'Jung and Religion: The Opposing Self'. In *The Cambridge Companion to Jung*. Eds. Polly Young-Eisendrath and Terence Dawson. Cambridge: Cambridge University Press, 1997, 296-313.

Updike, John. 'Remarks upon Receiving the Campion Medal'. In *John Updike and Religion: The Sense of the Sacred and Notions of Grace*. Ed. James Yerkes. Grand Rapids and Cambridge: William B. Eerdmans, 1999, 3-6.

Van Voorst, Robert E. *Jesus Outside the New Testament*. Grand Rapids: William B. Eerdmans, 2000.

VanderMolen, Ronald J. 'The Christian Historian: Apologist or Seeker'. *Fides et Historia* 3, 1 (Fall 1970): 41-56.

Veith, Gene Edward. *Postmodern Times: A Christian Guide to Contemporary Thought and Culture*. Wheaton: Crossway, 1994.

Verheyden, Joseph. 'The Unity of Luke-Acts: Where are we up to?'. In *The Unity of Luke-Acts*. Ed. J. Verheyden. Leuven, Belgium: Leuven University Press, 1999, 3-56.

Volz, James W. *What does this Mean? Principles of Biblical Interpretation in the Post-Modern World*. 2nd ed. Saint Louis: Concordia, 1995.

Von Campenhausen, Hans. *Ecclesiastical Authority and Spiritual Power in the Church of the First Three Centuries*. Trans. J. A. Baker. London: Adam and Charles Black, 1969.

Waite, A.E. *The Key to the Tarot*. Rev. ed. London: Rider, 1993.

Waite, Arthur Edward. *The Pictorial Key to the Tarot*. Stamford: U.S. Games Systems, 1991.

Waller, L. 'Patients and their Doctors'. *Issues Paper 4*. Australian Institute of Health, Law and Ethics, Canberra. 1997.

Walsh, Brian and Richard Middleton. *Truth is Stranger than it used to Be*. Downers Grove: InterVarsity, 1995.

Wampler, Dee. *The Trial of Christ: A Criminal Lawyer Defends Jesus*. Springfield, Missouri: Dee Wampler, n.d..

Ward, Kevin. 'Religion in a PostAquarian Age'. *Stimulus* 9, 1 (February 2001): 12-21.

Warren, Rick. *The Purpose Driven Church*. Grand Rapids: Zondervan, 1995.

Waters, Malcolm. *Globalization*. London: Routledge, 1995.

Webb, W.D. *The Trial of Jesus Christ*. Atchison, Kansas: Schauer & Burbank, 1907.

Webster, Daniel. *A Defense of the Christian Religion*. New York: M.H. Newman, 1844.

Webster, William. *The Credibility of the Resurrection of Christ upon the Testimony of the Apostles*. London: J. Wilford, 1735.

----------------------. *The Fitness of the Witnesses of the Resurrection of Christ Considered*. London: James Lacy, 1731.

Weiner, Harold M. *The Origin of the Pentateuch*. Oberlin, Ohio: Bibliotheca Sacra; London: Elliot Stock, 1910.

Welchel, James. 'Connecting in General: What is Truth in a Post-Metaphysical World?'. *Journal of Christian Apologetics* 2, 1 (Summer 1998): 44-77.

Wells, A.N. *Evidence and Advocacy*. Sydney: Butterworths, 1988.

Wells, David F. 'Living Tradition'. In *Where Shall my Wond'ring Soul Begin? The Landscape of Evangelical Piety and Thought*. Eds. Mark A. Noll and Ronald F. Thiemann. Grand Rapids and Cambridge: William B. Eerdmans, 2000, 87-96.

Wenham, John. *Easter Enigma*. 2nd ed. Grand Rapids: Baker, 1992.

——————. *Redating Matthew, Mark and Luke*. London: Hodder & Stoughton, 1991.

West, Andrew. 'Meet Mr Westie, the Man who put Howard in Power'. *The Sun Herald*. 18 November 2001, 21.

West, Emery Scott. *Impeachment of the Bible*. Chicago: n.p., 1923.

Westermann, Claus. *The Structure of the Book of Job*. Trans. Charles A. Muenchow. Philadelphia: Fortress Press, 1981.

Wharton, Francis. *A Treatise on Theism and on Modern Skeptical Theories*. Philadelphia: Lippincott; London: Trubner, 1859.

——————. 'Recent Changes in Jurisprudence and Apologetics'. *The Princeton Review* 2, 1 (July-December 1878): 149-168.

Whately, Richard. *Historic Doubts Relative to Napoleon Buonaparte*. 6th ed. London: B. Fellowes, Ludgate Street, 1837.

White, R.E.O. *Luke's Case for Christianity*. London: The Bible Reading Fellowship, 1987.

Whitlow, Robert. *The Trial*. Nashville: Word, 2001.

Whitworth, John Ford. *Legal and Historical Proof of the Resurrection of the Dead with an Examination of the Evidence in the New Testament*. Harrisburg, Pennsylvania: The United Evangelical Church, 1912.

Wiebe, Phillip H. 'Evidence for a Resurrection'. *Journal of Christian Theological Research* 6, 2 (2001). <http://home.apu.edu/~CTRF/jctr.html>.

Wigmore, John H. *Treatise on Evidence*. Vol. 1. Boston: Little, Brown, 1904.

Wigmore, John Henry. *Evidence in Trials at Common Law*. Vol 4. Rev. James H. Chadbourn. Boston and Toronto: Little, Brown, 1972.

——————. *Evidence in Trials at Common Law*. Vol. 5. Rev. James H. Chadbourn. Boston: Little, Brown, 1974.

——————. *Evidence in Trials at Common Law*. Vol. 7. Rev. James H. Chadbourn (Boston: Little, Brown, 1978).

Wilcox, Phineas Bacon. *A Few Thoughts by a Member of the Bar*. Columbus, Ohio: T.B. Cutler, 1836.

Wilhelm, Kate. *For the Defense*. London: HarperCollins, 1997.

Wilkinson, David. 'The Art of Apologetics in the Twenty-first Century'. *Anvil* 19, 1 (2002): 5-17.

Wilkinson, Loren. 'Circles and the Cross: Reflections on Neo-paganism, Postmodernity and Celtic Christianity'. *Evangelical Review of Theology* 22, 1 (January 1998): 28-47.

Wilkinson, Loren. 'The Bewitching Charms of Neo-Paganism'. *Christianity Today* 43, 13 (15 November 1999): 54-63.

Williams, Charles. *The Greater Trumps*. Grand Rapids: William B. Eerdmans, 1976.

Williams, Stephen D. *The Bible in Court or Truth vs Error*. Dearborn, Michigan: Dearborn Book, 1925.

Wilson, Ian. *The Blood and the Shroud*. London: Weidenfeld & Nicolson, 1998.

Wilson, Robert Dick. *A Scientific Investigation of the Old Testament*. Philadelphia: Sunday School Times, 1926.

Wilson, Thomas Frew. *The Trial of Jesus of Nazareth from an Historical and Legal Standpoint*. New York: T. Whittaker, 1906.

Wingo, Earl L. *The Illegal Trial of Jesus*. Indianapolis & New York: Bobbs-Merrill, 1962.

Winter, Bruce W. 'Official Proceedings and the Forensic Speeches in Acts 24-26'. In *The Book of Acts in its Ancient Literary Settings*. Vol. 1. Eds. Bruce W. Winter and Andrew D. Clarke. Grand Rapids: William B. Eerdmans, 1994, 305-336.

Witcher, Walter Campbell. *Legal Proof being an Answer to Thomas H. Huxley and Other Sceptics Demand for Legal Proof of the Resurrection of Christ from the Dead*. Fort Worth: Christian Forum, 1937.

Witherington, Ben. *Conflict and Community in Corinth*. Grand Rapids: William B. Eerdmans; Carlisle: Paternoster, 1995.

Wolterstorff, N. 'Can Belief in God be Rational if it has no Foundations?'. In *Faith and Rationality*. Eds. A. Plantinga and N. Wolterstorff. Notre Dame: University of Notre Dame Press, 1983, 135-186.

Wright, N.T. 'Grave Matters'. *Christianity Today* 4, 2 (April 6 1998): 51-53.

Wuthnow, Robert. 'World Order and Religious Movements'. In *New Religious Movements: A Perspective for Understanding Society*. Ed. Eileen Baker. New York and Toronto: Edwin Mellen, 1982, 47-65.

Wykstra, Stephen J. 'The Problem of Miracle in the Apologetic from History'. *Journal of the American Scientific Affiliation* 30, 4 (December 1978): 154-163.

Yamauchi, Edwin M. *The Stones and the Scriptures*. Grand Rapids: Baker, 1981.

Yamauchi, Edwin. *Persia and the Bible*. Grand Rapids: Baker, 1990.

Yarmey, A. Daniel and Hazel P. Tressillian Jones. 'Is the Psychology of Eyewitness Identification a Matter of Common Sense'. In *Evaluating Witness Evidence*. Eds. Sally M.A. Lloyd-Bostock and Brian R. Clifford. Chichester, New York, Brisbane, Toronto and Singapore: John Wiley, 1983, 15-33.

Zacharias, Ravi. 'The Touch of Truth'. In *Telling the Truth*. Ed. D.A. Carson. Grand Rapids: Zondervan, 2000, 30-43.

www.ingramcontent.com/pod-product-compliance
Lightning Source LLC
Chambersburg PA
CBHW050617300426
44112CB00012B/1537